MATERIAL FEMINISMS

Edited by Stacy Alaimo & Susan Hekman

INDIANA UNIVERSITY PRESS
BLOOMINGTON & INDIANAPOLIS

This book is a publication of

Indiana University Press
601 North Morton Street
Bloomington, IN 47404-3797 USA

http://iupress.indiana.edu

Telephone orders 800-842-6796
Fax orders 812-855-7931
Orders by e-mail iuporder@indiana.edu

The paper used in this publication meets the minimum requirements of American National Standard for Information Sciences—Permanence of Paper for Printed Library Materials, ANSI Z39.48-1984.

Manufactured in the United States of America

Library of Congress Cataloging-in-Publication Data

Material feminisms / edited by Stacy Alaimo and Susan Hekman.
p. cm.
Includes bibliographical references and index.
ISBN-13: 978-0-253-34978-1 (cloth : alk. paper)
ISBN-13: 978-0-253-21946-6 (pbk. : alk. paper) 1. Feminist theory.
2. Body, Human. I. Alaimo, Stacy, date II. Hekman, Susan J.
HQ1190.M3775 2008
305.4201—dc22 2007019295

2 3 4 5 13 12 11 10 09

To Justin and Jeanne

CONTENTS

ACKNOWLEDGMENTS · XI

INTRODUCTION: EMERGING MODELS OF MATERIALITY IN FEMINIST THEORY · 1
Stacy Alaimo and Susan Hekman

PART 1. MATERIAL THEORY

1. DARWIN AND FEMINISM: PRELIMINARY INVESTIGATIONS FOR A POSSIBLE ALLIANCE · 23
Elizabeth Grosz

2. ON NOT BECOMING MAN: THE MATERIALIST POLITICS OF UNACTUALIZED POTENTIAL · 52
Claire Colebrook

3. CONSTRUCTING THE BALLAST: AN ONTOLOGY FOR FEMINISM · 85
Susan Hekman

4. POSTHUMANIST PERFORMATIVITY: TOWARD AN UNDERSTANDING OF HOW MATTER COMES TO MATTER · 120
Karen Barad

PART 2. MATERIAL WORLD

5. OTHERWORLDLY CONVERSATIONS, TERRAN TOPICS, LOCAL TERMS · 157
Donna J. Haraway

6. VISCOUS POROSITY: WITNESSING KATRINA · 188
Nancy Tuana

7. NATURAL CONVERS(AT)IONS: OR, WHAT IF CULTURE WAS REALLY NATURE ALL ALONG? · 214
Vicki Kirby

8. TRANS-CORPOREAL FEMINISMS AND THE ETHICAL SPACE OF NATURE · 237
Stacy Alaimo

9. LANDSCAPE, MEMORY, AND FORGETTING: THINKING THROUGH (MY MOTHER'S) BODY AND PLACE · 265
Catriona Mortimer-Sandilands

PART 3. MATERIAL BODIES

10. DISABILITY EXPERIENCE ON TRIAL · 291
Tobin Siebers

11. HOW REAL IS RACE? · 308
Michael Hames-García

12. FROM RACE/SEX/ETC. TO GLUCOSE, FEEDING TUBE, AND MOURNING: THE SHIFTING MATTER OF CHICANA FEMINISM · 340
Suzanne Bost

13. ORGANIC EMPATHY: FEMINISM, PSYCHOPHARMACEUTICALS, AND THE EMBODIMENT OF DEPRESSION · 373
Elizabeth A. Wilson

14. CASSIE'S HAIR · 400
Susan Bordo

LIST OF CONTRIBUTORS · 425

INDEX · 429

Acknowledgments

Permission granted by The University of Chicago Press to reprint Karen Barad's essay "Posthumanist Performativity: Toward an Understanding of How Matter Comes to Matter," as it appeared in *Signs* 28:3 (2003), 801–31.

Permission granted by Routledge Publishing, Inc. to reprint Donna J. Haraway's essay "Otherworldly Conversations, Terran Topics, Local Terms," as it appeared in *The Haraway Reader*, by Donna J. Haraway. New York: Routledge, 2004.

Permission granted by aunt lute Books to reprint Gloria Anzaldúa's poem "*Cihuatlyotl*, Woman Alone" from *Borderlands/La Frontera*. San Francisco: aunt lute Books, 1987.

Linda G. Hardnett's poem "If Hair Makes Me Black, I Must Be Purple" appeared in *Black Hair*, edited by Ima Ebong. New York: Universe Publishing, 2001.

Permission granted by Debraha Watson to reprint her poem "Good Hair" as it appeared in *Black Hair*, edited by Ima Ebong. New York: Universe Publishing, 2001.

MATERIAL FEMINISMS

INTRODUCTION: EMERGING MODELS OF MATERIALITY IN FEMINIST THEORY

Stacy Alaimo and Susan Hekman

The purpose of this anthology is to bring the material, specifically the materiality of the human body and the natural world, into the forefront of feminist theory and practice. This is no small matter indeed, and we expect this collection to spark intense debate. Materiality, particularly that of bodies and natures, has long been an extraordinarily volatile site for feminist theory—so volatile, in fact, that the guiding rule of procedure for most contemporary feminisms requires that one distance oneself as much as possible from the tainted realm of materiality by taking refuge within culture, discourse, and language. Our thesis is that feminist theory is at an impasse caused by the contemporary linguistic turn in feminist thought. With the advent of postmodernism and poststructuralism, many feminists have turned their attention to social constructionist models. They have focused on the role of language in the constitution of social reality, demonstrating that discursive practices constitute the social position of women. They have engaged in productive and wide-ranging analyses and deconstructions of the concepts that define and derogate women.

The turn to the linguistic and discursive has been enormously productive for feminism. It has fostered complex analyses of the interconnections between power, knowledge, subjectivity, and language. It has allowed feminists to understand gender from a new and fruitful perspective. For example, it has allowed feminists to understand how gender has been articulated with other volatile markings, such as class, race, and sexuality, within cultural systems of difference that function like a language (à la Ferdinand de Saussure). The rigorous deconstructions of Jacques Derrida and Luce Irigaray (especially within *Speculum of the Other Woman*) have exposed the pernicious logic that casts woman as subordinated, inferior, a mirror of the same, or all but invisible. At the forefront of this turn to the linguistic is the influence of postmodern thought in feminist theory. The strength of postmodern feminism is to reveal that since its inception, Western thought has been structured by a series of gendered dichotomies. Postmodern feminists have argued that the male/female dichotomy informs all the dichotomies that ground Western thought: culture/nature, mind/body, subject/object, rational/emotional, and countless others. Postmodern feminists have further argued that it is imperative not to move from one side of the dichotomy to the other, to reverse the privileging of concepts, but to deconstruct the dichotomy itself, to move to an understanding that does not rest on oppositions.

Feminist theory and practice have been significantly enriched by these postmodern insights. Postmodern analysis has revealed the liability of defining and fixing the identity of "woman" in any location or of attempting to assert the superiority of the feminine over the masculine. Indeed, within queer theory, especially, the "feminine" and the "masculine" have been productively unmoored, contested, and redeployed. But it is now apparent that the move to the linguistic, particularly in its postmodern variant, has serious liabilities as well as advantages. In short, postmodernism has not fulfilled its promise as a theoretical grounding for feminism. Although postmoderns claim to reject all dichotomies, there is one dichotomy that they appear to embrace almost without question: language/reality. Perhaps due to its centrality in modernist thought, postmoderns are very uncomfortable with the concept of the real or the material. Whereas the epistemology of modernism is grounded in objective access to a real/natural world, postmodernists argue that the real/material is entirely constituted by language; what we call the real is a product of language and has its reality only in language. In their zeal to reject the modernist grounding in the material, postmoderns have turned to the discursive pole as the exclusive source of the constitution of nature, society, and reality. Far from deconstructing the dichotomies of language/reality or culture/nature, they have rejected one side and embraced the other. Even though many social constructionist theories grant the existence of material reality, that reality is often posited as a realm entirely separate from that of language, discourse, and culture. This presumption of separation has meant, in practice, that feminist theory and cultural studies have focused almost entirely on the textual, linguistic, and discursive.

Defenders of postmodernism would argue that this is a misreading of the postmodern position or even that we cannot identify a single postmodern position in any case. Theorists such as Gilles Deleuze and Michel Foucault do, in fact, accommodate the material in their work. Their use of the material, furthermore, has been reflected in the work of other theorists. William Connolly, for example, employs the materiality of Deleuze in his *Neuropolitics* (2002). And feminist theorists such as Claire Colebrook and Ladelle McWhorter have drawn upon Deleuze and Foucault to enable them to engage with materiality in significant and revealing ways. Nonetheless, the material force of the work of Deleuze, and especially of Foucault, is often overlooked because of the exclusive focus on the discursive. Furthermore, the tendency to focus on the discursive at the expense of the material has been particularly evident in feminist versions of postmodernism. Judith Butler, perhaps the most notable feminist postmodern, is frequently criticized for her "loss" of the material, specifically the materiality of the body. The feminist debate over her *Gender Trouble* (1990) and *Bodies That Matter* (1993) is evidence, in the eyes of many feminists, that postmodern feminism has retreated from the material.[1]

This retreat from materiality has had serious consequences for feminist theory and practice. Defining materiality, the body, and nature as products of discourse has skewed discussions of these topics. Ironically, although there has been a tremendous outpouring of scholarship on "the body" in the last twenty years, nearly all of the work in this area has been confined to the analysis of discourses *about* the body. While no one would deny the ongoing importance of discursive critique and rearticulation for feminist scholarship and feminist politics, the discursive realm is nearly always constituted so as to foreclose attention to lived, material bodies and evolving corporeal practices. An emerging group of feminist theorists of the body are arguing, however, that we need a way to talk about the materiality of the body as itself an active, sometimes recalcitrant, force. Women *have* bodies; these bodies have pain as well as pleasure. They also have diseases that are subject to medical interventions that may or may not cure those bodies. We need a way to talk about these bodies and the materiality they inhabit. Focusing exclusively on representations, ideology, and discourse excludes lived experience, corporeal practice, and biological substance from consideration. It makes it nearly impossible for feminism to engage with medicine or science in innovative, productive, or affirmative ways—the only path available is the well-worn path of critique. Moreover, bracketing or negating materiality can actually inhibit the development of a robust understanding of discursive production itself, since various aspects of materiality contribute to the development and transformation of discourses. Note Donna Haraway's formulation in this volume of the "material-discursive," which refuses to separate the two.

Environmental feminists have long insisted that feminism needs to take the materiality of the more-than-human world seriously. The mainstream of feminist theory, however, has, more often than not, relegated ecofeminism to the backwoods, fearing that any alliance between feminism and environmentalism could only be founded upon a naïve, romantic account of reality.[2] As Stacy Alaimo argues in *Undomesticated Ground: Recasting Nature as Feminist Space* (2000), predominant feminist theories, from Simone de Beauvoir to Gayle Rubin and Monique Wittig, have pursued a "flight from nature," relentlessly disentangling "woman" from the supposed ground of essentialism, reductionism, and stasis. The problem with this approach, however, is that the more feminist theories distance themselves from "nature," the more that very "nature" is implicitly or explicitly reconfirmed as the treacherous quicksand of misogyny. Clearly, feminists who are also environmentalists cannot be content with theories that replicate the very nature/culture dualism that has been so injurious—not only to nonhuman nature but to various women, Third World peoples, indigenous peoples, people of color, and other marked groups. Rather than perpetuate the nature/culture dualism, which imagines nature to be the inert ground for the exploits of Man, we must reconceptualize nature itself. Nature can no longer be imagined as a pliable resource for industrial production or social construction. Nature is agentic—it acts, and those actions have consequences for both the human and nonhuman world. We need ways of understanding the agency, significance, and ongoing transformative power of the world—ways that account for myriad "intra-actions" (in Karen Barad's terms) between phenomena that are material, discursive, human, more-than-human, corporeal, and technological. Since the denigration of nature and the disregard for materiality cannot be entirely disaggregated, material feminism demands profound—even startling—reconceptualizations of nature.

One of the most significant areas of discontent within feminism is feminist science studies. Initially, feminist critiques of science focused on the androcentrism of science—the masculine constructions, perspectives, and epistemologies that structure scientific practice. Following the social studies of science, feminists argued that scientific concepts constitute the reality they study, that science, like all other human activities, is a social construction. Despite the persuasiveness of this position, however, questions began to arise about the viability of this approach. Feminist and other critics of science began to explore alternative approaches that bring the material back into science without losing the insights of social constructionism. The "new empiricism" of feminist science critics like Sandra Harding, Helen Longino, Lorraine Code, and Lynne Hankinson Nelson represents attempts to retain an empirical, material element without abandoning social construction.

Significant as this work has been, recent work in science studies promises to "make matter matter" in more significant ways. Theorists such as Bruno Latour and Andrew Pickering have begun to develop innovative theories that combine social construction with an understanding of the ontology and agency of the material world. Instead of focusing on the epistemology of scientific concepts, they have turned the focus to ontology and materiality. Feminist science critics Donna Haraway and Karen Barad have developed theories that define the human, nonhuman, technological, and natural as agents that jointly construct the parameters of our common world. They have demonstrated that this interaction has wide-ranging implications for the place of women and others in that world. Elizabeth A. Wilson also insists on the ongoing, mutual, co-constitution of mind and matter. Her book

Psychosomatic: Feminism and the Neurological Body (2004) refuses to merely critique neuroscience from a cultural perspective, but instead brings detailed accounts of the neurological body to bear on feminist thought.

Our intent in this anthology is to address the dis-ease in contemporary feminist theory and practice that has resulted from the loss of the material. But our intervention in this debate is a very specific one. Many within the feminist community have railed against the loss of the material. Many have argued that we must develop theories that bring the material back into feminist theory and practice; however, few have been successful in developing these theories. Our intention in compiling this anthology has been to seek out those few. We have sought theorists who do not simply lament the loss of the material but, rather, attempt to formulate approaches that address this problem. The essays we have collected here are seeking to define what Bruno Latour calls a "new settlement," a new way of understanding the relationship between discourse and matter that does not privilege the former to the exclusion of the latter. Karen Barad has argued that we must "construct a ballast" against the tendency in feminism to define theory as unconstrained play. This collection is intended to be a key element of that construction.

We have brought together thinkers who are attempting to move beyond discursive construction and grapple with materiality. A central element of that attempt, however, is to build on rather than abandon the lessons learned in the linguistic turn. The new settlement we are seeking is not a return to modernism. Rather, it accomplishes what the postmoderns failed to do: a deconstruction of the material/discursive dichotomy that retains both elements without privileging either. The theorists assembled here have been working to revise the paradigms of poststructuralism, postmodernism, and cultural studies in ways that can more productively account for the agency, semiotic force, and dynamics of bodies and natures. The most daunting aspect of such projects is to radically rethink materiality, the very "stuff" of bodies and natures. The innovative work of these theorists and many others constitutes what we are calling the "material turn" in feminist theory, a wave of feminist theory that is taking matter seriously.[3]

The material turn in feminist theory opens up many fundamental questions about ontology, epistemology, ethics, and politics, questions that are explored in the essays in this volume. "Material feminists" want to know how we can define the "real" in science and how we can describe nonhuman agency in a scientific context. The theories emerging from feminists who explore this perspective are redefining our understanding of the relationships among the natural, the human, and the nonhuman. They are developing theories in which nature is more than a passive social construction but is, rather, an agentic force that interacts with and changes the other elements in the mix, including the human. For these theorists, nature "punches back" at humans and the machines they construct to explore it in ways that we cannot predict. Feminist theorists of the body want definitions of human corporeality that can account for how the discursive and the material interact in the constitution of bodies. They explore the question of nonhuman and post-human nature and its relationship to the human. One of the central topics in this approach is the question of agency, particularly the agency of bodies and natures. Material feminists explore the interaction of culture, history, discourse, technology, biology, and the "environment," without privileging any one of these elements.

Material feminism opens up new ethical and political vistas as well. Redefining the human and nonhuman has ethical implications: discourses have material consequences that require ethical responses. Ethics must be centered not only on those discourses but on the material consequences as well. Material feminism suggests an approach to ethics that displaces the impasse of cultural relativism. Cultural relativism entails that all ethical positions are equal, that we cannot make any cross-cultural judgments. This impasse has stymied feminists who want to reveal the abuses against women in other cultures. A material ethics entails, on the contrary, that we can compare the very real material consequences of ethical positions and draw conclusions from those comparisons. We can, for example, argue that the material consequences of one ethics is more conducive to human and nonhuman flourishing than that of another. Furthermore, material ethics allows us to shift the focus from ethical principles to ethical practices. Practices are, by nature, embodied, situated actions. Ethical practices, which unfold in time and take place in particular contexts, invite the recognition of and response to expected as well as unexpected material phenomena. Particular ethical practices, situated both temporally and physically, may also allow for an openness to the needs, the significance, and the liveliness of the more-than-human world. Ethical practices—as opposed to ethical principles—do not seek to extend themselves over and above material realities, but instead emerge from them, taking into account multiple material consequences. Although a focus on ethical practices is not foundational in the modernist sense, it allows us to compare the material effects of those practices in a way disallowed by a strictly discursive approach.

Material feminism also requires a new political dimension. Political decisions are scripted onto material bodies; these scripts have consequences that demand a political response on the part of those whose bodies are scripted. Karen Barad's (1998) discussion of the political consequences of the invention and use of the sonogram to study the unborn fetus is an excellent example of the politics entailed by material feminism. The use of the sonogram on female pregnant bodies has political repercussions for all women in our society, redefining both "life" and "rights" in a political context. Barad's work also illustrates another aspect of material feminism: the interface between the scientific, technological, political, and human. It is impossible to neatly separate these elements; they are "mangled" together (in Andrew Pickering's terms) in the mix of political and social practice, and this mangle has material, political, and ethical dimensions.

Material feminism also transforms environmental politics, which is, of course, intimately related to environmental science. Indeed, the "truth" of scientific statements about the environment affects the direction of political decisions. Defining all scientific statements as equally valid social constructions does not provide environmentalists with a means of arguing for their positions. Current "debates" about global warming in which political conservatives attempt to discredit a veritable avalanche of scientific data from around the globe stand as a case in point. Clearly, environmental politics demands a renewed understanding that science can disclose indispensable knowledge about nonhuman creatures, ecosystems, and other natural forces. Unlike modernist or even postmodernist accounts that "background," in Val Plumwood's terms, the natural world—imagining it as a mere resource for technological progress or social construction—material feminism must insist that nature be considered a noteworthy actor within the realm of politics as well as science. Catriona Sandilands, in *The Good-Natured Feminist: Ecofeminism and the Quest for Democracy,* proposes, for example, a radical democratic project that would make space for nature in politics, not as a "positive, human-constructed presence, but as an enigmatic, active Other" (1999, 181). Sandilands recasts the political landscape in order to imagine ongoing democratic conversations in which nonhuman nature can participate in nondiscursive ways.

Moreover, thinking through the co-constitutive materiality of human corporeality and nonhuman natures offers possibilities for transforming environmentalism itself. Rather than centering environmental politics on a wilderness model, which severs human from nature and undergirds anti-environmentalist formulations that pit, say, spotted owls against loggers, beginning with the co-extensive materiality of humans and nonhumans offers multiple possibilities for forging new environmental paths. Environmental justice movements, for example, locate "the environment" not in some distant place, but within homes, schools, workplaces, and neighborhoods. These movements reveal that lower-class peoples, indigenous peoples, and people of color carry a disproportionate toxic load. Tracing the traffic in toxins involves scientific/economic/political/ethical analyses of realms and interest groups heretofore imagined separately, for example, those of health, medicine, occupational safety, disability rights, and environmental justice, as well as "traditional" environmentalisms devoted to the welfare of wild creatures. The same material substance, in this case, a particular toxin such as mercury or dioxin, may affect the workers who produce it, the neighborhood in which it is produced, the domesticated and wild animals that ingest it, and the humans who ingest the animals who have ingested it. Beginning with material substances rather than already constituted social groups may, in fact, allow for the formation of unexpected political coalitions and alliances.

The emerging theories of materiality developed in material feminisms are crucial for every aspect of feminist thought: science studies, environmental feminisms, corporeal feminisms, queer theory, disability studies, theories of race and ethnicity, environmental justice, (post-) Marxist feminism, globalization studies, and cultural studies. The essays in this anthology are a first step toward not just articulating these theories but integrating them into what amounts to a new paradigm for feminist thought. It is our thesis that this paradigm is currently emerging and that it is a necessary and exhilarating move for contemporary feminism. While this volume brings together some of the most thought-provoking and innovative theorists of the new "material feminism," no single volume can hope to represent every point of emergence; thus, this volume should be read in dialogue with the work of Luce Irigaray, Rosi Braidotti, Myra J. Hird, Susan Wendell, Ladelle McWhorter, Val Plumwood, Susan Squier, Lynda Birke, Mette Bryld, Nina Lykke, Gloria Anzaldúa, and others. We hope that this collection will encourage readers to forge their own connections between the essays included here and the work of other feminist scholars who insist upon the meaning, force, and value of materiality.

The essays in the first part of the book, "Material Theory," outline the broad parameters of the issues confronting material feminisms. Elizabeth Grosz takes on an issue that has been taboo in feminist accounts of science—Darwin's evolutionary theory—and argues that it can be useful to feminism. Grosz argues that feminists need a complex and subtle account of what biology is and how biology facilitates and makes possible cultural existence. To achieve this goal, she asserts, feminists should incorporate the most influential biological theory of the nineteenth century—Darwin's theory of evolution. Grosz identifies aspects of Darwin's thought that can be used to develop a feminist approach to biology. Her argument offers a kind of template for how the "new" feminist critiques of science should operate. Nothing is out-of-bounds; all possibilities are considered. And most importantly, the materiality of the subject of science is paramount.

The subject of Claire Colebrook's essay is what she calls the "new vitalism." Although she rejects the conservative vitalism of thinkers such as Bergson, Colebrook asserts that a radical feminist materialism must be grounded in a redefined vitalism. Colebrook discusses the work of Elizabeth Grosz along with that of Marx, Hegel, Bergson,

Judith Butler, Michel Foucault, and Gilles Deleuze, analyzing the philosophical and political reverberations of their conceptions of matter. Each analysis yields important insights into the redefinition of matter. Regarding Marx, Colebrook argues that the Marxist concept of dialectical materialism counters the depoliticizing of history by emphasizing bodily needs. Her rereading of feminist critiques of matter leads her to reform matter as "positive difference." Her bold formulations take the matter of corporeality seriously by refusing to posit the substance of the body as a mere blank slate for cultural constructions. Indeed, Colebrook emphasizes the extent to which matter can itself alter those systems. She concludes with an image of feminist art criticism and a feminist politics that "frees matter from the human through the human."

Susan Hekman's essay presents an argument for the movement from epistemology to ontology in contemporary feminist thought. Arguing that the focus on epistemology has had detrimental effects, Hekman asserts that we should embrace an ontological perspective that brings the material back into the forefront of feminism. Hekman's key argument is that we should replace a view of language as constituting reality to one that defines this relationship in terms of disclosure. If we define language as disclosing reality, she argues, we can retain a notion of the materiality of the world without abandoning the insights of social construction. Hekman uses this perspective to develop what she calls a social ontology of the subject, an approach that defines identity as both material and social.

Many of the authors in this collection rely on the work of Karen Barad to ground their approaches. Her essay included here makes it clear why her theory is so central to this emerging perspective. Barad's goal is to articulate "how matter comes to matter" and to define what she calls "posthumanist performativity." Her concept incorporates the material and the discursive, the human and the nonhuman, the natural and the cultural, while challenging these dichotomies and the givenness of the categories. Barad identifies her position as "agential realism," a position she derives from the work of Niels Bohr. Far from rejecting poststructuralist insights about language, Barad incorporates these insights while at the same time revealing where theorists such as

Foucault and Butler fall short. Barad's powerful and influential theory reveals the unique strengths of the "material feminism" we are advocating.

The second part of the book, "Material World," addresses the principal subject of science: nature. The "nature" of science, however, is entangled with the nature of philosophy, politics, literature, and popular culture. The multiple, overdetermined, and potent notions of nature have hardly been neutral when it comes to race, gender, or sexuality. Feminists have long had to combat the "nature" of misogyny—the very bedrock of essentialism, biological determinism, homophobia, and racism. Thus, the longstanding, pernicious associations between "woman" and "nature" in Western culture—associations that are rarely advantageous to either woman or nature—have made "nature" a treacherous terrain for feminism. Yet as several of us have argued, distancing feminism from the category of nature only serves to calcify nature as a solid ground for heterosexist infrastructure. Whereas most postmodern and poststructuralist feminisms have sought to disentangle "woman" from "nature"—for significant reasons, to be sure—material feminism seeks a thorough redefinition and transvaluation of nature. Nature, as understood by material feminism, is rarely a blank, silent resource for the exploits of culture. Nor is it the repository of sexism, racism, and homophobia. Instead, it is an active, signifying force; an agent in its own terms; a realm of multiple, inter- and intra-active cultures. This sort of nature—a nature that is, expressly, *not* the mirror image of culture—is emerging from the overlapping fields of material feminism, environmental feminism, environmental philosophy, and green cultural studies.

Donna Haraway's work, which has been essential for the development of all of the aforementioned fields, offers comprehensive and compelling transformations of the category of nature. The nature-culture divide is unthinkable within Haraway's conceptual universe, a universe that is replete with "material-semiotic actors" and such rich and revealing figures as the cyborg, the trickster coyote, and the Onco Mouse. Her essay in this volume takes on the question of what "nature" means in the complex practices of contemporary society. The stories with which she begins the essay illustrate that our understanding of nature must be able to incorporate historically located people, other organisms, and technological artifacts. "Nature" must encompass demarcation and continuity among actors that are both human and nonhuman, organic and inorganic. The practice of "otherworldly conversations"—in which various nonhuman entities participate as subjects rather than objects—provides one model for ethical relations that respect difference and allow for mutual transformation.

In "Viscous Porosity: Witnessing Katrina," Nancy Tuana brings together the key themes of this collection. First, she articulates the theoretical basis that inspires *Material Feminisms:* what she calls the interactionist ontology of viscous porosity. This theoretical position rematerializes the social and takes seriously the agency of the natural. It attends to the process of becoming in which unity is dynamic and always interactive, and agency is diffusely enacted in complex networks of relations. Second, she provides a brilliant illustration of how viscous porosity works by "witnessing" Katrina. Her analysis includes levees, the Army Corp of Engineers, global warming, the hurricane, the local politics of New Orleans, shell middens, the federal government, racial politics, and the poor and disabled populations of New Orleans. In a compelling argument, Tuana illustrates how the "dance of agency" brings all these elements together in the phenomenon we call "Katrina" and how their interaction destroys our neat divisions between human and nonhuman, biological and cultural. Tuana's essay graphically articulates the theoretical and practical implications of the perspective we are developing.

Vicki Kirby offers an intrepid argument for reconceptualizing the nature of nature by considering the possibility that what we have been calling culture "was really nature all along." Indeed, understanding nature via the values and terms of contemporary (cultural) criticism, such as articulation, reinvention, and the cacophony of multiple signifying agents, allows Kirby to dislodge the assumption that all naturalizing arguments are inherently conservative. Once nature is no longer presumed to be the realm of prescriptive, immutable, and retrogressive truths, feminism can carefully reconsider whether the heretofore negative conflation of "woman" and "nature" may actually offer possibilities for discussing the question of origins.

Both Stacy Alaimo and Catriona Mortimer-Sandilands situate human bodies within specific environmental contexts, reading human processes and events as inseparable from specific biophysical relations and interconnections. Alaimo's essay argues that imagining human corporeality as trans-corporeality, in which the human opens out into a more-than-human world, underlines the extent to which the corporeal substance of the human is ultimately inseparable from "the environment." The space-time of trans-corporeality is a site of both pleasure and danger—the pleasures of desire, surprise, and lively emergence, as well as the dangers of pain, toxicity, and death. Alaimo focuses, however, on toxic bodies, arguing that although they are not something to celebrate, toxic bodies may help lead feminist theory out of the false dilemma of having to choose between a romanticized valorization of bodies and natures or an anti-essentialist flight from the grounds of our being. As a particularly vivid example of trans-corporeal space, toxic bodies insist that environmentalism, human health, and social justice cannot be severed, since they are all continually emergent from zones of intra-activity (in Barad's terms) that are as biological as they are political, as material as they are social. Alaimo promotes trans-corporeal feminisms that encourage us to imagine ourselves in constant interchange with the "environment" and, paradoxically, perhaps, to imagine an "epistemological space" that allows for both the unpredictable becomings of other creatures and the limits of human knowledge.

Catriona Mortimer-Sandilands begins her essay, "Landscape, Memory, and Forgetting: Thinking through (My Mother's) Body and Place," by analyzing recent debates in environmental phenomenology that highlight the "relations between body, mind, and landscape." She departs from most environmental phenomenology by insisting upon the "particular techno-historical relationships between human bodies and others." Her wide-ranging essay weaves together environmental philosophy, an analysis of Jane Urquhart's novel *A Map of Glass,* scientific accounts of Alzheimer's disease, and a personal, poetic account of her mother's life with Alzheimer's. She argues, against David Abram, that we have not, in fact, "lost all traces of the environmental physicality of our memories." And she urges us to consider how we can "cultivate an awareness of and respect for this process through our environmental philosophies and activisms."

The final group of essays, "Material Bodies," focuses on the question of how feminist theory can rethink the materiality of human corporeality. Although there has been a veritable explosion of scholarship within feminist theory and feminist cultural studies about "the body," the overwhelming majority of that work analyzes discourses and representations—exclusively. This textual universe sometimes seems worlds apart from lived materiality and the often obdurate substance and unexpected agencies of corporeality. However, material feminisms that take the physicality of the human body into account are emerging.

Tobin Siebers's discussion of disability takes on one of the pillars of poststructuralist thought: the rejection of experience. Siebers questions the poststructuralist banishing of experience, asking whether this strategy is radical or reactionary. Relying on the emerging realist theory of identity, Siebers argues that social identities are both constructed and real. He concludes that the experience of disabled people embodies identities that may contain legitimate claims to knowledge and that this knowledge, once verified, is a valuable weapon against the oppression of minority people.

The question of identity and identity politics is also the focus of Michael Hames-García's essay. Examining the contradictions between social and biological conceptions of race, Hames-García argues that what is needed now is creative experimentation with racial identities rather than their abandonment. Against the critics of identity politics, Hames-García develops the thesis that racial identities can be useful, productive, and transformative; their progressive political potential can benefit from a substantive account of their material reality. Turning to Castells's theory of "project identities," Hames-García concludes that we need creative racial identity projects more than we need philosophical arguments against race.

Suzanne Bost turns her attention to bodies as they appear in the recent autobiographical writings of Chicana feminists. Bost's intervention is to use disability studies to examine the shifting matter of bodies in the work of Gloria Anzaldúa and Cherrie Moraga. Exploring a territory previously defined exclusively in terms of race and sex, Bost reveals how these authors' accounts of pain, illness, and disability uncover new dimensions in Chicana feminism. Using the "permeable and migratory politics of disability," she argues that the disabled subjects in the works of Anzuldúa and Moraga speak to the aims of Chicana feminism better than identity politics.

Elizabeth A. Wilson questions the way feminist critiques of psychopharmaceuticals emphasize the social rather than the biological. These accounts, in both academic and popular feminist writing, criticize the medical and pharmaceutical establishments—as well as the wider culture—for tranquilizing women's (social) discontent. Wilson takes a very different approach to the question of psychopharmaceuticals. By focusing directly on the specific biological effects of the SSRI and SNRI antidepressants, Wilson constructs innovative feminist positions that confound traditional understandings of mind and body. Most remarkably, perhaps, she suggests that it is possible to understand the psychoanalytic process of "transference" occurring at a microbiological level. If the "talking cure" can be understood as organic, as biological as well as mental, then our most basic understandings of "mind" and "matter" need be radically rewritten. Wilson's essay demonstrates how an unflinching engagement with biological specificities can allow feminist science studies to productively challenge established feminist positions.

Susan Bordo's piece, "Cassie's Hair," provides a fitting conclusion to the volume. Like Tuana's analysis of Katrina, Bordo provides an example of how the biological and the social interact. Bordo contrasts abstract conceptions of "difference" with the sense of difference that develops from specific practices that bring one into contact with materiality—in this case, the materiality of her biracial daughter's hair. Feminism has long held that even intimate, familial relations can be infused with political forces, but Bordo's essay suggests that the physicality of bodies can itself beckon us toward more complex understandings of how the personal, the political, *and* the material are braided together.

One of the most exciting aspects of this particular volume is that it reveals the remarkable intersections between scholars working in separate areas. In so doing, it encourages fruitful conversations between the fields of corporeal feminism, environmental feminism, and feminist science studies. The reader may notice, for example, that most of the essays in this volume address not only the topic of the part in which they appear, but the topics of the other two parts as well. Categories and organizational schemes are always provisional, to be sure, but perhaps the overlap and emerging dialogue between the essays is also a result of the topic itself, for attending to materiality erases the commonsensical boundaries between human and nature, body and environment, mind and matter. In short, taking matter seriously entails nothing less than a thorough rethinking of the fundamental categories of Western culture. In the process, these categories may become nearly unrecognizable. Thus, it is our hope that this volume will offer a substantial response to Teresa de Lauretis's recent call in *Critical Inquiry* to "break the piggy bank of saved conceptual schemata and reinstall uncertainty in all theoretical applications, starting with the primacy of the 'cultural' and its many 'turns'" (2004, 368). Such uncertainty requires risk, to be sure, as the specter of essentialism continues to haunt feminism. We think the risks are worth taking, however, since the emerging body of thought we are calling "material feminism" promises bold, provocative, and potent reconceptualizations of the material terrains of our shared worlds.

NOTES

1. More evidence of discontent can be found in recent critiques of feminist anti-essentialism. Many have argued that at this point the denouncement of essentialism has become a rigid orthodoxy, more prohibitive and policing than productive. The debates over essentialism are almost always, at some level, debates about the nature and force of materiality.

2. It is ironic that feminist poststructuralism and postmodernism tend to distance themselves from the category of nature if, as Verena Andermatt Conley contends, "the driving force of poststructuralist thought is indissolubly linked to ecology" (1997, 7). By demonstrating how ecology influenced poststructuralist thinkers, Conley radically revised predominant understandings of these theories.

3. Other important discussions of the "new materialism" include Susan Squier and Melissa M. Littlefield (2004) and Myra J. Hird (2004a, 2004b). The "new materialism" overlaps with what we term "material feminism." See also the special issue of *Feminist Theory* (5.2, 2004) edited by Squier and Littlefield that

focuses on the "new materialism" within science studies. "Material feminisms" and "new materialism" also overlap with what Iris van der Tuin (2006) terms "Third Wave Materialism." It is important to distinguish what we are calling "material feminism"—which is emerging primarily from corporeal feminism, environmental feminism, and science studies—from "materialist" feminism, which emerges from, or is synonymous with, Marxist feminism. Even as many of the theorists of what we are calling "material feminism" have been influenced by Marxist theory, post-Marxism, and cultural studies, their definition of "materiality" is not, or is not exclusively, Marxist. For more on "materialist" feminism, see the work of Christine Delphy, Michele Barrett, Annette Kuhn, Ann Marie Wolpe, and Rosemary Hennessy. Gerald Landry and Donna MacLean distinguish "materialist feminism" from Marxist feminism by noting that the latter "holds class contradictions and class analysis to be central," whereas the former also focuses on "race, sexuality, imperialism and colonialism, and anthropocentrism" (1993, 229). Teresa Ebert, in *Ludic Feminism and After: Postmodernism, Desire, and Labor in Late Capitalism,* critiques poststructuralist and postmodern feminisms, arguing that their "ludic matterism" perceives materiality as "sign/textuality or as the matter of the body," thus displacing the Marxist conception of matter as "the praxis of labor and the contradictions and class conflicts in which it is always involved" (1996, 34, 35). Even as labor and class remain essential concepts for feminist analysis and critique, they cannot encompass the materiality of human corporeality or, certainly, of nonhuman nature.

REFERENCES

Alaimo, Stacy. 2000. *Undomesticated Ground: Recasting Nature as Feminist Space.* Ithaca, N.Y.: Cornell University Press.

Barad, Karen. 1998. "Getting Real: Technoscientific Practices and the Materialization of Reality." *differences: A Journal of Feminist Cultural Studies* 10.2: 87–128.

Butler, Judith. 1993. *Bodies That Matter: On the Discursive Limits of "Sex."* New York: Routledge.

———. 1990. *Gender Trouble: Feminism and the Subversion of Identity.* New York: Routledge.

Conley, Verena Andermatt. 1997. *Ecopolitics: The Environment in Poststructuralist Thought.* New York: Routledge.

De Lauretis, Teresa. 2004. "Statement Due." *Critical Inquiry* 30.2: 365–68.

Ebert, Teresa. 1996. *Ludic Feminism and After: Postmodernism, Desire, and Labor in Late Capitalism.* Ann Arbor: University of Michigan Press.

Hird, Myra J. 2004a. "Feminist Matters: New Materialist Considerations of Sexual Difference." *Feminist Theory* 5.2: 223–32.

———. 2004b. *Sex, Gender and Science.* New York: Palgrave.

Irigaray, Luce. 1985. *Speculum of the Other Woman.* Trans. Gillian Gill. Ithaca, N.Y.: Cornell University Press.

Landry, Donna, and Gerald MacLean. 1993. *Materialist Feminisms.* Cambridge: Blackwell.

Sandilands, Catriona. 1999. *The Good-Natured Feminist: Ecofeminism and the Quest for Democracy.* Minneapolis: University of Minnesota Press.
Squier, Susan, and Melissa M. Littlefield. 2004. "Feminist Theory and/of Science." *Feminist Theory* 5.2 (special issue): 123–26.
Van der Tuin, Iris. 2006. "Third Wave Materialism." Paper presented at the Society for the Study of Science, Literature, and the Arts in Amsterdam.
Wilson, Elizabeth A. 2004. *Psychosomatic: Feminism and the Neurological Body.* Durham, N.C.: Duke University Press.

PART 1. MATERIAL THEORY

1

DARWIN AND FEMINISM: PRELIMINARY INVESTIGATIONS FOR A POSSIBLE ALLIANCE

Elizabeth Grosz

> [Darwin has] not succeeded in explaining living beings, but in constituting them as witnesses to a history, in understanding them as recounting a history whose interest lies in the fact that one does not know a priori what history it is a question of.
>
> —Isabelle Stengers, *Power and Invention*

There has traditionally been a strong resistance on the part of feminists to any recourse to the question of nature. Within feminist scholarship and politics, nature has been regarded primarily as a kind of obstacle against which we need to struggle, as that which remains inert, given, unchanging, and resistant to historical, social, and cultural transformations.[1] The suspicion with which biological accounts of human and social life are treated by feminists, especially feminists not trained in the biological sciences, is to some extent understandable. "Biology" not only designates the *study* of life but also refers to the body, to organic processes or activities that are the *objects* of that study. Feminists may have had good reasons to object to the ways in which the *study,* the representations and techniques used to understand bodies and their processes and activities, have been undertaken—there is clearly much that is problematic about many of the assumptions, methods, and criteria used in some cases of biological analysis, which have been actively if unconsciously used by those with various paternalistic, patriarchal, racist, and class commitments to rationalize their various positions. But there is a certain absurdity in objecting to the notion of nature or biology itself if this is (even in part) what we are and will always be. If we *are* our biologies, then we need a complex and subtle account of that biology if it is to be able to more adequately explain the rich variability of social, cultural, and political life. How does biology, the bodily existence of individuals (whether human or nonhuman), provide the conditions for culture and for history, those terms to which it is traditionally opposed? What are the virtualities, the potentialities, within biological existence that enable cultural, social, and historical forces to work with and actively transform that existence? How does biology—the structure and organization of living systems—facilitate and make possible cultural existence and social change?

FEMINISM AND BIOLOGY

It seems remarkable that feminists have been so reluctant to explore the theoretical structure and details of one of the most influential and profound theoretical figures of the modern era, Charles Darwin. For the last three decades or more, there has been an increasingly widening circle of male texts that have enthralled and preoccupied the work of many feminist theorists: Hegel, Nietzsche, Spinoza, Heidegger, Althusser, Lacan, Derrida, and Deleuze are just some of the more recent and philosophically oriented additions to this ever-expanding pantheon. This makes the virtual ignorance and neglect of Darwin's work even more stark and noticeable. It is not clear why Darwin—whose enduring impact on knowledge and politics is at least as strong as that of Hegel, Marx, or Freud—has been left out of feminist readings. It is perhaps time that feminist theorists begin to address with some rigor and depth the usefulness and value of his work in rendering our conceptions of social, cultural, political, and sexual life more complex, more open to questions of materiality and biological organization, more nuanced in terms of understanding both the internal and external constraints on behavior as well as the impetus to new and creative activities.

Some feminist theorists have made tentative approaches to a theoretical analysis of Darwin's scientific contributions. The most open has been Janet Sayers, in *Biological Politics: Feminist and Anti-Feminist Perspectives* (1982). She carefully distinguishes Darwin's theory from the more pointedly politicized and self-serving readings of the social Darwinists of Darwin's own times, and their current counterparts, sociobiologists. Darwin's theory of evolution, she suggests, implies "that the species characters are not fixed but change as the effect of chance variation and of selection of those variations that prove relatively well adapted to prevailing environmental conditions" (1982, 55). She sees it as a model that signals an open-ended becoming, a mode of potentially infinite transformation, which may prove helpful in feminist struggles to transform existing social relations and their concomitant value systems. Sadly, while she notes the relative openness of Darwin's understanding of evolution, she leaves its social and political implications largely unanalyzed. There is, however, perhaps only in the last few years, an increasing dis-ease with the rejection of biology in some more postmodern feminist concerns and the beginning of a more serious intellectual engagement with biological and scientific discourses.[2]

Other feminists, especially those working within evolutionary biology, have actively welcomed a Darwinian mode of explanation but have commonly reduced Darwinism to a form of determinism, to a partial explanation to be placed alongside of, or in parallel with, social and cultural accounts. This seems to be the most pervasive feminist position for those working *within* evolutionary Darwinism. Patricia Adair Gowaty, the editor of the only anthology specifically directed to exploring the relations between Darwinism and feminism, may serve here as representative of this trend. She claims that Darwinism is a discourse parallel with feminist social and political analyses. It functions in a different but contiguous conceptual space, outside the political interests of feminists. In attributing to it a *neutral,* noninfecting position vis-à-vis political, psychological, and cultural theory, she has effectively secured Darwinism against its own most radical insights (a fundamental *indetermination* seems one of the most exciting elements of Darwin's contributions to both science and politics) and has insulated feminism against any theoretical impact on, and from being transformed by, Darwinism:

> There are multiple foci of analysis in the modern biological study of behavior (including social behavior and social organization of both human and nonhuman animals). We ask questions about neuronal causation (How do sensory signals contribute to "cause" behavior?), about hormonal causation (How do hormonal signals "cause" behavior?). How do cognitive processes "cause" behavior? How do genes cause behavior? How do emotions or feelings cause behavior? None of these levels of foci of analysis are alternative to one another, meaning that each of these levels of causation or foci of analysis might (probably) simultaneously work to "cause" the expression of this or that behavior (including sexist behavior of all kinds). (Gowaty 1997, 5)

Clearly uneasy at the notion of causation in these accounts (this explains her use of quotation marks in all cases where the word *cause* is used—except in the case of "genes . . . emotions or feelings"), Gowaty reduces both Darwinism and feminism to positions on two sides of a mutual divide. They occupy different levels or "foci"; each provide a "proximate explanation" of their own fields of endeavor, which do not come into direct contact with each other. The social is uninfected by the biological; the biological is secured from intrusion by the social. They are assumed to act simultaneously without, however, any adequate explanation of how they affect and transform each other, how they integrate together or influence each other. Gowaty's use of Darwin implies both a reduced view of feminism (feminism as the struggle for social parity) and a reduced view of science (science as the search for causal relations), as well as a commitment to the impossibility of their interaction—indeed, a revelry in their neutral indifference to each other.

Sue V. Rosser outlines the way many other feminists have regarded Darwin's apparent androcentrism. She seems to endorse the common assumption that because Darwin's work is "biased," it requires a corrective lens that focuses on the active position of females rather than naturally assumes the perspective of the male as active evolutionary or sexual agent. Her position functions as an inverted Darwinism: if Darwin's theory could somehow be made more open to the position of females, if it could more adequately deal with both sexes, its "bias" could be redressed. She affirms a kind of Darwinist liberal reformism:

> [M]any feminist scientists have critiqued Darwin's theory of sexual selection for its androcentric bias. The theory of sexual selection reflected and reinforced Victorian social norms regarding the sexes. . . . Expanding considerably on the theory first presented in the *Origin,* Darwin specified, in the *Descent of Man,* how the process functions and what roles males and females have in it. . . . According to the theory, the males who triumph over their rivals will win the more desirable females and will have the most progeny, thereby perpetuating and increasing, over numerous generations, those qualities that afforded them victory. (Rosser 1992, 57)

In shorthand, Darwin's is a theory of "winners and losers," of the dominating and those who have succumbed to domination or extinction, a theory that, on the face of it, seems to provide a perfect justification for the relations of phallocentric and racist domination that constituted Eurocentric, patriarchal culture in his time as much as in ours. Darwinism, it is implicitly claimed in accounts such as Rosser's, justifies, rather than provides the tools by which to problematize relations of domination and subordination between races and sexes as well as the domination of the human over the natural.

These claims are strikingly similar to those that surrounded Freudian psychoanalysis in the estimation of feminists openly hostile to its possible theoretical contributions three decades ago: what Freud (Darwin) says about women is phallocentric, rooted in the assumption of a natural subordination of women to men; it is sexist and biased. Each privileges the masculine and positions the feminine as its subordinated and complementary counterpart. While this is undoubtedly true, more or less, of any discourse written before the development of feminism as a theoretical and political movement, it evades the more interesting question: without necessarily minimizing these investments in male and white privilege, do these discourses provide theoretical models, methods, questions, frameworks, or insights that nevertheless, in spite of their recognizable limitations, could be of some use in understanding and transforming the prevailing structures of (patriarchal) power and in refining and complexifying feminist analyses of and responses to these structures? Psychoanalytically oriented feminists have demonstrated, even while recognizing many of the limits of Freud's work, that it provides an account of the unconscious and of the acquisition of sexual identity that has proved crucial, if not indispensable, to the ways feminist theorists have come to understand subjectivity and desire. It seems timely to suggest that Darwin may himself prove to be as complex, ambivalent, and rewarding a figure for feminists to investigate as Freud has been. His writings may provide feminism with richer and more workable concepts of nature, the body, time, and transformation than those available to it from the discourses of cultural and political theory, history, or philosophy alone. Darwin's work may prove as rich, if not even more productive, for feminist thought as Freud's has been, in spite of its nineteenth-century conceptions of the relations between the sexes because, like Freud, Darwin opened up a new way of thinking, a new mode of interpretation, new connections and forms of explanation—indeed, a new discipline—that may prove useful in highlighting and explaining the divisions and connections between nature and culture.

I will argue that Darwin's work offers a subtle and complex critique of both essentialism and teleology. It provides a dynamic and open-ended understanding of the intermingling of history and biology (indeed, it is Darwin's work that most actively affirms the irreversibility of time within the natural sciences, the centrality of chance, and the accumulation of temporally sensitive characteristics), and a complex account of the movements of difference, bifurcation, and becoming that characterize all forms of life. His work develops an anti-humanist, that is, a broadly mechanical or fundamentally mindless and directionless, understanding of biological dynamics that refuses to assume that the temporal movement forward can be equated with development or progress. His work affords us an understanding of the productivity, the generative surprise, that the play of repetition and pure difference—the ongoing movement of biological differences and their heritable reproduction through slight variation, which he affirms as "individual variation"—effects the becoming of species. He is perhaps the most original thinker of the link between difference and becoming, between matter and its elaboration as life, between the past and the future. Moreover, his work pays specific attention to the question of sexual difference, to which he grants prominence as a quasi-autonomous feedback loop within the larger and more overarching operations of natural selection. The status and function of sexual selection and the intense variability, or difference, that he sees both within each sex and between the two sexes, as well as within and between species and genera, occupy a central, if ambiguous, position in his work that is worthy of serious feminist investigation.

These seem to provide at least prima facie reasons why it may prove fruitful for feminists to cast their critical gaze at Darwin, not simply with the a priori aim of dismissing his work, as has been the case in many feminist responses to any kind of biological analysis, or of simply accepting it and developing scientific research projects and paradigms that function to illustrate or refine its principles, as seems to have occurred with the largely revisionist ambitions of many feminist approaches within evolutionary biology. Rather, we need to look again at his texts with the desire to see what may be of value for providing feminist theory with richer and more subtle intellectual resources to both attain its aims and refine its goals.

DARWINIAN EVOLUTION

Although the most essential elements of Darwin's understanding of evolution are relatively straightforward and generally well known, there is a great deal of contention regarding the ways in which scientists and nonscientists have interpreted its most basic precepts. *The Origin of Species* (1859) has two aims: first, to demonstrate that contemporary species and forms of life are descended from earlier forms: if there is an "origin" of species, it is in earlier species and their transformations. And second, to demonstrate how such an evolution, a "descent with modification," is possible, and what processes and mechanisms enable both modification and descent to produce viable new species from the mutability and transformability of existing species. In this sense, Darwin offers an account of the *genesis of the new* from the play of repetition and difference within the old, the generation—of history, movement, and the dynamism of evolutionary change—from the impetus and mobility of existing species.

Darwin claims that three basic and closely linked principles explain the contrary forces at play in the evolution of species: individual variation, the heritability of the characteristics of individual variation that lead to the proliferation of species and individuals, and natural selection. The evolution of life is possible only through the irreversible temporality of genealogy, which requires an abundance of variation, mechanisms of indefinite, serial, or recursive replication/reproduction, and criteria for the selection of differential fitness. When put into dynamic interaction, these three processes provide an explanation of the dynamism, growth, and transformability of living systems, the impulse toward a future that is unknown in, and uncontained by, the present and its history. I will briefly outline each of these three principles.[3]

First, there is the postulate of a vast but often minute and possibly insignificant series of individual variations that may eventually lead to the formation of different species, that is, the postulate of diversity, which Darwin calls individual variation. This is the proliferation of individuating characteristics, differences, and features that may prove more or less significant in the successful adaptation of individuals or species to their environments. While a large number, the majority, of variations are either irrelevant to or positively harmful for the ongoing existence of species, there are random variations that are, or will prove to be, positive improvements relative to the environment, whether it is fixed or changing: "No one supposes that all the individuals of the same species are cast in the very same mould. These individual differences are highly important for us as they afford materials for natural selection to accumulate, in the same manner as man can accumulate in any given direction individual differences in his domesticated production" (Darwin 1996 [1859], 39).

Second, there is an invariable tendency to superabundance, excessiveness, the generation of large numbers of individuals, in the rates of reproduction and proliferation of individuals and species. Even if they merely reproduce their own numbers, they will eventually encounter scarcity and thus a hostile environment. This superabundance can be understood, negatively, as the struggle for existence, in which this excess drives species and individuals to compete with each other for increasingly limited resources, eventually eliminating the weaker and less successful in order to allow the proliferation of the stronger and the more successful. In more positive terms, it can be understood as the intensification of difference or variation: "There is no exception to the rule that every organic being naturally increases at so high a rate that if not destroyed, the earth would soon be covered by the progeny of a single pair" (Darwin 1996, 54).

This teaming proliferation of individuals and species suggests that the greater the proliferation of diversity, the more natural selection is able to take effect. If species reproduced themselves in ever-diminishing numbers, natural selection would be unable to weed out the less fit and provide space for the selection and profusion of the more fit.[4] The proliferation of numbers and the production of greater and greater variability does not occur untrammeled; it is restrained by a number of factors. While variation and proliferation are the very motors of the production of evolutionary change, there are nevertheless a series of limits on the type and degree of variability that any particular region or location can sustain.[5] The range and scope of diversity and variability cannot be determined in advance, but it is significant that there are inherent, if unknown, limits to tolerable, that is to say, sustainable variation: "monstrosities," teratological variations, may be regularly produced, but only those that remain both viable and reproductively successful, and only those that attain some evolutionary advantage, either directly or indirectly, help induce this proliferation.

Taken together, the two principles of individual variation and the heritability of this variation imply that if there is a struggle for existence in circumstances where resources may be harsh or scarce, then any variation, however small and apparently insignificant, may provide an individual with advantages that may differentiate and privilege it relative to other individuals. Even minute variations may provide major advantages for individuals, especially in unexpected and changing circumstances or environments. Moreover, if individual variations are inherited, whatever small advantages were bestowed on an individual may be amplified over time. It is in this capacity for individual variation that Darwin locates the origin of species and genera. Once individual variations are selected and become a force in heritable characteristics, and if there is some separation, geographical or ecological, between such individually differentiated groups, the conditions under which a new species, or several, emerge from common ancestors become clear:

> New species are formed by new varieties arising, which have some advantage over older forms; and those forms, which are already dominant, or have some advantage over the other forms in their own country, would naturally oftenest give rise to new varieties or incipient species; for these latter must be victorious in a still higher degree in order to be preserved and to survive. (Darwin 1996, 263)

Third, and as a counterbalancing yet interrelated force to these ongoing interactions between individual variation, the struggle for existence, and the inheritance of variation, is the postulate of natural selection. Natural selection functions either by inducing proliferation or by providing a hostile, or conducive, environment to select from the variety of life forms those that survive and provide reproductive continuity with succeeding generations. As its name suggests, natural selection is the process, or rather the processes (for it includes both artificial and sexual selection, discussed below) that provide selective criteria that serve to give significance and value to individual variations:

> If . . . variations useful to any organic being do occur, assuredly individuals thus characterized will have the best chance of being preserved in the struggle for life; and from the strong principle of inheritance they will tend to produce offspring similarly characterized. This principle of preservation, I have called, for the sake of brevity, Natural Selection; and it leads to the improvement of each creature in relation to its organic and inorganic conditions. (Darwin 1996, 104–105)

Darwin describes natural selection as the "principle of preservation," but this preservation is quite ambiguous and multilayered. It preserves only those variations that can viably function within its parameters or conditions and that show some marked or significant advantage over their competitors. The principle of preservation is the preservation of the fittest, of the most appropriate existences in given *and* changing circumstances, not the victorious species—the "winners" of evolutionary struggle at any particular moment—but those most open and amenable to change. Through its selective capacities, natural selection provides both a negative mechanism, which functions to eliminate much of the proliferation generated by the hyper-abundance of individual variation, indirectly sorting or sifting through the variations between individuals and species; and also a more positive productivity, when it functions as the source of a pressure on those individuals and species that survive to even greater proliferation and divergence:[6]

> [Natural Selection] entails extinction; and how largely extinction has acted in the world's history, geology plainly declares. Natural selection, also, leads to divergence of character: for more living beings can be supported on the same area the more they diverge in structure, habits, and constitution, of which we see proof by looking to the inhabitants of any small spot or to naturalised production. (Darwin 1996, 105)

Natural selection is rendered more intricate and complicated through the input of its two particular variations and complexifications, artificial selection and sexual selection. Artificial selection, the selective breeding of life forms through the human introduction of selection criteria, provides for Darwin a model for understanding the more general, overarching, but less visible relations of natural selection. Rather than being construed as polar opposites, as cultural and natural binaries, natural and artificial selection are regarded as two versions of the same thing, the artificial functioning according to the same principles as natural selection but varying the criteria for selection according to the aesthetic, material, or experimental investments of human breeders. The artificial illustrates the natural because it is subjected to its forces and principles though it simplifies it and renders explicit the selective criteria utilized.

Sexual selection functions, not in opposition to or as a separate stream from natural selection, but as one of its offshoots, as one of its more specific techniques for ensuring the detailed elaboration and functioning of the criteria of survival and reproductive success. It is significant that the bulk of feminist literature on Darwinism is devoted to a discussion, usually a critique, of Darwin's account of sexual selection, with relatively little attention paid to natural selection.[7] Yet sexual selection is clearly both a sub-branch of natural selection (those beings that reproduce sexually have an evolutionary advantage over their hermaphroditic counterparts in most but not all situations by virtue of the maximum variation generated by sexual reproduction), and an additional inflection, an intricate feedback loop, further complexifying natural selection processes, adding other criteria (primarily, attractiveness to the opposite sex) to its operations. Sexual selection adds more aesthetic and immediately or directly individually motivating factors to the functioning of natural selection, and it deviates natural selection through the expression of the will, or desire, or pleasure, of individuals. Sexual selection, while conforming in the long run to the principles of natural selection, nonetheless may exert a contrary force to the pure principle of successful survival, for reproductive success cannot be rendered equivalent to mere survival, though it requires it to operate.

Darwin notes that many features of animal appearance and adornment, even those that may in some way render the being less able to survive, more noticeable to predators, less able to protect or disguise itself than its dowdier yet fitter counterparts, nevertheless have survival value. In the case of the spectacular plumage of the peacock relative to the plainness of the peahen, Darwin's explanation is that even if its plumage and adornment make the peacock more vulnerable to attack, the more magnificent its coloring, the more bright, striking, and numerous its tail feathers, the more the attractiveness of the peacock to the peahen is enhanced and the more likely it is to leave numerous progeny that may inherit its sexual successes. While it is or may be disadvantaged in the stakes of natural survival, it is positively advantaged in the stakes of sexual selection.[8]

SEXUAL SELECTION AND RACIAL DIFFERENCES

It is significant that Darwin wants to link the question of sexual selection to the descent of the different races of man. Sexual selection—taste, individual choice—may have dictated that what were once slight individual variations, not yet classifiable as racial variation—variations in color, features, proclivities—would, if linked to sexual selection, and repeated for a number of generations, provide criteria by which males and females choose each other as sexual and reproductive partners. Racial differences cannot be attributed directly or solely to the selective pressures imposed by environments, Darwin argues, but may be the result of a preference for particular characteristics evolved through sexual selection: "If . . . we look to the races of man, as distributed over the world, we must infer that their characteristic differences cannot be accounted for by the direct action of different conditions of life, even after exposure to them for an enormous period of time" (Darwin 1981(1), 246).

Rather than claim that racial differences are the simple result of the selective capacities of extremes or particularities of environment, Darwin suggests that it may be precisely the sexual appeal or attractiveness of individual racial variations, however slight they may have been to begin with, that explains the historical variability and the genealogical emergence of racial differences. Racial differences may have been those differences that have been actively selected by individuals and perhaps amplified through geographical dispersion and the subsequent geographical and/or cultural isolation from our racially less-differentiated primordial ancestors:[9]

> We have thus far been baffled in all our attempts to account for the differences between the races of man; but there remains one important agency, namely Sexual Selection, which appears to have acted as powerfully on man, as on any other animal. I do not intend to assert that sexual selection will account for all the differences between races. An unexplained residuum is left. . . . It can be shewn that the differences between the races of man, as in colour, hairyness, form of features etc. are of the nature which it might have been expected would have been acted on by sexual selection. (Darwin 1981(1), 249–50)

Sexual selection inflects, and may be productive of, racial differences in the more stark and clear-cut forms that racial difference takes today, even if it is not the only contributing factor. What were once small, possibly biologically insignificant but sexually significant, characteristics exert a force in the functioning of sexual attraction, and it is this sexual appeal that gives these otherwise insignificant characteristics a key role to play in inheritance and long-term survival. Darwin makes explicit that skin color and racially signifying characteristics exert a *beauty,* an aesthetic force, which has had a major impact on phenotype and long-term survival. Sexual selection exerts a powerful force on the operations of natural selection: while it may sometimes work in congruence with natural selection, where the "fittest" individuals coincide with the most sexually attractive individuals, at other times it deviates natural selection through the detour of individual sexual preference and individual taste or discernment, even at the peril of individuals:

> The best kind of evidence that the colour of skin has been modified through sexual selection is wanting in the case of mankind; for the sexes do not differ in this respect, or only slightly and doubtfully. On the other hand, we know from many facts already given that the colour of the skin is regarded by the men of all races as a highly important element in their beauty; so that it is a character which would likely be modified through selection, as has occurred in innumerable instances with the lower animals. (Darwin 1996, 381)

Natural selection is the active, selective, and ever-transforming milieu of evolutionary change. It consists in what we understand as the biological context of any living being, which is comprised largely, but not entirely, of the other living beings in their various interactions with each other. It also consists in the geographical, climatological, and highly specific material context for each existent, which may be as geographically wide-ranging as continents for some species, or as small as a nest or tree for others. These conditions enable natural selection to provide ever-changing criteria by which both fitness or survival and sexual or reproductive success are measured.[10] Natural selection is not simply the passive background or context in which individual variation unfolds, a mere landscape that highlights and positions the living being; rather, it is a dynamic force that sets goals and provides resources and incentives for the ever-inventive functioning of species in their self-proliferation.

Between them, these three principles, on the one hand, provide an explanation of a series of processes and interactions that are fundamentally mindless and automatic, without plan, direction, or purpose, which are, on the other hand, entirely unpredictable and inexplicable in causal terms. Daniel Dennett (1996) has described this as Darwin's "dangerous idea": that the "excellence of design," the apparently perfect adaptation of species to the specificities of their environment and for long-term survival, is the result of both serendipity or chance of individual variation, which produces variation or difference for its own sake, randomly, and the fundamentally blind and mindless system of selection that inadvertently yet relentlessly weeds out and diminishes the effects and operations of the less-adapted, thus providing an evolutionary advantage to the more- and better-adapted.[11] As long as the timescale of evolutionary unfolding is long enough, the mindless automatism of natural selection and the spontaneous production and inheritance of variation have time to ensure that experiments in living, as they might be called, living in a variety of environments under a variety of conditions, produce maximal results from given and changing resources. These results then feed into the operations of natural selection to actively transform them, which in turn transforms the stakes involved in selection and which therefore work themselves out on new individuals and evolving species.

Darwin has outlined an ingenious temporal machine for the production of the new, which constrains the new only through the history that made it possible and the present that it actively transforms but that leaves its directions, parameters, and destinations unknown and unknowable, discernible only in retrospect or artificially through analysis and reconstruction. Where variation tends to occur through small, slow accretion—that is, where variation and inheritance tend to function slowly, over a large timescale requiring many successive generations—natural selection, which generally functions with a certain regularity and predictability, may, at times, function through catastrophic leaps; major climatological, geological, or population changes; and sudden and unpredictable upheavals. Its temporality is more (but not only) short-term, intensified, linked to the impact of events. It is in part the clash between the generally (but not universally) slow relentlessness of genetic variability and change, and the cataclysmic or irregular time of natural selection—that is, between two durational forms, two different rhythms of becoming—that the new, both new species and new environments, is generated.

If Darwin locates chance at the center of natural selection, as that which indicates an organism's openness, its potentially mortal susceptibility to changing environments, environments hitherto unseen or not yet in existence ("fitness" designating not superiority in a given milieu or environment but rather the adaptability of the organism, in its given state, to changing environments—a notion of fitness more in keeping with Darwin's own writings than socio-biological readings of evolutionary theory, which assume a pre-given notion of fitness, will allow), then from this time on, the random, the accidental, that which befalls an individual entity, becomes an essential ingredient in the history and development of that entity and in the group in which it lives and interacts. Chance erupts at both the level of random variation and at the level of natural selection, and perhaps more interestingly, in the gap or lag that commonly exists in their interaction. At the level of individual variation, chance emerges in the processes, unknown to Darwin at the time and still today, of genetic reproduction and recombination, which produces multiplicious, usually minute and insignificant variations in organisms. What dictates these variations is both unknown and in some sense irrelevant, at least as far as natural selection is concerned, for it works only on the viable and inherited results of such randomness. At the level of natural selection, Darwin suggests that changes in the environment and in the various pressures facing organisms within that environment are also unpredictable. But more significant than the randomness of either individual variation or the randomness of natural (or artificial) selection is the randomness of individual variation *relative to* natural selection. Furthermore, the randomness of individual variation, while in no sense causally connected to the randomness of natural selection, may actively transform the criteria by which natural selection functions.[12] In other words, evolution is a fundamentally open-ended system that pushes toward a future with no real direction, no promise of any particular result, no guarantee of progress or improvement, but with every indication of inherent proliferation and transformation.

NATURAL AND CULTURAL EVOLUTION

It is not clear that Darwin wanted to differentiate natural and cultural systems in his understanding of the differential selection of surviving variation. Evolution functions through reproduction, variation, and natural selection. As such, it should also, in principle, be able to explain the function of cultural phenomena such as languages, technologies, and social practices as readily as it can natural systems or biological species.

Darwin was fascinated by the evolutionary resemblances between species and languages. The "origin" and history of languages functions according to the same logic as biological species: proliferation, competition, natural selection, and the temporal dispersion of development are as much at the origin and history of languages as they are of species. In a sense, the matter through which such a logic operates, whether it is the matter of biology or of spoken and written languages, is of less significance than the principles of organization or emergence that govern it. And these principles are fundamentally bound up with the effectivity or use of that matter, and the weeding-out effects that this effectivity generates in its confrontation with an environment. It is thus not entirely surprising, though it seems to have evaded the reflections of some scientists working in the area, that Darwin has posited the same processes of production in natural as well as in avowedly cultural activities. His refusal to restrict the forces of evolution to biological or natural categories and activities, while deeply resented and questioned by some feminists, may prove to be part of the strength of his understanding and of its value for feminist and cultural theory. The force of his argument resides in the fact that, as Dennett makes clear, evolution, if it functions as an explanatory model at all, functions all the way up, from the lowliest species to the most elevated of cultural and intellectual activities.[13] The systematic cohesion of modes of reproduction (forms of repetition) with their resulting mutations, which are imperfect or innovative copies (forms of difference), and modes of "natural" selection (systems of differentiation), produces a system—or rather, an asystematic systematicity—that is co-extensive with all of life in its political, cultural, and even artificial as well as its natural forms.

What can feminists learn from Darwin? Of what use can Darwin's work be for feminist intellectual and political struggles? If Darwin's work provides a fundamental, indeed, canonical model for the biological sciences, is Darwin worth serious investigation for those feminists who do not work in the area of biology? These are difficult questions that require not only an openness to texts and positions that many feminists have asserted, sometimes dogmatically, are hostile to feminist interests (the discourses of nature and biology), they also require a different understanding of feminism itself. It is only if feminist theory puts itself at risk in what we might understand as its own "evolutionary" modes of self-overcoming, where it is confronted with its own limits, where it is placed in new situations and contexts, that its own explanatory power, its power to enhance both understanding and action, is tested against others and, ideally, is transformed. A more open feminist inquiry into the value and relevance of *any* discourse, not just Darwin's, involves not only feminist critique, not simply inspection for errors and points of contention, but more passively and thus dangerously, a preparedness to provisionally accept the framework and guiding principles of that discourse or position in order to access, understand, and possibly transform it, even knowing that it may remain problematic in many of its assumptions and claims. One must risk the seductive appeals of the key discourses of various disciplines and knowledges, even those that may appear hostile or antithetical to feminist concerns, in order to be able to use them rather than simply criticize them or seek to avoid them. Biological discourses are no more "dangerous," "ideological," "biased," or "misleading" than any other discourses or models; we ignore them only at the expense of our own disciplinary discourses and political models, only at the expense of our own growth and self-transformation.

I will suggest here in broad outline some of the possible ramifications that Darwin's understanding of evolution may have for the reevaluation (transvaluation?) of feminist discourses and methods.

1. Darwin's model of evolutionary unfolding provides a striking response to various theories of oppression. Oppression is the result of operations of systems of harm and injustice that privilege the bodies and activities of some at the expense of others. What Darwin's work makes clear is that what has occurred to an individual in the operations of a milieu or environment (it matters little here if it is natural or cultural) is the force or impetus that propels that individual to processes, not of remediation (remediation literally involves undoing what cannot be undone) but of self-transformation. The struggle for existence is pre-

cisely that which induces the production of ever more viable and successful strategies, strategies whose success can only be measured by the degree to which they induce transformation in the criteria by which natural selection functions.[14] This means that feminism itself must undergo continuous revision and revitalization, a thorough self-transformation of its basic presumptions, methods, and values, including its understanding of the harms and wrongs done to women. Evolution and growth, in nature as in politics, are precisely about overcoming what has happened to the individual through the history, memory, and innovation open to that individual. This is true of the survival of species as much as it is of the survival of political strategies and positions, historical events, and memories. It is only insofar as past wrongs, "injuries," are the spur to forms of self-overcoming that feminist or antiracist struggles are possible and have any hope of effectivity. Darwin makes it clear that self-overcoming is incessantly if slowly at work in the life of all species. Politics is an attempt to mobilize these possibilities of self-overcoming in individuals and groups. The logic by which this self-overcoming occurs is the same for natural as for social forces, and social forces borrow the energy and temporality of natural systems for political modes of resistance and overcoming.

Darwin's open-ended understanding of struggle and development seems to anticipate, rather than the liberal political discourses with which it is commonly associated (e.g., John Stuart Mill), a more "postmodern" concept of emergence. Indeed, there are some remarkable convergences between Darwin's understanding of the movements of evolution and Foucault's understanding of the fundamentally bottom-up, open-ended, strategic, or opportunistic dynamics of power. In Darwin, as in Foucault, there is a fundamental commitment to the intangibility of the hold of domination and its ongoing and transforming susceptibility to resistance and realignment in virtue of the very forms of distribution or patterning that power itself takes. Power generates resistance as much as species' development generates and in turn produces natural selection, from within, as variation or difference. For Foucault, power produces resistance, which transforms power, which produces resistances . . . in a never-ending spiral of self-transformation.

Resistances do not come from without but are actively generated by the forms that power itself takes, which are thereby vulnerable to the transforming effects of resistance. Neither power nor resistance has ongoing stability or a pre-given form; each is the ramifying effect of the other. In Darwin's work too, there is a sense in which the domination of individuals or species is precarious and necessarily historically limited, that the very successes of dominant groups produce the conditions for the domination of other groups that differ from them and serve to transform them. In both theorists, there is an understanding of the inherent productivity of the subordinated groups—precisely *not* a theory of victors who abolish the vanquished, but a theory of how transformation and change remains in principle open because of the position of the subordinated, because domination remains precariously dependent on what occurs not only "above" but also "below."[15]

2. This logic of self-overcoming, the motor of Darwinian evolution, must be recognized not only as a distribution of (geographical and geological) spacing, processes of spatial dispersion through migration and exchange, periodic isolation, and relations of proximity and contact with other groups; above all, and more commonly unrecognized, it is a form of temporization, in which the pull of the future exerts a primary dispersing force. Beings are impelled forward to a future that is unknowable and relatively uncontained by the past; they are directed into a future for which they cannot prepare and where their bodies and capacities will be open to recontextualization and re-evaluation. It is only retrospection that can determine what direction the paths of development, of evolution or transformation, have taken; and it is only an indefinitely deferred future that can indicate whether the past or the present provides a negative or positive legacy for those that come. This means that history and its related practices (geology, archaeology, anthropology, psychoanalysis, medical diagnosis, etc.) are required for understanding the current, always partial and residual situation as an emergence from a train of temporal events already given, which set the terms for, but in no way control, cause, or direct a future fanning out or proliferation of the present. The future follows directions latent or virtual in, but not necessarily actualized by, the present. Evolution represents a force of spatial and temporal dis-

persion rather than linear or progressive development, movements rather than goals, processes rather than ends.

3. One of the more significant questions facing contemporary feminist theory, and indeed all political discourses, is precisely what generates change; how change is facilitated; what ingredients, processes, and forces are at work in generating the conditions for change; and how change functions in relation to the past and the present. Darwin presents, in quite developed if not entirely explicit form, the elements of an account of the place of futurity, the direction forward as the opening up, diversification, or bifurcation of the latencies of the present, which provide a kind of ballast for the induction of a future different but not detached from the past and present. The future emerges from the interplay of a repetition of cultural/biological factors, and the emergence of new conditions of survival. It must be connected, genealogically related, to what currently exists, but it is capable of many possible variations in current existence, the exploration of its virtual tendencies as well as its actualized products. The new is the generation of a productive monstrosity, the deformation and transformation of prevailing models and norms, so that what has been unrecognized in the past and present, as well as what deformations the present can sustain, will elaborate themselves in the future.

4. Darwin provides feminist theory with a way of reconceptualizing the relations between the natural and the social, between the biological and the cultural, outside the dichotomous structure in which these terms are currently enmeshed. Culture cannot be seen as the overcoming of nature, as its ground or mode of mediation, the representational form that, through retrospection, produces the natural as its precondition. According to Darwinian precepts, culture is not different in kind from nature. Culture is not the completion of an inherently incomplete nature (this is to attribute to Man, to the human, and to culture the position of destination of evolution, its telos or fruition, when what Darwin makes clear is that evolution is not directed toward any particular goal). Culture cannot be viewed as the completion of nature, its culmination or end, but can be seen as the ramifying product and effect of a nature that is ever-prodigious in its techniques of production and selection, and whose scope is capable of infinite and

unexpected expansion. Nature and culture can no longer be construed as dichotomous or oppositional terms when nature is understood as the very field on which the cultural elaborates and develops itself. Language, culture, intelligence, reason, imagination, memory—terms commonly claimed as defining characteristics of the human and the cultural—are all equally effects of the same rigorous criteria of natural selection: unless they provide some kind of advantage to survival, some strategic value to those with access to it, there is no reason why they should be uniquely human or unquestionably valuable attributes. Darwin affirms a fundamental continuity between the natural and the social, and the complicity, not just of the natural with the requirements of the social, but also of the social with the selective procedures governing the order and organization of the natural.

5. Darwin's work may add some welcome layers of complexity to understanding the interlocking and entwinement of relations of sexual and racial difference. His work makes clear how sexual selection, that is to say, relations of sexual difference, may have played a formative role in the establishment of racial differences in the terms in which we know them today, and moreover, how racial variations have fed into and acted to transform the ways in which sexual difference, subjected to the laws of heredity, is manifested. Darwin provides an ironic and indirect confirmation of the Irigarayan postulation of the irreducibility, indeed, ineliminability, of sexual difference, and its capacity to play itself out in all races and across all modes of racial difference.[16] He makes sexual difference one of the ontological characteristics of life itself, not merely a detail, a feature that will pass. Although sexual difference—the requirement of genetic material from two sexes—emerges for Darwin contingently or randomly, an ingenious "invention" of primitive life that maximizes individual variation by ensuring that each generation varies from the previous one, it is now so well adapted to the generation of variation that it would be hard to imagine an invention life might generate to compete with and supersede it. Sexual difference is an ineliminable characteristic of life because of its peculiar economy of combination, exchange, and variation and because of its pervasive historical force and effectivity. Darwin's work indirectly demonstrates the way

racial and bodily differences are bound up with, and complicated by, sexual difference and the various transforming criteria of sexual selection. This is not to suggest any political or logical secondariness of racial and other differences, but only their fundamental reliance on sexual difference, the ways in which they are fundamentally bound up with the historicity of sexual relations.

6. Darwin's work, with the centrality it attributes to random variation, to chance transformations, and to the unpredictable, has provided and will continue to provide something of a bridge between the emphasis on determinism that is so powerful in classical science and the place of indetermination that has been so central to the contemporary postmodern forms of the humanities. Evolution is neither free and unconstrained, nor determined and predictable in advance. It is neither commensurate with the temporality of physics and the mathematical sciences, nor is it unlimited in potential and completely free to develop in any direction. Rather, it implies a notion of overdetermination, indetermination, and a systemic openness that precludes precise determination. This is the temporality of retrospection, of reconstruction, but a reconstruction whose aim is never the faithful reproduction of the past so much as the forging of a place for the future as the new.

7. Darwin had provided a model of history that resorts neither to the telos or a priorism of the dialectic, nor to a simple empiricism that sees history simply as the accumulation of variously connected or unconnected events. History is fundamentally open but also regulated within quite strict parameters. There are historical—that is, temporal, genealogical—constraints on what becomes a possible path of biological/cultural effectivity: it is only that which has happened, those beings in existence, now or once, that provide the germs or virtualities whose divergence produces the present and future. That which has happened, the paths of existence actualized, preempt the virtualities that other existences may have brought with them; they set different paths and trajectories than those that might have been. While time and futurity remains open-ended, the past provides a propulsion in directions, unpredictable in advance, that in retrospect have emerged from the unactualized possibilities that it yields.

While I am not suggesting that feminists now need to become adherents and followers of Darwin, as in the past it seemed imperative to embrace the discourses of Marx or Freud or Lacan, I am claiming that there is much of significance in Darwin's writings that may be of value for developing a more politicized, radical, and far-reaching feminist understanding of matter, nature, biology, time, and becoming—objects and concepts usually considered outside the direct focus of feminist analysis. His work is not "feminist" in any sense, but as a profound and complex account of the organic becoming of matter, of the strategies of survival and the generation of multiple modes of becomings in the face of the obstacles or problems of existence that life poses for them, it is or should be of some direct interest and value for feminists.

NOTES

1. There is, of course, no unanimity in any feminist endeavor. There are certainly a number of feminists who have actively lauded the virtues of women's connections with nature. These have been variously described as cultural feminists, radical feminists, and ecofeminists. This project must be carefully differentiated from the interests of ecofeminism and its cognates on several grounds: (1) it is directed primarily at ontological and epistemological claims, while ecofeminism seems largely oriented to ethical, moral and economic issues; (2) it disputes the a priori commitment to holism, the presumption that the interconnectedness of ecological orders forms a systematic whole that lies at the basis of much ecological and ecofeminist thought. It argues that Darwin's work stresses difference, divergence, bifurcation, and division, the fracturing of a social and biological field rather than interconnectedness and wholeness. It is the *asystematicity* of the Darwinian system that is of interest to me here. Finally, (3) this project is not concerned with placing women in a different position from men in their relations to nature; women have no more, or any less, connection to the natural (or the social) order. The question here is not to explore women's particular connection to nature but rather the role that different, critically revitalized conceptions of nature may play in our understandings of the becomings open to each sex.

2. There is, of course, considerable feminist scholarship involved in science itself (e.g., Keller, Fausto-Sterling, Oyama), but it is only recently that feminist theorists in the humanities and social sciences have exhibited an openness to the relevance of biological research in the analysis of the social relations between the sexes. See, for example, the work of Elizabeth A. Wilson (1998, 2004), Margrit Shildrick and Janet Pryce (eds., 1999), Griet Vandermassen (2004), and Catherine Waldby (1996, 1999, 2000).

3. It is not entirely clear whether there are three or two principles governing the movement of evolution. Most scientists regard evolution as governed by

two broad principles—individual variation and natural selection—and they subsume under the category of individual variation the idea of the heritability of variation. I prefer here, in a nonscientific, philosophical context, to make as explicit as I can the conceptual nuances involved in his account. The heritability of individual variation is not conceptually contained in an understanding of individual variation (as Lamarckianism attests), so I will consider it a separate principle and deal with it separately.

4. "A high degree of variability is obviously favorable, as freely giving the materials for selection to work on; not that mere individual differences are not amply sufficient, with extreme care, to allow of the accumulation of a large amount of modification. . . . When the individuals of any species are scanty, all the individuals, whatever their quality may be, will generally be allowed to breed, and this will effectively prevent selection" (Darwin 1996, 35).

5. Stephen Jay Gould (1989) makes it clear from his analysis of the Burgess Shale—a discovery of ancient fossils with bodily forms of a type never seen before or since—that there is the possibility (indeed, the actuality) of almost unimaginable morphological variations, of creatures so unlike those usually discovered in fossil records or living today that they appear otherworldly.

6. While the teratological influence on mutation and genetic transformation is commonly noted, there is currently a body of research on epigenetic markers that indicates a more direct relation between the forces of natural selection, or at least, environmental effects, and the heritability of genetic variations they produce: "Over the course of evolutionary time, a variety of mechanisms, mediated by epigenetic factors, have emerged to generate new variation with the potential of 'bailing out' organisms that have become dysfunctional under conditions of stress. Selection—intracellular, cell lineage, or organismic—provides the conditions under which adaptive variants can become fixed. For many organisms that normally reproduce asexually, a switch to sexual reproduction can provide this diversity" (Keller 1998, 116).

7. "Aside from noting its statement in terms of upper-class Victorian values and decrying the misuse of his theory of natural selection by social Darwinists, feminist scientists by and large have not critiqued the theory of natural selection. As scientists, they have recognized the significance of the theory for the foundations of modern biology. Given the strong attacks on natural selection by creationists and other groups not known for their profeminist stances, most feminist scientists who might have critiqued some minor points have been reluctant to provide creationists with evidence they might misuse. In contrast to accepting his theory of natural selection, many feminist scientists have critiqued Darwin's theory of sexual selection for its androcentric bias. The theory of sexual selection reflected and reinforced Victorian social norms regarding the sexes" (Rosser 1992, 57).

8. See Darwin 1981(2), 135, 157–58.

9. There has been a tremendous amount of literature on the question of the biology of race, and it is significant that a good deal of it devoted to the critique of Eurocentrism has suggested that racial categories are social constructs. I have no doubt that the various distinctions and categories that mark race today and in the past are historically variable, politically motivated, and highly volatile in their operations; but it is also clear that there are systematic, visible differences between

groups of individuals that we can mark in various, perhaps arbitrary, ways. Darwin's understanding of race in no way preempts the study of the history and politics of racialized categories. Nor does it preempt further analysis of bodily differences, including genetic differences. What these differences are remains unclear. Darwin's work does, however, imply that what we understand as racial differences are primarily, or in the first instance, bodily variations, variations that in themselves may have no particular or a priori social significance and that come to acquire their significance and value only in social contexts. These bodily variations do not in themselves form racial categories, which imply conceptual discontinuities from other races, for they constitute individual variations, variations in a continuum of bodies and bodily types.

10. The rate by which the ever-changing status of natural selection functions is quite variable and specific: Darwin's position is closely tied to the presumption that many of these changes are imperceptible over generations and only come to acquire significance when measured in geological or cosmological time.

11. See Dennett 1996, 51:

> What Darwin discovered was not really *one* algorithm, but rather, a large class of related algorithms that he had no clear way to distinguish. We can now reformulate his fundamental idea as follows:
>
> Life on earth has been generated over billions of years in a single branching tree—the Tree of Life—by one algorithmic process.
>
> That there is something fundamentally mindless and automatic about the Darwinian system is certainly one its explanatory advantages. And Dennett is quite correct to recognize that the mindlessness of these processes renders no category, including the most hallowed of philosophy, untouched. Reason, conscience, nobility—all the human virtues and inventions are the long-term effects of the same kind of automatism that regulates the existence of the most humble bacteria. What is dangerous about Darwinism is that it sets the whole of cosmology into a framework of forces that are incapable of being controlled by its participants.

12. In some of the recent literature, there has been an argument that there is a nonrandom variation induced by natural selection—an epigenetic inheritance—that natural selection may have a more direct impact on selectable and heritable variations:

> One of our major themes is that the variation on which evolutionary change is based is affected by instructive processes that have themselves evolved. In addition to random genetic change, natural selection has produced systems that alter the base sequence of DNA by responding to special external stimuli.
>
> Other sources of heritable variation that have clearly been molded by natural selection are the epigenetic inheritance system, which transmits information between individuals through social learning. The adaptability that these additional inheritance systems allow can be the basis of long-term genetic adaptations (Jablonka and Lamb 1998, 120–21).

13. While Dennett provides one of the more rigorous philosophical readings of Darwinism and has, furthermore, acknowledged and explored the "danger" (his term) of Darwin's idea, the threat it poses, not only to received religions but also to those humanists who wish to attribute a post- or nonevolutionary status for the products of mind or reason—this, after all, was the limit of Alfred Russel Wallace's version of evolution: he exempted mind from the operations of evolution—Dennett himself submits to the same exigency when he distinguishes the biological evolution of species from what he describes, following Richard Dawkins's (1976) usage, as the "memetic" evolution of cultural and mental concepts. Dennett effectively reproduces precisely the mind/body split that he so convincingly criticizes in Wallace, Stephen Gould, and a series of other evolutionary thinkers. He argues that the evolution of concepts is subject to the same principles of evolution as the evolution of biological entities. With this claim, I have no disagreement. However, he presents the evolution of ideas in a separate landscape than the evolution of biological beings, when the evolution of concepts and cultural activities can be regarded simply as the latest spiral or torsion in the function of one and the same biological evolution. For Dennett, as for Dawkins, memes are "analogues" of genes, rather than, as Darwin himself would imply, the ramifying products of genes (see Dennett 1996, 345, 347). Memes are to mind what genes are to bodies! I have further developed my criticisms of Dennett's understanding of evolution in Grosz 2004.

14. I am not suggesting, to put it bluntly, that the violent persecution of various individuals or minorities is a good thing; rather, I am suggesting that, given that oppressions, harms, injustice have occurred and cannot be undone, the political task is not simply to mourn or lament them, but to use them, their memory, precisely as a spur to transformation, to difference. It is this violence, this memory of injustice and pain, that is the ballast that may serve to produce a different future.

15. See *The History of Sexuality*, Vol. 1 (1978), particularly the section called "Method."

16. As Irigaray claims,

> Without doubt, the most appropriate content for the universal is sexual difference. . . . Sexual difference is an immediate natural given and it is a real and irreducible component of the universal. The whole of human kind is composed of women and men and of nothing else. The problem of race is, in fact, a secondary problem—except from a geographical point of view— . . . and the same goes for other cultural diversities—religious, economic, and political ones.
>
> Sexual difference probably represents the most universal question we can address. Our era is faced with the task of dealing with this issue, because, across the whole world, there are, there are only, men and women. (1996, 47)

I do not believe that Irigaray here denies the centrality of other differences, other modes of oppression. Racial relations and oppressions based on sexual preference or religious affiliation clearly have a relative autonomy from the question of sexual difference. Where Darwinism confirms Irigaray's position is in claiming that the structures of racial, religious, and sexual orientation are open to potentially infinite historical transformation, given a long enough period of time, in ways that may or may not be true for sexual difference. This in no way places sexual difference outside historical or biological transformation, nor does it render it any more significant than other forms of oppression in explaining the complexities of social and cultural evolution; it simply insists that whatever other factors are at work, sexual difference must be a consideration, a relevant factor.

REFERENCES

Darwin, Charles. 1981 [1871]. *The Descent of Man, and Selection in Relation to Sex.* Princeton, N.J.: Princeton University Press.

———. 1996 [1859]. *The Origin of Species.* Oxford: Oxford University Press.

Dennett, Daniel. 1996. *Darwin's Dangerous Idea: Evolution and the Meaning of Life.* New York: Touchstone.

Foucault, Michel. 1978. *The History of Sexuality.* Vol. 1: *An Introduction.* Trans. Robert Hurley. London: Allen Lane.

Gould, Stephen Jay. 1989. *Wonderful Life: The Burgess Shale and the Nature of History.* New York: Norton.

Gowaty, Patricia Adair, ed. 1997. *Feminism and Evolutionary Biology: Boundaries, Intersections, and Frontiers.* New York: Chapman and Hall.

Grosz, Elizabeth. 2004. *The Nick of Time: Politics, Evolution and the Untimely.* Durham, N.C.: Duke University Press.

Irigaray, Luce. 1996. *I Love to You. Sketch of a Possible Felicity in History.* Trans. Alison Martin. New York: Routledge.

Jablonka, Eva, and Marion J. Lamb. 1998. "Bridges between Development and Evolution." *Biology and Philosophy* 13.1: 119–24.

Keller, Evelyn Fox. 1996. *Reflections on Gender and Science.* New Haven, Conn.: Yale University Press.

Rosser, Sue V. 1992. *Biology and Feminism: A Dynamic Interaction.* New York: Twayne.

Sayers, Janet. 1982. *Biological Politics: Feminist and Anti-Feminist Perspectives.* London: Tavistock.

Shildrick, Margrit, and Janet Pryce, eds. 1999. *Vital Signs: Feminist Reconfigurations of the Bio/logical Body.* Edinburgh: University of Edinburgh Press.

Stengers, Isabelle. 1997. *Power and Invention: Situating Science.* Trans. Paul Bains. Minneapolis: University of Minnesota Press.

Vandermassen, Griet. 2004. "Sexual Selection: A Tale of Male Violence and Feminist Denial." *European Journal of Women's Studies* 11.1: 9–26.

Waldby, Catherine. 1996. *AIDS and the Body Politic: Biomedicine and Sexual Difference.* London: Routledge.

———. 1999. "IatroGenesis: The Visible Human Project and the Reproduction of Life." *Australian Feminist Studies* 14: 29, 77–90.

———. 2000. *The Visible Human Project: Informatic Bodies and Posthuman Medicine.* London: Routledge.
Wilson, Elizabeth A. 1998. *Neural Geographies: Feminism and the Microstructure of Cognition.* New York: Routledge.
———. 2004. *Psychosomatic: Feminism and the Neurological Body.* Durham, N.C.: Duke University Press.

2

ON NOT BECOMING MAN: THE MATERIALIST POLITICS OF UNACTUALIZED POTENTIAL

Claire Colebrook

THE NEW VITALISM

Why would feminism turn to vitalism, and how could vitalism today become a way of politicizing problems? To feel the force of these questions, we might begin to consider why, until recently, "vitalism" was a pejorative term. Only then can we begin to see how and why the reworkings of the vitalist tradition have been so beneficial—and perilous—for feminist thought.

When feminists turn to vitalism today, they do so with a full sense of the exhaustion and limits of the linguistic paradigm. The idea that the world is constructed through language merely repeats a centuries-old privilege of the formal and logical over the material (Gatens 1996). It is not surprising, then, that having returned the body to philosophy, by arguing that we should not just see the body as the vehicle through which mind or activity makes its way in the world, feminism is now appealing to more radically impersonal vital processes—such as the evolutionary forces through which bodies become, or the somatic responses that cannot be referred back to the agency of the organism (Grosz 2005; Wilson 2004). At a broader level, the work of Gilles Deleuze, with its emphasis on mind and language as *emergent,* has led critical theory to take up recent and fashionable work in the sciences regarding the brain, life processes, and the dynamism of matter (Protevi 2001). However we regard the "waves" of feminism, and however many waves we deem there to be, we do appear to be at the threshold of a new wave, and this would be the result of contingent but revolutionary confluences. Just as critical theory is recognizing that poststructuralism, far from being a theory of language, was a rigorous philosophy of life, the life sciences themselves—through new imaging technologies—are turning to problems of emotion, affect, distributed cognition, and emergence.

Once considered to be radical feminist questions, the problem of the embodiment of thinking and the passions of reason are now central to new developments in cognitive science and neuro-philosophy. General arguments about supposedly abstract and constructed phenomena—such as the relation between male and female, reason and passion—can now be given a material basis. Such a material basis is far from being reductive. If there is a biological and evolutionary basis to aesthetics, this is not because works of art bear a timeless value, but because they are composed in response to the brain's recognition mechanisms, which themselves have a history and malleability. If there is an evolutionary imperative at the heart of our emotional and rational tendencies, then this is not because of hard-wiring but because the brain is adaptive and dynamic (LeDoux 2002). Brain science is not a question of finding "the" gay gene, the emotional center of the brain, or the relation between nature and nurture. For the contemporary picture of the brain is one of networks, so that one's reasoning and emotional capacities are both formed through time and grounded in the body and its processes.

The turn to life, the vital, and materialism is therefore also a turn away from the ways in which matter (as the bearer of properties) and the vital (as the spirit that infuses matter) have been defined. In this chapter I will argue that despite such caveats some aspects of a less critical vitalism remain in cognitive archaeology, neuroscience, and some of the best feminist work on life. In order to make this argument, I will suggest that we need to attend to the subtle criticisms of vitalism that defined poststructuralism.

Both Edmund Husserl and Henri Bergson—philosophers whom Jacques Derrida (1978a) and Gilles Deleuze (1988) began their careers researching—were related curiously to vitalism. Husserl insisted that as long as logic and language circulated as repeatable and efficient systems, detached from the sense of their origin, they could only diminish the life and potential of reason (Husserl 1970). Husserl was also critical of the then fashionable *Lebensphilosophie.* The idea that we can explain formal and eternal truths by appealing to life processes is a category error. It may be the case that we require some desiring, living, fleshy, and located individual to formalize and inscribe the truths of logic, mathematics, and geometry; but once those truths have been given form or written down, they take on a spiritual being—a pure truth for all time that is available for any later subject who can re-live the original intuition.

Bergson was also critical of simple material notions of life, rejecting the idea that evolutionary change occurs in a mechanical manner. Unlike contemporary proponents of evolution such as Daniel Dennett (2003), for whom it is possible to explain the freedom of life as the interaction of random elements, Bergson defined life as explosive, creative, and *intensive:* belied by the perception we have of it in terms of quantities *of* this or that (Bergson 1911). Life for Bergson is the production of difference, and the responsive and dynamic relation among differences. We can explain organisms as the outcome of a process of creativity. Life produces change but also maintains a relative stability for the sake of further creation. The mind, for example, responds to the dynamism of life by creating relatively stable concepts, but doing so allows it to create further difference. Without language, the mind would be bombarded with intense difference; with language, the mind can master difference and then go on to create further potentials for production (through science, philosophy, or art). We should not, therefore, see life as a realm of matter that produces change through mechanical and random interaction; nor should we regard matter as bearing some intrinsic form that would unfold through time. Life ought not to be conceived as matter, for matter is nothing more than the relatively stable form taken on by a life that is truly and fundamentally a potentiality for change (Bergson 1912). Life is spirit in two senses: it is not a thing or body so much as a potential for difference and creation that traverses bodies; accordingly, the true understanding of a body is achieved, not by regarding what it *is,* but by understanding the movements or problems that animate it. Bergson therefore argued for the sense of spirit and the spirit of sense: we can grasp the meaning of a word or action, experience a particular memory, and understand evolutionary change only because of spirit. If I can understand what you say or have a *sense* of what you are doing, then it is only because I intuit the spirit that animates you to speak or move. If I want to understand an organism, I do not classify it in relation to other living beings, but I consider how it came into being. In the case of evolution, Bergson gives the example of the emergence of the eye: if life were merely the contingent and random interaction of elements, then nothing as complex as the eye could emerge. Instead, life must be creative and marked by striving; we understand the life of the eye by understanding it as a response to the problem of light, as a created and achieved power.

It is just this appeal to spirit or the virtual that made Bergson so attractive for Deleuze, and in turn for feminism. It was also the concept most criticized by Derrida and Deleuze. For Derrida, the Husserlian appeal to a spirit of sense that could always be re-intuited was the epitome of a Western architectonic metaphysics (1978a). For Derrida, Husserl was radical in arguing that mathematics and logic must have emerged from temporal and flowing life. However, by insisting that one could always return to the emergence of sense and logic from life, Husserl precluded a consideration of all those radically material elements—in the sense of inanimate, unproductive, and inert—that would be resistant to comprehension. For Derrida, Western metaphysics has always been critical of the subjection of the flow of life and time to discrete units or quantities. What cannot be admitted, Derrida insists, is some mark, trace, or scar that could not be included within the self-recognition of one all-inclusive life that recognizes, masters, and senses itself.

Deleuze's criticism of Bergson also focused on Bergson's resistance to the mathematical and quantification. In *Time and Free Will,* Bergson argues against the existence of intensive quantities. The moment we try to give a quantity to temporal qualities, we materialize, or render extensive, movements through time that are belied by the establishment of fixed points. (Mapping degrees of color or light misses irreducible quantities.) In *Difference and Repetition* (1994), however,

Deleuze argues for "an ethics of intensive quantities." There is not a spiritual, flowing life on the one hand, and then the systems of the intellect that reify that life on the other. On the contrary, "our" life—the life within which we think and do philosophy—must attend to the points that matter: how much of a quality can we discern, at what thresholds do we become conscious or begin to think? Crucial to this question is the machine; the cinematic eye, for example, can allow thinking to make connections that are no longer those of the synthesizing and ordering brain. Literary language, by deforming the syntax and grammar that enables efficient, striving, and self-maintaining life, frees human thought from its own rhythms and propensities. Deleuze's ethics of intensive quantities resists a "cerebral vitalism" (Deleuze and Guattari 1994, 194), where there is a life or spirit liberated from any fixity or inertia, and instead confronts a passive vitalism in which the points of perception, consciousness, or spirit always depend upon systems—such as language—that are never fully alive.

It is only if we understand the early and conservative forms of vitalism that we can understand how and why radical feminist materialism must at one and the same time retrieve the vitalist criticism of the world as mere matter, while at the same time also resisting traditional vitalist appeals to an expressive and creative life force. In this essay I will argue that some of the best work in feminist philosophy takes the form of vitalism: refusing the idea that matter needs to be granted meaning by thought. I will also argue that as long as the "life" of vital matter is deemed to be creative, productive, and intensive, then we remain caught in an age-old moral resistance to those aspects of life that remain without relation, thereby repeating the gender binary that privileges act and production over inertia and passivity.

The explicit articulation of vitalism as a philosophy reached its highest pitch in the early decades of the twentieth century (Lovejoy 1912), and was then confined to intellectual history by scientists and philosophers who argued against any appeal to some life spirit or life force that would give meaning and directional order to life. The idea that the material world is accompanied by, infused by, animated by, or differentiated by a vital force has always been a way of resisting a reduction of life to matter and its predictable causal relations. In the seventeenth century, against Cartesian materialism and its definition of the world as extended matter that could be mapped and mastered geometrically, vitalists appealed to a divine and spiritual force that endowed matter with its own properties of movement (Rogers 1996). Vitalism was a way of retaining one of philosophy's most traditional principles: a world of mere matter, with no properties other than those of mechanical interaction, would be contingent and devoid of meaning. Matter, if reduced to the *res extensa* of Cartesian philosophy, must be supplemented by a synthetic, creative, and sense-giving power. Descartes no longer regarded matter as the way in which true forms or essences exist in this sensual world; the world was material and was accompanied by the mental substance of mind, which has no other quality or property than that of representing material substance and its relations.

The appeal to the vital, to spirit, to life, to divine force or immaterial essences was a way, both before and after Descartes, of avoiding the reduction of life to mere matter: to that which has no intrinsic form or identity and which is devoid of striving, purpose, expression, or meaning. In that respect, vitalism is one of the most intense expressions of the desire and imperative for life to be productive and creative, and it is just this desire that has most often articulated itself in an axiology of gender. If the feminine is deemed to be of lesser or dependent value, this is because woman provides the material support for the actualization of male form. Furthermore, as long as the feminine is productive, fertile, and directed toward the masculine power of synthesis, then it has its rightful place in the logic of life. If, however, the feminine remains within itself, deflected from production, relation, and reflection, then it becomes the very image of evil.

MATERIALIST POLITICS

If in traditional metaphysics matter was deemed to be the lesser, dependent, and not fully real partner to form, this is because matter was merely the vehicle through which form became actual. Matter, as potentiality, is on its way to actualization, and that actuality is determined in advance as what matter *ought* to be. In Platonic metaphysics, forms are eternal—and truly have being—and it is their instantiation in matter that allows them to be perceived in this world. In Aristotelian metaphysics, there is no such simple distinction between the eternal reality of forms and the mere dross of matter that can only take on being by participating in forms. Instead, forms do not exist independent of their material actualization, and matter also bears a potentiality for form: in this sense, matter can be said to have a *proper potentiality*—the form toward which it tends and which brings out its fullest being (Irwin 1988). Human beings, for example, do have a material and bodily being and a nutritive soul that sustains that bodily being. But man's proper potentiality—that which defines the human *as human*—is what the human soul achieves when it actualizes its utmost power (Agamben 1999, 232). When we reason, we fulfill the highest power of what we can be, so that even when we are not actually reasoning—even when we are at rest or even when we are dead—we are defined by our capacity to reason (Witt 2003). While we are necessarily embodied and material, it is our form—or the full actualization of what we can do (in reason)—that defines the types of beings we are. The hierarchy of form, spirit, and reason over matter is not, therefore, a simple binary in which the embodied is devalued. Rather, the hierarchy is organized according to a metaphysical commitment to life: matter *is* only insofar as it is formed, forms itself, or actualizes itself into the form that it *properly and potentially is.*

If, in modern thought, there is an apparent reversal of the form/matter moral binary, this deeper metaphysical commitment to "living on" remains the same: what has true being and truly is, is that which maintains itself through time. If we champion matter as that which lives, acts, creates, produces, connects, realizes itself, and *gives form,* then we remain within a norm of life in which action, production, dynamism, and being are privileged over unactualized potential. It is worth bearing in mind that our modern notion of dynamism carries over the ancient Greek *dynamis* (or potentiality) that was always on its way to actualization or *energeia.* If we think of a potentiality that might *not* act or bring itself into being, then we might—I would suggest—think of the virtual. In contrast with Bergson, for whom matter is fully actualized and devoid of any potentiality, we could (and should) think of matter as virtual, but not a virtual that animates matter so much as a virtual that remains unproductive and devoid of relations. If matter in ancient metaphysics was neither pure actuality nor pure potentiality but the medium through which forms could come into actualization, Bergson creates a stricter distinction between potentiality and actuality: matter is mere actuality and can never become or be other than it is, while spirit is pure potentiality that can bring itself to actualization through matter but is never reducible to any of its material instances (Bergson 1911). Whereas language, for Bergson, rigidifies and fixes life through time and is exemplary of the divide between the selfsame inertia of matter and the fluidity of spirit, I would argue that literary language destroys this opposition between the deathly reification of matter and the animating life of a purely potential spirit. In this essay I want to take up the notion of the materiality of language, *not* to draw language back to its emergent human, systemic, and life-serving conditions. On the contrary, it is when language is *material*—or literary—that it resists relations and vibrates in itself.

It might at first appear that a celebration of the body and materiality—those aspects normally associated with the feminine—would overturn a gender hierarchy that has always attributed active mind to man and passive body to woman. What we have *not* overturned, though, is a horror of the inert, the unproductive, and the radically *different:* that which cannot be comprehended, enlivened, rendered fertile or dynamic. I would argue therefore that we need to be wary of taking the resurgence of interest in life, vitalism, evolution, and creative matter as a prima facie good for feminism. The true politics of matter lies not in matter now occupying the position that was once attributed to God (and the man who is made in his image)—the position of being that has no determination or limit other than its own coming into existence (Gilson 1957)—but in a matter that fails to come to life.

Perhaps no work has done more to make clear the ways in which the metaphysics of matter is connected with the history of gender politics than Thomas Laqueur's *Making Sex* (1990). According to Laqueur, whereas premodern Aristotelian science had regarded the male role in reproduction as form-giving, immaterial, and active (with the female body as mere material vehicle for the coming into being of form), modern science recognizes two material sexes. Accordingly, modern arguments regarding sexual difference become possible, and the difference between men and women becomes bodily and material. It is this modern recognition of the possibly positive contribution of matter to the unfolding of the world that Foucault also recognizes in *The Order of Things:* whereas premodern thought had regarded the world as a site where forms were unfolded in relations of analogy, modern thought could posit something like "life" that would be the hidden force that would produce everything from man in his laboring relations, to man as a speaking and desiring being. Foucault suggests that this positing of life—particularly as it is expressed in Marxism and the later human sciences—fails to confront the *being* of language: this would not be language as expressive of life *or* as constitutive or constructive of life, but language as that which cannot be returned to speech, action, production, or "man." Although we no longer posit matter as the inert stuff that is formed by mind or language, we remain within this modern post-Marxist tradition of appealing to material life as the truth of our being, as that which might be re-lived and recognized as the origin of normativity (Foucault 1970, 128).

MARXIST MATERIALISM

The Marxist assertion of the materiality of history challenged two fundamental depoliticizing strategies. First, if history is material, then we need to understand where we are now, what we think, what is possible—and even what we desire—not only as historically located but also as structured by the ways in which our human material being—our needs—inaugurates a certain relation to matter. Because of our species needs, we are required to produce, and the mastery of production will demand ever more sophisticated technologies. Crucial to the development of technology will be the division of labor. This very commitment to efficiency, repeatability, and maximization of effort will eventually lead to those ideological categories of class and gender. Our consciousness will be *class* consciousness precisely because what we take the world to be will be determined by just how we relate to the distribution of production. For the capitalist, the world of matter includes human labor, technology, and raw material; other human bodies are so much quantifiable power, available for increased production and to be managed like any other resource. For the proletariat, the world is both matter upon which one must exert labor and those relations of production that are not purely material. Relations of production—the very fact that my body must exert effort beyond my need and must expend more material force than is required to live—are lived by the proletariat (in false consciousness) as natural, as nothing more than the way things are. Matter is lived as existing only in itself. But in revolutionary class consciousness, the worker's relation to matter—his bodily being—is understood as an outcome of dynamic or dialectical materiality. Our subjection to the system of capital has occurred precisely because our material needs required production, division of labor, struggle, and technology; but once we recognize the needs of life, we also recognize that the production of human relations are not material *simpliciter* but have to do with our comportment to matter through time. Even gender, on this understanding, needs to be understood, not as a fact of life—what simply is—but as a consequence of how material life has determined certain developments. Laboring man, who is subjected to technology, the market, and the struggle between the value of his work and those to whom he sells that work, relies upon a system of reproduction: woman is just that being who will not be expected to produce, but only because she is required to reproduce and maintain the private sphere (Pateman 1988).

The Marxist concept of dialectical materialism therefore insists upon the dynamism of matter: it is because we must *live* as bodily beings that we are required to work, so the very relation to being will be structured by the ways in which our work is structured. But Marxism—if it is dialectical—also insists on a certain irreducibility of the material. In addition to demonstrating that our historical location and the ways in which we live our lives are the outcome of human relations and are neither immutable nor universal, Marxism will also attack all forms of history that do not consider our bodily life. This is precisely Marx's objection to Hegel, for whom material life is merely the externalization of an absolute spirit that must eventually recognize matter as spirit's own externalization and medium of becoming through time. For Marx, we need to see matter, not as a mere epiphenomenon of spirit, but as itself active in relation to spirit: spirit's relation to matter is not one of mastery but of dynamic interaction.

Just as Hegel had corrected Kant for positing "mind" as an already given and distinct being that would then come to know the world, Marx countered Hegel for the detachment of absolute spirit: dialectical materialism would describe the genesis of spirit from material life, and the history of materiality through the labors of spirit. Hegel had countered Kant's assertion of pure freedom with a historical corrective: consciousness cannot simply determine itself until it understands itself historically. We cannot just assert the freedom of mind—or pure decision without foundation—in opposition to a material world that is governed by predictable, transcendental, and knowable laws. For Hegel, that idea of an external and determined reality is not other than mind but is given only in mind's history of positing what is other than itself *as other* (Hegel 1977). It is mind that has split itself into the freely determining and the materially determined; absolute idealism will overcome this diremption of mind and matter. Mind can only be *immaterial* if it sets itself against a matter that is inert, "in itself" and devoid of all decision or relation. The other of mind is therefore mind's own condition; freedom is recognition, not of the distinction between mind and matter, but their mutual imbrication. Mind or freedom *is* only in its relation to what is not itself. Once this relation is recognized, mind not only *knows* that it exists in and through the material. Matter itself is transformed as just that which was required for mind to be other than itself and to come to know itself.

Marxist *materialism* will argue that matter has not yet achieved this position of dialectical sublation. Only when matter is truly that which allows mind to develop for itself, only when the self really is capable of deciding and determining itself—only then will the liberal ideal of a mind without any law other than its own be a fact and not an ideology.[1] A materialist politics in the Marxist sense will therefore accuse philosophy of ideology as long as its takes as already achieved—

the pure mind of self-determination—what really requires material action. In utopia we will be those self-creating, self-determining, and self-governing beings of liberal ideology (Jameson 1981); but the realm of pure mind or freedom has material conditions. The political appeal to *materialism* is always twofold: we must both recognize how bodily life has unfolded historically to produce certain relations, and we must acknowledge that freedom from those relations requires recognition of our materiality.

Considered in terms of feminist politics, such commitments to materialism could also be deployed to challenge Marxist notions of laboring man as well as liberal ideals of the pure self without foundations. We need to transform the relations of *social* labor, so that we are no longer divided between those who produce and those who have the time to enjoy the meditative life that comes from freedom from work. But the transformation of *domestic* labor will be no less necessary. As long as woman remains as that bodily being whose daily life is regarded as part of a natural cycle of reproduction, the image of self-deciding humanity will remain mythic (Mitchell 1971). One can only be a man selling labor to other men if woman has already taken up the burden of domestic life (Pateman 1988). The unencumbered self of liberalism who must will only that which could, in principle, be willed by any other is a self without particular ties, allegiances, or affections: those private virtues are catered for by woman. Such freedom is possible for women, but only with material conditions that would include birth control, child care, and shared domestic labor.

For all its criticism of Hegelianism's idealization of matter—its taking as fully subjective what is actually alien, material, and not yet human—Marxism maintains as its goal the overcoming of an alien matter and a humanization and internalization of our material conditions. If we were once compelled to subject ourselves to the exigencies of matter, and if the technology that ameliorated that subject has in turn become alien, a Marxist recognition of our journey from matter will return us, finally, to a world in which matter is truly humanized and internalized. Matter must not remain in itself, nor must it simply be wished away as already human. Recognition of matter's own dynamism—its role in the trajectory of human history—will allow us to harness matter's potentiality such that human life can live in accord with its own material nature.

What is brought to the fore in this Marxist imperative is both monism and vitalism. Monism: matter and spirit must not be accepted as distinct beings but must be thought of as the outcome of an ongoing and active genesis. Vitalism: neither matter nor spirit should be accepted as simply *being,* but they should be viewed as nothing more than the process of always-productive becoming. It is this movement toward vitalism and monism that sustains a traditional metaphysical commitment toward life, fertility, production, and the overcoming of *techne,* and that anticipates some trends in recent feminism. When feminists criticized or rejected the notion of women as mired in material embodiment, they did so because matter was deemed to be devoid of dynamism. When, subsequently, that phobia regarding matter was questioned, it was precisely because the border between mind and matter was deemed to be the effect of a prior linguistic or social production. And when "linguisticism," in turn, was challenged, this was because language had been erroneously taken to be a fixed, determining, and inhuman grid imposed upon life, rather than a living force.

COUNTER-MATERIALISM

When the prima facie political value of the appeal to matter came under question, this was due primarily to the critique of the philosophy of life that had sustained Marxist and feminist materialisms. The call to "materialism" had always been a call to consider those aspects of our being that were both irreducibly natural *and* undeniably human. It is fully materialist to question the very notion of gender: by what right do we assume that there is one group of bodies whose being is structured by the biological capacities of childbirth and child-rearing? Such questioning will, though, reintroduce the human into matter: what we took to be natural—the binary between producing man and reproducing woman—is the outcome of a history and a struggle. The materialist response to the history of our biological life combined recognition and refutation: recognition of our material history and the ways in which women's biology had produced a gender system, *and* refutation that such a history is inevitable. Our biology can and should be lived otherwise. The distinction between sex and gender is therefore a distinction between the biology that needs to be recognized (sex, or the matter that is too often ignored in dreams of a purely rational "man") and biology as historically and socially lived (gender, or the simple transition from matter to norm).

If we question the sex/gender distinction today, we also question the political function of "materialism." For Judith Butler, any appeal to a material condition of life has to posit as *simply other* that which is given as other only through *being lived.* Butler draws upon both Hegel and Foucault to criticize any notion of matter, in itself, that might provide a critical lever for the ways in which life is lived. To return to Hegel *after* Marx, as Butler does, is to take up the cause of post-1968 French thought and the problem of desire (Butler 1987). For Butler, desire is the problem of relationality: whatever our material existence or species being, we always live that materiality with and through others. The Hegelianism that Butler identifies in twentieth-century French thought—and that she defends against Deleuzian and Spinozist turns to positive life—maintains the gap between a supposedly material and determinate life and the human relation toward, or fantasy of, that life (Butler 2004).

In *The Order of Things,* Foucault notes that up until the eighteenth century, "life did not exist." Life in nineteenth-century thought is not one concept among others but a style of thinking, a way in which being is folded (Foucault 1970, 244). Mind is not the simple picture or double of a world that bears its own truth; there is no longer a simple distinction between the world of matter perceived and the mind that forms ideas or perceptions. Rather, "man" is now understood as a living being whose existence requires that he work (labor) and that he speak (language); his specific being needs to be understood, then, as part of a broader process of life. Only when man understands his living existence will he understand why he needs to speak and work with others. "Life" in Marxism, psychoanalysis, anthropology, ethnography, and other transcendental enterprises explains how it is that a material being such as man emerges as a mind who can speak about, master, and know his world.

Foucault's own genealogy will therefore demonstrate all the practices, relations, and discursive events that allow life to be studied as that which will normalize our being. "Man" is posited as "empirico-transcendental": a being whose material existence will allow for the formation of cultures that enable him to know and master his own materiality (Foucault 1970, 318). Modern bio-power can then take the form of the management of life: far from asking *how* we might live, what we might do, or what counts as a good life, life is now that which will ground political decisions. For Foucault it is the discourse of sexuality that will express most vividly this new fold between inner and outer; sex becomes the truth of our being, and that which we must liberate in order to be who we are (Foucault 1978). If it was once possible, with Aristotle, to distinguish between our bodily life and our political and decided social existence, it is now the case that our political being must follow from our status as living: what polity will maximize life, allow for the effective and efficient health of populations? What we fail to question in this appeal to the material life that gives us our being, and what is forgotten in this assurance that we are speaking beings only because we are compelled to live, is the *being of language* (Foucault 1970, 382). To consider language as construction or mediation of life is to remain within a Hegelian dialectic of desire in which that which is other than the self can be grasped as the medium through which the self becomes. We can only really begin to think beyond Hegel—only really think the outside of thought—when desire does not realize, maximize, and master itself. The very technologies of language that allow us to maintain life have *being*. It is this being of language—its irreducibility to thinking—that will allow us once again to think ethically. Far from a material existence that differs from itself through speech only to turn back and know itself, the self will be required to think all those relations, technologies, practices, and distributions that are never fully its own. Sexuality is not a material ground that we might come to know and recognize, but a fold, one way in which the self organizes its own being and relations with regard to what is not itself.

FEMINIST CRITIQUES OF MATTER

Judith Butler is vigilant in maintaining this Foucaultian critique of material and normalizing life. The sex or matter that would supposedly grant us the truth of our existence can only be given as our authentic sexuality through lived practices (Butler 1993). Foucault had already argued that as long as we maintained a politics of life Hegel would hold the upper hand: that supposed brute otherness that holds the truth of our desire is only posited *as brute and other* through the desire it tries to explain. We need to ask about the desires—in the plural—through which the self constitutes itself and the relations it establishes between mastery and subjection. There is not *a* life whose logic we might turn back and know, whose desire we might recognize, but lives through which various technologies enable various styles of subject. Like Foucault, Butler will not simply accept that sex is some underlying matter that must be lived through the meanings and practices of gender. What is other than the act and desire of practice is effected through the relations of practice; matter is not a foundation that precedes relations but is always already given through relations. But Butler adds to her Foucaultian critique of a transcendent and normalizing materiality a Hegelian insistence on recognition (Butler 2004). Foucault's commitment to immanence establishes the subject, not as the being who constitutes, synthesizes, and unfolds the world, but as a being who lives within folds. There are practices, relations, distributions, and technologies within which selves pose questions and problems. For Butler, however, this immanent dispersion of folds fails to take into account the problem of subjection (Butler 1997). To be a self, to take oneself as having a life, requires some degree of recognition; one is always this or that self.

If Foucault can overcome the question of sexuality—what one supposedly *is*—through the question of ethics, or what one may or may not do, for Butler there can be no easy exit. To have a sex—to be recognized as male or female—is one way in which one is recognized as human. While such normalizing regimes of recognition need to be restructured, the living of one's life requires that one be a subject (Butler 2004). And subjectivity matters in a double sense. To have a body that matters, that can be recognized, requires that we answer to this or that style of self. But those conditions of recognition that will grant some bodies material import are themselves material. The self may be performative—having no being that grounds its life other than its own doing—but those performances are materially constrained. Bodies matter, not because they cause our being, but because the living of them *as material*—as the very nature that is our own—is made possible only through regarding ourselves as subjects, as beings who have some recognizable, repeatable, and accountable identity. And to have identity, or to be *someone,* is to possess some minimal degree of self-definition. Our bodily relations—our comportments, affections, habits, and perceptions—are subject, not just to an other who recognizes me, but to one who will recognize me *as* this or that social being. To call such practices and processes material—to refer to the materiality of the signifier—is both to locate all relations and productions beyond the myth of self-present mind *and* to define matter as a process of relations, as that which unfolds from itself to produce its own "before" and "after."

In this regard, far from being simply discursive or linguistic, Butler's critique of an appeal to life before mediation, recognition, performance, or system follows from poststructuralism's critique of the language paradigm. There is not a presence, life, and substance that *is,* in itself, and then requires difference and relation in order to be known. All those features that supposedly mark the secondary signifier characterize life as such. Even so, those feminists who have offered the most persuasive and stringent criticisms of Butler's work have drawn attention to Butler's inability to transcend the linguistic paradigm. Butler does not want to see language or difference as a form imposed upon matter, but she nevertheless allows matter to remain that which can only be posited after the event—as that which must have been "before" the recognized performance of the self. By contrast, Vicki Kirby (2002) does not see life as that which can only be known or posited after the event of performance, for embodiment or matter itself partakes of all those features usually attributed to writing. Life is not something that is differentiated by systems of writing but is itself productive of difference and relations. Taking up the more "positive and productive vicissitudes of biology," Elizabeth A. Wilson has also argued that Butler remains too committed to the concept of gender that is *critical* of biology, without thinking the politics of biology as it is, rather than as it is mediated (Wilson 1998, 54, 62).

The scandal of Butler's linguisticism, her perceived failure of nerve, lies—so Wilson, Kirby, Cheah, and Grosz argue—in allowing the performance and difference of material life to be located in the acting human subject and not in the dynamic life of which that subject is an effect. Whereas a conservative Hegelianism would ultimately conclude that absolute consciousness can recognize itself as that which must experience what is other than itself, and then recognize itself as that which can posit and know otherness, Butler remains with a desire for recognition—a self who *is* only in not being at one with itself—but refuses any sublation of that diremption (Butler 1987). Thus, one must be taken to have a gender, mode, or style of being in order to be recognized; at the same time, the self who will be recognized as one who performs or acts must always be anticipated as in excess of any of its actual performances (Butler 1993).

We can make sense of what is at stake in Butler's insistence on the performative—or that act which must create what is other than itself—through her debt to Hegel, and thereby assess just where a radical nondialectical materialism might be formulated. Hegel's absolute idealism is critical of any supposed substance that might simply *be* in itself without relation. Consider as an example Hume's empiricism in which all ideas, concepts, and even the self are effects of a series of experiences. For Hume, there is only synthesizing, connecting, and relating, not an ultimate *who* or *what* that synthesizes. The mind is not some spiritual substance added on to life, but just one part of life that, through time, has been the site of a network of connections. Hegel's response to an empiricism that regards material life as all that is, is to argue that it must exclude the act of knowing or relating. The very idea that there could be matter before cognition, ideas, or experience must posit some absolutely simple "this." Not only could we only *know* such a simple "this" through a relation—this is Kant's idealism—Hegel goes further to argue that nothing ever *is* such a finite, nonrelational being. Consciousness in its simplicity might take itself to be mind that must grasp a world or might imagine itself as just a part of material life, but the condition for either of these positions is absolute idealism. There can only be an idea or mind if there is an idea *of* some being, and there can only be being—something that *is*—if there is that which establishes relations. Life is relationality, connection, and difference, and absolute consciousness is the recognition of that difference.

For Butler, though, that recognition of difference cannot arrive precisely because consciousness is not the master of difference. Difference is not something consciousness (or anything) *does;* there are acts of difference—performances—from which one posits a subject or substance. But that supposed subject, if she turns back to recognize herself as nothing other than her acts, or as pure performance or mask without sex, nature, or matter, will be stalled by two problems. First, practically, we live in a culture in which performance is legitimated only if it is the act or performance *of* someone; we can never arrive at that Hegelian moment of difference recognizing itself as difference, liberated from all that is not itself and not pure act (Butler 2004). Second, ontologically, Butler maintains a primarily linguistic vocabulary, despite her critique of the idea of language as secondary, supplementary, or parasitic. It is not that there is pure life or presence that must then be taken *as matter* through some linguistic system, for matter is just that which is not itself. For Hegel all life—all being—was difference and relation, but only consciousness could come to know relationality. For Butler all matter is iteration and performance—that which must not be itself only to be taken to *be* at all—so this means that we must think of life and matter *as performative.* Something *is* only insofar as it is maintained and recognizable through time, but this repetition *of* itself is always repetition of an identity, and such identity requires subjection to that which remains the same.

A radically nondialectical materialism would need to challenge the deeper ontological claims regarding relations that underpin Butler's critique of sex. Butler's political and practical wariness of simply arriving at a world beyond recognition is premised on just what is required for something to be. Recognition is at once a political predicament, for Butler details the ways in which those seeking surgery, partnership rights, and familial bonds have to submit to claims of naturalness and sexual identity (Butler 2004). But recognition is also a material condition: to matter, to be taken to *be*, requires that ongoing performance be the performance *of* this or that being (Butler 1993).

MATTER AS POSITIVE DIFFERENCE

Butler was not alone in her critique of the linguisticism that was assumed by the sex/gender distinction. The idea of a materiality awaiting inscription, with the body acting as some passive surface upon which culture might do its work, was targeted rigorously by Elizabeth Grosz's assertion of the positivity of the body. Drawing on psychoanalysis, but not its emphasis on the psyche, Grosz argued that affective and bodily relations—touch, movement, perceptions of morphology, the experience of fluids—produced an interiority (Grosz 1994). The body does not cause mind, for the body has to go through desiring encounters in order to achieve some minimal stability; nor does mind cause the body to be sexed *as* this or that. For Grosz sexual difference, even in her early psychoanalytically oriented works, is a recognition of life's relationality: that something *becomes what it is only through desire.* One cannot, therefore, posit "man" as that being who subjects himself to social relations. More importantly, one cannot posit woman and man as beings who must approach each other through desire. If one's being as male or female is achieved through relations among bodies, then it follows both that sexual difference or relations of desire produce one's sexual identity *and* that different bodies will produce different styles of relation.

Grosz's more recent work on Darwin emphasizes, radicalizes, and extends the claims of sexual difference. Grosz rejects the notion of an inert matter that goes through time. We could understand this in a more nuanced manner, though, not by contrasting it with facile biological determinisms, but with Butler's notion of iterability. Such a contrast will bring us to the heart of what is at stake in feminist politics of materiality. For Butler, matter—or what we posit before culture, act, performance, and relations—is not a substance that exists in itself and is then represented and repeated in various ways. Rather, in order for some identifiable thing to be repeated it must already *be,* and something *is* only insofar as it is iterable. Matter is therefore always the effect of a process of performing *as* something. So the acting self is not a subject who then performs; rather, there is performance or acting *from which* we posit some subject who must have been. If this is so, then performance is itself a splitting; in the beginning there is a not-being-at-one. It is not that language mediates, constructs, or constitutes matter; for matter—what is—is that nonidentity which has traditionally been confined to the signifier but which really characterizes all that is. If there is materiality, it is not that which is masked or hidden by language, for language itself is materiality, always relating to what is not-itself:

> This is not to say that, on the one hand, the body is simply linguistic stuff or, on the other hand, that it has no bearing on language. It bears on language all the time. The materiality of language, indeed, of the very sign that attempts to denote materiality, suggests that it is not the case that everything, including materiality, is always already language. On the contrary, the materiality of the signifier (a "materiality" that comprises both signs and their significatory efficacy) implies that there can be no reference to a pure materiality except via materiality. Hence, it is not that one cannot get outside of language in order to grasp materiality in and of itself; rather, every effort to refer to materiality takes place through a signifying process which, in its phenomenality, is always already material. (Butler 1993, 68)

Butler, in her recent engagements with her feminist critics, has remained committed to the structures of recognition and negation: something *is* or matters only by being recognized or relating to what is not itself (Butler 2004). For Butler a rigorous materialism focuses on the conditions of intelligibility and recognition: what bodies are allowed to matter? But if mattering occurs through iteration—through what is being constituted as recognizable and as the same through time—then the time of politics is a time of recognizing significant differences. How do some sexualities—such as normative familial heterosexuality—come to be constituted as the foundational human identities that ground history and politics? How might other identities come to have a consistency through time, come into time? Time, in a politics of iteration and recognition, is both a time out of joint—for the repetition of any identity is also a minor and possibly destabilizing difference of that identity—and a time that gives matter. Only with performing itself through time, acting itself out, can something be said to be or have time.

Elizabeth Grosz's recent work is, like Butler's, critical of any matter that would provide the foundation for politics, either acting as some ultimate cause or as some moral touchstone. Grosz also takes up the post-structuralist critique of the linguistic paradigm. Matter is not that upon which culture works; nor is it that which is known through language or construction. If we take Butler's work to be a deconstructive radicalization of the nature/culture binary, we can then see how Grosz refuses a critical deconstruction. For Butler, we cannot say that language constructs matter, nor can we see the mind as constituting its world; for those supposedly ideal constructing terms—language or mind—are themselves material, and this materiality is just that of the act or performance. In the beginning is that which splits or differs from itself, effecting a before and after. The problem with this critical approach for Grosz is its failure of nerve (2005, 47). By placing biology, matter, and life in brackets, by insisting that they are always known through relations and binaries, and by allowing the politics of gender—or what is recognized—to limit discussion, we preclude the discussion of sexual difference.

For Grosz sexual difference is literally *material.* In order for life to *be* it does not *go through time,* and time is not constituted as a marking out, tracing, or constituting of the same. Rather, life—biological, evolving, dynamic life—is the production of potential relations. Life does not have a process, development, or trajectory that unfolds in time taken or time lived; rather, there are random, unthinking, mechanical, and directionless changes that may or may not produce relations. Natural selection describes the way in which changes occur between organisms and environment so that certain changes of bodies might be repeated because they allow for further growth, change, and proliferating potentials. Sexual selection describes the ways in which the changes of bodies, such as lighter or darker skin, come to be desired and thus produce the groupings of bodies. For Grosz, then, one must go further than problematizing the nature/culture binary: culture *is* nature, and nature *is* culture. Culture is nature, because without those tendencies to change, adapt, increase complexity, and newness, there would be no arenas of thought, beauty, or political grouping. Nature is culture because all those features that were once deemed to be elevated and human—invention, force, relations, activity—characterize life in general. Nature, far from being that timeless essence that might once have been used to halt human liberation—in claims, say, that women are naturally passive—is actually that which can introduce dynamism and radicalism into claims regarding what may or may not be human. Once nature is accepted as dynamic, active, and unpredictably open, we have arrived at a liberating anti-humanism. The human is not some spiritual substance set over and against matter, nor is it merely material—quantifiable as so much biologically or genetically determinate stuff—for human culture is matter that has acquired organizations so complex as to constitute culture.

Grosz therefore sees her work as in many ways compatible with the recent turns away from language and mentalism that have characterized more analytic approaches. Grosz is keen to make the political connections that are hinted at in Daniel Dennett's (1996) description of Darwinism as "dangerous." Not only should feminism understand the more difficult scientific ideas that might explain sexual politics and oppression, but there is also a clear sense in which the Darwinian understanding of life is immediately radical: precluding any appeals to timeless nature, precluding biological determinism, and confronting thought with the challenge to live up to the potentials for newness. Contrasting her work with other evolutionists such as Dennett, Grosz makes a forceful claim regarding culture. We should not just *liken* cultural change to natural evolutionary change; cultural relations do not occupy a separate sphere from living material relations (Grosz 2005, 219). We can understand cultural forms by looking at the desires and tendencies of bodies, just as we can understand bodies by looking at the ways in which they have unfolded into cultural forms, such as gender. Thus, Grosz's Darwinism renders clear, apposite, and disseminable her long-standing claim about the dynamism and complexity of the body. The biological is neither determining nor determined. Nor is it—as in Butler—that which is posited as determined after events that have rendered some beings as determinate. "Matter," "life," and "embodiment" name that which differs to produce complex morphologies, such as the male/female binary, and intricate structures, such as the beauty of art and the systems of language, reference, and knowledge.

What is at stake in Grosz's disagreement with both Butler and Dennett is the status of life. Life gives itself in culture. Sexual difference, or the productivity of life, can therefore be understood as the motor for political change. Grosz argues that we need to overcome not only the idea of matter as passive and inert in opposition to the activity and force of culture, but also the very distinction between nature and culture as two domains. Her work here is clearly indebted both to Bergson's vitalism and Deleuze's monism, and it is precisely through these difficult and highly charged concepts that I would like to conclude by suggesting the ways in which the current politics of life intensifies, rather than overcomes, humanism—a humanism that I would also argue is intensely theological, insofar as the central image is that of a life that generously gives and creates in order to yield an image of itself. Grosz's monism and vitalism is in line with the normative image of life that has underpinned traditional metaphysics: beyond distinct and determined beings there is the one life that is pure act and brings those beings into existence. By contrast, Deleuze's monism suggests a critique of theologism, and does so in his "ethics of intensive difference" (Deleuze 1994). Here, although there is still only one substance—not mind *and* matter, not being *and* relations—this substance yields divergent, unproductive, nonactualized, and *unlived* singularities that remain beyond all presentation. One way of understanding this notion of intensity is through literary language, for it is in the "stuttering" of literary language—when language fails to speak or no longer operates as the instrument of a willing organism—that language stands alone and is no longer the expression *of* a preceding subject nor the indication *of* a fulfilling sense. Deleuze's monism is therefore a pluralism, not because the one life actualizes itself in a diversity that it can ultimately come to know and master, but because life produces singularities that may remain detached, unlived and devoid of relationality. Philosophy, science, and art approach the problem of these singularities in different ways. Science gives some order to chaos by mapping the way singular potentials are lived in this actual world; very simply, scientific laws generalize potentials and relations. Philosophy creates intensive concepts, so that the *concept* of matter is not the set of all the material things that exist but a way of posing a problem: we have seen that the concept of matter allows us to think that which precedes ongoing forms and identities.

Literature does not create concepts—the ideal or immaterial orientation or problem that must be expressed through some material language—for literature, like all art, allows matter to stand alone or vibrate. Whereas the language of life is productive, vital, and extensive—so that our lexicon allows us to stabilize the world and relations around us into an ongoing, predictable, and lived time—the language of literature is material and *dead.* The word is no longer part of an acting, living body and its communicative relations but stands alone, as a monument or fragment of time in its pure state. Consider, for example, two ways of approaching a literary materiality. The first is to see the text as a signifier, as the mark or trace through which communicative and lived relations are organized; the aim of reading is actualization—to take the matter of the text and unfold all its potentialities. We could take a novel, *Pride and Prejudice,* and trace the text back to conditions of women, the marriage market, expectations of romantic love, reading publics, and conditions of distribution and then also see the ways in which future cinematic actualizations also realize the text. The represented romantic and social relations can be re-lived, re-transcribed in the present, with the language of the text living on in time, allowing the present to revive the past. Alternatively, we can read the text as a fragment of "time in its pure state"; rather than extending itself through time, the text is intensive. When Deleuze and Guattari argue that all language begins as "indirect"—as a style or noise that organizes bodies and produces points of stability and subjection, they directly refute the idea of language as the expression *of* life, as the material mediation or differentiation of being. At the same time, by tearing the matter of language from its relations and from the positions and subjections that have unfolded as styles of speech, we are given the expression of matter itself—separate, vibrating, stuttering, and unproductive. To read in this way, one isolates style from reference—the world from which it emerged—and intuits its sense. How does a word inscribed in a text, given a material separateness and isolation, halt ongoing and extended life? Words such as "virtue," "marriage," "fortune," and "love" come to function in the nineteenth-century novel *not* as expressions of speaking subjects, but as pure affects. The phrases, words, and linguistic gestures of the bourgeois marriage market lose all sense of reference: words such as "virtue" and "marriage" become linguistic tokens. We are given a word that has *sense*—where marriage is the desire for a certain stabilization and equilibrium of time, the overcoming of struggle and markets, the fulfillment of a self in relation to an other—but no reference. Language is taken from life as it is lived (in relations) and given a separate, monumental, and intensive being.

CONCLUSION

All art, Deleuze argues, is an incarnation of an Idea. Deleuze takes the notion of the Idea from Kant as that which lies ideally beyond the concept: the concept is the determination or definition of the manifold—a subject actively recognizing an object—but the Idea is the ideal and virtual reality that makes such an actual distribution possible. Thus we could say that before there is a painting of a specific landscape, there is the Idea of painting: the potential for the human eye to be related to a brain that thinks what is not perceived, which in turn is related to a history of other painted objects, to the virtual powers of the color spectrum, to the range of textures of paint and canvas, and to the emergence of figures. The Idea unfolds from singular points, or potentials, to produce reciprocally determining relations (Deleuze 1994, 254). When we look at a work of art, we should see beyond its actual differences to the differentiation from which it has emerged and which expresses all the singularities (which themselves are eternal possibilities for change, mutation, and creation). The actualized work of art—its colors, syntax, relations, and distributions—gives form to what lies beyond actuality and exposes the *genesis* of the actual, which is not itself lived.

> When it is claimed that works of art are immersed in a virtuality, what is being invoked is not some confused determination but the completely determined structure formed by its genetic differential elements, its "virtual" or "embryonic" elements. The elements, varieties of relations and singular points coexist in the work or the object, in the virtual part of the work or object, without it being possible to designate a point of view privileged over others, a centre which would unify the other centres. (Deleuze 1994, 260)

Once conceptual, functional, and affective singularities can be freed from the lived, to be experienced in their pure state, we arrive at a new notion of becoming, "the pure form of empty time in general" (Deleuze 1994, 207). Becoming-woman, for example, could be considered as the anti-vitalist concept par excellence. In his book on Francis Bacon, Deleuze (2003) describes the "northern line," which in fine art is not a line between two spaces or bodies, and is not the separation of this from that, but is just the movement of paint across a canvas: not representing a figure—figuration—but creating a figure (Deleuze 2003). In *A Thousand Plateaus,* Deleuze and Guattari (1987) write of the "feminine line" that gives a sense of sense: whereas concepts usually have a sense, or orient thought, the feminine line gives the sense *that there is something to be thought,* but with no sense of a concept, or *what* is to be thought. Becoming-woman is that concept that opens the conceptuality of concepts—the idea of arriving at or fulfilling a potentiality—to a certain nonfulfillment. Woman is not she who gives herself form, becomes what she is, or realizes her proper potential in animating her materiality with the sense of who she properly is; woman is that which does not master or comprehend it/herself. We might refer to woman, then, as a type of "higher deterritorialization." Could we, Deleuze and Guattari ask, from the various planes through which we think, and through the various images of what counts as good thinking, achieve a sense of that which remains without orientation? This would be thought "without an image" or the thought of the plane of immanence.

We can consider all concepts to be deterritorializations of maps. All animals have a map of the world: I eat this, do not eat that; I fear this, do not fear that; I dwell here, do not move there. Such maps mark out a territory, a space of potential movement that is the animal's world. The concept takes such *actual* and extended orientations in order to create sense, which is a survey "all at once," not taking actual time in order to be lived, but occurs at infinite speed. Thus, the concept of man is not merely a territory—all those bodies of a set—nor is it a group of predicates; it is an orientation or milieu, consisting of problems. The human is a sense of what might be, of potentiality or proper realization. To be human is to be burdened with giving oneself a world, with forming oneself and deciding on one's own being. I can recognize an other as human, as one of my kind, but dispute his or her humanity: it is possible to ask whether he or she is living up to the potentiality of the human. The concept of man is therefore one of intense *re*-territorialization. A territory is a grouping or assemblage of bodies marking out a certain terrain. Such an assemblage is de-territorialized when its immanent relations—say, each body feeling the other's pain in a ritual of scarring, or each body pulsing with the same rhythm in traditional dance—are rendered transcendent. The assemblage is viewed from on high by a despot who enjoys the pain of incision or by a god to whom the dance is offered. Relations among bodies are referred to some higher body that also anticipates what those bodies may or may not do—through an expectation of the despot's possible punishment or the god's retribution. But the concept of man organizes bodies, not as an extended set—we who are governed by this power—but by *intensity*. To be "man" is to be governed by certain affective relations, a power of self over self, of dominating one's body and passions: not for this or that authority or end, but in and for itself as the very *sense* of the human. The concept of the human has always been marked by this style of relation; one obeys not this or that given and determined rule, for humanity is just this giving a law to oneself, determining oneself. The deterritorialization of bodies in external power is re-territorialized when our bodies are organized, assembled, and oriented by nothing other than a sense of ourselves as properly oriented only to our own becoming. The matter of the human body is just that which can *give itself* any form whatever.

We see this reterritorialization in specific claims regarding the self-transcendence of the brain: in Bergson's (1911) claim that there will be some point in immanent flowing life that has the potential to intuit life as such. We see it also in recent neuroscientific and cognitive scientific claims that would deny human life any intrinsic material determination regarding the self's formation of logic, language, art, and morality as extensions of technologies that manipulate and organize environments (Clark 2003). We can see it also in Butler's claim that matter has no essence or intrinsic property that would orient it to perform in this or that manner, for matter just is that which is always different from or other than itself.

Elizabeth Grosz's work is perhaps one of the few feminist critiques to think beyond a matter that is either that through which form-giving life becomes, or that which gives itself its own form. Grosz raises a possibility of a mindless, mechanical, ateleological, and radically external force. This, I would argue, is the most audacious and valuable aspect of her work. However, she wants to see culture as an *extension* of nature, as nature giving itself a manner through which it can think itself:

> Is it possible to understand culture not as the completion of nature but as the endlessly ramified and open product of nature: that is, is it possible, and productive, to understand culture as the way in which nature reflects on and articulates itself, as nature's most generous and complex self-reflection? Is culture nature's way of thinking itself, of gaining consciousness of itself, of representing itself, and of acting on itself? (Grosz 2004, 50)

This strand of her work posits a life that differs from itself and arrives at an (albeit contingent) culture in order to see itself, think itself. Against this aspect of Grosz's work I would argue that the true radicalism of monism is to posit an anti-vitalism: how the one life can produce, through differences of degree, that which is opposed to life, or a difference in kind. Culture would not be an extension of nature but, *through its very materiality,* that which acts demonically in opposition to nature's potentiality.

How can a power be deflected from its potentiality, or *not* realize itself? The human has traditionally been conceived as that which not only passes from potentiality into actuality but has the potential to actualize itself as any existence whatever. So how is it, then, that this potential has *not* been realized, that humanity all too often subjects itself to images of a proper or normative self? The answer of traditional political and liberal theory is that man must arrive at his pure and open potential, and must free himself from all external determinants and images. Against the "man" who is pure potentiality and who falls into the inauthenticity of determination, Deleuze and Guattari argue that life's potential for just this deflection from itself or *not* arriving at itself—its "stupidity" or mindlessness—is precisely where one might affirm a politics beyond the lived. Far from lamenting the fall into deterritorialization or the capacity for a techne to free itself from its emergence in vital life, Deleuze and Guattari (1994) affirm the nature of art as monument. Just as philosophy should strive to think thought without an image, so art should—through the use of material—give a form or monument to the sensible.

If man is that matter who, through life, can give himself form, turn back, and then recognize himself as the very eminence of life, woman is a becoming who does not go through time to differ from herself but remains *without relation*. In *A Thousand Plateaus*, Deleuze and Guattari contrast the "gray eminence"—the ultimate ground of traditional metaphysics—with the "gray immanence," or that which does not demarcate itself in relation to otherness; and they also identify this immanence with the becoming-woman who does not figure the secret of our being precisely because she *is* the secret. Deleuze and Guattari create "becoming-woman" as a concept that frees conceptuality from the plane of transcendence. In contrast with man, "woman" is a becoming that is not the becoming *of* a subject prior to its relations, nor is it a becoming toward realization. Concepts are orientations but tend to be territorialized as orientations *of* this thinking being, emerging through this persona. A radical or properly philosophical concept would thereby be liberated from the lived, giving a sense *that* there is thinking, without a fulfillment of *what* is to be thought. In terms of philosophy, concepts that encounter art lead the way beyond the life that recognizes itself through itself. The disruption of "man" or the subject as the plane of transcendence occurs through art's *inhuman* materiality. Such a materiality would figure nothing other than itself, giving "time in its pure state" only by allowing matter to vibrate without forward movement, production, creation, or relation. Art allows for a certain thinking of the material that is liberated from actualization or a "becoming-toward."

This possibility, I would argue, yields both an image of feminist art criticism and a feminist politics. First, art criticism has always tended to be vitalist and historicist, returning a work to its condition of emergence in order that it might live, for us, again. By contrast, a criticism liberated from the concept of "man" would acknowledge that fragile materiality of a work that resists comprehension, inclusion, recognition, and interpretation. Second, as a politics, we might recognize all the positive ways in which life issues in technologies that break with their original or lived intention. It may be the case, as evolutionary psychologists and some neurologically oriented art historians have argued, that beauty and aesthetic value emerge from processes of sexual selection that maximize life (Ramachandran 2003). But it is also the case that art has the capacity to recognize its origin in the lived and—far from striving to maintain itself—turn against beauty, pleasure, and the proliferation of relations. Similarly, while certain industries and technologies, such as reproductive medicine and cosmetic surgery, may have their origin in reterritorializing life, they might also allow us to free life from any notion of that which *strives to live.* It is *this* potentiality of nonrealization, of dispersion, of remaining inert and refusing to be oneself that frees matter from the human, through the human.

NOTES

1. The very concept of ideology, in all its complex senses, relies on materialist critique. If ideology is the distorted or imaginary relation we bear to the real conditions of existence, then a critique of ideology will have to make some reference to that which lies beyond mediation. Even Louis Althusser's concept of ideology—in which the real is posited only after the event of its imaginary structuring—defines Marxism as the science capable of yielding a critique of the imaginary (Althusser 1971).

REFERENCES

Agamben, Giorgio. 1999. *Potentialities: Collected Essays in Philosophy.* Ed. and trans. Daniel Heller-Roazen. Stanford, Calif.: Stanford University Press.

Althusser, Louis. 1971. *Lenin and Philosophy, and Other Essays*. Trans. Ben Brewster. London: New Left Books.
Bergson, Henri. 1911. *Creative Evolution*. Trans. Arthur Mitchell. New York: Henry Holt.
———. 1912. *Matter and Memory*. London: G. Allen.
Butler, Judith. 1987. *Subjects of Desire: Hegelian Reflections in Twentieth-Century France*. New York: Columbia University Press.
———. 1993. *Bodies that Matter: On the Discursive Limits of 'Sex'*. New York: Routledge.
———. 1997. *The Psychic Life of Power: Theories in Subjection*. Stanford, Calif.: Stanford University Press.
———. 2004. *Undoing Gender*. New York: Routledge.
Clark, Andy. 2003. *Natural Born Cyborgs: Minds, Technologies, and the Future of Human Intelligence*. Oxford: Oxford University Press.
Deleuze, Gilles. 1988. *Bergsonism*. Trans. Hugh Tomlinson and Barbara Habberjam. New York: Zone Books, 1988.
———. 1994. *Difference and Repetition*. Trans. Paul Patton. New York: Columbia University Press.
———. 2003. *Francis Bacon: The Logic of Sensation*. Trans. Daniel Smith. London: Continuum.
Deleuze, Gilles, and Félix Guattari. 1987. *A Thousand Plateaus: Capitalism and Schizophrenia*. Trans. Brian Massumi. Minneapolis: University of Minnesota Press.
———. 1994. *What Is Philosophy?* Trans. Hugh Tomlinson and Graham Burchill. London: Verso.
Dennett, Daniel. 1996. *Darwin's Dangerous Idea: Evolution and the Meaning of Life*. New York: Touchstone.
———. 2003. *Freedom Evolves*. New York: Viking.
Derrida, Jacques. 1978. *Edmund Husserl's Origin of Geometry: An Introduction*. Trans. John P. Leavey Jr. Ed. David B. Allison. Lincoln: University of Nebraska Press.
Foucault, Michel. 1970. *The Order of Things: An Archaeology of the Human Sciences*. London: Tavistock.
———. 1978. *The History of Sexuality*. Vol. 1. *An Introduction*. Trans. Robert Hurley. London: Allen Lane.
Gatens, Moira. 1996. *Imaginary Bodies: Ethics, Power and Corporeality*. London: Routledge.
Gilson, Etienne. 1957. *The Christian Philosophy of St. Thomas Aquinas*. Trans. L. K. Shook. London: V. Gollancz.
Grosz, Elizabeth. 1994. *Volatile Bodies: Toward a Corporeal Feminism*. Sydney: Allen and Unwin.
———. 2005. *Time Travels: Feminism, Nature, Power*. Sydney: Allen and Unwin.
Hegel, G. W. F. 1977. *Hegel's Phenomenology of Spirit*. Trans. A. V. Miller. Ed. J. N. Findlay. Oxford: Clarendon.
Husserl, Edmund. 1970. *The Crisis of European Sciences and Transcendental Phenomenology: An Introduction to Phenomenological Philosophy*. Trans. David Carr. Evanston, Ill.: Northwestern University Press.

Irwin, Terence. 1988. *Aristotle's First Principles.* Oxford: Clarendon.
Jameson, Fredric. 1981. *The Political Unconscious: Narrative as a Socially Symbolic Act.* London: Methuen.
Kant, Immanuel. 1990. *Foundations of the Metaphysics of Morals and What Is Enlightenment?* Trans. Lewis White Beck. 2nd ed., rev. New York: Macmillan.
Kirby, Vicki. 2002. "When All That Is Solid Melts Into Language: Judith Butler and the Question of Matter." *International Journal of Sexuality and Gender Studies* 7.4: 265–80.
Laqueur, Thomas. 1990. *Making Sex: Body and Gender from the Greeks to Freud.* Cambridge, Mass.: Harvard University Press.
LeDoux, Joseph E. 2002. *Synaptic Self: How Our Brains Become Who We Are.* New York: Viking.
Lovejoy, A. O. 1912. "The Meaning of Driesch and the Meaning of Vitalism." *Science: New Series* 36.933 (Nov. 1912): 672–75.
Mitchell, Juliet. 1971. *Women's Estate.* New York: Pantheon.
Pateman, Carole. 1988. *The Sexual Contract.* Stanford, Calif.: Stanford University Press.
Protevi, John. 2001. *Political Physics: Deleuze, Derrida, and the Body Politic.* New Brunswick, N.J.: Athlone.
Ramachandran, V. S. 2003. *The Emerging Mind: The Reith Lectures 2003.* London: Profile.
Rogers, John. 1996. *The Matter of Revolution: Science, Poetry, and Politics in the Age of Milton.* Ithaca, N.Y.: Cornell University Press.
Wilson, Elizabeth A. 1998. *Neural Geographies: Feminism and the Microstructure of Cognition.* New York: Routledge.
———. 2004. *Psychosomatic: Feminism and the Neurological Body.* Durham, N.C.: Duke University Press.
Witt, Charlotte. 2003. *Ways of Being: Potentiality and Actuality in Aristotle's Metaphysics.* Ithaca, N.Y.: Cornell University Press.

3

CONSTRUCTING THE BALLAST: AN ONTOLOGY FOR FEMINISM

Susan Hekman

THE CRISIS

The purpose of this essay is to tell a story. It is a story that attempts to explain why feminists in particular and critical theorists in general are facing a theoretical and practical crisis. In order to tell this story we have to understand the origin of the crisis, where we are now, and where we might be going in the future. It is a story that has a beginning, although not an origin. The events of the story have precipitated a crisis that has not yet been resolved, although the parameters of the resolution are emerging. It is a story that has immense consequences for both feminism and critical theory because its resolution will determine the future direction of these approaches.

I begin my story by describing the publication of two articles that give the story its frame. The first is an influential feminist article by Donna Haraway first published in 1985. The article, "A Manifesto for Cyborgs: Science, Technology, and Socialist Feminism in the 1980's," was a kind of rallying cry for an emerging feminist paradigm. The goal of her article, Haraway claims, is to "build an ironic political myth faithful to feminism, socialism, and materialism" (1990, 190). Haraway's thesis is that feminism is at a crossroads. The universal theories that informed feminism at the beginning of the second wave, most notably socialism, are, she claims, no longer relevant. Indeed, Haraway asserts, universal, totalizing theory is a "major mistake" because it misses most of reality (1990, 223). Haraway employs the cyborg as the metaphor to describe the new situation that feminism must address. The cyborg, Haraway claims, is our ontology. It is committed to partiality, irony, intimacy, and perversity. It violates the dichotomies of modernism: public/private, nature/culture (1990, 192). The cyborg defines women's experience in the 1980s, an experience that is "a fiction and fact of the most crucial, political kind" (1990, 191).

The task Haraway sets for herself is not easy. She does not want to adopt an anti-science metaphysics or one that rejects technology. She wants to develop an approach that takes account of real relations, one that is specifically material but at the same time specifically political. Complicating things even further is her desire to incorporate a discourse that was gaining ascendancy in feminism, a discourse of fiction and partiality. The facts and materiality she wants to define are at the same time both fictional and real: "Social reality is lived social relations, our most important political construction, a world-changing fiction" (1990, 191). Exactly how facts and fiction can be merged in this new paradigm, Haraway admits from the outset, is problematic. Also problematic is a specific danger that this approach incurs: "We risk lapsing into boundless difference and giving up on the confusing task of making partial, real connection" (1990, 202).

The next several decades of feminist theory proved that Haraway was right: the task was indeed difficult. In the postmodern idiom that soon came to dominate feminist theory, what Haraway is trying to do is to deconstruct the discourse/reality dichotomy. She is trying to redefine the materiality that informed socialist feminism in discursive terms. She is trying to hold fiction and fact together in a new paradigm in which, as she puts it, discursive constructions are no joke (1990, 203).

With the hindsight of more than twenty years of feminist theory and practice, it seems fair to conclude that Haraway's project has failed. Instead of deconstructing the discourse/reality dichotomy, instead of constructing a new paradigm for feminism that integrates the discursive and the material, feminism has instead turned to the discursive pole of the discourse/reality dichotomy. Inspired by theorists such as Haraway who revealed the discursive constitution of scientific "reality" and by postmodern theorists who examined the discursive constitution of social reality, many feminists turned to discourse at the expense of the material. Haraway's desire to define a feminist discourse of materialism was lost in the linguistic turn of feminism and critical theory as a whole. It is significant that Haraway's article is reprinted and reaches its widest audience in a volume, *Feminism/Postmodernism* (Nicholson 1990), that examines the question of the relevance of postmodernism for feminism. By the time the volume was published, the question was already a moot point: postmodernism had transformed feminism.

The second publication that frames my story is an article by Bruno Latour in *Critical Inquiry* in 2004, "Why Has Critique Run Out of Steam? From Matters of Fact to Matters of Concern." Latour, like Haraway, has been at the forefront of the intellectual effort to reveal the social construction of scientific facts. But almost twenty years after Haraway's clarion call to construct a new paradigm that is rooted in this insight, Latour wants to assess where this critique has led critical theory. In an issue of *Critical Inquiry* devoted to the question of the future of critical theory, Latour's answer is stunning: our approach is fundamentally flawed. "What," he asks, "if explanations resorting automatically to power, society, discourse have outlived their usefulness and deteriorated to the point of now feeding the most gullible sort of critique?" (2004, 229).

Latour's assessment of the situation is blunt:

> My argument is that a certain form of critical spirit has sent us down the wrong path, encouraging us to fight the wrong enemies and, worst of all, to be considered as friends by the wrong sort of allies because of a little mistake in the definition of its main target. The question was never to get *away* from facts but *closer* to them, not fighting empiricism but, on the contrary, renewing empiricism. (2004, 231)

Latour's suggestion of what is to be done is equally radical: we need a new paradigm, a "new settlement," as he puts it elsewhere, that will cultivate a "stubbornly realist attitude," a realism dealing with matters of concern, not matters of fact (2004, 231). His error, Latour argues, was to believe that there was no way to criticize matters of fact except by moving away from them and analyzing the conditions that made them possible. To counter this tendency, he now concludes that we need a "second empiricism," a return to a realist attitude. We need a new critical attitude rooted in new critical tools, a new definition of the critic, not as one who "debunks," but as one who "assembles" (2004, 246).

Latour's article is a frontal assault on the linguistic turn in critical theory and feminism that was beginning when Haraway published her article. Latour's radical thesis is that this turn was a mistake, that it led us to a place where we cannot say anything about the real, much less the true. It is a place that, in Haraway's terms, has abandoned the material in favor of the discursive. For both Haraway and Latour the point of critique is not to abandon reality but to redefine it in discursive terms. The point is not to privilege the discursive over the material but to understand the material in discursive terms. But if Latour is right, then that goal has not been realized in either feminism, critical theory, or science studies.

I believe that Latour *is* right, that we have gone down the wrong path, and that in order to correct this error, we must return to the goal Haraway stated so clearly in 1985: redefining the material in discursive terms. The linguistic turn has been immensely fruitful for feminism. We have learned much about the social construction of "woman" and "reality." But the loss of the material is too high a price to pay for that gain. What we need now is not a return to a modernist conception of reality as an objective given, but rather an understanding of reality informed by all we have learned in the linguistic turn. We need a "new settlement" of the question posed by modernism. We need, in Karen Barad's terms, to construct "a ballast against current tendencies that confuse theorizing with unconstrained play" (1998, 124 n. 20).

Revolutions in the intellectual world do not come out of nowhere. Latour's broadside against social studies of science was rooted in several decades of work by philosophers and sociologists of science who were discontented with a strict social constructionist position. Proponents of the sociology of scientific knowledge (SSK) made a persuasive case for the social construction of scientific concepts. But what is entailed by this movement was difficult for many philosophers of science to accept. If there is, quite literally, no "objective" way of distinguishing among various scientific theories, then the whole purpose of science is called into question. If everything is a social construction, then how is science different from any other social construction? Is there any way of setting apart the exploration of nature that defines science from anything else that humans do?

Feminists have been at the forefront of the SSK movement. Their approach to these studies, however, is distinctive. They argue that the reality constructed by scientific concepts is a specifically masculine reality. Bringing gender into SSK has extended the scope of its constructionist argument in significant ways. Yet discontent with the conclusions entailed by the social studies of science has been particularly pronounced among feminist philosophers of science. Feminists have attempted to define science as a distinctive activity without abandoning the insights of the social studies of science. Helen Longino, for example, argues that social studies of science are premised on an absolute dichotomy: either nature imposes its character directly on our cognitive processes or scientists' cognitive processes are mediated in various ways (2002, 23). Longino argues that we need to overcome this dichotomy. The solution she proposes involves overcoming the opposition between rationality and sociality. Both sides in the debate, she claims, accept this opposition. Against this, she argues that rationality and sociality are equal aspects of knowledge (2002, 143).

Attempts to overcome this dichotomy characterize the work of several other feminist philosophers of science. Sandra Harding seeks to define a "constructivist materialism" (2004, 38). Lynne Hankinson Nelson (1990) redefines empiricism as community-based knowledge. Lorraine Code (1991) calls for a "regulative realism." All of these accounts are attempts to negotiate the problem outlined by Latour. But these formulations do not attack the problem at its root. Specifically, they do not succeed in moving to the new settlement that he defines. Instead, these accounts remain within the epistemological terrain that constitutes the problem in the first place. Although the solutions offered by these theorists are persuasive, they all entail a redefinition of epistemological concepts—rationality, objectivity, and so forth. They do not move beyond the epistemological sphere to attempt to grapple with the reality that the concepts describe.[1]

Discontent with the social constructionist orthodoxy has also been evident in epistemology. Ian Hacking, in *The Social Construction of What?* (1999), summarized this discontent with his usual irony. If everything is socially constructed, he argues, then "social construction" is both obscure and overused. He concludes: "The metaphor of social construction once had excellent shock value, but now it has become tired" (1999, 35). Richard Bernstein (1992) looks for a middle ground between the modernists who espouse rational grounding and the postmoderns who reject it as an illusion. Feminist epistemologists have been equally concerned. Louise Antony (2002) argues for a version of naturalized epistemology that is appropriate for feminism. She and other feminist epistemologists argue that giving up on objectivity and rationality is too high a price to pay. If we as feminists want to represent accounts of the social world as true and accurate, we must have an epistemology that allows us to assert this (Crary 2002). Linda Alcoff, in her attempt to deal with the slippery concept of identity, argues for a "postpositivist realism" (2000).

Feminist discontent with social construction has also emerged in feminist considerations of the body. Many feminists were concerned that if we embrace the postmodern conception of "woman" as a discursive construct the result will be "The Incredible Shrinking Woman" (Di Stefano 1987). What is at issue here emerges in a debate between Judith Butler and Susan Bordo on the materiality of the body. Butler claims that feminists must reject the metaphysical assumptions of materiality; she asserts that a discursive understanding of the body is both sufficient and appropriate for feminism. Bordo's counter is that the hegemonic gender discourses of our society, the discourses that Butler foregrounds, create a very real reality for gendered bodies and that feminism must take account of this reality (Hekman 1998).

Feminist discontent with social construction and postmodernism, then, has coalesced around the definition of the "real." Like Latour, many feminists came to the conclusion that we should be able to account for the real beyond discourse, but exactly how this accounting should be expressed remains elusive. Furthermore, the attempts on the part of feminist philosophers of science, epistemologists, and theorists of the body to bring in the real have not, for the most part, succeeded.

There appears to be a consensus that something is amiss, but there is as yet no consensus on how the problem can be fixed.

THE SETTLEMENTS

The linguistic turn, social constructionism, and postmodernism are all attempts to combat the fundamental presuppositions of modernist thought. At the root of modernism is an absolute distinction between objective reality on one hand and social construction on the other. Latour defines this as the "modernist settlement." It is this settlement that science studies addresses. Their goal has been to question the objective reality of the world, to bring it under the rubric of the "constructed" rather than the absolute and objective. Latour's thesis is that this effort has not succeeded in creating an alternative to the modernist settlement and is, furthermore, untenable. He argues that we have yet to provide a viable alternative to the "fateful distinction" between construction and reality (1999, 16). It follows that what we need is a new settlement, one that takes a path different from that of social construction without abandoning its insights.

Defining this new settlement, however, is a daunting task. The social constructionist paradigm is deeply entrenched in the contemporary intellectual world. Discussions of the "real" and the "material" are anathema to many in the intellectual community (the scare quotes are necessary). Establishing a new paradigm, as Kuhn (1962) has taught us, is nothing short of revolutionary. Kuhn has also taught us that when paradigms are first proposed, their parameters are vague. This is certainly true of the new settlement that is emerging. Although, as this collection attests, a number of contemporary thinkers are attempting to formulate this settlement, exactly what it will entail remains unclear.

What is clear, however, is that the new settlement cannot involve a return to modernism. The dichotomy between construction and reality is untenable.[2] Privileging reality over construction, the modernist settlement, is not preferable to privileging construction over reality, the social constructionist alternative. What we need is a conception that does not presuppose a gap between language and reality that must be bridged, that does not define the two as opposites. We have learned much from the linguistic turn. Language *does* construct our reality. What we are discovering now, however, is that this is not the end of the story. Language interacts with other elements in this construction; there is more to the process than we originally thought. What we need is not a theory that ignores language as modernism did, but rather a more complex theory that incorporates language, materiality, and technology into the equation.

Obviously, not everyone will agree with this assessment of the intellectual crisis we are facing. The social constructionist paradigm is pervasive and hegemonic. Furthermore, it has been politically effective for feminists, gays, lesbians, and antiracist projects. Its adherents will not abandon their position easily. My argument, however, is that we should take seriously the signs of discontent with this paradigm. Something significant is wrong here. The material is not only a social construction; it is not only a passive object of our linguistic creation. Feminists, philosophers of science, environmental philosophers, epistemologists, and critical theorists need a new way to understand the relationship between language and reality.

That many of these thinkers are concerned with the loss of the material is evident from even a casual perusal of contemporary theory. The theorists I cited above are representative of a wide-ranging reassessment of social constructionism. But there is more going on than grousing about the problems with social constructionism. There are also theorists whose work moves beyond criticism to an attempt to formulate the new settlement to which Latour refers. My thesis is that there are four settlements emerging in contemporary theory that are beginning to define this new paradigm. All of these efforts are in some sense incomplete; there are gaps in the conceptions that must be addressed in subsequent work. What is important about these efforts, however, is that they are moving ahead rather than looking back. With Latour I am arguing that defining this new settlement is imperative if critical theory is to overcome its present stagnation.

The first settlement that is emerging is rooted in the philosophy of science. Latour's work is at the forefront of this effort. His formulation of the settlement takes various forms, but his clearest articulation is found in *Pandora's Hope* (1999). There Latour begins with the assumption that we must provide an alternative to the opposition between construction and reality in science studies. He proposes "the collective" to replace the conception of society operative in contemporary theory. He argues that while society was an artifact imposed by the modernist settlement, "collective" refers to the association between humans and nonhumans. Central to the collective is a political process by which the cosmos is collected in one livable whole (1999, 304).

In opposition to the correspondence theory that has dominated social studies of science, Latour proposes a conception he calls "circulating reference." Phenomena, he asserts, are not found in the meeting point between things and the forms of the human mind, but rather, phenomena are what circulate all along the reversible chain of transformations (1999, 71). One of the most radical elements of Latour's theory is his assertion that nonhuman entities *act*. Action, he claims, is not a property of humans but an association of actants. Humans and nonhumans belong to a collective that involves the exchange of human and nonhuman properties inside a corporate body (1999, 193). For Latour, nonhuman entities have both agency and ontology.

Latour would be the first to admit that his definition of the new settlement is vague. Despite the overriding influence of Latour's thought, it is another contemporary philosopher of science, Andrew Pickering, who provides the best description of what the new settlement would look like for the natural sciences. Like Latour, Pickering's goal is to try to bring the material world back into the equation of science, and also like Latour, his method of doing so is to argue for the agency of the material world. A useful way of thinking about science, Pickering argues, is that the world is filled with agency; it is continually doing things that bear on us. But he argues that it is not accurate to describe this doing as observation statements upon disembodied intellects, but rather as forces upon material beings (1995, 6). Adopting a theme that is common to many of the new settlements, Pickering appeals to our everyday life experiences to ground his conception. Much of everyday life, he asserts, involves coping with the material agency of the natural world. Science, he argues, should be seen as a continuation and extension of that coping with material agency (1995, 6).

Pickering's goal is to develop a theory of science, technology, and society that will result in what he calls a "performative" image of science.

> Scientists are human agents in a field of material agency which they struggle to capture in machines. Further, human and material agency are reciprocally and emergently intertwined in this struggle. Their contours emerge in the temporality of practice and are definitional of and sustain one another. Existing culture constitutes the surface of emergence for the intentional structure of scientific practice and such practice consists in the reciprocal tuning of human and material agency, tuning that can itself reconfigure human intentions. (1995, 21)

The metaphor that Pickering employs to characterize this theory is the mangle. Pickering's mangle evokes the unpredictability of the transformations worked on whatever is fed into the device. He uses the term as both a noun and a verb. Used as a noun, the mangle represents the transformative process of science, the way in which disparate elements are combined in unexpected ways. Used as a verb, "mangle" describes the way in which the contours of material and social agency are transformed in that process (1995, 23).

Employing the metaphor of the mangle to describe scientific practice allows Pickering to break down the rigid distinctions between the human and the nonhuman, science and society, the discursive and the material. In Pickering's settlement, these opposites are inextricably intertwined. The human scientist is "no longer at the center of the action calling the shots." Rather, "the world makes us in the same process by which we make the world" (1995, 26). One of the key advantages of Pickering's theory is that it can accommodate what he calls the "resistances" of nature, the instances in which nature does not do what it is expected to do and scientists are forced to deal with this. Pickering asserts that this resistance occurs, not in the nonhuman realm of instruments or in the human realm of scientific concepts, but in the boundary of the two realms (1995, 92).

Pickering defines the mangle as "impure": mangles mix everything up and produce unpredictable results. Connections between scientific knowledge and the world are "interactive stabilizations of machinic performances and conceptual strata" (1995, 182). What Pickering calls his "mangle realism" is grounded in the thesis that "how the material world is leaks into and infects our representations of it in a nontrivial and consequential fashion" (1995, 183). Unlike the conceptions he is opposing, Pickering's settlement is not monocausal. The modernists claimed that the world dictates our theories. The social constructionists claimed that our theories dictate the world. Mangle realism asserts that it is more complicated, that science, technology, and society, all of which possess agency, interact in complex ways to give us an understanding of the world. The mangle brings the world back in, but in a way that acknowledges its interaction with the other actors in the drama.

Other contemporary philosophers of science are formulating theories compatible with those of Latour and Pickering. Niels Bohr provides the inspiration for the feminist settlement articulated by Karen Barad. The work of Joseph Rouse has also been influential. Like Pickering and Latour, Rouse wants to break down dichotomies, in his case between naturalism and anti-naturalism. One of the most significant aspects of Rouse's thesis is that he defines a distinction between social studies of science and feminist studies of science. While the proponents of the social studies of science argued for the constitution of the natural world through scientific concepts, Rouse argues that feminist studies of science have developed a different ontology of knowing (2002, 138). Another significant aspect of Rouse's thought is his argument that we should understand the natural world as "disclosed" through scientific interaction (2002, 272). For Rouse, although scientific practice is a human activity, it is a distinctive human activity in that it aspires to point beyond itself to make intelligible the supposed brute unintelligibility of the natural world (2002, 16).

My discussion here is not exhaustive. Several other philosophers of science have developed approaches compatible with those discussed above. My point is to highlight a trend that is significant in that it is moving toward a new understanding of our relationship with the natural world. It is a complicated understanding. Pickering's mangle mixes everything up. The notion of nonhuman agency is difficult to conceptualize. The parameters of the settlement defy simple description. This is the case, however, because it is breaking new ground. It is a conception that is defining an understanding of the human and the nonhuman, the material and the discursive, that offers a much more fruitful way of grasping all of the elements of the equation. Furthermore, the settlement emerging in the philosophy of science is central to the other versions of the settlement being articulated. Because science is so important to the modernist settlement, resolving the question of science and society is a necessary first step in defining a new settlement.[3]

A second settlement is emerging in contemporary discussions of epistemology. The parameters of this settlement are structured by the long-standing antagonism between Continental and Anglo-American analytic philosophy. Continental philosophy has been dominated by the discursive turn of postmodernism, the source, by most accounts, of the problem of the loss of the material. Anglo-American analytic philosophy, on the other hand, has been unwilling to abandon their traditional modernist concern with realism and naturalism. The result has been an unproductive confrontation in which each side rejects the position of the other as untenable. What has been emerging in recent years, however, is a position that bridges the gap between the real and the discursive. It constitutes a new way of characterizing the relationship between language and reality that avoids the pitfalls of each camp.

Linda Alcoff, in her *Real Knowing* (1996), outlines what is at stake in this attempt to formulate a new settlement. Alcoff argues that we are witnessing a paradigm shift in epistemology and the emergence of a new conception of knowledge. This conception unites the need for a normative theory of knowledge that allows us to make evaluative distinctions between competing claims with an account of the interconnection between knowledge and power (1996, 2). What she attempts to do in her book is to initiate a dialogue between Continental and analytic philosophy in which this new paradigm can be articulated.

In order to formulate her thesis, Alcoff draws on major figures from both the Continental and analytic traditions. Her representatives from the Continental tradition are Gadamer and Foucault. In her analysis of these thinkers, Alcoff is at pains to argue that their positions are not nihilistic or idealistic, but rather that for both philosophers the real world and truth matter a great deal. Gadamer's theory, Alcoff claims, can be interpreted as a procedural argument for coherence. Gadamer defines understanding as ontologically dependent on an evolving tradition; beliefs subsist in an ever-evolving web of belief (1996, 52). Foucault, likewise, is concerned to improve the epistemic status of thought itself, not to eliminate the possibility of knowledge. His goal is to understand and evaluate knowledges in their specificity (1996, 159).

Alcoff's choices on the analytic side are Davidson and Putnam. She argues that Davidson's theory of the web of belief has significant similarities to Gadamer's position on tradition. Davidson argues that we judge the truth or error of belief against the background of a web of true beliefs (1996, 104). Hilary Putnam's internal realism, Alcoff argues, accomplishes much the same thing. For Alcoff the advantage of Putnam's position is that he describes coherentism in ontological terms. Putnam's internal realism preserves a mind-independent reality but also asserts that the question of what objects the world consists in is always answered within a theory (1996, 166). Once again, concepts and reality are not separate but inextricably intertwined.

Alcoff's analysis constitutes a significant breakthrough in epistemological discussions. Her argument for the convergence of Continental and analytic philosophy illustrates the liabilities of each position. If Alcoff is right, then both Continental and analytic philosophers are coming to realize that staking out a position on either side of the real/discursive divide will not work. The alternative that Alcoff articulates, what she calls "immanent realism," is an attempt to deconstruct this dichotomy, and in so doing, to articulate a new paradigm.

An even more important aspect of Alcoff's work is her argument for a shift in emphasis from epistemology to ontology. She discusses this shift in the context of her argument for a "robust coherentism" that avoids the problems of both foundational philosophy and epistemological nihilism (1996, 6). The movement from epistemology to ontology is of immense significance. As many commentators have argued, the linguistic turn in philosophy and critical theory has entailed an almost exclusive emphasis on epistemology. But this emphasis on epistemology necessarily skews philosophical discussions in the direction of words rather than matter; the real takes a backseat to the discursive. The move from epistemology to ontology that Alcoff both describes and advocates corrects this imbalance. Ontological theories are about matter; unlike epistemological theories, they cannot "lose" the real—it is their subject matter. The ontological theories that Alcoff describes, however, do not entail a return to modernism. Rather, they are rooted in the conviction that our only access to ontology is through the discursive. The best way of articulating this approach is that, for the new ontology, our language structures how we apprehend the ontological but it does not constitute it.

As Alcoff's analysis indicates, there are a variety of different philosophers from both sides of the Continental/analytic divide that are formulating a new settlement in Latour's terms. There are important differences among these theorists. Putnam would most likely be shocked to be put in the same category as Foucault. But there is a common thread here that is expressed succinctly by John Searle: there is no contradiction between conceptual relativism and external realism (1995, 161). The theorists Alcoff discusses, and several she does not, concur on this thesis although they may approach it in different ways.

Ludwig Wittgenstein, although he is mentioned by some of these philosophers, rarely takes center stage in these discussions. This is unfortunate, for Wittgenstein's approach has much to contribute to the formulation of a new settlement. Wittgenstein's work is commonly identified as the epitome of the linguistic turn in philosophy. His work on language is seen as one of the major causes of the turn to discourse and away from the real. This interpretation of his work, however, is seriously misguided. Far from arguing that language constitutes reality, Wittgenstein defined language as an activity, a game, something that human beings, because we are the kind of beings we are, practice. Wittgenstein, like the postmoderns, is trying to break philosophy away from the modernist conception of language as the mirror of nature. But Wittgenstein does not move in the direction of epistemological nihilism, of a conception in which language constitutes our world. Rather, his view is that language is what we do *in* the world. It is a central part, but not the only part, of our form of life. For Wittgenstein, language and the world are always intimately connected and interacting.

There is a further dimension to Wittgenstein's understanding of the connection between language and the world: it is fundamental to human life itself. Language is part of human beings' "natural history"; it is rooted in "general facts of nature" (Wittgenstein 1958, 230; Hekman 2002). These references have posed difficulties for those Wittgenstein interpreters who want to place him in the discursive camp. Despite his emphasis on language, Wittgenstein appears to be moving back in the direction of a foundationalist philosophy with these references. The question becomes how these comments can be reconciled with the obvious linguistic emphasis of Wittgenstein's approach.

In the context of contemporary discussion of a new settlement, however, these references constitute the strength rather than the weakness of Wittgenstein's thought. Wittgenstein never intended to initiate a "linguistic turn" in philosophy. He did not intend to sever language from reality, to argue that language constitutes reality. Although his work was used to that effect, his texts do not entail linguistic determinism. For Wittgenstein language is an embedded activity—embedded in the way of life of the human species. Although he rejects the definition of language as the mirror of nature, it does not follow that he defines language as constitutive of reality. Rather, like the proponents of the new settlement, Wittgenstein sees language and the real as complexly intertwined. Language does not constitute our world but makes it possible for us to live in it in a certain way determined by the parameters of our existence as human beings.

Wittgenstein's linguistic philosophy and postmodernism are generally identified as the principal causes of the linguistic turn of contemporary thought. I have argued that Wittgenstein's work does not, in fact, privilege the linguistic, but rather, it offers a way of integrating language with reality. A similar argument can be made regarding certain aspects of postmodernism. Although postmodernism as a whole is certainly guilty of the privileging of the discursive, it is nevertheless the case that some postmodern thinkers do precisely what postmodernism claims to accomplish: the deconstruction of the dichotomy. They offer a theory, in other words, that deconstructs the dichotomy between the real and the discursive, a theory that constitutes a third version of the new settlement.

The work of Gilles Deleuze is one instance of this other aspect of postmodernism. A common characteristic of the settlements I have described thus far is the movement from epistemology to ontology. Deleuze embraces this shift in his work. He looks to Spinoza for philosophical guidance precisely because he provides an ontological conception of practice. The focus of Deleuze's work is not language but experience, and, most notably, practice. His interest is in "life," not language alone, but in the complex interaction between life and language (Deleuze and Guattari 1987, 76). The result is what he calls "transcendental empiricism," the experience of life that has no ground outside itself (Colebrook 2002, 69).

In *A Thousand Plateaus* (1987) Deleuze and Guattari formulate the concept of the "assemblage": "An assemblage, in its multiplicity necessarily acts on semiotic flows, material flows, and social flows simultaneously" (1987, 22). An assemblage establishes connections with previously separate entities, reuniting them into a complex whole. "Assemblages are necessary for states of force and regimes of signs to intertwine their relations" (1987, 71). Assemblages, like Pickering's mangle, mix everything up. They posit an interaction and intertwining of forces, not a determination of one force by another. For Deleuze, as the elements of the assemblage change, so does the realm of practice and experience.

The work of Michel Foucault, however, provides an even stronger case for the definition of a new settlement in what has been labeled postmodern thought. Although Foucault is strongly associated with the turn to the discursive that characterizes postmodernism, it is possible, as with Wittgenstein, to interpret his thought in a different light as an effective deconstruction of the discourse/matter dichotomy. The goal of Foucault's analyses of discourses in all of his works is to reveal how discourses shape the material reality in which we live. For Foucault, changes in discourses result in very real changes in our physical world. Foucault's concern is with those material changes. His history of the present is designed to show how the world in which we live today has been shaped by discourses that are deeply rooted in our culture and extend to the thought and practice of the ancient Greeks.

But perhaps the strongest case for the effectiveness of Foucault's deconstruction of discourse/reality is his theory of bio-power. More than any other contemporary theorist, Foucault has turned our attention to bodies and to the interaction between discourses and bodies. His brilliant analyses of the carceral society are predicated on the assumption that bodies are crafted by discourse and that this crafting has very real consequences for how those bodies inhabit cultural space. For Foucault, it is impossible to detach the discourse of bodies from the bodies we inhabit. We *are* our bodies; the discourse and the matter become one in our bodily existence. But it is also a central aspect of Foucault's theory that the relationship between bodies and discourse that now structures our lives could be arranged differently. A different discourse of bodies would result in a different bodily reality. This is the sense of Foucault's critique of what he calls carceral society. Foucault suggests that changing the discourse of bodies would change the material reality of those bodies. And it is this change that is the whole point of his analyses (1979, 1980).

What I am arguing with regard to the work of Deleuze and Foucault, but particularly of Foucault, is that what postmodernism has come to represent in contemporary thought is an inaccurate interpretation of some thinkers who have been placed under this label. Postmodernism began as an attempt to deconstruct dichotomies, especially the discourse/reality dichotomy. In their zeal to reject modernism, many postmoderns have moved from privileging reality to privileging discourse. But not all. A sympathetic reading of Foucault yields a perspective that does not privilege either side, that articulates the complex interaction between the elements of the dichotomy. Rereading Foucault can and does produce an understanding of the way in which the material and the discursive participate in defining a particular social reality. This understanding makes a significant contribution to the new settlement.

The fourth settlement that is emerging in contemporary thought has its origins in feminist thought. Despite the advantages produced by discursive analysis, feminists have been uneasy with the discursive turn from the outset. Discursive analysis has enabled feminists to probe the linguistic constitution of "woman" and related concepts in our society. It has provided insight into the structure of the subordination women face. But the limitations of this analysis have also been all too apparent. Many feminists have argued that we must remain focused on the material reality of women's lives, on their bodies and their biology, in order to formulate a viable feminism. Consequently, many feminists have sought another avenue for feminist theory and practice than that provided by discursive analysis.

In confronting the issues raised by the discursive turn, philosophers of science and feminists have addressed similar concerns. Science cannot afford to entirely lose material reality, and feminists cannot afford to entirely lose women's bodily reality. Thus feminist critics of science in particular, like philosophers of science such as Latour and Pickering, have moved away from the social studies of science to a position that brings matter back into the equation. The work of Donna Haraway is exemplary in this respect. Haraway resists the temptation to move to the discursive pole of the discourse/matter dichotomy. She develops a theory that takes matter seriously without forgetting the lessons of social construction:

> Cells, organisms, and genes are not "discovered" in a vulgar realist sense, but they are not made up. . . . The world takes shape in specific ways and cannot take shape in just any way. (1997, 143)

One commentator argues that Haraway's position results in "ontological gerrymandering," an epistemological position that accepts the constructionist account but at the same time positions its own knowledge claims as accurate descriptions of reality (K. Campbell 2004, 172).

In their introduction to a volume of *Hypatia* devoted to feminist science studies, Lynn Hankinson Nelson and Alison Wylie (2004, x) argue that a new position is emerging in feminist science studies based on the conviction that an unqualified social constructionism is just as inadequate as objectivism. The feminist science critic who has done the most to define a position that avoids both of these pitfalls is Karen Barad. Barad is very critical of the tendency in contemporary feminist theory to engage in what she calls "unconstrained play," the "unqualified social construction" to which Nelson and Wylie refer. But what is most significant about Barad's work is that she has accomplished what few others have achieved: a precise outline of what is entailed by "making matter matter" in feminist science studies.

A key advantage of Barad's work is that she is very clear on the nature of the problem confronting contemporary feminist theory:

> Language has been granted too much power. The linguistic turn, the semiotic turn, the interpretive turn, the cultural turn: it seems that at every turn lately every "thing"—even materiality—is turned into a matter of language or some other form of cultural representation. (2003, 801)

She concludes: the only thing that does not seem to matter is matter. The goal of Barad's work is to counter this tendency, to "provide a ballast against current tendencies that confuse theorizing with unconstrained play" (1998, 124 n. 20). At the center of Barad's critique of postmodernism and poststructuralism is her claim that these approaches reinscribe the active-culture/passive-nature dualism that they claim to deconstruct (2001b, 77). By defining materiality solely as an effect of discursive practices, she claims, these accounts leave the discourse/matter dichotomy in place.[4]

Barad's strategy for addressing these problems is to move the discussion from epistemology to ontology. But Barad's ontology is not the "old" ontology of modernism. Rather, it entails the "crafting of ontologies," the exploration of technologies by which nature and culture interact (1996, 163). What is needed, she claims, is a rejection of the epistemological/ontological distinction and a move toward what she calls "onto-epistem-ology," the study of practices of knowing (2003, 829). The vehicle for her articulation of this approach is her interpretation of the work of Niels Bohr, specifically Bohr's argument that scientific theories describe "agential reality," the position that matter is given agency by a particular theory. Out of Bohr's approach, Barad formulates what she calls "agential realism":

> Agential realism is an epistemological and ontological framework that extends Bohr's insights and takes as its central concerns the nature of materiality, the relationship between the material and the discursive, the nature of "nature" and "culture," and the relationship between them, the nature of agency, and the effects of boundary, including the nature of exclusions that accompany boundary projects. (1998, 89)

The brilliance of Barad's concept lies in her integration of the insights of social construction/postmodernism/poststructuralism with a new approach to materiality. The traditional realism of modernism privileges matter, presupposing an independent reality about which we have knowledge. Discursive theories privilege language and deny the materiality of matter. Agential realism, in contrast, proposes the "intra-action" of matter and discourse—the inseparability of objects and agencies of observation (1998, 96). She argues:

> Which material-discursive practices are enacted matters for ontological as well as epistemological reasons: a different material-discursive apparatus materializes a different agential reality, as opposed to simply producing a different description of a fixed observation-independent world. (2001c, 236)

Agential realism is not about the representation of an independent reality, but about the real consequences of intra-action with the world (1996, 188).

Barad is very conscious of the relationship between her theory and that of the postmoderns. Far from rejecting postmodernism, she accepts its basic premises and tries to correct its defects. Agential realism, she argues, is a form of social constructionism that is not relativist, does not reduce knowledge to power plays or language, but rather accounts for the real, material consequences of knowledge (1996, 183–86). Although Barad is sympathetic to the position taken by Foucault, she criticizes him for failing to treat the materialization of human bodies on a par with that of nonhuman bodies. Foucault, she argues, defines disciplinary power as exercised through various apparatuses, but he does not see the inseparability of these observing apparatuses and the observed (1998, 99–103).

Barad's critique of the work of Judith Butler is even more revealing. Barad develops a theory of what she calls "performativity" that can only be understood as an explicit challenge to Butler's concept. For Barad performativity is a "materialist, naturalist, and posthumanist elaboration that allows matter its due as an active participant in the world's becoming" (2003, 804). Barad's concept of "post-humanist performativity" incorporates the material and discursive; it questions the human/nonhuman distinction. The problem with Butler's approach, Barad argues, is that she cannot explain how discursive practices produce material bodies. She argues that we need to explain not only how the body is discursively constructed but how the discursive construction is related to nondiscursive practices that vary widely from one society to another. Butler's theory, she concludes, reinscribes matter as a passive product of discursive practices (2003, 821 n. 26). What we need instead is an alternative to the metaphysics of words and things (2003, 812).

The significance of Barad's position and its advantages in relation to those of Butler and Foucault are revealed in a pathbreaking article published in *differences* in 1998. Barad's article supplies an illustration of how agential realism works in both theory and practice. At the core of agential realism is the thesis that theories make particular aspects of reality agentic and that this agency has real, material—and, most notably—political consequences. Her example in this article is the technological-discursive-material practice of fetal imaging. The technological capability of fetal imaging makes it possible to "see" the fetus at a very early stage in its development. This "seeing," a product of both technology and theory, makes an aspect of nature—the very early fetus—agentic in several significant ways. First, it "becomes" matter; it did not exist as matter before the technology could "see" it. Second, and very significantly, it becomes politically significant. The fetus, which can now be "seen," has political significance that it lacked before it attained the status of matter. In other words, the technology that allows us to "see" the fetus at an early stage has material, political, and ethical consequences that are both real and significant. Furthermore, the material arrangement of fetal imaging is facilitated and in part conditioned by a political discourse presupposing the autonomy of the fetus. The construction of the fetus as a self-contained, free-floating object under the eye of the scientific observer reinforces this presupposition of the subject's autonomy and the objectivity of the scientific observer (1998, 110–14).

Barad concludes her account by arguing that the "fetus" designates an element of agential reality, a phenomenon constituted and reconstituted out of the historically and culturally situated intra-actions of material-discursive apparatuses of bodily production (1998, 115). In another article, Barad contrasts her analysis of the sonogram to Butler's analysis in *Bodies That Matter* (1993). Her point is that Butler's theory can only explain how discourse comes to matter, but not how matter comes to matter (2001a, 103–105). Barad's example of the sonogram, more than any other aspect of her work, demonstrates the power of agential realism. It explains how the intra-action of the discursive, technological, and material produce a new configuration that has agency. And, most significantly, it demonstrates not only the material but the political and ethical implications of this agency. The sonogram makes the fetus a political actor, and this fact has profound consequences for feminist politics.[5]

The settlement that emerges from Barad's work moves the discussion of the relationship between discourse and the material to a new level. Her description of the relationship between the human and the nonhuman, the technological and the material, the social and the political constitutes a new understanding of the intra-action of these elements. Barad's approach provides a kind of template for the new paradigm that is emerging in contemporary thought. Her settlement applies not just to feminism but to all aspects of critical thought. It can provide a solid foundation for the new paradigm that we are seeking.

The new settlement emerging in feminist science studies is evident in other aspects of feminism as well. Feminist discussions of the body are beginning to move beyond the restrictions imposed by linguistic construction. The starting point for many of these discussions is the effort to counter Judith Butler's claim that the body is not prior to discourse, but rather, its effect (1993, 30). Against this, Elizabeth Grosz argues that we must start thinking about the body in terms that transcend this dualism. Thinking of the body either as pure culture or as pure biology, she argues, is untenable. Instead, she proposes defining the body as "open materiality"—"a set of (possible infinite) tendencies and potentialities which may be developed yet whose development will necessarily hinder or induce other developments and other trajectories" (1994, 191).

Moira Gatens (1996) also wants to pry feminist discussions of the body away from dualisms. Arguing against the "degendering feminists," she asserts that the body is not a neutral, passive element that absorbs discursive scripts. The significance of discursive formations will be different on a male than on a female body. What we need, she argues, is an analysis of the body as *lived* (1996, 11). The approach to the body that these feminist theorists embrace is another instance of the movement that characterizes the new settlement: from the epistemological to the ontological. Commenting on these theorists, Claire Colebrook remarks, "The pervasiveness of textuality is not an argument for rejecting real or material being" (2000, 81). What these feminist theorists of the body are doing is bringing the materiality of the body into feminist discussions without losing the insights of discursive analysis.

Elizabeth A. Wilson extends this discussion into the broader issue of biology as a whole. Wilson is very explicit in her criticism of the limitation of discursive analysis. Biology, she argues, remains an "established adversary" of feminist theory, and as a result, certain fundamental aspects of the body, biology, and materiality have been foreclosed in feminist discussions (1999, 8–16). Wilson seeks to challenge this foreclosure in her book *Neural Geographies* (1998). Using a biological discussion of cognition as a springboard, Wilson argues that biology and neurology are not natural enemies of politics and that feminists can find a greater critical productivity in biology than our current theories of gender will allow (1998, 62). Her goal is not to prohibit biology but to remove it as origin (1998, 100). Wilson's aim is, once more, to overcome dualisms in a way that does not privilege either side of the opposition.

The settlement that is emerging in feminism is in many respects more developed and explicit than that which is emerging in other fields. The reason for this is the political commitment that lies at the root of feminism. This political commitment has two aspects. First, feminists want to be able to talk about the reality of women's bodies and their lived experiences in a patriarchal world. Extreme linguistic determinism precludes such discussions. Second, feminists want to assert the truth of their statements regarding women's status in that world. Embracing social constructionism and the relativism that it entails makes it impossible to make such truth claims.

Sharyn Clough takes on these challenges for feminism directly in *Beyond Epistemology* (2003). Clough argues that "our investment in epistemological critique is beginning to yield diminishing returns" (2003, 2). Clough's thesis is that the root of the problem is what she calls representationalism, a set of assumptions informing both correspondence and coherentist theories of truth. Representationalism entails, although it can be characterized in different ways, that language is always a representation of reality. Clough and an increasing number of contemporary theorists are arguing that it is this assumption that has led us in the wrong direction. As long as we assume that language is representational, we will be caught up with issues of relativism and objectivity, truth and skepticism. The only way to overcome these intractable problems is to abandon the assumptions of representationalism.

As an alternative, Clough turns to the pragmatic approach of Donald Davidson. Davidson's position, she asserts, does not answer skepticism, but dodges it and thus makes the need for epistemology less compelling (2003, 14). The center of Clough's theory is her reliance on Davidson's concept of the "web of belief." It is significant that Clough compares her use of Davidson to Barad's reliance on Bohr. The point here is not that these feminist theorists are looking to male theorists to ground their theories, but rather, that both are seeking a foundation for feminist truth claims and are willing to go wherever they can to find this foundation. The Davidson/Clough web of belief urges us to view potential beliefs as members of the same holistic web of evidence as empirical beliefs (2003, 60). False beliefs can be detected only from a background of true beliefs. This is possible because we live in a world composed of a shared background of true beliefs (2003, 106). Thus Clough can conclude: "Our scientific theories and our beliefs about oppression and justice are not merely relative to our feminist conceptual schemes, they are justified by the evidence and they are true" (2003, 127).

Clough is not the only feminist philosopher who is turning away from epistemology, social constructionism, and postmodernism. Nancy Tuana, Vicki Kirby, Jacinta Kerin, and many others are formulating positions similar to that taken by Barad and Clough.[6] My point in analyzing these theories is not to decide which one is right, but rather to emphasize that they sound a common theme: a rejection of the dualisms of modernism and an attempt to move to a position that does not privilege either side of the dualisms. My thesis is that this feminist attempt will be the driving force behind the formulation of a new settlement not only for feminism but for critical thought as a whole.

FROM EPISTEMOLOGY TO ONTOLOGY

I have argued in several contexts that one of the themes that emerges in the new settlements discussed above is the move from epistemology to ontology. But what is entailed by this move is not entirely clear. Social constructionists, postmodernists, and other adherents of the linguistic turn are very leery of ontology. They associate discussions of ontology with a modernist version of realism, the assumption of a fixed reality about which we seek absolute knowledge. The conception of ontology that is emerging in the new settlements, however, does not conform to this definition. The "new ontology" *does* assume that "there is a world out there." It is an ontology in this sense. But it also assumes that our only access to that world is linguistic: we know the world through the concepts and theories we have formulated. But it is also the case that the world shapes and constrains our knowledge. As Richard Rorty puts it, "The world can, once we have programmed ourselves within a language, cause us to hold beliefs" (1988, 69). Vocabularies are tools employed by natural creatures in a natural world. Different vocabularies equip us with beliefs that are more or less useful in coping with our environment.

Modernist ontology assumes that we can have unmediated knowledge of an objective world. The new ontology assumes that knowledge is always mediated by concepts and, in many cases, technology as well. It is, in Barad's terms, an intra-action. But unlike social constructionism, the new ontology assumes that concepts and theories have material consequences. If we employ one set of concepts, we will be able to cope with our environment more or less usefully. There is a world out there that shapes and constrains the consequences of the concepts we employ to understand it. Another important aspect of the new ontology is that these consequences can be compared. We can compare the usefulness of one set of concepts to another set of concepts in terms of how well they allow us to cope with our environment. Two points are important here. First, the new ontology is moving away from relativism. We *can* compare conceptual schemes, and our standard of comparison is the material consequences of these schemes. Second, we have not abandoned the insights of the linguistic turn. We know our world through our concepts. The difference is that in this conception there is a world that we know.

Naomi Scheman's discussion of photography (1993) demonstrates the point I am making here. Scheman points out that a photo is a visual trace of an act of seeing. But photos are not passive. A photo does not depict the one true reality of the object photographed, but rather, different photos can depict the same object in very different ways. The different intentions of the photographer produce very different versions of the same reality (1993, 161). The point is that the photo is *of something.* There is something out there that the photo records. It is not wholly a product of the photographer's imagination. It is a piece of reality that is depicted differently, given the different intentions of the photographers. This applies to ontological understandings as well. We access the world through our concepts and theories. Different conceptual schemes are going to produce very different versions of the world. But these concepts do not *constitute* the world; they depict it. This difference is very significant.

In his discussion of feminist science studies, Joseph Rouse argues that we should understand the natural as "disclosed" through scientific interaction (2002, 272). What he means by this is that science does not appeal to a given concept of nature, but rather that we are located in the midst of scientific and technological practices that continue to reshape what it is to *be* nature (2002, 360). Rouse does not elaborate on his concept of disclosure, nor does he specify which of the different meanings of the word he is employing. In the following, like Rouse, I adopt the concept of disclosure because I think it captures much of what is going on in the new settlements that are emerging. Moving from an understanding of the world as linguistically constituted to a conception in which the world is disclosed is an essential component of the new settlement. Disclosure brings in the ontological element that is missing in constitution without abandoning the role of epistemology. Disclosure captures Barad's "onto-epistem-ology" by bringing epistemology and ontology into intra-action.

Unlike Rouse, however, I think it is important to specify what disclosure means in the context of the new settlements. There are two definitions of disclosure that I want to reject. One is the definition of disclosure as "to uncover, to expose to view" (*OED*). This understanding of disclosure comes dangerously close to modernism. It entails that we are "getting it right" in a modernist sense. Another definition I want to reject is Heidegger's definition of the concept. For Heidegger, disclosure has a mystical component—the showing forth of Being throughout the ages.

The definition of disclosure that I want to embrace is the intransitive definition: to show itself, to come to light (*OED*). This intransitive definition captures the sense of disclosure that I want to build on. Disclosure does not entail uncovering, getting reality right, but bringing to light. Different aspects of reality can be disclosed from different perspectives. One of these aspects is not right and the others wrong, but rather they represent different aspects of the same reality. But, importantly, it is possible to compare the consequences of the different disclosures of the same reality.

My thesis is that this definition is operative in the new settlements I discussed above. It is particularly evident in Foucault's analyses. Foucault reveals that different epistemes disclose different worlds. As those epistemes change, so do the worlds they disclose. But for Foucault, this does not result in endless relativism. Foucault's analysis of carceral society is designed to reveal the dire material consequences of this particular disclosure. It is also designed to suggest that under a different episteme we might be different—and better—subjects.

Disclosure is not a refutation of relativism or skepticism, but a new way of approaching the issues of knowledge and reality. It avoids the problems of representationalism by offering another way of understanding the relationship between language and reality. Disclosure entails that perspectives/concepts/theories matter—that they are our means of accessing reality. But disclosure also entails that we do not constitute that reality with our concepts, but rather portray it in varying ways. An important aspect of this understanding is that the reality, like the object in the photograph or the subject of the scientist's experiment, is agentic. It pushes back, it effects the result. Another important aspect of this understanding is that there *is* a result. There are different material consequences to different disclosures. We can compare those material consequences and make arguments about which ones are more useful. We will not convince everyone with these arguments. We cannot appeal to an objective reality to trump the argument. But we have something to argue *about*.

SOCIAL ONTOLOGY

Although it is possible to make a plausible case for bringing ontology back into discussions of the material world, when we turn to the social world, the case for ontology seems much less compelling. The argument that the social world is a thoroughly social construction is very persuasive. The existence of the entities within the social world is wholly dependent on the definitions that the particular social group imposes on them; what an entity is, is wholly constituted in the linguistic realm. Here it seems that the postmoderns are right: when it comes to the social, and particularly the key social construct, the subject, there is no "there" there. It is all the performance of the social script.

Against this, I will argue that positing a social ontology is a necessary and useful aspect of the new settlement. Even though societies vary hugely in their constitution, it is possible to identify certain constant elements. All societies are composed of individuals arranged in groups. These individuals accomplish the basic goals necessary for the survival of the group. The elements that constitute society are disclosed in widely different ways in different societies. What constitutes the economic or the political system in a given society, for example, is defined by the terms for the economic and the political operative in that society. The connection between words and things is more intimate in the social world than in the material. But there is a "there" there: there are bodies and groups upon which the social concepts are deployed.

The element of the social world that has received the most attention in recent decades is the subject. Trying to understand the subject in ontological terms is particularly difficult. For the subject, the connection between the concept and that which is disclosed is unique. Subjects are particularly vulnerable to social definitions, and the consequences of those definitions structure the life of all subjects within the society. What it means to be a subject, furthermore, is central to the character of any society; defining the individual is a fundamental element of social organization. The definition of a subject in any given society provides individuals with the possibility of an identity. Those who do not meet the definition of the subject extant in society, or those who challenge that definition, lose their identity as subjects; they cease to be subjects altogether.

The advantage of looking at the subject from an ontological perspective is that it allows us to see the necessity of identity and how it functions in a social setting. Bodies in social groups are not just bodies. They require an identity to make sense of their lives and to operate as human beings in a social setting. Human bodies in social groups require viable identities, but they can only obtain those identities from the social script extant in the society in which they live. The definitions of the subject in any particular society either give the individual body a viable identity or they do not. Either I become a subject or I do not. If I am excluded from subjecthood, I am deprived of an identity that can provide me with a possible life in my society. Having a viable identity, being accepted by my society as a subject, is necessary to social existence. Without it I am, quite literally, no one.

Foucault suggests that what he is doing and what we should be doing is a "critical ontology of ourselves." It is in this spirit that I am suggesting a social ontology. As Foucault's work makes so clear, different ontologies of the subject have vastly different material effects. The conception of the subject that defines contemporary society makes possible the carceral society that Foucault describes. Understanding this ontology of the subject is what Foucault's work is all about. It is also about understanding that another ontology of the subject would result in a very different social world. The death of "man," he argues, might lead to a world in which the relationship between bodies and pleasures would be quite different.

> The critical ontology of ourselves has to be considered not, certainly, as a theory, a doctrine, nor even as a permanent body of knowledge that is accumulating; it has to be conceived as an attitude, an ethos, a philosophical life in which the critique of what we are is at one and the same time the historical analysis of the limits that are imposed on us and an experiment in the possibility of going beyond them. (Foucault 1984, 50)

Foucault's critical ontology is about bodies and practices, where they came from and what effects they have. His point is that subjectivity today is constituted by the material practices of prisons, barracks, schools, and hospitals. A critical ontology of ourselves entails a historico-practical test of the limits beyond which we cannot go (1984, 47).

What, then, does feminism gain by adopting the social ontology that I am advocating? Moira Gatens suggests an answer to this question when she states, "One cannot take up a place in society unless one is designated 'female' or 'male'" (2000, 69). What Gatens and other feminist theorists are suggesting is a feminist social version of Pickering's mangle. Instead of assuming, as do the social constructionists, that language creates social reality, we assume instead that language, bodies, technologies, and other elements interact to create "collective assemblages of enunciation/utterance" (Gatens 2000, 70). This perspective has the advantage of bringing bodies and the material back into the discussion of social reality. It also serves another important function: it breaks down the division between the natural and the cultural. Assuming that the material is appropriate to the natural but not the social world reifies the natural/cultural division that we are trying to avoid.

Feminist and other critical theorists have a long way to go in the effort to formulate a social ontology. Many of the resources cited above can be useful in this effort, however. Foucault's focus on bodies is an important first step. Foucault wants to explain how power works on bodies and how that power has material effects. Wittgenstein's work can also be one of the building blocks. Wittgenstein considers language as part of the natural history of human beings. Language, he asserts, is something we do as human beings, just like walking and breathing; language games are practices. In her feminist interpretation of Wittgenstein, Deborah Orr argues that for Wittgenstein the body and lived experiences are the weft into which language is woven to create the pattern of our lives (2002, 323). What she calls this "holistic view" of the human has much in common with the assemblages of the mangle.

One of the most significant advantages of embracing a feminist social ontology is that it allows us to talk about something that has been lost in the linguistic turn: identity. For the postmoderns, identity is suspect, a throwback to the errors of modernism. But, as even Judith Butler tentatively admits in her recent work, we "appear to require" identity to function in society (2004, 187). Butler's tentativeness here is insufficient. What we need is a core sense of self in order to function in the social world. Just as importantly, we need a way to theorize about that identity (Hekman 2004; Alcoff 2000).

The problem, of course, is that society's norms define our identities; they define us as normal or deviant, moral or immoral. What do I do if the identity I am given by my society is not viable, defining me as deviant or even subhuman? I cannot appeal to my "true nature" and thus reject the identity imposed on me. What I can argue is that we should conceive of my identity in another way. I can resist the identity in society's script. If we move, for example, from a negative to a positive definition of "lesbian," everything changes for the material life of the lesbian woman. It is possible to arrange the body/language connection in a different way and disclose a different reality for lesbians. The advantage of this perspective is that it does not deny the female body of the lesbian; it does not reduce her to the social script. Instead, this perspective incorporates both bodies and social scripts.

The creation of a feminist social ontology has yet to be realized. For those of us trained in postmodernism, the journey is a scary one. We have been so convinced that the world, and especially the social world, is a linguistic construction that discussions of the "real" seem like heresy. But the social world is very real; there are bodies and matter and real consequences of this materiality. If feminists are to understand—and change—that social reality, we must bring the material back in. We must make matter matter, not only in science but in society as well.

NOTES

1. A recent collection of feminist critiques of science goes so far as to return to the modernist conception of science in order to overcome the problems posed by social construction (Pinnick 2003).

2. This is Latour's argument in his 1993 book, *We Have Never Been Modern.*

3. See especially Stengers (1997) and the theorists writing about Actor Network Theory (Law 1999).

4. See Alaimo, Haraway, and Merchant for related arguments.

5. For a related analysis of the construction of the fetus, see Casper (1994).

6. I do not include in this list Richmond Campbell's advocacy of an almost unreconstructed empiricism, a position that constitutes a return to modernism (1998).

REFERENCES

Alcoff, Linda. 1996. *Real Knowing: New Versions of the Coherence Theory.* Ithaca, N.Y.: Cornell University Press.

———. 2000. "Who's Afraid of Identity Politics?" In Paula Moya et al., eds., *Reclaiming Identity: Realist Theory and the Predicament of Postmodernism,* 312–44. Berkeley: University of California Press.

Antony, Louise. 2002. "Quine as Feminist: The Radical Import of Naturalized Epistemology." In Louise Antony and Charlotte Witt, eds., *A Mind of One's Own,* 2nd ed., 110–53. Boulder, Colo.: Westview.

Barad, Karen. 1996. "Meeting the University Halfway." In Lynn Hankinson Nelson and Jack Nelson, eds., *Feminism, Science, and the Philosophy of Science,* 161–94. Dordrecht: Kluwer.

———. 1998. "Getting Real: Technoscientific Practices and the Materialization of Reality." *differences* 10.2: 87–128.

———. 2001a. "Performing Culture/Performing Nature: Using the Piezoelectric Crystal of Ultrasound Technologies as a Transducer between Science Studies and Queer Theories." In Christina Lammar, ed., *Digital Anatomy,* 98–114. Vienna: Turia and Kant.

———. 2001b. "Reconfiguring Space, Time, and Matter." In Mariane DeKoven, ed., *Feminist Lacations: Global and Local, Theory and Practice,* 75–109. New Brunswick, N.J.: Rutgers University Press.
———. 2001c. "Scientific Literacy, Agential Literacy=(Learning + Doing) Science Responsibly." In Maralee Mayberry et al., eds., *Feminist Science Studies: A New Generation,* 226–46. New York: Routledge.
———. 2003. "Posthumanist Performativity: Toward an Understanding of How Matter Comes to Matter." *Signs* 28.3: 801–31.
Bernstein, Richard. 1992. *The New Constellation.* Cambridge: MIT Press.
Butler, Judith. 1993. *Bodies That Matter.* New York: Routledge.
———. 2004. "Bodies and Power Revisited." In Dianna Taylor and Karen Vintges, eds., *Feminists and the Final Foucault.* Urbana: University of Illinois Press, 183–94.
Campbell, Kristen. 2004. "The Promise of Feminist Reflexivities: Developing Donna Haraway's Project for Feminist Science Studies." *Hyptia* 19.1: 162–82.
Campbell, Richmond. 1998. *Illusions of Paradox: A Feminist Epistemology Naturalized.* Lanham, Md.: Rowman and Littlefield.
Casper, Monica. 1994. "Reframing and Grounding Nonhuman Agency: What Makes a Fetus an Agent?" *American Behavioral Scientist* 37.6: 839–56.
Clough, Sharyn. 2003. *Beyond Epistemology: A Pragmatist Approach to Feminist Science Studies.* Lanham, Md.: Rowman and Littlefield.
Code, Lorraine. 1991. *What Can She Know? Feminist Theory and the Construction of Knowledge.* Ithaca: Cornell University Press.
Colebrook, Claire. 2000. "From Radical Representation to Corporeal Becomings: The Feminist Philosophy of Lloyd, Grosz, and Gatens." *Hypatia* 15.2: 76–93.
Crary, Alice. 2002. "What Do Feminists Want in an Epistemology?" In Naomi Scheman and Peg O'Connor, eds., *Feminist Interpretations of Ludwig Wittgenstein,* 97–118. University Park: Penn State Press.
Deleuze, Gilles, and Félix Guattari. 1987. *A Thousand Plateaus: Capitalism and Schizophrenia.* Trans. Brian Massumi. Minneapolis: University of Minnesota Press.
Di Stefano, Christine. 1987. "Postmodernism/Postfeminism? The Case of the Incredible Shrinking Woman." Paper delivered at the American Political Science Association Convention.
Foucault, Michel. 1979. *Discipline and Punish.* New York: Random House.
———. 1980. *Power/Knowledge.* New York: Pantheon.
———. 1984. "What Is Enlightenment?" In Paul Rabinow, ed., *The Foucault Reader,* 32–50. New York: Pantheon.
Gatens, Moira. 1996. *Imaginary Bodies: Ethics, Power, and Corporeality.* New York: Routledge.
———. 2000. "Feminism as 'Password': Re-thinking the 'Possible' with Spinoza and Deleuze." *Hypatia* 15.2: 59–75.
Grosz, Elizabeth. 1994. *Volatile Bodies: Toward a Corporeal Feminism.* Bloomington: Indiana University Press.
Hacking, Ian. 1999. *The Social Construction of What.* Cambridge: Harvard University Press.

Haraway, Donna. 1990 [1985]. "A Manifesto for Cyborgs: Science, Technology, and Socialist Feminism in the 1980's." In Linda Nicholson, ed., *Feminism/Postmodernism,* 190–233. New York: Routledge.

———. 1997. *Modest_Witness@Second_Millennium.FemaleMan©_Meets_OncoMouse™: Feminism and Technoscience.* New York: Routledge.

Harding, Sandra. 2004. "A Socially Relevant Philosophy of Science? Resources from Standpoint Theory's Controversiality." *Hypatia* 19.1: 25–47.

Hekman, Susan. 1998. "Material Bodies." In Donn Welton, ed., *Body and Flesh,* 61–70. Oxford: Blackwell.

———. 2002. "The Moral Language Game." In Naomi Scheman and Peg O'Connor, eds., *Feminist Interpretations of Ludwig Wittgenstein.* University Park: Penn State Press, 159–75.

———. 2004. *Private Selves, Public Identities: Reconsidering Identity Politics.* University Park: Penn State Press.

Kuhn, Thomas. 1962. *The Structure of Scientific Revolutions.* Chicago: University of Chicago Press.

Latour, Bruno. 1993. *We Have Never Been Modern.* Trans. Catherine Porter. Cambridge: Harvard University Press.

———. 1999. *Pandora's Hope: Essays on the Reality of Science Studies.* Cambridge, Mass.: Harvard University Press.

———. 2004. "Why Has Critique Run out of Steam? From Matters of Fact to Matters of Concern." *Critical Inquiry* 30.2: 225–48.

Law, John. 1999. "After ANT: Complexity, Naming and Topology." In John Law and John Hassard, eds., *Actor Network Theory and After,* 1–14. Oxford: Blackwell.

Longino, Helen. 2002. *The Fate of Knowledge.* Princeton, N.J.: Princeton University Press.

Nelson, Lynne Hankinson. 1990. *Who Knows? From Quine to a Feminist Empiricism.* Philadelphia: Temple University Press.

Nelson, Lynne Hankinson, and Alison Wylie. 2004. Introduction. *Hypatia* 19.1: vii–xii.

Nicholson, Linda, ed. 1990. *Feminism/Postmodernism.* New York: Routledge.

Orr, Deborah. 2002. "Developing Wittgenstein's Picture of the Soul." In Naomi Scheman and Peg O'Connor, eds., *Feminist Interpretations of Ludwig Wittgenstein,* 322–43. University Park: Penn State Press.

Pickering, Andrew. 1995. *The Mangle of Practice: Time, Agency, and Science.* Chicago: University of Chicago Press.

Pinnick, Cassandra, et al., eds. 2003. *Scrutinizing Feminist Epistemology: An Examination of Gender in Science.* New Brunswick, N.J.: Rutgers University Press.

Rorty, Richard. 1988. *Contingency, Irony, and Solidarity.* Cambridge: Cambridge University Press.

Rouse, Joseph. 2002. *How Scientific Practices Matter: Reclaiming Philosophical Naturalism.* Chicago: University of Chicago Press.

Scheman, Naomi. 1993. *Engenderings: Constructions of Knowledge, Authority, and Privilege.* New York: Routledge.

Searle, John. 1995. *The Construction of Social Reality.* New York: The Free Press.

Stengers, Isabelle. 1997. *Power and Invention: Situating Science.* Minneapolis: University of Minnesota Press.
Wilson, Elizabeth A. 1998. *Neural Geographies: Feminism and the Microstructure of Cognition.* New York: Routledge.
———. 1999. "Introduction: Somatic Compliance—Feminism, Biology, and Science." *Australian Feminist Studies* 14.29: 7–18.
Wittgenstein, Ludwig. 1958. *Philosophical Investigations.* New York: Macmillan.

4

POSTHUMANIST PERFORMATIVITY: TOWARD AN UNDERSTANDING OF HOW MATTER COMES TO MATTER

Karen Barad

> Where did we ever get the strange idea that nature—as opposed to culture—is ahistorical and timeless? We are far too impressed by our own cleverness and self-consciousness. . . . We need to stop telling ourselves the same old anthropocentric bedtime stories.
>
> —Steve Shaviro, *Doom Patrols*

Language has been granted too much power. The linguistic turn, the semiotic turn, the interpretative turn, the cultural turn: it seems that at every turn lately every "thing"—even materiality—is turned into a matter of language or some other form of cultural representation. The ubiquitous puns on "matter" do not, alas, mark a rethinking of the key concepts (materiality and signification) and the relationship between them. Rather, it seems to be symptomatic of the extent to which matters of "fact" (so to speak) have been replaced with matters of signification (no scare quotes here). Language matters. Discourse matters. Culture matters. There is an important sense in which the only thing that does not seem to matter anymore is matter.

What compels the belief that we have a direct access to cultural representations and their content that we lack toward the things represented? How did language come to be more trustworthy than matter? Why are language and culture granted their own agency and historicity while matter is figured as passive and immutable, or at best inherits a potential for change derivatively from language and culture? How does one even go about inquiring after the material conditions that have led us to such a brute reversal of naturalist beliefs when materiality itself is always already figured within a linguistic domain as its condition of possibility?

It is hard to deny that the power of language has been substantial. One might argue too substantial, or perhaps more to the point, too substantializing. Neither an exaggerated faith in the power of language nor the expressed concern that language is being granted too much power is a novel apprehension specifically attached to the early twenty-first century. For example, during the nineteenth century Nietzsche warned against the mistaken tendency to take grammar too seriously: allowing linguistic structure to shape or determine our understanding of the world, believing that the subject and predicate structure of language reflects a prior ontological reality of substance and attribute. The belief that grammatical categories reflect the underlying structure of the world is a continuing seductive habit of mind worth questioning. Indeed, the representationalist belief in the power of words to mirror preexisting phenomena is the metaphysical substrate that supports social constructivist as well as traditional realist beliefs. Significantly, social constructivism has been the object of intense scrutiny within both feminist and science studies circles where considerable and informed dissatisfaction has been voiced.[1]

A *performative* understanding of discursive practices challenges the representationalist belief in the power of words to represent preexisting things. Performativity, properly construed, is not an invitation to turn everything (including material bodies) into words; on the contrary, performativity is precisely a contestation of the excessive power granted to language to determine what is real. Hence, in ironic contrast to the misconception that would equate performativity with a form of linguistic monism that takes language to be the stuff of reality, performativity is actually a contestation of the unexamined habits of mind that grant language and other forms of representation more power in determining our ontologies than they deserve.[2]

The move toward performative alternatives to representationalism shifts the focus from questions of correspondence between descriptions and reality (e.g., do they mirror nature or culture?) to matters of practices/doings/actions. I would argue that these approaches also bring to the forefront important questions of ontology, materiality, and agency, while social constructivist approaches get caught up in the geometrical optics of reflection where, much like the infinite play of images between two facing mirrors, the epistemological gets bounced back and forth, but nothing more is seen. Moving away from the representationalist trap of geometrical optics, I shift the focus to physical optics, to questions of diffraction rather than reflection.

Diffractively reading the insights of feminist and queer theory and science studies approaches through one another entails thinking the "social" and the "scientific" together in an illuminating way. What often appears as separate entities (and separate sets of concerns) with sharp edges does not actually entail a relation of absolute exteriority at all. Like the diffraction patterns illuminating the indefinite nature of boundaries—displaying shadows in "light" regions and bright spots in "dark" regions—the relation of the social and the scientific is a relation of "exteriority within." This is not a static relationality but a doing—the enactment of boundaries—that always entails constitutive exclusions and therefore requisite questions of accountability.[3] My aim is to contribute to efforts to sharpen the theoretical tool of performativity for science studies and feminist and queer theory endeavors alike, and to promote their mutual consideration. In this article, I offer an elaboration of performativity—a materialist, naturalist, and posthumanist elaboration—that allows matter its due as an active participant in the world's becoming, in its ongoing "intra-activity."[4] It is vitally important that we understand how matter matters.

FROM REPRESENTATIONALISM TO PERFORMATIVITY

> People represent. That is part of what it is to be a person. . . . Not *homo faber*, I say, but *homo depictor*.
>
> —Ian Hacking, *Representing and Intervening*

Liberal social theories and theories of scientific knowledge alike owe much to the idea that the world is composed of individuals—presumed to exist before the law or the discovery of the law—awaiting/inviting representation. The idea that beings exist as individuals with inherent attributes, anterior to their representation, is a metaphysical presupposition that underlies the belief in political, linguistic, and epistemological forms of representationalism. Or, to put the point the other way around, representationalism is the belief in the ontological distinction between representations and that which they purport to represent; in particular, that which is represented is held to be independent of all practices of representing. That is, there are assumed to be two distinct and independent kinds of entities—representations, and entities to be represented. The system of representation is sometimes explicitly theorized in terms of a tripartite arrangement. For example, in addition to knowledge (i.e., representations), on the one hand, and the known (i.e., that which is purportedly represented), on the other, the existence of a knower (i.e., someone who does the representing) is sometimes made explicit. When this happens, it becomes clear that representations serve a mediating function between independently existing entities. This taken-for-granted ontological gap generates questions of the accuracy of representations. For example, does scientific knowledge accurately represent an independently existing reality? Does language accurately represent its referent? Does a given political representative, legal counsel, or piece of legislation accurately represent the interests of the people allegedly represented?

Representationalism has received significant challenge from feminists, poststructuralists, postcolonial critics, and queer theorists. The names of Michel Foucault and Judith Butler are frequently associated with such questioning. Butler sums up the problematics of political representationalism as follows:

> Foucault points out that juridical systems of power *produce* the subjects they subsequently come to represent. Juridical notions of power appear to regulate political life in purely negative terms. . . . But the subjects regulated by such structures are, by virtue of being subjected to them, formed, defined, and reproduced in accordance with the requirements of those structures. If this analysis is right, then the juridical formation of language and politics that represents women as "the subject" of feminism is itself a discursive formation and effect of a given version of representationalist politics. And the feminist subject turns out to be discursively

> constituted by the very political system that is supposed to facilitate its emancipation. (1990, 2)

In an attempt to remedy this difficulty, critical social theorists struggle to formulate understandings of the possibilities for political intervention that go beyond the framework of representationalism.

The fact that representationalism has come under suspicion in the domain of science studies is less well known but of no less significance. Critical examination of representationalism did not emerge until the study of science shifted its focus from the nature and production of scientific knowledge to the study of the detailed dynamics of the actual practice of science. This significant shift is one way to coarsely characterize the difference in emphasis between separate multiple disciplinary studies of science (e.g., history of science, philosophy of science, sociology of science) and science studies. This is not to say that all science studies approaches are critical of representationalism; many such studies accept representationalism unquestioningly. For example, there are countless studies on the nature of scientific representations (including how scientists produce them, interpret them, and otherwise make use of them) that take for granted the underlying philosophical viewpoint that gives way to this focus—namely, representationalism. On the other hand, there has been a concerted effort by some science studies researchers to move beyond representationalism.

Ian Hacking's *Representing and Intervening* (1983) brought the question of the limitations of representationalist thinking about the nature of science to the forefront. The most sustained and thoroughgoing critique of representationalism in philosophy of science and science studies is to be found in the work of philosopher of science Joseph Rouse. Rouse has taken the lead in interrogating the constraints that representationalist thinking places on theorizing the nature of scientific practices.[5] For example, while the hackneyed debate between scientific realism and social constructivism moved frictionlessly from philosophy of science to science studies, Rouse (1996) has pointed out that these adversarial positions have more in common than their proponents acknowledge. Indeed, they share representationalist assumptions that foster such endless debates: both scientific realists and social constructivists believe that scientific knowledge (in its multiple representational forms such as theoretical concepts, graphs, particle tracks, photographic images) mediates our access to the material world; where they differ is on the question of referent, whether scientific knowledge represents things in the world as they really are (i.e., "Nature") or "objects" that are the product of social activities (i.e., "Culture"), but both groups subscribe to representationalism.

Representationalism is so deeply entrenched within Western culture that it has taken on a commonsense appeal. It seems inescapable, if not downright natural. But representationalism (like nature itself, not merely our representations of it!) has a history. Hacking traces the philosophical problem of representations to the Democritean dream of atoms and the void. According to Hacking's anthropological philosophy, representations were unproblematic prior to Democritus: "The word 'real' first meant just unqualified likeness" (1983, 142). With Democritus's atomic theory emerges the possibility of a gap between representations and represented—"appearance" makes its first appearance. Is the table a solid mass made of wood or an aggregate of discrete entities moving in the void? Atomism poses the question of which representation is real. The problem of realism in philosophy is a product of the atomistic worldview.

Rouse identifies representationalism as a Cartesian by-product—a particularly inconspicuous consequence of the Cartesian division between "internal" and "external" that breaks along the line of the knowing subject. Rouse brings to light the asymmetrical faith in word over world that underlines the nature of Cartesian doubt:

> I want to encourage doubt about [the] presumption that representations (that is, their meaning or content) are more accessible to us than the things they supposedly represent. If there is no magic language through which we can unerringly reach out directly to its referents, why should we think there is nevertheless a language that magically enables us to reach out directly to its sense or representational content? The presumption that we can know what we mean, or what our verbal performances say, more readily than we can know the objects those sayings are about is a Cartesian legacy, a linguistic variation on Descartes' insistence that

> we have a direct and privileged access to the contents of our thoughts that we lack towards the "external" world. (1996, 209)

In other words, the asymmetrical faith in our access to representations over things is a contingent fact of history and not a logical necessity; that is, it is simply a Cartesian habit of mind. It takes a healthy skepticism toward Cartesian doubt to be able to begin to see an alternative.[6]

Indeed, it is possible to develop coherent philosophical positions that deny that there are representations on the one hand and ontologically separate entities awaiting representation on the other. A performative understanding, which shifts the focus from linguistic representations to discursive practices, is one such alternative. In particular, the search for alternatives to social constructivism has prompted performative approaches in feminist and queer studies as well as in science studies. Judith Butler's name is most often associated with the term *performativity* in feminist and queer theory circles. And while Andrew Pickering has been one of the very few science studies scholars to take ownership of this term, there is surely a sense in which science studies theorists such as Donna Haraway, Bruno Latour, and Joseph Rouse also propound performative understandings of the nature of scientific practices.[7] Indeed, *performativity* has become a ubiquitous term in literary studies, theater studies, and the nascent interdisciplinary area of performance studies, prompting the question as to whether all performances are performative.[8] In this essay, I propose a specifically posthumanist notion of performativity—one that incorporates important material and discursive, social and scientific, human and nonhuman, and natural and cultural factors. A posthumanist account calls into question the givenness of the differential categories of "human" and "nonhuman," examining the practices through which these differential boundaries are stabilized and destabilized.[9] Donna Haraway's scholarly opus—from primates to cyborgs to companion species—epitomizes this point.

If performativity is linked not only to the formation of the subject but also to the production of the matter of bodies, as Butler's account of "materialization" and Haraway's notion of "materialized refiguration" suggest, then it is all the more important that we understand the nature of this production.[10] Foucault's analytic of power links discursive practices to the materiality of the body. However, his account is constrained by several important factors that severely limit the potential of his analysis and Butler's performative elaboration, thereby forestalling an understanding of precisely *how* discursive practices produce material bodies.

If Foucault, in queering Marx, positions the body as the locus of productive forces, the site where the large-scale organization of power links up with local practices, then it would seem that any robust theory of the materialization of bodies would necessarily take account of *how the body's materiality*—for example, its anatomy and physiology—*and other material forces actively matter to the processes of materialization.* Indeed, as Foucault makes crystal-clear in the last chapter of *The History of Sexuality* (Vol. 1), he is not out to deny the relevance of the physical body but, on the contrary, to

> show how the deployments of power are directly connected to the body—to bodies, functions, physiological processes, sensations, and pleasures; far from the body having to be effaced, what is needed is to make it visible through an analysis in which the biological and the historical are not consecutive to one another . . . but are bound together in an increasingly complex fashion in accordance with the development of the modern technologies of power that take life as their objective. Hence, I do not envision a "history of mentalities" that would take account of bodies only through the manner in which they have been perceived and given meaning and value; but a "history of bodies" and the manner in which what is most material and most vital in them has been invested. (1980a, 151–52)

On the other hand, Foucault does not tell us in what way the biological and the historical are "bound together" such that one is not consecutive to the other. What is it about the materiality of bodies that makes it susceptible to the enactment of biological and historical forces simultaneously? To what degree does the matter of bodies have its own historicity? Are social forces the only ones susceptible to change? Are not biological forces in some sense always already historical ones? Could it be that there is some important sense in which historical forces are always already biological? What would it mean to even ask such a question, given the strong social constructivist undercurrent in certain interdisciplinary circles in the early twenty-first century?

For all Foucault's emphasis on the political anatomy of disciplinary power, he too fails to offer an account of the body's historicity in which its very materiality plays an *active* role in the workings of power. This implicit reinscription of matter's passivity is a mark of extant elements of representationalism that haunt his largely post-representationalist account.[11] This deficiency is importantly related to his failure to theorize the relationship between "discursive" and "nondiscursive" practices. As materialist feminist theorist Rosemary Hennessey insists in offering her critique of Foucault, "a rigorous materialist theory of the body cannot stop with the assertion that the body is always discursively constructed. It also needs to explain how the discursive construction of the body is related to nondiscursive practices in "ways that vary widely from one social formation to another" (1993, 46).

Crucial to understanding the workings of power is an understanding of the nature of power in the fullness of its materiality. To restrict power's productivity to the limited domain of the "social," for example, or to figure matter as merely an end product rather than an active factor in further materializations, is to cheat matter out of the fullness of its capacity. How might we understand not only how human bodily contours are constituted through psychic processes but how even the very atoms that make up the biological body come to matter and, more generally, how matter makes itself felt? It is difficult to imagine how psychic and sociohistorical forces alone could account for the production of matter. Surely it is the case—even when the focus is restricted to the materiality of "human" bodies—that there are "natural," not merely "social," forces that matter. Indeed, there are a host of material-discursive forces—including ones that get labeled "social," "cultural," "psychic," "economic," "natural," "physical," "biological," "geopolitical," and "geological"—that may be important to particular (entangled) processes of materialization. If we follow disciplinary habits of tracing disciplinary-defined causes through to the corresponding disciplinary-defined effects, we will miss all the crucial intra-actions among these forces that fly in the face of any specific set of disciplinary concerns.[12]

What is needed is a robust account of the materialization of *all* bodies—"human" and "nonhuman"—and the material-discursive practices by which their differential constitutions are marked. This will require an understanding of the nature of the relationship between discursive practices and material phenomena, an accounting of "non-human" as well as "human" forms of agency, and an understanding of the precise causal nature of productive practices that takes account of the fullness of matter's implication in its ongoing historicity. My contribution toward the development of such an understanding is based on a philosophical account that I have been calling "agential realism." Agential realism is an account of techno-scientific and other practices that takes feminist, antiracist, poststructuralist, queer, Marxist, science studies, and scientific insights seriously, building specifically on important insights from Niels Bohr, Judith Butler, Michel Foucault, Donna Haraway, Vicki Kirby, Joseph Rouse, and others.[13] It is clearly not possible to fully explicate these ideas here. My more limited goal in this essay is to use the notion of performativity as a diffraction grating for reading important insights from feminist and queer studies and science studies through one another while simultaneously proposing a materialist and posthumanist reworking of the notion of performativity. This entails a reworking of the familiar notions of discursive practices, materialization, agency, and causality, among others.

I begin by issuing a direct challenge to the metaphysical underpinnings of representationalism, proposing an agential realist ontology as an alternative. In the following section, I offer a posthumanist performative reformulation of the notion of discursive practices and materiality and theorize a specific causal relationship between them. In the final section, I discuss the agential realist conceptions of causality and agency that are vital to understanding the productive nature of material-discursive practices, including techno-scientific ones.

TOWARD A PERFORMATIVE METAPHYSICS

As long as we stick to things and words we can believe that we are speaking of what we see, that we see what we are speaking of, and that the two are linked.

—Gilles Deleuze, *Foucault*

"Words and things" is the entirely serious title of a problem.

—Michel Foucault, *The Archaeology of Knowledge*

Representationalism separates the world into the ontologically disjointed domains of words and things, leaving itself with the dilemma of their linkage such that knowledge is possible. If words are untethered from the material world, how do representations gain a foothold? If we no longer believe that the world is teeming with inherent resemblances whose signatures are inscribed on the face of the world, things already emblazoned with signs, words lying in wait like so many pebbles of sand on a beach there to be discovered, but rather that the knowing subject is enmeshed in a thick web of representations such that the mind cannot see its way to objects that are now forever out of reach and all that is visible is the sticky problem of humanity's own captivity within language, then it begins to become apparent that representationalism is a prisoner of the problematic metaphysics it postulates. Like the frustrated would-be runner in Zeno's paradox, representationalism never seems to be able to get any closer to solving the problem it poses because it is caught in the impossibility of stepping outward from its metaphysical starting place. Perhaps it would be better to begin with a different starting point, a different metaphysics.[14]

Thingification—the turning of relations into "things," "entities," "relata"—infects much of the way we understand the world and our relationship to it.[15] Why do we think that the existence of relations requires relata? Does the persistent distrust of nature, materiality, and the body that pervades much of contemporary theorizing and a sizable amount of the history of Western thought feed off of this cultural proclivity? In this section, I present a relational ontology that rejects the metaphysics of relata, of "words" and "things." On an agential realist account, it is once again possible to acknowledge nature, the body, and materiality in the fullness of their becoming without resorting to the optics of transparency or opacity, the geometries of absolute exteriority or interiority, and the theorization of the human as either pure cause or pure effect while at the same time remaining resolutely accountable for the role "we" play in the intertwined practices of knowing and becoming.

The postulation of individually determinate entities with inherent properties is the hallmark of atomistic metaphysics. Atomism hails from Democritus.[16] According to Democritus the properties of all things derive from the properties of the smallest unit—atoms (the "uncuttable" or "inseparable"). Liberal social theories and scientific theories alike owe much to the idea that the world is composed of individuals with separately attributable properties. An entangled web of scientific, social, ethical, and political practices, and our understanding of them, hinges on the various and differential instantiations of this presupposition. Much hangs in the balance in contesting its seeming inevitability.

Physicist Niels Bohr won the Nobel Prize for his quantum model of the atom, which marks the beginning of his seminal contributions to the development of the quantum theory.[17] Bohr's philosophy-physics (the two were inseparable for him) poses a radical challenge not only to Newtonian physics but also to Cartesian epistemology and its representationalist triadic structure of words, knowers, and things. Crucially, in a stunning reversal of his intellectual forefather's schema, Bohr rejects the atomistic metaphysics that takes "things" as ontologically basic entities. For Bohr, things do not have inherently determinate boundaries or properties, and words do not have inherently determinate meanings. Bohr also calls into question the related Cartesian belief in the inherent distinction between subject and object, and knower and known.

It might be said that the epistemological framework that Bohr develops rejects both the transparency of language and the transparency of measurement; however, even more fundamentally, it rejects the presupposition that language and measurement perform mediating functions. Language does not represent states of affairs, and measurements do not represent measurement-independent states of being. Bohr develops his epistemological framework without giving in to the despair of nihilism or the sticky web of relativism. With brilliance and finesse, Bohr finds a way to hold on to the possibility of objective knowledge while the grand structures of Newtonian physics and representationalism begin to crumble.

Bohr's break with Newton, Descartes, and Democritus is not based in "mere idle philosophical reflection" but on new empirical findings in the domain of atomic physics that came to light during the first quarter of the twentieth century. Bohr's struggle to provide a theoretical understanding of these findings resulted in his radical proposal that an entirely new epistemological framework is required. Unfortunately,

Bohr does not explore crucial ontological dimensions of his insights, but rather, he focuses on their epistemological import. I have mined his writings for his implicit ontological views and have elaborated on them in the development of an agential realist ontology. In this section, I present a quick overview of important aspects of Bohr's account and move on to an explication of an agential realist ontology. This relational ontology is the basis for my posthumanist performative account of the production of material bodies. This account refuses the representationalist fixation on "words" and "things" and the problematic of their relationality, advocating instead *a causal relationship between specific exclusionary practices embodied as specific material configurations of the world* (i.e., discursive practices/(con)figurations rather than "words") *and specific material phenomena* (i.e., relations rather than "things"). This causal relationship between the apparatuses of bodily production and the phenomena produced is one of "agential intra-action." The details follow.

According to Bohr, *theoretical concepts* (e.g., "position" and "momentum") are not ideational in character but rather *are specific physical arrangements.*[18] For example, the notion of "position" cannot be presumed to be a well-defined abstract concept, nor can it be presumed to be an inherent attribute of independently existing objects. Rather, "position" only has meaning when a rigid apparatus with fixed parts is used (e.g., a ruler is nailed to a fixed table in the laboratory, thereby establishing a fixed frame of reference for specifying "position"). And furthermore, any measurement of "position" using this apparatus cannot be attributed to some abstract independently existing "object" but rather is a property of the *phenomenon*—the inseparability of "observed object" and "agencies of observation." Similarly, "momentum" is only meaningful as a material arrangement involving movable parts. Hence, the simultaneous indeterminacy of "position" and "momentum" (what is commonly referred to as the Heisenberg uncertainty principle) is a straightforward matter of the material exclusion of "position" and "momentum" arrangements (one requiring fixed parts and the complementary arrangement requiring movable parts).[19]

Therefore, according to Bohr, the primary epistemological unit is not independent objects with inherent boundaries and properties, but rather, *phenomena*. On my agential realist elaboration, phenomena do not merely mark the epistemological inseparability of "observer" and "observed"; rather, *phenomena are the ontological inseparability of agentially intra-acting "components."* That is, phenomena are ontologically primitive relations—relations without preexisting relata.[20] The notion of *intra-action* (in contrast to the usual "interaction," which presumes the prior existence of independent entities/relata) represents a profound conceptual shift. It is through specific agential intra-actions that the boundaries and properties of the "components" of phenomena become determinate and that particular embodied concepts become meaningful. A specific intra-action (involving a specific material configuration of the "apparatus of observation") enacts an *agential cut* (in contrast to the Cartesian cut—an inherent distinction—between subject and object) effecting a separation between "subject" and "object." That is, the agential cut enacts a *local* resolution *within* the phenomenon of the inherent ontological indeterminacy. In other words, relata do not preexist relations; rather, relata-within-phenomena emerge through specific intra-actions. Crucially then, intra-actions enact *agential separability*—the local condition of *exteriority-within-phenomena*. The notion of agential separability is of fundamental importance, for in the absence of a classical ontological condition of exteriority between observer and observed, it provides the condition for the possibility of objectivity. Moreover, the agential cut enacts a local causal structure among "components" of a phenomenon in the marking of the "measuring agencies" ("effect") by the "measured object" ("cause"). Hence, *the notion of intra-actions constitutes a reworking of the traditional notion of causality.*[21]

In my further elaboration of this agential realist ontology, I argue that phenomena are not the mere result of laboratory exercises engineered by human subjects. Nor can the apparatuses that produce phenomena be understood as observational devices or mere laboratory instruments. Although space constraints do not allow an in-depth discussion of the agential realist understanding of the nature of apparatuses, since apparatuses play such a crucial, indeed constitutive, role in the production of phenomena, I present an overview of the agential realist theorization of apparatuses before moving on to the question of the nature of phenomena. The proposed elaboration enables an exploration of the implications of the agential realist ontology beyond those specific to understanding the nature of scientific practices. In fact, agential realism offers an understanding of the nature of material-discursive practices, such as those very practices through which different distinctions get drawn, including those between the "social" and the "scientific."[22]

Apparatuses are not inscription devices, scientific instruments set in place before the action happens, or machines that mediate the dialectic of resistance and accommodation. They are neither neutral probes of the natural world nor structures that deterministically impose some particular outcome. In my further elaboration of Bohr's insights, apparatuses are not mere static arrangements in the world, but rather, *apparatuses are dynamic (re)configurings* of *the world, specific agential practices/intra-actions/performances through which specific exclusionary boundaries are enacted.* Apparatuses have no inherent "outside" boundary. This indeterminacy of the "outside" boundary represents the impossibility of closure—the ongoing intra-activity in the iterative reconfiguring of the apparatus of bodily production. Apparatuses are open-ended practices.

Importantly, apparatuses are themselves phenomena. For example, as scientists are well aware, apparatuses are not preformed interchangeable objects that sit atop a shelf waiting to serve a particular purpose. Apparatuses are constituted through particular practices that are perpetually open to rearrangements, rearticulations, and other reworkings. This is part of the creativity and difficulty of doing science: getting the instrumentation to work in a particular way for a particular purpose (which is always open to the possibility of being changed during the experiment as different insights are gained). Furthermore, any particular apparatus is always in the process of intra-acting with other apparatuses, and the enfolding of locally stabilized phenomena (which may be traded across laboratories, cultures, or geopolitical spaces only to find themselves differently materializing) into subsequent iterations of particular practices constitutes important shifts in the particular apparatus in question and therefore in the nature of the intra-actions that result in the production of new phenomena, and so on. Boundaries do not sit still.

With this background, we can now return to the question of the nature of phenomena. Phenomena are produced through agential intra-actions of multiple apparatuses of bodily production. Agential intra-actions are specific causal material enactments that may or may not involve "humans." Indeed, it is through such practices that the differential boundaries between "humans" and "nonhumans," "culture" and "nature," the "social" and the "scientific" are constituted. Phenomena are constitutive of reality. Reality is not composed of things-in-themselves or things-behind-phenomena, but of "things"-in-phenomena.[23] The world *is* intra-activity in its differential mattering. It is through specific intra-actions that a differential sense of being is enacted in the ongoing ebb and flow of agency. That is, it is through specific intra-actions that phenomena come to matter—in both senses of the word. The world is a dynamic process of intra-activity in the ongoing reconfiguring of locally determinate causal structures with determinate boundaries, properties, meanings, and patterns of marks on bodies. This ongoing flow of agency through which "part" of the world makes itself differentially intelligible to another "part" of the world and through which local causal structures, boundaries, and properties are stabilized and destabilized does not take place in space and time but in the making of space-time itself. The world is an ongoing open process of mattering through which "mattering" itself acquires meaning and form in the realization of different agential possibilities. Temporality and spatiality emerge in this processual historicity. Relations of exteriority, connectivity, and exclusion are reconfigured. The changing topologies of the world entail an ongoing reworking of the very nature of dynamics.

In summary, the universe is agential intra-activity in its becoming. The primary ontological units are not "things" but phenomena—dynamic topological reconfigurings/entanglements/relationalities/(re)articulations. And the primary semantic units are not "words" but material-discursive practices through which boundaries are constituted. This dynamism is agency. Agency is not an attribute but the ongoing reconfigurings of the world. On the basis of this performative metaphysics, in the next section

I propose a posthumanist refiguration of the nature of materiality and discursivity and the relationship between them, and a posthumanist account of performativity.

A POSTHUMANIST ACCOUNT OF MATERIAL-DISCURSIVE PRACTICES

Discursive practices are often confused with linguistic expression, and meaning is often thought to be a property of words. Hence, discursive practices and meanings are said to be peculiarly human phenomena. But if this were true, how would it be possible to take account of the boundary-making practices by which the differential constitution of "humans" and "nonhumans" are enacted? It would be one thing if the notion of constitution were to be understood in purely epistemic terms, but it is entirely unsatisfactory when questions of ontology are on the table. If "humans" refers to phenomena, not independent entities with inherent properties but rather beings in their differential becoming, particular material (re)configurings of the world with shifting boundaries and properties that stabilize and destabilize along with specific material changes in what it means to be human, then the notion of discursivity cannot be founded on an inherent distinction between humans and nonhumans. In this section, I propose a posthumanist account of discursive practices. I also outline a concordant reworking of the notion of materiality and hint at an agential realist approach to understanding the relationship between discursive practices and material phenomena.

Meaning is not a property of individual words or groups of words. Meaning is neither intra-linguistically conferred nor extra-linguistically referenced. Semantic contentfulness is not achieved through the thoughts or performances of individual agents but rather through particular discursive practices. With the inspiration of Bohr's insights, it would also be tempting to add the following agential realist points: meaning is not ideational but rather specific material (re)configurings of the world, and semantic indeterminacy, like ontological indeterminacy, is only locally resolvable through specific intra-actions. But before proceeding, it is probably worth taking a moment to dispel some misconceptions about the nature of discursive practices.

Discourse is not a synonym for language.[24] Discourse does not refer to linguistic or signifying systems, grammars, speech acts, or conversations. To think of discourse as mere spoken or written words forming descriptive statements is to enact the mistake of representationalist thinking. Discourse is not what is said; it is that which constrains and enables what can be said. Discursive practices define what counts as meaningful statements. Statements are not the mere utterances of the originating consciousness of a unified subject; rather, statements and subjects emerge from a field of possibilities. This field of possibilities is not static or singular, but rather, it is a dynamic and contingent multiplicity.

According to Foucault, discursive practices are the local sociohistorical material conditions that enable and constrain disciplinary knowledge practices such as speaking, writing, thinking, calculating, measuring, filtering, and concentrating. Discursive practices produce, rather than merely describe, the "subjects" and "objects" of knowledge practices. On Foucault's account, these "conditions" are immanent and historical rather than transcendental or phenomenological. That is, they are not conditions in the sense of transcendental, ahistorical, cross-cultural, abstract laws defining the possibilities of experience (Kant), but rather, they are actual historically situated social conditions.

Foucault's account of discursive practices has some provocative resonances (and some fruitful dissonances) with Bohr's account of apparatuses and the role they play in the material production of bodies and meanings. For Bohr, apparatuses are particular physical arrangements that give meaning to certain concepts to the exclusion of others; they are the local physical conditions that enable and constrain knowledge practices such as conceptualizing and measuring; they are productive of (and part of) the phenomena produced; they enact a local cut that produces "objects" of particular knowledge practices within the particular phenomena produced. On the basis of his profound insight that "concepts" (which are actual physical arrangements) and "things" do not have determinate boundaries, properties, or meanings apart from their mutual intra-actions, Bohr offers a new epistemological framework that calls into question the dualisms of object/subject, knower/known, nature/culture, and word/world.

Bohr's insight that concepts are not ideational but rather are actual physical arrangements is clearly an insistence on the materiality of meaning making that goes beyond what is usually meant by the frequently heard contemporary refrain that writing and talking are material practices. Nor is Bohr merely claiming that discourse is "supported" or "sustained" by material practices, as Foucault seems to suggest (though the nature of this "support" is not specified), or that nondiscursive (background) practices determine discursive practices, as some existential-pragmatic philosophers purport.[25] Rather, Bohr's point entails a much more intimate relationship between concepts and materiality. In order to better understand the nature of this relationship, it is important to shift the focus from linguistic concepts to discursive practices.

On an agential realist elaboration of Bohr's theoretical framework, apparatuses are not static arrangements in the world that embody particular concepts to the exclusion of others; rather, apparatuses are specific material practices through which local semantic and ontological determinacy are intra-actively enacted. That is, apparatuses are the exclusionary practices of mattering through which intelligibility and materiality are constituted. Apparatuses are material (re)configurings/discursive practices that produce material phenomena in their discursively differentiated becoming. A phenomenon is a dynamic relationality that is locally determinate in its matter and meaning as mutually determined (within a particular phenomenon) through specific causal intra-actions. Outside of particular agential intra-actions, "words" and "things" are indeterminate. Hence, the notions of materiality and discursivity must be reworked in a way that acknowledges their mutual entailment. In particular, on an agential realist account, both materiality and discursive practices are rethought in terms of intra-activity.

On an agential realist account, *discursive practices are specific material (re)configurings of the world through which local determinations of boundaries, properties, and meanings are differentially enacted. That is, discursive practices are ongoing agential intra-actions of the world through which local determinacy is enacted within the phenomena produced. Discursive practices are causal intra-actions*—they enact local causal structures through which one "component" (the "effect") of the phenomenon is marked by another "component" (the "cause") in their differential articulation. Meaning is not a property of individual words or groups of words but an ongoing performance of the world in its differential intelligibility. In its causal intra-activity, "part" of the world becomes determinately bounded and propertied in its emergent intelligibility to another "part" of the world. Discursive practices are boundary-making practices that have no finality in the ongoing dynamics of agential intra-activity.

Discursive practices are not speech acts, linguistic representations, or even linguistic performances, bearing some unspecified relationship to material practices. Discursive practices are not anthropomorphic place-holders for the projected agency of individual subjects, culture, or language. Indeed, they are not human-based practices. On the contrary, agential realism's posthumanist account of discursive practices does not fix the boundary between "human" and "nonhuman" before the analysis ever gets off the ground, but rather, it enables (indeed demands) a genealogical analysis of the discursive emergence of the "human." "Human bodies" and "human subjects" do not preexist as such; nor are they mere end products. "Humans" are neither pure cause nor pure effect, but part of the world in its open-ended becoming.

Matter, like meaning, is not an individually articulated or static entity. Matter is not little bits of nature, or a blank slate, surface, or site passively awaiting signification; nor is it an uncontested ground for scientific, feminist, or Marxist theories. Matter is not a support, location, referent, or source of sustainability for discourse. Matter is not immutable or passive. It does not require the mark of an external force like culture or history to complete it. Matter is always already an ongoing historicity.[26]

On an agential realist account, matter does not refer to a fixed substance; rather, *matter is substance in its intra-active becoming—not a thing, but a doing, a congealing of agency. Matter is a stabilizing and destabilizing process of iterative intra-activity.* Phenomena—the smallest material units (relational "atoms")—come to matter through this process of ongoing intra-activity. That is, *matter refers to the materiality/materialization of phenomena,* not to an inherent fixed property of abstract, independently existing objects of Newtonian physics (the modernist realization of the Democritean dream of atoms and the void).

Matter is not simply "a kind of citationality" (Butler 1993, 15), the surface effect of human bodies, or the end product of linguistic or discursive acts. Material constraints and exclusions and the material dimensions of regulatory practices are important factors in the process of materialization. The dynamics of intra-activity entails matter as an *active* "agent" in its ongoing materialization.

Boundary-making practices, that is, discursive practices, are fully implicated in the dynamics of intra-activity through which phenomena come to matter. In other words, materiality is discursive (i.e., material phenomena are inseparable from the apparatuses of bodily production: matter emerges out of and includes as part of its being the ongoing reconfiguring of boundaries), just as discursive practices are always already material (i.e., they are ongoing material (re)configurings of the world). Discursive practices and material phenomena do not stand in a relationship of externality to one another; rather, the material and the discursive are mutually implicated in the dynamics of intra-activity. But neither are they reducible to one another. The relationship between the material and the discursive is one of mutual entailment. Neither is articulated/articulable in the absence of the other; matter and meaning are mutually articulated. Neither discursive practices nor material phenomena are ontologically or epistemologically prior. Neither can be explained in terms of the other. Neither has privileged status in determining the other.

Apparatuses of bodily production and the phenomena they produce are material-discursive in nature. *Material-discursive practices are specific iterative enactments—agential intra-actions—through which matter is differentially engaged and articulated (in the emergence of boundaries and meanings), reconfiguring the material-discursive field of possibilities in the iterative dynamics of intra-activity that is agency.* Intra-actions are causally constraining, nondeterministic enactments through which matter-in-the-process-of-becoming is sedimented out and enfolded in further materializations.[27]

Material conditions matter, not because they "support" particular discourses that are the actual generative factors in the formation of bodies, but rather because *matter comes to matter* through the iterative intra-activity of the world in its becoming. The point is not merely that there are important material factors in addition to discursive ones; rather, the issue is the conjoined material-discursive nature of constraints, conditions, and practices. The fact that material and discursive constraints and exclusions are intertwined points to the limited validity of analyses that attempt to determine individual effects of material or discursive factors.[28] Furthermore, the conceptualization of materiality offered by agential realism makes it possible to take account of material constraints and conditions once again without reinscribing traditional empiricist assumptions concerning the transparent or immediate given-ness of the world and without falling into the analytical stalemate that simply calls for a recognition of our mediated access to the world and then rests its case. The ubiquitous pronouncements proclaiming that experience or the material world is "mediated" have offered precious little guidance about how to proceed. The notion of mediation has for too long stood in the way of a more thoroughgoing accounting of the empirical world. The reconceptualization of materiality offered here makes it possible to take the empirical world seriously once again, but this time with the understanding that the objective referent is phenomena, not the seeming "immediately givenness" of the world.

All bodies, not merely "human" bodies, come to matter through the world's iterative intra-activity—its performativity. This is true not only of the surface or contours of the body but also of the body in the fullness of its physicality, including the very "atoms" of its being. Bodies are not objects with inherent boundaries and properties; they are material-discursive phenomena. "Human" bodies are not inherently different from "nonhuman" ones. What constitutes the "human" (and the "nonhuman") is not a fixed or pre-given notion, but nor is it a free-floating ideality. What is at issue is not some ill-defined process by which human-based linguistic practices (materially supported in some unspecified way) manage to produce substantive bodies/bodily substances, but rather it is a material dynamics of intra-activity: material apparatuses produce material phenomena through specific causal intra-actions, where "material" is always already material-discursive—*that is what it means to matter.* Theories that focus exclusively on the materialization of "human" bodies miss the crucial point that the very practices by which the differential boundaries of the "human" and the "nonhuman" are drawn are always already implicated in particular materializations. The differential constitution of the "human" ("nonhuman") is always accompanied by particular exclusions and always open to contestation. This is a result of the nondeterministic causal nature of agential intra-actions, a crucial point that I take up in the next section.

THE NATURE OF PRODUCTION AND THE PRODUCTION OF NATURE: AGENCY AND CAUSALITY

What is the nature of causality on this account? What possibilities exist for agency, for intervening in the world's becoming? Where do the issues of responsibility and accountability enter in?

Agential intra-actions are causal enactments. Recall that an agential cut effects a local separability of different "component parts" of the phenomenon, one of which ("the cause") expresses itself in effecting and marking the other ("the effect"). In a scientific context this process is known as a "measurement." (Indeed, the notion of "measurement" is nothing more or less than a causal intra-action.)[29] Whether it is thought of as a "measurement" or as part of the universe making itself intelligible to another part in its ongoing differentiating intelligibility and materialization is a matter of preference.[30] Either way, what is important about causal intra-actions is the fact that marks are left on bodies. Objectivity means being accountable to marks on bodies.

This causal structure differs in important respects from the common choices of absolute exteriority and absolute interiority and of determinism and free will. In the case of the geometry of absolute exteriority, the claim that cultural practices produce material bodies starts with the metaphysical presumption of the ontological distinction of the former set from the latter. The inscription model of constructivism is of this kind: culture is figured as an external force acting on passive nature. There is an ambiguity in this model as to whether nature exists in any prediscursive form prior to its marking by culture. If there is such an antecedent entity, then its very existence marks the inherent limit of constructivism. In this case, the rhetoric should be softened to more accurately reflect the fact that the force of culture "shapes" or "inscribes" nature but does not materially *produce* it. On the other hand, if there is no preexistent nature, then it behooves those who advocate such a theory to explain how it is that culture can materially produce that from which it is allegedly ontologically distinct, namely nature. What is the mechanism of this production? The other usual alternative is also not attractive: the geometry of absolute interiority amounts to a reduction of the effect to its cause, or in this case, nature to culture, or matter to language, which amounts to one form or another of idealism.

Agential separability presents an alternative to these unsatisfactory options.[31] It postulates a sense of "exteriority within," one that rejects the previous geometries and opens up a much larger space that is more appropriately thought of as a changing topology.[32] More specifically, *agential separability* is a matter of *exteriority within (material-discursive) phenomena.* Hence, no priority is given to either materiality or discursivity.[33] There is no geometrical relation of absolute exteriority between a "causal apparatus" and a "body effected," nor an idealistic collapse of the two, but rather an ongoing topological dynamics that enfolds the space-time manifold upon itself, a result of the fact that the apparatuses of bodily production (which are themselves phenomena) are (also) part of the phenomena they produce. Matter plays an active—indeed, agential—role in its iterative materialization, but this is not the only reason that the space of agency is much larger than that postulated in many other critical social theories.[34] Intra-actions always entail particular exclusions, and exclusions foreclose any possibility of determinism, providing the condition of an open future.[35] Therefore, intra-actions are constraining but not determining. That is, intra-activity is neither a matter of strict determinism nor unconstrained freedom. The future is radically open at every turn. This open sense of futurity does not depend on the clash or collision of cultural demands; rather, it is inherent in the nature of intra-activity—even when apparatuses are primarily reinforcing, agency is not foreclosed. Hence, the notion of

tions reformulates the traditional notion of causality and opens ace—indeed, a relatively large space—for material-discursive f agency.

A posthumanist formulation of performativity makes evident the importance of taking account of "human," "nonhuman," and "cyborgian" forms of agency (indeed, all such material-discursive forms). This is both possible and necessary because agency is a matter of changes in the apparatuses of bodily production, and such changes take place through various intra-actions, some of which remake the boundaries that delineate the differential constitution of the "human." Holding the category "human" fixed excludes an entire range of possibilities in advance, eliding important dimensions of the workings of power.

On an agential realist account, agency is cut loose from its traditional humanist orbit. Agency is not aligned with human intentionality or subjectivity. Nor does it merely entail resignification or other specific kinds of moves within a social geometry of antihumanism. Agency is a matter of intra-acting; it is an enactment, not something that someone or something has. Agency cannot be designated as an attribute of "subjects" or "objects" (since they do not preexist as such). Agency is not an attribute whatsoever—it is "doing"/"being" in its intra-activity. Agency is the enactment of iterative changes to particular practices through the dynamics of intra-activity. Agency is about the possibilities and accountability entailed in reconfiguring material-discursive apparatuses of bodily production, including the boundary articulations and exclusions that are marked by those practices in the enactment of a causal structure. Particular possibilities for acting exist at every moment, and these changing possibilities entail a responsibility to intervene in the world's becoming, to contest and rework what matters and what is excluded from mattering.

CONCLUSIONS

Feminist studies, queer studies, science studies, cultural studies, and critical social theory scholars are among those who struggle with the difficulty of coming to terms with the weightiness of the world. On the one hand, there is an expressed desire to recognize and reclaim matter and its kindred reviled Others exiled from the familiar and comforting domains of culture, mind, and history, not simply to altruistically advocate on behalf of the subaltern, but in the hopes of finding a way to account for our own finitude. Can we identify the limits and constraints, if not the grounds, of discourse-knowledge in its productivity? But despite its substance, in the end, according to many contemporary attempts at its salvation, it is not matter that reels in the unruliness of infinite possibilities; rather, it is the very existence of finitude that gets defined as matter. Caught once again looking at mirrors, it is either the face of transcendence or our own image. It is as if there are no alternative ways to conceptualize matter: the only options seem to be the naïveté of empiricism or the same old narcissistic bedtime stories.

I have proposed a posthumanist materialist account of performativity that challenges the positioning of materiality as either a given or a mere effect of human agency. On an agential realist account, materiality is an active factor in processes of materialization. Nature is neither a passive surface awaiting the mark of culture nor the end product of cultural performances. The belief that nature is mute and immutable and that all prospects for significance and change reside in culture is a reinscription of the nature/culture dualism that feminists have actively contested. Nor, similarly, can a human/nonhuman distinction be hardwired into any theory that claims to take account of matter in the fullness of its historicity. Feminist science studies scholars in particular have emphasized that foundational inscriptions of the nature/culture dualism foreclose the understanding of how "nature" and "culture" are formed, an understanding that is crucial to both feminist and scientific analyses. They have also emphasized that the notion of "formation" in no way denies the material reality of either "nature" or "culture." Hence, any performative account worth its salt would be ill-advised to incorporate such anthropocentric values in its foundations.

A crucial part of the performative account that I have proposed is a rethinking of the notions of discursive practices and material phenomena and the relationship between them. On an agential realist account, discursive practices are not human-based activities, but rather, specific material (re)configurings of the world through which local determinations of boundaries, properties, and meanings are differentially enacted. And matter is not a fixed essence; rather, matter is substance in its intra-active becoming—not a thing but a doing, a congealing of agency. And performativity is not understood as iterative citationality (Butler), but rather as iterative intra-activity.

On an agential realist account of techno-scientific practices, the "knower" does not stand in a relation of absolute externality to the natural world being investigated—there is no such exterior observational point.[36] It is therefore not absolute exteriority that is the condition of possibility for objectivity, but rather, agential separability—exteriority within phenomena.[37] "We" are not outside observers of the world. Nor are we simply located at particular places *in* the world; rather, we are part *of* the world in its ongoing intra-activity. This is a point Niels Bohr tried to get at in his insistence that our epistemology must take account of the fact that we are a part of that nature that we seek to understand. Unfortunately, however, he cuts short important posthumanist implications of this insight in his ultimately humanist understanding of the "we." Vicki Kirby eloquently articulates this important posthumanist point: "I'm trying to complicate the locatability of human identity as a here and now, an enclosed and finished product, a causal force upon Nature. Or even . . . as something within Nature. I don't want the human to be in Nature, as if Nature is a container. Identity is inherently unstable, differentiated, dispersed, and yet strangely coherent. If I say 'this is Nature itself,' an expression that usually denotes a prescriptive essentialism and that's why we avoid it, I've actually animated this 'itself' and even suggested that 'thinking' isn't the other of nature. Nature performs itself differently."[38]

The particular configuration that an apparatus takes is not an arbitrary construction of "our" choosing, nor is it the result of causally deterministic power structures. "Humans" do not simply assemble different apparatuses for satisfying particular knowledge projects but are themselves specific local parts of the world's ongoing reconfiguring. To the degree that laboratory manipulations, observational interventions, concepts, or other human practices have a role to play, it is as part of the material configuration of the world in its intra-active becoming. "Humans" are part of the world-body space in its dynamic structuration.

There is an important sense in which practices of knowing cannot be fully claimed as human practices, not simply because we use nonhuman elements in our practices, but because knowing is a matter of part of the world making itself intelligible to another part. Practices of knowing and being are not isolatable, but rather, they are mutually implicated. We do not obtain knowledge by standing outside of the world; we know because "we" are *of* the world. We are part of the world in its differential becoming. The separation of epistemology from ontology is a reverberation of a metaphysics that assumes an inherent difference between human and nonhuman, subject and object, mind and body, matter and discourse. *Onto-epistem-ology*—the study of practices of knowing in being—is probably a better way to think about the kind of understandings that are needed to come to terms with how specific intra-actions matter.

NOTES

I would like to thank Sandra Harding and Kate Norberg for their patient solicitation of this article. Thanks also to Joe Rouse for his helpful comments, ongoing support, and encouragement, and for the inspiration of his work.

1. Dissatisfaction surfaces in the literature in the 1980s. See, e.g., Donna Haraway's "Gender for a Marxist Dictionary: The Sexual Politics of a Word" (originally published 1987) and "Situated Knowledges: The Science Question in Feminism and the Privilege of Partial Perspective" (originally published 1988); both reprinted in Haraway 1991. See also Butler 1989.

2. This is not to dismiss the valid concern that certain specific performative accounts grant too much power to language. Rather, the point is that this is not an inherent feature of performativity but an ironic malady.

3. Haraway proposes the notion of diffraction as a metaphor for rethinking the geometry and optics of relationality: "[F]eminist theorist Trinh Minh-ha . . . was looking for a way to figure 'difference' as a 'critical difference within,' and not as special taxonomic marks grounding difference as apartheid. . . . Diffraction does not produce 'the same' displaced, as reflection and refraction do. Diffraction is a mapping of interference, not of replication, reflection, or reproduction. A diffraction pattern does not map where differences appear, but rather maps where the *effects* of differences appear" (1992, 300). Haraway (1997) promotes the notion of

diffraction to a fourth semiotic category. Inspired by her suggestions for usefully deploying this rich and fascinating physical phenomenon to think about differences that matter, I further elaborate the notion of diffraction as a mutated critical tool of analysis (though not as a fourth semiotic category) in *Meeting the Universe Halfway* (2007).

4. See Rouse 2002 on rethinking naturalism. The neologism *intra-activity* is defined below.

5. Rouse begins his interrogation of representationalism in *Knowledge and Power* (1987). He examines how a representationalist understanding of knowledge gets in the way of understanding the nature of the relationship between power and knowledge. He continues his critique of representationalism and the development of an alternative understanding of the nature of scientific practices in *Engaging Science* (1996). Rouse proposes that we understand science practice *as* ongoing patterns of situated activity, an idea that is then further elaborated in *How Scientific Practices Matter* (2002).

6. The allure of representationalism may make it difficult to imagine alternatives. I discuss performative alternatives below, but these are not the only ones. A concrete historical example may be helpful at this juncture. Foucault points out that in sixteenth-century Europe, language was not thought of as a medium; rather, it was simply "one of the figurations of the world" (1970, 56), an idea that reverberates in a mutated form in the posthumanist performative account that I offer.

7. Andrew Pickering (1995) explicitly eschews the representationalist idiom in favor of a performative idiom. It is important to note, however, that Pickering's notion of performativity would not be recognizable as such to poststructuralists, despite their shared embrace of *performativity* as a remedy to representationalism, and despite their shared rejection of humanism. Pickering's appropriation of the term does not include any acknowledgment of its politically important—arguably inherently queer—genealogy (see Sedgwick 1993) or why it has been and continues to be important to contemporary critical theorists, especially feminist and queer studies scholars/activists. Indeed, he evacuates its important political historicity along with many of its crucial insights. In particular, Pickering ignores important discursive dimensions, including questions of meaning, intelligibility, significance, identity formation, and power, which are central to poststructuralist invocations of "performativity." And he takes for granted the humanist notion of agency *as a property* of individual entities (such as humans, but also weather systems, scallops, and stereos), which poststructuralists problematize. On the other hand, poststructuralist approaches fail to take account of "nonhuman agency," which is a central focus of Pickering's account. See Barad (2007) for a more detailed discussion.

8. The notion of performativity has a distinguished career in philosophy that most of these multiple and various engagements acknowledge. Performativity's lineage is generally traced to the British philosopher J. L. Austin's interest in speech acts, particularly the relationship between saying and doing. Jacques Derrida is usually cited next as offering important poststructuralist amendments. Butler elaborates Derrida's notion of performativity through Foucault's understanding of the productive effects of regulatory power in theorizing the notion of identity performatively. Butler introduces her notion of gender performativity in

Gender Trouble, where she proposes that we understand gender, not as a thing or a set of free-floating attributes, not as an essence—but rather as a "doing": "Gender is itself a kind of becoming or activity . . . gender ought not to be conceived as a noun or a substantial thing or a static cultural marker, but rather as an incessant and repeated action of some sort" (1990, 112). In *Bodies That Matter* (1993) Butler argues for a linkage between gender performativity and the materialization of sexed bodies. Eve Kosofsky Sedgwick (1993) argues that performativity's genealogy is inherently queer.

9. This notion of posthumanism differs from Pickering's idiosyncratic assignment of a "*posthumanist* space [as] a space in which the human actors are still there but now inextricably entangled with the nonhuman, no longer at the center of the action calling the shots" (1995, 26). However, the decentering of the human is but one element of posthumanism. (Note that Pickering's notion of "entanglement" is explicitly epistemological, not ontological. What is at issue for him in dubbing his account "posthumanist" is the fact that it is attentive to the mutual accommodation, or responsiveness, of human and nonhuman agents.)

10. Diffractively reading Butler's (1993) and Haraway's (1997) accounts of materialization through one another highlights their very different patterns of engagement with post-Foucaultian understandings of power's production of bodies and subjectivities.

11. See also Butler 1989.

12. The conjunctive term *material-discursive* and other agential realist terms like *intra-action* are defined below.

13. This essay outlines issues I developed in earlier publications, including Barad 1996, 1998a, 1998b, and 2001b; see also Barad (2007).

14. It is no secret that *metaphysics* has been a term of opprobrium through most of the twentieth century. This positivist legacy lives on even in the heart of its detractors. Poststructuralists are simply the newest signatories of its death warrant. Yet, however strong one's dislike of metaphysics, it will not abide by any death sentence, and so it is ignored at one's peril. Indeed, new "experimental metaphysics" research is taking place in physics laboratories in the United States and abroad, calling into question the common belief that there is an inherent boundary between the "physical" and the "metaphysical" (see Barad 2007). This fact should not be too surprising to those of us who remember that the term *metaphysics* does not have some highbrow origins in the history of philosophy, but rather, it originally referred to the writings of Aristotle that came after his writings on physics in the arrangement made by Andronicus of Rhodes about three centuries after Aristotle's death.

15. *Relata* are would-be antecedent components of relations. According to metaphysical atomism, individual relata always preexist any relations that may hold between them.

16. Atomism is said to have originated with Leucippus and was further elaborated by Democritus, devotee of democracy, who also explored its anthropological and ethical implications. Democritus's atomic theory is often identified as the most mature pre-Socratic philosophy, directly influencing Plato and Epicurus, who transmitted it into the early modern period. Atomic theory is also said to form the cornerstone of modern science.

17. Niels Bohr (1885–1962), a contemporary of Einstein, was one of the founders of quantum physics and also the most widely accepted interpretation of the quantum theory, which goes by the name of the Copenhagen interpretation (after the home of Bohr's internationally acclaimed physics institute that bears his name). On my reading of Bohr's philosophy-physics, Bohr can be understood as proposing a proto-performative account of scientific practices.

18. Bohr argues on the basis of this single crucial insight, together with the empirical finding of an inherent discontinuity in measurement "intra-actions," that one must reject the presumed inherent separability of observer and observed, knower and known. See Barad 1996 and 2007.

19. The so-called uncertainty principle in quantum physics is not a matter of "uncertainty" at all, but rather of indeterminacy. See Barad 1995, 1996, and 2007.

20. That is, relations are not secondarily derived from independently existing "relata," but rather the mutual ontological dependence of "relata"—the relation—is the ontological primitive. As discussed below, relata only exist *within* phenomena as a result of specific intra-actions (i.e., there are no independent relata, only relata-within-relations).

21. A concrete example may be helpful. When light passes through a two-slit diffraction grating and forms a diffraction pattern, it is said to exhibit wave-like behavior. But there is also evidence that light exhibits particle-like characteristics, called *photons.* If one wanted to test this hypothesis, the diffraction apparatus could be modified in such a way as to allow a determination of which slit a given photon passes through (since particles only go through a single slit at a time). The result of running this experiment is that the diffraction pattern is destroyed! Classically, these two results together seem contradictory—frustrating efforts to specify the true ontological nature of light. Bohr resolves this wave-particle duality paradox as follows: the objective referent is not some abstract, independently existing entity, but rather, the phenomenon of light intra-acting with the apparatus. The first apparatus gives determinate meaning to the notion of "wave," while the second provides determinate meaning to the notion of "particle." The notions of "wave" and "particle" do not refer to inherent characteristics of an object that precedes its intra-action. *There are no such independently existing objects with inherent characteristics.* The two different apparatuses effect different cuts, that is, draw different distinctions delineating the "measured object" from the "measuring instrument." In other words, they differ in their local material resolutions of the inherent ontological indeterminacy. There is no conflict because the two different results mark different intra-actions. See Barad 1996 and 2007 for more details.

22. This elaboration is not based on an analogical extrapolation. Rather, I argue that such anthropocentric restrictions to laboratory investigations are not justified and indeed defy the logic of Bohr's own insights. See Barad 2007.

23. Because phenomena constitute the ontological primitives, it makes no sense to talk about independently existing things as somehow behind or as the causes of phenomena. In essence, there are no noumena, only phenomena. Agential realist phenomena are neither Kant's phenomena nor the phenomenologist's phenomena.

24. I am concerned here with the Foucaultian notion of discourse (discursive practices), not with formalist and empirical approaches stemming from Anglo-American linguistics, sociolinguistics, and sociology.

25. Foucault makes a distinction between "discursive" and "nondiscursive" practices, where the latter category is reduced to social institutional practices: "The term 'institution' is generally applied to every kind of more-or-less constrained behaviour, everything that functions in a society as a system of constraint and that isn't utterance, in short, *all the field of the non-discursive social, is an institution*" (1980b, 197–98; my italics). This specific social science demarcation is not particularly illuminating in the case of agential realism's posthumanist account, which is not limited to the realm of the social. In fact, it makes no sense to speak of the "nondiscursive" unless one is willing to jettison the notion of causality in its intra-active conception.

26. In her critique of constructivism within feminist theory Judith Butler puts forward an account of materialization that seeks to acknowledge these important points. Reworking the notion of matter as a process of materialization brings to the fore the importance of recognizing matter in its historicity and directly challenges representationalism's construal of matter as a passive blank site awaiting the active inscription of culture and the representationalist positioning of the relationship between materiality and discourse as one of absolute exteriority. Unfortunately, however, Butler's theory ultimately reinscribes matter as a passive product of discursive practices rather than as an active agent participating in the very process of materialization. This deficiency is symptomatic of an incomplete assessment of important causal factors and an incomplete reworking of "causality" in understanding the nature of discursive practices (and material phenomena) in their productivity. Furthermore, Butler's theory of materiality is limited to an account of the materialization of human bodies or, more accurately, to the construction of the contours of the human body. Agential realism's relational ontology enables a further reworking of the notion of materialization that acknowledges the existence of important linkages between discursive practices and material phenomena without the anthropocentric limitations of Butler's theory.

27. The nature of causal intra-actions is discussed further in the next section.

28. See Barad 1998b, 2001a, 2001b, and 2007 for examples.

29. I am grateful to Joe Rouse for putting this point so elegantly (private conversation). Rouse (2002) suggests that *measurement* need not be a term about laboratory operations, that before answering whether or not something is a measurement, a prior question must be considered: What constitutes a measurement of what?

30. Intelligibility is not a human-based affair. It is a matter of differential articulations and differential responsiveness/engagement. Vicki Kirby (1997) makes a similar point. See Barad (2007) for more details.

31. Butler also rejects both of these options, proposing an alternative that she calls the "constitutive outside." The "constitutive outside" is an exteriority *within language*—it is the "that which" to which language is impelled to respond in the repeated attempt to capture the persistent loss or absence of that which

cannot be captured. It is this persistent demand for, and inevitable failure of, language to resolve that demand that opens up a space for resignification—a form of agency—within the terms of that reiteration. But the fact that language itself is an enclosure that contains the constitutive outside amounts to an unfortunate reinscription of matter as subservient to the play of language and displays a commitment to an unacceptable anthropocentrism, reducing the possibilities for agency to resignification.

32. Geometry is concerned with shapes and sizes (this is true even of the non-Euclidean varieties, such as geometries built on curved surfaces like spheres rather than on flat planes), whereas topology investigates questions of connectivity and boundaries. Although spatiality is often thought of geometrically, particularly in terms of the characteristics of enclosures (like size and shape), this is only one way of thinking about space. Topological features of manifolds can be extremely important. For example, two points that seem far apart geometrically may, given a particular connectivity of the spatial manifold, actually be proximate to one another (as, e.g., in the case of cosmological objects called "wormholes").

33. In contrast to Butler's "constitutive outside," for example.

34. For example, the space of agency is much larger than that postulated by Butler's or Louis Althusser's theories. There is more to agency than the possibilities of linguistic resignification, and the circumvention of deterministic outcome does not require a clash of apparatuses/discursive demands (i.e., overdetermination).

35. This is true at the atomic level as well. Indeed, as Bohr emphasizes, the mutual exclusivity of "position" and "momentum" is what makes the notion of causality in quantum physics profoundly different from the determinist sense of causality of classical Newtonian physics.

36. Others have made this point as well, e.g., Haraway 1991; Kirby 1997; Rouse 2002; and Bohr.

37. The notion of agential separability, which is predicated on the agential realist notion of intra-actions, has far-reaching consequences. Indeed, it can be shown to play a critical role in the resolution of the "measurement problem" and other long-standing problems in quantum theory. See Barad 2007.

38. Vicki Kirby (private communication, 2002). Kirby's sustained interrogation of the tenacious nature/culture binary is unparalleled. See Kirby 1997 for a remarkable "materialist" (my description) reading of Derridean theory.

REFERENCES

Barad, Karen. 1995. "A Feminist Approach to Teaching Quantum Physics." In *Teaching the Majority: Breaking the Gender Barrier in Science, Mathematics, and Engineering,* ed. Sue V. Rosser, 43–75. Athene Series. New York: Teacher's College Press.

———. 1996. "Meeting the Universe Halfway: Realism and Social Constructivism without Contradiction." In *Feminism, Science, and the Philosophy of Science,* ed. Lynn Hankinson Nelson and Jack Nelson, 161–94. Dordrecht, Holland: Kluwer Press.

———. 1998a. "Agential Realism: Feminist Interventions in Understanding Sci-entific Practices." In *The Science Studies Reader,* ed. Mario Biagioli, 1–11. New York: Routledge.
———. 1998b. "Getting Real: Technoscientific Practices and the Materialization of Reality." *differences: A Journal of Feminist Cultural Studies* 10.2: 87–126.
———. 2001a. "Performing Culture/Performing Nature: Using the Piezoelectric Crystal of Ultrasound Technologies as a Transducer between Science Studies and Queer Theories." In *Digital Anatomy,* ed. Christina Lammar, 98–114. Vienna: Turia and Kant.
———. 2001b. "Re(con)figuring Space, Time, and Matter." In *Feminist Locations: Global and Local, Theory and Practice,* ed. Marianne DeKoven, 75–109. New Brunswick, N.J.: Rutgers University Press.
———. 2007. *Meeting the Universe Halfway: Quantum Physics and the Entanglement of Matter and Meaning.* Durham, N.C.: Duke University Press.
Butler, Judith. 1989. "Foucault and the Paradox of Bodily Inscriptions." *Journal of Philosophy* 86.11: 601–607.
———. 1990. *Gender Trouble: Feminism and the Subversion of Identity.* New York: Routledge.
———. 1993. *Bodies That Matter: On the Discursive Limits of "Sex."* New York: Routledge.
Deleuze, Gilles. 1988. *Foucault.* Trans. Sean Hand. Minneapolis: University of Minnesota Press.
Foucault, Michel. 1970. *The Order of Things: An Archaeology of the Human Sciences.* New York: Vintage Books.
———. 1972. *The Archaeology of Knowledge and the Discourse on Language.* Trans. A. M. Sheridan Smith. New York: Pantheon Books.
———. 1980a. *The History of Sexuality.* Vol. 1: *An Introduction.* Trans. Robert Hurley. New York: Vintage Books.
———. 1980b. *Power/Knowledge: Selected Interviews and Other Writings, 1972–1977.* Ed. Colin Gordon. New York: Pantheon Books.
Hacking, Ian. 1983. *Representing and Intervening: Introductory Topics in the Philosophy of Natural Science.* Cambridge: Cambridge University Press.
Haraway, Donna. 1991. *Simians, Cyborgs, and Women: The Reinvention of Nature.* New York: Routledge.
———. 1992. "The Promises of Monsters: A Regenerative Politics for Inappropriate/d Others." In *Cultural Studies,* ed. Lawrence Grossberg, Cory Nelson, and Paula Treichler, 295–337. New York: Routledge.
———. 1997. *Modest_Witness@Second_Millennium.FemaleMan©_Meets_Onco Mouse™: Feminism and Technoscience.* New York: Routledge.
Hennessey, Rosemary. 1993. *Materialist Feminism and the Politics of Discourse.* New York: Routledge.
Kirby, Vicki. 1997. *Telling Flesh: The Substance of the Corporeal.* New York: Routledge.
Pickering, Andrew. 1995. *The Mangle of Practice: Time, Agency, and Science.* Chicago: University of Chicago Press.
Rouse, Joseph. 1987. *Knowledge and Power: Toward a Political Philosophy of Science.* Ithaca, N.Y.: Cornell University Press.

…gaging *Science: How to Understand Its Practices Philosophically.* …Cornell University Press.
… *Scientific Practices Matter: Reclaiming Philosophical Naturalism.* …ersity of Chicago Press.
…ofsky. 1993. "Queer Performativity: Henry James's *The Art of* … 1.1: 1–16.
…. 1997. *Doom Patrols: A Theoretical Fiction about Postmodernism.* New York: Serpent's Tail. Available online at http://www.dhalgren.com/Doom/.

PART 2. MATERIAL WORLD

5

OTHERWORLDLY CONVERSATIONS, TERRAN TOPICS, LOCAL TERMS

Donna J. Haraway

Therefore the Lord God sent him forth from the garden of Eden, to till the ground from whence he was taken. So he drove out the man; and he placed at the east of the garden of Eden Cherubim, and a flaming sword which turned every way, to keep the way to the tree of life.

—Genesis 3:23–24

Nothing is ultimately contextual; all is constitutive, which is another way of saying that all relationships are dialectical.

—Robert Young, *Darwin's Metaphor*

Animals are not lesser humans; they are other worlds.

—Barbara Noske, *Humans and Other Animals*

Although, of course, I longed in the normal human way for exploration, I found my first world oddly disconcerting. . . . It is only in circumstances like these that we realise how much we ourselves are constructed bilaterally on either-or principles. Fish rather than echinoderms. . . . It was quite a problem to get through to those radial entities.

—Naomi Mitchison, *Memoirs of a Spacewoman*

Nature is for me, and I venture for many of us who are planetary fetuses gestating in the amniotic effluvia of terminal industrialism and militarism, one of those impossible things characterized during a talk in 1989 in California by Gayatri Spivak as that which we cannot not desire. Excruciatingly conscious of nature's constitution as Other in the histories of colonialism, racism, sexism, and class domination of many kinds, many people who have been both ground to powder and formed in European and Euro-American crucibles nonetheless find in this problematic, ethno-specific, long-lived, and globally mobile concept something we cannot do without but can never "have." We must find another relationship to nature besides reification, possession, appropriation, and nostalgia. No longer able to sustain the fictions of being either subjects or objects, all the partners in the potent conversations that constitute nature must find a new ground for making meanings together.[1]

Perhaps to give confidence in its essential reality, immense resources have been expended to stabilize and materialize nature, to police its/her boundaries. From one reading of Genesis 3:23–24, it looks like God established the first nature park in the Neolithic First World, now become the oil-rich Third World, complete with an armed guard to keep out the agriculturalists. From the beginning such efforts have had disappointing results. Efforts to travel into "nature" become tourist excursions that remind the voyager of the price of such displacements—one pays to see fun-house reflections of oneself. Efforts to preserve "nature" in parks remain fatally troubled by the ineradicable mark of the founding expulsion of those who used to live there, not as innocents in a garden, but as people for whom the categories of nature and culture were not the salient ones.

Expensive projects to collect "nature's" diversity and bank it seem to produce debased coin, impoverished seed, and dusty relics. As the banks hypertrophy, the nature that feeds the storehouses disappears. The World Bank's record on environmental destruction is exemplary in this regard. Finally, the projects for representing and enforcing human "nature" are famous for their imperializing essences, most recently replicated in the Human Genome Project. It seems appropriate that a core computer project for storing the record of human unity and diversity, GenBank, the U.S. depository for DNA sequence data, is located at the national laboratories at Los Alamos, New Mexico, site of the Manhattan Project and a major U.S. weapons laboratory since the Second World War.

So nature is not just a physical place to which one can go, or a treasure to fence in or to bank, or an essence to be saved or violated. Nature is not hidden and so does not need to be unveiled. Nature is not a text to be read in the codes of mathematics and biomedicine. It is not the Other who offers origin, replenishment, and service. Neither mother, nurse, lover, nor slave, nature is not matrix, resource, mirror, or tool for the reproduction of that odd, ethnocentric, phallogocentric, putatively universal being called Man. Nor for his euphemistically named surrogate, the "human."

Nature is, however, a *topos,* a place, in the sense of a rhetorician's place or topic for consideration of common themes; nature is, strictly, a commonplace. We turn to this topic to order our discourse, to compose our memory. As a topic in this sense, nature also reminds us that in seventeenth-century English the "topick gods" were the local gods, the gods specific to places and peoples. We need these spirits rhetorically if we can't have them any other way. We need them in order to reinhabit, precisely, common places—locations that are widely shared, inescapably local, worldly, enspirited—that is, topical. In this sense, nature is the place in which to rebuild public culture.[2]

Nature is also a *trópos,* a trope. It is figure, construction, artifact, movement, displacement. Nature cannot preexist its construction, its articulation in heterogeneous social encounters, where all of the actors are not human and all of the humans are not "us," however defined. Worlds are built from such articulations. Fruitful encounters depend on a particular kind of move—a *trópos,* or "turn." Faithful to the Greek, as *trópos,* nature is about turning. Troping, we turn to nature as if to the earth, to the tree of life—geotropic, physiotropic. We turn in the hope that the park police, the cherubim, are on strike against God and that both swords and ploughshares might be beaten into other tools, other metaphors for possible conversations about inhabitable terran other-worlds. Topically, we travel toward the earth, a commonplace. Nature is a topic of public discourse on which much turns, even the earth.

THREE STORIES

Less grandly, I turn to a little piece of this work of world building—telling stories. When I grow up, or, as we used to say, "after the revolution,"

I know what I want to do. I want to have charge of the animal stories in the *Reader's Digest* reaching twenty or so million people monthly in over a dozen languages. I want to write the stories about morally astute dogs, endangered people, instructive beetles, marvelous microbes, and co-habitable houses of difference. With my friends, I want to write natural history at the end of the second Christian millennium to see if some other stories are possible, ones not premised on the divide between nature and culture, armed cherubim, and heroic quests for secrets of life and secrets of death.[3]

Following Ursula LeGuin, and inspired by some of the chapters in the evolutionary tales of woman-the-gatherer, I want to engage in a carrier-bag practice of storytelling, in which the stories do not reveal secrets acquired by heroes pursuing luminous objects across and through the plot matrix of the world. Bag-lady storytelling would instead proceed by putting unexpected partners and irreducible details into a frayed, porous carrier bag. Encouraging halting conversations, the encounter transmutes and reconstitutes all the partners and all the details. The stories do not have beginnings or ends; they have continuations, interruptions, and reformulations—just the kind of survivable stories we could use these days. And perhaps my beginning with the transmogrification of LeGuin's "Carrier-Bag Theory of Fiction" (1989) to the bag-lady practice of storytelling can remind us that the lurking dilemma in all of these tales is comprehensive homelessness, the lack of a common place, and the devastation of public culture.

In the United States, storytelling about nature, whatever problematic kind of category that is, remains an important practice for forging and expressing basic meanings. The profusion of nature television specials is a kind of collective video–Bridgewater Treatise, producing secularized natural theology within late capitalism. A recent visit to the San Diego Zoo confirmed my conviction that people reaffirm many of their beliefs about each other and about what kind of planet the earth can be by telling each other what they think they are seeing as they watch the animals. So I would like to begin this meditation on three books—by Robert Young, Barbara Noske, and Naomi Mitchison—with a few stories that reveal some of the investments I bring to reading their work.

A few years ago I was visiting my high-school friend, who lived with her husband and three sons, aged sixteen, fourteen, and eleven, near Milwaukee, Wisconsin. Periodically throughout the weekend, the two older boys teased each other mercilessly about a high-school dance that was coming up; each boy tried to get under his brother's skin by queer-baiting him relentlessly. In this middle-class, white, American community, their patent nervousness about dating girls was enacted in "playful" insults about each other's not-yet-fully-consolidated gender allegiances and identities. In confused, but numbingly common moves, they accused each other of being simultaneously a girl and a queer. From my point of view, they were performing a required lesson in the compulsory heterosexuality of my culture and theirs.

I found the whole scene personally deeply painful for many reasons, not least the profoundly poor manners and disrespect the parents allowed, knowing the gay, lesbian, and bisexual makeup of my life, family, and community. My world is sustained by queer confederacies. Lacking courage and feeling disoriented, late in the weekend I told my friend what I thought was happening. Shocked, she said the boys were much too young to be taught anything about homosexuality and homophobia, and that in any case what they were doing was just natural. Despite the fact that I was the godmother of the older boy, I culpably shut up, leaving his moral education to the proven sensibilities of his milieu.

Later that day, knowing my interest in another kind of nature and hoping to heal our dis-ease with each other by a culturally appropriate, therapeutic trip "outside civilization," my friend and her husband took me to a beautiful small lake in the wooded countryside. With high spirits, if little zoological erudition, we began talking about some ducks across the lake. We could see very little, and we knew less. In instant solidarity, my friend and her husband narrated that the four ducks in view were in two reproductive, heterosexual pairs. It quickly sounded like they had a modest mortgage on the wetlands around that section of the lake and were about to send their ducklings to a good school to consolidate their reproductive investment. I demurred, mumbling something about the complexity and specificity of animal behavior and society. Meanwhile, I, of course, held that the ducks were into queer communities. I knew better; I knew they were *ducks,* even though I was embarrassed not to know their species. I knew ducks deserved our recognition of their *nonhuman* cultures, subjectivities, histories, and material lives. They had enough problems with all the heavy metals and organic solvents in those lakes without having to take sides in our ideological struggles too. Forced to live in our ethno-specific constructions of nature, the birds could ill-afford the luxury of getting embroiled in what counts as natural for the nearby community.

Nonetheless, furious at each other, both my friends and I were sure we were right in our self-interested and increasingly assertive stories about the ducks. After all, we could see what they were doing; they were right across the lake; we had positive knowledge about them. They were objects performing on our stage, called nature. They had been appropriated into our shamefully displaced struggle, which belonged where earlier in the day we were too "chicken" to put it—directly over the homophobia, compulsory heterosexuality, and commitments to normalizing particular kinds of families in *our* lives. We avoided building needed, contested, situated knowledges among ourselves by—once again, in ways historically sanctioned in middle-class, Anglo cultures—objectifying nature.

More sophisticated scientific accounts of animal behavior published in the best technical journals and popularized in the most expensive public television series patently do much the same thing. But not always. Sometimes, rarely and preciously, we—those of us gestating in techno-scientific media—manage to tell some very non-innocent stories about, and even with, the animals, rather than about our "natural" selves. Meanwhile, I'm still sure I was more right than my friends about those ducks, whoever they were. And while queer-bashing remains a popular sport, I still feel the pain and know my complicity in those particular boys' natural development.

A second story: once upon a time, early in graduate school in biology in the mid-1960s, I was tremendously moved, intellectually and emotionally, by an ordinary lecture on the enzymes of the electron transport system (ETS). These biological catalysts are involved in energy-processing in cells complicated enough to have elaborate, internal, membrane-bound organelles (little organs) to partition and enlarge their activities. Using new techniques, the process was being studied experimentally *in vitro* in structural-functional complexes of membrane subunits prepared from the cellular organelles, called mitochondria. The membrane subunits were dis-assembled and re-assembled to be analyzed both by electron microscopy and biochemistry. The result was a stunning narrative and visual imagery of structural-functional complexity of the type that has always made biology, including molecular biology, a beautiful science for me. The apparatus of production of these written and oral accounts and visual artifacts was rigorously analytical and biotechnical. There was no way around elaborate machine mediations, complete with all their encasements of dead labor, intentional and unintentional delegations, unexpected agencies, and past and present, pain-fraught socio-technical histories.

After the lecture, on a walk around town, I felt a surging high. Trees, weeds, dogs, invisible gut parasites, people—we all seemed bound together in the ultra-structural tissues of our being. Far from feeling alienated by the reductionistic techniques of cell biology, I realized to my partial embarrassment, but mainly pleasure, that I was responding *erotically* to the connections made possible by the knowledge-producing practices, and their constitutive narratives, of techno-science. So who is surprised: when were love and knowledge not co-constitutive? I refused, then and now, to dismiss the specific pleasure experienced on that walk as epistemological sadomasochism, rooted in alienation and objectifying scientific reductionism or in ignorant denial of the terrible histories of domination built into what we politely call "modern science." I was *not* experiencing a moment of romantic postmodern rapture in the techno-sublime. Machine, organism, and human embodiment all were articulated—brought into a *particular* co-constitutive relationship—in complex ways that forced me to recognize a historically specific, conjoined discipline of love, power, and knowledge. Through its enabling constraints, that is, through lab practice in cell biology, this discipline was making possible—unequally—particular kinds of subjectivity and systematic artifactual embodiments for which people in my worlds had to be responsible.

This knowing love could not be innocent; it did not originate in a garden. But neither did it originate in *expulsion* from a garden. Not about secrets—of life or death—this knowing love took shape in quite particular, historical-social intercourse, or "conversation," among machines, people, other organisms and parts of organisms. All those feminists like me still in the closet—that is, those who have not come out to acknowledge the viscous, physical, erotic pleasure we experienced from dis-harmonious conversations about abstract ideas, auto repair, and possible worlds that took place in local consciousness-raising groups in the early 1970s—might have a thrill of self-recognition in thinking about the electron transport system. Our desires are very heterogeneous indeed, as are our embodiments. We may not be ducks, but as natural-technical terran constructs, we are certainly ETs.

And a final story: when Alexander Berkman and Sojourner Truth, my and my lover's half-Labrador mutts, were just over a year old, we all went to obedience training together in a small town in northern California. Although we had discoursed on dog training from library books for a year, none of us had ever before been to obedience training, that amazing institution that domesticates people and their canine companions to agree to cohabit particular stories important to civic peace. It was late in our lives together to seek institutionalized obedience training. One of us already showed signs of criminality, or at least bore the marks of a shared incoherent relation to authority of the kind that could result in mayhem and legally mandated death sentences for dogs and nasty fines for people. That is, one of us seemed intent on murdering con-specifics (other dogs) in any and all circumstances, and the rest of us were handling the situation badly.

In some important situations in the 1980s in California, we four didn't seem to speak the same language, either within or across species boundaries. We needed help. So, with a motley assortment of other cross-specific pairs of mammals, of types that had shared biological and social histories for a couple of tens of thousands of years, we entered a commercial pedagogical relationship with the dog, Goody-goody, and her human, Perfection, who seemed to have mastered the political problem of paying consequential attention to each other. They seemed to have a story to tell us.

In her discussion of the language games of training, Vicki Hearne invoked Wittgenstein's injunction that "to imagine a language is to imagine a form of life" (1986, 4). A professional trainer and an incurable intellectual, Hearne was looking for a philosophically responsible language for talking about the stories inhabited by trainers and companion animals like dogs and horses. She was convinced that the training relationship is a moral one that requires the personhood of all the partners. But, although Hearne did not affirm this point, the moral relationship cannot rely on a shared *anthropomorphic* personhood. Only some of the partners are people, and the form of life the conversants construct is neither purely canine nor purely human. Furthermore, personhood is only one local, albeit historically broadly important, way of being a subject. And, like most moral relationships, this one cannot rely on ignorance of radical heterogeneity in the commitment to equality-as-sameness.

Certainly, however, in the training relationship animals and people are constructing a historically specific form of life, and therefore a language. They are engaged in making some effective meanings rather than others. Hearne's moral universe had such premises as: dogs have the right to the consequences of their actions, and biting (by the dog) is a response to incoherent authority (the human's). She envisioned certain civil rights, like those enjoyed by seeing-eye dogs and their people, for other dogs and people who had achieved superb off-lead control.

I quibble about discussing this matter in terms of people's control of the dogs, not out of a fetishized fear of control and of naming who exercises it over whom, but out of a sense that my available languages for discussing control and its directional arrows misshape the forms of attention and response achieved by serious dogs and trainers. By *misshape,* I do not mean *misrepresent,* but more seriously, I mean that the language of unidirectional "human control over dog" instrumentally is part of producing an incoherent and even dangerous relationship that is not conducive to civil peace within or across species. A convinced skeptic about the ideologies of representation anyway, I am not interested in worrying too much about the accurate portrayal of training relationships. But I am very much concerned about the instrumentality of languages, since they are forms of life.

Sojourner, Alexander—the canine reincarnation of the lover of Emma Goldman and the anarchist who shot Frick in 1892 after the Homestead strike—Rusten, and I were serious about training, but we were very unskilled. We should have met Vicki Hearne, but at that point we had only read her in *The New Yorker.* We needed more on-the-ground skill.

Instead, we blundered into an appalling conversation that makes those heterosexually construed ducks look untouched by human tongues. As long as you didn't listen to the English that Perfection used to explain to the other humans what was happening, but attended only to the other semiotic processes, like gesture, touch, and unadorned verbal command, Goody-goody and Perfection had a pretty good story for lots of ordinary events in inter-species life. But, like lots of sheltered folk, they weren't good with anarchists and criminals; they relied, or at least Perfection did, on escalating force and languages of stripped-down subjugation. The result was stunning escalation of the potential for violence in our dog. The conversation was going quite wrong. We later met some trainer humans and social-worker dogs who taught us how to work on reliable obedience in challenging circumstances—such as the mere existence of other dogs in the world. But our first encounter with obedience training posed in stark terms the fact that forms of inter-species domestic life can go very wrong.

My growing suspicions that our incoherence was only increasing in this particular attempt at training reached their apogee near graduation time, when Goody-goody and Perfection demonstrated how a human could examine any spot on a dog's body if necessary. This exercise could be crucial in emergencies, where pain and injury to the dog could put both human and animal at risk. The class was very attentive. While Perfection was touching Goody-goody in every imaginable place, opening and closing orifices, and generally showing how few boundaries were necessary when trust and good authority existed, the conversants seemed to me to be involved in a complex intercourse of gesture, touch, eye movement, tone of voice, and many other modalities. But, while grasping a paw and holding it up for our view, what Perfection was saying to us went something like this: "See this paw? It may look like Goody-goody's paw, but it's really my paw. I own this paw, and I can do anything I want with it. If you are to be able to do what you see us doing, you too must accept that form of appropriation of your dog's body."

It was my opinion that day, and still is, that if Perfection had really acted on her explicit words, Goody-goody and she would have achieved nothing. Their other conversation belied the discourse she provided the students. If my lover and I had been better at attending to that other conversation, we might have been able to get further on our needed communication with Alexander and Sojourner on difficult subjects. We were actually very good at the physical examination language game. In our harder task, the one involving our dog's tendency to attack other dogs, with his sister aiding and abetting, we were deterred by misshaping words that Perfection did not follow in her relations with Goody-goody but did impose in both physical and verbal relationships with at least some other dogs and people. Maybe she just had that trouble with criminals, anarchists, and socialists. That population is, it must be said, quite large. Unpromisingly, my household went to obedience-training graduation wearing "question authority" buttons. We had not yet built a coherent conversation, inter- or intra-specific, for the crucial subject of authority.

So my opening stories have been about three forms of life and three conversations involving historically located people and other organisms or parts of organisms as well as technological artifacts. All of these are stories about demarcation and continuity among actors, human and not, organic and not. The stories of the "wild ducks in nature," of the "reductive" methodologies and the ETS in cell biology, and of the problem of "discourse" between people and companion species collectively raise the problems that will concern us for the rest of this essay as we turn to Young, Noske, and Mitchison. Is there a common context for discussion of what counts as nature in techno-science? What kind of topic is the "human" place in "nature" by the late twentieth century in worlds shaped by techno-science? How might inhabitable narratives about science and nature be told, without denying the ravages of the dedication of techno-science to militarized and systematically unjust relations of knowledge and power, while refusing to replicate the apocalyptic stories of Good and Evil played out on the stages of Nature and Science?

DIGESTING DISCOURSES

In *Darwin's Metaphor: Nature's Place in Victorian Culture* (1985), a richly textured, scholarly, and politically passionate book that collects a series of still vitally important essays written across the 1970s on the nineteenth-century British debates on "man's place in nature,"[4] Robert Young depicts the structure and consequences of the broad, common cultural context within which the intellectuals' struggle over the demarcation between man, God, and nature took place. The twentieth-century phrase "science *and* society" would not have made much sense to the participants in earlier debates, for whom the parts were not two preconstituted, oppositional entities, *science* and *society,* held apart by a deceiving conjunction. The phrase should not make sense in the 1990s either, but for different reasons from those that pertained in Darwin's world. My debased goal of writing the animal stories for the *Reader's Digest* should be seen in the context of a social scene very different from the nineteenth-century contestation for shared meanings and inhabitable stories. In those halcyon days, I might have aspired instead to have written for the *Edinburgh Review.*

Young's fundamental insistence is that probing deeper into a scientific debate leads inexorably to the wider issues of a culture. If we inquire insistently enough—if we take doing cultural studies seriously—"we may learn something about the nature of science itself, and thereby illuminate the way societies set agendas in their broad culture, including science, as part of the pursuit of social priorities and values" (1985, 122). For Young, to understand the nineteenth-century debates that he is exploring and, more generally, to engage any important issues in the history of science as culture, to sequester the scientific debate from the social, political, theological, and economic ones is to falsify all the parts and "to mystify oppression in the form of science" (1985, 192).

Young's reference in the 1970s for these arguments was the debate over "internalist versus externalist" approaches to the history of science that exercised scholars throughout the decade. Can science be understood to have "insides" and "outsides" that justify separating off "contents" of scientific "discovery" from "contexts" of "construction"? All of Young's essays are rigorous, principled objections to the dichotomy as scholarly obfuscation and political mystification. In 1992, I would still be hard put to recommend a more richly argued invitation to, and enactment of, politically engaged, holistic, scholarly work than Young's 1973 essay, "The Historiographic and Ideological Contexts of the Nineteenth-century Debate on Man's Place in Nature." I found in the 1970s, and still find, Robert Young's cogency about the need to confront the content of the sciences with a nonreductionist, social-historical analysis and to avoid easy answers to the relations of science and ideology indispensable to all my projects as a critical intellectual.

That cogency is certainly indispensable to understanding science *as* culture, rather than science *and* culture. As he put it much earlier than those now cited in science studies for injunctions that sound similar but lack Young's crucial political edge, "Nothing is ultimately contextual; all is constitutive, which is another way of saying that all relationships are dialectical" (1985, 241). Following a Marxist tradition, especially in the work of Georg Lukacs, "whose analysis of reification provides the tools for looking more closely at the ways in which science has been used for the purpose of reconciling people to the status quo," Young builds his book around the premise that "nature is a social category" (1985, 242). I will come back to this indispensable and highly problematic assertion.

Young's general view of the nineteenth-century debate is that its questions were not allocated to specialist disciplines, but were deeply embedded in a shared (although class-differentiated) cultural context, for which the relation of God and his creation, that is, theism and the fate of natural theology, was the organizing center. For example, the fine structure of Darwin's scientific discourse on "selection" shows that theological and philosophical issues were constitutive, not contextual. The common intellectual context of the debate about "man's place in nature" from the early 1800s to the 1880s took shape in a widely read periodical literature in which theological, geological, biological, literary, and political questions were complexly knotted together. The debate about "man's place in nature" was not an integrated whole but a rich web. The threads were sustained by a material apparatus of production of a common culture among the intelligentsia, including potent reading, writing, and publishing practices.

Through the 1870s and 1880s, the breakup of the common intellectual context through specializations and disciplinizations familiar to an observer from the *late* twentieth century was reflected by—and partly *effected* by—a very different structure of writing and publishing practices. As Young put it, "The common intellectual context came to pieces in the 1870s and 1880s, and this fragmentation was reflected in the development of specialist societies and periodicals, increasing professionalization, and the growth of general periodicals of a markedly lower intellectual standard" (1985, 128). Thus was born my desire to write for *National Geographic, Omni,* and, to return to the deepest shame and hope for an academic used to audiences of a few hundred souls, the *Reader's Digest,* or even *The National Enquirer.*

But if there has been a disruption in one context—and its constitutive literary, social, and material technologies—Young notes a stream of continuity from the early nineteenth to the late twentieth century that is fed by the very specializations in practice and the literary debasements that he describes: current biotechnology, perhaps especially genetic engineering and the profusion of genome projects to appropriate an organism's DNA sequences in a particular historical form—one amenable to property and commodity relations—must be seen as, in significant part, the "harvest of Darwinism" that has reshaped biological culture at its roots. "The current context for reflecting on these matters is a period in which biotechnology is harvesting and commercializing the long-term fruits of Darwinism and making commodities out of the least elements of living nature—amino acids and genes" (1985, 247). "Darwinism provides the unifying thread and themes from Malthus to the commodification of the smallest elements of living nature in genetic engineering. With this set of interrelations go the social forms of technocracy, information processing, and the disciplines that are recasting how we think of humanity in terms of cybernetics, information theory, systems theory, and 'communication and control'" (1985, xiii).

So our "common context" is not theism—the relations of a creator God to his product—but constructivism and productionism. Constructivism and productionism are the consequences of the material relocation of the narratives and practices of creation and their ensuing legal relations onto "man" and "nature" in (how else can I say it?) white capitalist heterosexist patriarchy (hereafter WCHP, an acronym whose beauty fits its referent). The nineteenth-century debate about the demarcation between God's creative action and nature's laws, and so between man and nature, mind and body, was resolved by a commitment to the principle of the uniformity of nature and scientific naturalism. In the context of the founding law of the Father, nature's *capacities* and nature's *laws* were identical. Narratively, this identification entails the escalating dominations built into stories of the endless transgressions of forbidden boundaries—the erotic *frisson* of man's projects of transcendence, prominently including techno-science. "Science did not replace God: God became identified with the laws of nature" (1985, 240).

God did not interfere in his creation, not even in those previously reliable reservoirs for his action called biological design and mental function. But the deep European monotheist, patriarchal, cultural commitment to relating to the world as made, designed, and structured by the prohibitions of law remained. A recent element in the stories, *progress* was inserted into the body of nature and deeply tied to a particular kind of conception of the uniformity of nature as a *product.* By the late twentieth century, very few cracks, indeed, are allowed to show in the solid cultural complex of WCHP constructionism.

In March 1988, Charles Cantor, then head of the U.S. Department of Energy's Human Genome Center at the Lawrence Berkeley Laboratory, made these matters clear in his talk at the National Institute of Medicine entitled "The Human Genome Project: Problems and Prospects?" In the context of explaining the different material modes of existence of various kinds of genetic maps (genetic linkage maps, physical maps stored in Yeast Artificial Chromosome [YAC] libraries or "cosmid libraries," and database sequence information existing only in computers and their printouts), Cantor noted why having the physical maps mattered so much: "You own the genome at this point." I wanted

Cantor to explore further the socio-technical relations of physical libraries of sequence data; this exploration would show us something about the late-twentieth-century "common context" for demarcation debates between "nature," "man," and, if not God, at least the supreme engineer. The "realization" of the value of the genome requires its full materialization in a particular historical form. Instrumentalism and full constructivism are not disembodied concepts. To make and store the genome is to appropriate it as a specific kind of entity. This is historically specific human self-production and self-possession or ownership.

The long tradition of methodological individualism and liberty based in property in the self comes to a particular kind of fruition in this discourse. To patent something, one must hold the key to making it. That is what bestows the juridical right of private appropriation of the product of no longer simply *given,* but rather fully technically *replicated,* "nature." In the Human Genome Project, generic "man's place in nature" really does became the universal "human place in nature" in a particular form: species existence as fully specified process and product. The body is matrix, superfluous, or obstructive; the program is the prize.

In this mutated but still masculinist heroic narrative, the relation between sex and gender is one of the many worlds that is transformed in a concrete socio-technical project still under way in Europe, Japan, and the United States. Like toys in other games, Genes "R" Us, and "we" (who?) are our self-possessed products in this apotheosis of technological humanism. There is only one Actor, and we are It. Nature mutates into its binary opposite, culture, and vice versa, in such a way as to displace the entire nature/culture (and sex/gender) dialectic with a new discursive field, where the actors who count are their own instrumental objectifications. Context is content with a vengeance. Nature is the program; we replicated it; we own it; we are it. Nature and culture implode into each other and disappear into the resulting black hole. Man makes himself, indeed, in a cosmic onanism. The nineteenth-century transfer of God's creative role to natural processes, within a multiply stratified industrial culture committed to relentless constructivism and productionism, bears fruit in a comprehensive biotechnological harvest in which control of the genome is control of the game of life—legally, mythically, and technically. The stakes are very unequal chances for life and death on the planet. I honestly don't think Darwin would have been very happy about all this.

Let us return to Young's affirmation of Lukacs's proposition that nature is a social category. In the face of the implosion described above, that formulation seems inadequate in a basic way. In the Marxist radical science movement of the 1970s, Young formulated the problem in these terms: "In the nineteenth century, the boundaries between humanity and nature were in dispute. On the whole, nature won, which means that reification won. It is still winning, but some radicals are trying to push back the boundaries of reifying scientism as far as they can, and a critical study of the development of the models which underlie reifying rationalizations may be of service to them as they begin to place science in history—the history of people and events" (1985, 246). I would rather say, not that "nature" won, but that the man/nature game is the problem. But this is a quibble within my analysis so far; Young and I are united in identifying crucial parts of the structure of reification.

To oppose reification, Young appealed to a Marxist modification of the premise, "Man (i.e., human praxis) is the *measure* of all things" (1985, 241). But, deeply influenced by the practices of an anti-imperialist environmentalism that joins justice and ecology, and of a multicultural feminism that insists on a different imagination of relationality, both social movements that took deep root after Young wrote this essay, I think that human praxis formulated in this way is precisely part of the problem.

In 1973, Young sought a theory of mediations between nature and man. But nature remained either a product of human praxis (nature's state as transformed by the history of people and events) or a pre-social category not yet in relation to the transforming relation of human labor. What nature could not be in these formulations of Marxist humanisms is a social partner, a social agent with a history, a conversant in a discourse where all of the actors are not "us." A theory of "mediations" is not enough. If "human praxis is the measure of all things," then the conversation and its forms of life spell trouble for the planet.

And, less consequentially for others but dear to my heart, I'll never get to have a coherent conversation with my anarchist mongrel dog, Alexander Berkman. In Lukacs's and Young's story in the 1970s, nature could only be matrix or product, while man had to be the sole agent, exactly the masculinist structure of the human story, including the versions that narrate both the planting and the harvest of Darwinism.

We are in troubled waters, but not ones utterly unnavigated by European craft, not to mention other traditions. But animism has a bad name in the language games I need to enter as a critical intellectual in techno-science worlds, and besides, animism is patently a kind of human representational practice. Still, efforts to figure the world in lively terms pervade hermeticism in early modern Europe, and some important radical and feminist work has tried to reclaim that tradition. There is not really much help for us in that history, I fear. However, I think we must engage in forms of life with nonhumans—both machines and organisms—on livelier terms than those provided by harvesting Darwinism or Marxism. Refiguring conversations with those who are not "us" must be part of that project. We have to strike up a coherent conversation where humans are not the measure of all things and where no one claims unmediated access to anyone else. Humans, at least, need a different *kind* of theory of mediations.

OTHERWORLDLY CONVERSATIONS

It is that project that enlivens Barbara Noske's book *Humans and Other Animals: Beyond the Boundaries of Anthropology* (1989). Noske thoroughly warps the organizing field of humanist stories about nature and culture. Her situation as a radical Western intellectual in the late 1980s, where animal rights movements, environmentalism, feminism, and antinuclearism restructure the intellectual and moral heritage of the left, stands in historical contrast to Young's a decade earlier. Noske's discussion of Darwinism is much poorer scholarship compared to Young's fine-grained analysis, but she has her finger on a key political—epistemological—moral problem that I don't think the Young of those essays could broach. If he had broached the trouble in our relationship with other organisms in the way Noske does, he certainly could not have resolved the issue as she does.

Noske is consumed by the scandal of the particular kind of object status of animals enforced in the Western histories and cultures she discusses. In Marxist formulations, reification refers to the re-presentation to human laborers of the product of their labor—that is, of the means through which they make themselves historically—in a particular, hostile form. In capitalist relations of production, the human activity embodied in the product of labor is frozen, appropriated, and made to reappear as It, the commodity form that dominates and distorts social life. In that frame, reification is not a problem for domestic animals, but, for example, for tenant farmers, who objectify their labor in the products of animal husbandry and then have the fruit of that labor appropriated by another, who represents it to the worker in a commodity form. But more fundamentally, the farmer is represented to *himself* in the commodity form. The paradigmatic reification within a Marxist analysis is of the worker *himself*, whose own life-making activity, his labor power, is taken from him and represented in a coercive commodity form. He becomes It.

Noske is after another sense of objectification. For her, the Marxist analysis cannot talk about the animals at all. In that frame, animals have no history; they are matrix or raw material for human self-reformation, which can go awry, for example, in capitalist relations of production. Animals are not part of the *social* relationship at all; they never have any status but that of not-human; not subject, therefore object.

But the kind of "not subject, not human, therefore object" that animals are made to be is also not like the status occupied by women within patriarchal logics and histories. Feminist analysis that either affirms or resists women's identification with animals as nature and as object has not really gotten the point about animals either, from Noske's provocative point of view. In an important stream of Anglo-feminist theory, woman as such does not suffer reification in the way the Marxist describes the process for the worker.[5] In masculinist sexual orders, woman is not a subject separated from the product of her life-shaping activity; her problem is much worse. She *is* a projection of another's desire, who then haunts man as his always elusive, seductive, unreliable Other. Woman as such is a kind of illusionist's projection, while mere women bear the violent erasures of that history-making move. There is nothing of her own for her to reappropriate; she is an object in the sense of being another's project.

The kind of objectification of animals that Noske is trying to understand is also not like the history of racial objectification in the West, although the status of slavery in the New World came dizzyingly close to imposing on the enslaved the same kind of animal object status borne by beasts, and by nature in general within colonizing logics. In African American slavery, for example, slaves were fully alienable property. Slave women were not like white women—the conveyers of property through legitimate marriage.[6] Both slave men and women were the property itself. Slave women and men suffered both sexual and racial objectifications in a way that transformed both, but still the situation was not like that of nonhuman animals. Slave liberation depended on making the human subjecthood of the slaves an effective historical achievement. In that history-remaking process, what counts as human, that is, the story of "man," gets radically recast.

But no matter how recast, this human family drama is not the process of re-establishing the terms of relationality that concerns animals. The last thing they "need" is human subject status, in whatever cultural-historical form. That is the problem with much animal rights discourse. The best animals could get out of that approach is the "right" to be permanently represented, as lesser humans, in human discourse, such as the law—animals would get the right to be permanently "orientalized." As Marx put it in another context and for other beings, "They cannot represent themselves; they must be represented." Lots of well-intentioned, but finally imperialist ecological discourse takes that shape. Its tones resonate with the pro-life/anti-abortion question, "Who speaks for the fetus?" The answer is, anybody but the pregnant woman, especially if that anybody is a legal, medical, or scientific expert. Or a father. Facing the harvest of Darwinism, we do not need an endless discourse on who speaks for animals, or for nature in general. We have had enough of the language games of fatherhood. We need other terms of conversation with animals, a much less respectable undertaking. The point is not new representations but new *practices,* other forms of life rejoining humans and not-humans.

So in the human-animal relationship gone awry, the analogy to other objectifications so often invoked in radical discourse breaks down systematically. That is the beauty of Noske's argument. There is *specific* work to be done if we are to strike up a coherent form of life, a conversation, with other animals. "It may all boil down to a form of anthropocentric colonizing, where everything and everyone is still being measured by a human and Western yardstick. In the context of our law systems, animals are bound to appear as human underlings. However, animals are not lesser humans; they are other worlds, whose otherworldliness must not be disenchanted and cut to our size, but must be respected for what it is" (1989, xi; my punctuation). Great, but how? And how especially if there is no *outside* of language games?

Trying to get a grip on this matter, Noske achieves four things that I value highly. First, she starts out by formulating the historicity of all the partners in the stories. Animals have been active in their relations to humans, not just the reverse. Domestication, a major focus of Noske's discussion, is paradigmatic for her argument. Although an unequal relationship, domestication is a two-way matter. Domestication refers to the situation in which people actively force changes in the seasonal subsistence cycles of animals to make them coincide with particular human needs. Emphasizing the active aspect and the changing and specific ecologies of both species, the definition Noske uses insists on a historically dynamic continuum of human-animal relations of domestication. From this point of view, capture, taming, and reproductive isolation are relatively recent developments.

Second, in her analysis of contemporary factory-animal domestication, Noske formulates a very useful concept, the "animal-industrial complex."[7] Animals are forced to "specialize" in one "skill" in a way that would chill the harshest human labor-process de-skillers. "The animal's life-time has truly been converted into 'working-time': into round-the-clock production" (1989, 17). The design of animals as laboratory research models is one of the most extreme examples of domestication. Not only has the animal been totally incorporated into human technology; it has become a fully designed instance of human technology.

Noske doesn't discuss genetic engineering, but her argument would readily accommodate those intensifications of reshaping the animals (and humans) to productionist purposes. As indeed, from the point of view of dominant narratives about the human genome initiative, humans themselves are the reading and writing technologies of their genes. Nature *is* a technology, and that is a very particular sort of embodied social category. "We" (who?) have become an instance of "our" (whose?) technology. The "Book of Life" (the genome in the title image used by the Nova television program "Decoding the Book of Life," 1988) is the law of life, and the law is paradigmatically a technical affair. Noske agrees with the Dutch philosopher Ton Lemaire that this full objectification of "nature" could only be complete with the full "autonomization" of the human subject. Autonomy and automaton are more than aural puns. Fully objectified, we are at last finished subjects—or finished as subjects. The world of "autonomous" subjects is the world of objects, and this world works by the law of the annihilation of defended selves imploding with their deadly projections.

Here, Noske, Young, and I are very much in the same conversation. The notion of the "animal-industrial complex" makes it easy to discuss some of the crucial issues. The consequences of these forms of relating rest on humans and animals, but differently. At the very least, it must be admitted that "animal exploitation cannot be tolerated without damaging the principle of inter-subjectivity" (1989, 38). Here we are getting to the heart of the matter. What is inter-subjectivity between radically different kinds of subjects? The word subject is cumbersome, but so are all the alternatives, such as agent, partner, or person. How do we designate radical otherness at the heart of ethical relating? That problem is more than a human one; as we will see, it is intrinsic to the story of life on earth.

Noske's third achievement is, then, to state unequivocally that a coherent conversation between people and animals depends on our recognition of their "otherworldly" subject status. In a discussion of various concepts of culture in anthropology and biology, Noske notes that both traditions can only see animal behavior as the outcome of mechanisms. They cannot take account of animals socially constructing their worlds, much less constructing ours. Biology, in particular, does not have the methodological equipment to recognize "things socially and culturally created and which in turn shape the creators" (1989, 86).

In her final chapter, "Meeting the Other: Towards an Anthropology of Animals," Noske describes the history of Western writing about "wolf children," very young children believed to be somehow lost from human communities, raised by other social animals, and then found by people. She is interested in how to hear the stories of and about animal-adopted children. So she asks if, instead of asking if people can "deanimalize" the children by restoring, or teaching for the first time, fully human language, we can ask what kind of social thing happened when a human child acquired a specific nonhuman socialization? She imagines that the children did not become "human," but they did become social beings. Even in stories of less extreme situations, such as the tales of white, middle-class, professional homes that contain both young apes and human children, the children experience animal acculturation as well as the reverse. For Noske, these situations suggest not so much "human-animal communication" as "animal-human communication." None of the partners is the same afterwards.

Noske's fourth achievement for me was her use of Sandra Harding's *The Science Question in Feminism* to shift the focus to "the animal question in feminism" (1989, 102–16). Noske insists that some feminists' positive identification with animals, including their embracing our own femaleness, and other feminists' resistance to such supposed biological essentialism are both wrong-headed as long as the terms of the troubled relationship of "women and nature" are seen within the inherited ethnocentric subject/object frame that generates the problem of biological reductionism. Noske argues for a feminist position *vis-à-vis* animals that posits continuity, connection, and conversation, but without the frame that leads inexorably to "essentialism." "Essentialism" depends on reductive identification, rather than ethical relation, with other worlds, including with ourselves. It is the paradox of continuity *and* alien relationality that sustains the tension in Noske's book and in her approach to feminism. Once the world of subjects and objects is put into question, that paradox concerns the congeries, or curious confederacy, that is the self, as well as selves' relations with others. A promising form of life, conversation defies the autonomization of the self as well as the objectification of the other.

TRAVEL TALK

Science fiction (SF) offers a useful writing practice within which to take up Noske's arguments. Re-published in an explicitly feminist context by The Women's Press in London in 1985, *Memoirs of a Spacewoman* was the first SF novel written by Naomi Mitchison. The story of space exploration, told from the point of view of a woman xenobiologist and communications expert named Mary, was first copyrighted in 1962, when the author was sixty-three years old and in the midst of a rich career as a national and international political activist and writer. Her references in the 1960s were to a different generation of women's consideration of science and politics from that represented by her later publishers and readers. Daughter of the important British physiologist, J. S. Haldane, and sister of one of the architects of the modern evolutionary synthesis, J. B. S. Haldane, Mitchison could hardly have avoided her large concerns with forms of life. She came, in short, from the social world that produced the Darwins and the Huxleys, those familial arbiters of authoritative terran and otherworldly conversations. Sexual experimentation; political radicalism; unimpeded scientific literacy; literary self-confidence; a grand view of the universe from a rich, imperialist, intellectual culture—these were Mitchison's birthright. She wrote that legacy into her spacewoman's memoirs.

Foregrounding the problem of imperialism, which was the silent, if deeply constitutive, axis in Victorian debates on "man's place in nature," Mitchison set her xenobiologist a most interesting task: to make contact with "otherworlds," adhering to only one serious restriction in the deployment of her psychological, linguistic, physical, and technological skills—noninterference. Knowledge would not come from scientific detachment but from scientific connection. Exploring her garden of delights, spacewoman Mary had to obey only one little restriction.

"Contacts" could take any number of forms—linguistic, sexual, emotional, cognitive, mathematical, aesthetic, mechanical or, in principle, just about anything else. The novel's erotic fusions, odd couplings, and curious progeny structure both its humor and its serious side. Communication, naturally, is inherently about desire—but there's the rub. How could conversation occur, in any form, if the rule of noninterference were to be strictly interpreted? The question of power cannot be evaded, least of all in "communication": This was the moral problem for Mary's world: "Humans were beginning to run out of serious moral problems about the time that space exploration really got going" (1976, 16). But no more.

The rule of noninterference wasn't strictly interpreted, of course; so the story could continue. The delicate shades of interference turned out to be what really mattered narratively. "The difficulty seems to be that in the nursery world we take ourselves for granted as stable personalities, as completely secure. Impossible that we should ever deviate, that interference should ever be a temptation" (1976, 19). Every explorer found out otherwise rather quickly. So the imperative of noninterference constituted the law, the symbolic matrix within which subjects could be called into position for "conversation": To obey the founder's law is always impossible; that is the point of the tragicomic process of becoming a social subject webbed with others. Not to eat of the tree of life in Mitchison's book is not to know the necessary, impossible situation of the communicator's task. Communication, even with ourselves, *is* xenobiology: otherworldly conversation, terran topics, local terms, situated knowledges. "It all works out in the end. But the impact of other worlds on this apparently immovable stability comes as a surprise. Nobody enjoys their first personality changes" (1976, 19). Neither, presumably, do those with whom contact is made.

In Althusser's sense, in *Memoirs of a Spacewoman* subjects are interpellated, or hailed, into being in a world where the law is not the policeman's "Hey, you!" or the father's "Thou shalt not know," but a deceptively gentler moralist's command, "Be fruitful and multiply; join in conversation, but know that you are not the only subjects. In knowing each other, your worlds will never be the same." Interference is static, noise, interruption in communication; and yet, interference, making contact, is the implicit condition of leaving the nursery world. "Although, of course, I longed in the normal human way for exploration, I found my first world oddly disconcerting. . . . It is only in circumstances like these that we realise how much we ourselves are constructed bilaterally on either-or principles. Fish rather than echinoderms. . . . It was quite a problem to get through to those radial entities" (1976, 19, 20, 23). The subject-making action—and the moral universe—really begins once those bilateral and radial entities establish touch. And that's only the beginning: "I think about my children, but I think less about my four dear normals than I think about Viola. And I think about Ariel. And the other" (1976, 16).

THREE BILLION YEARS

But what if we went back to another beginning, to the early days of living organisms on earth a few billion years ago? That seems a good place to end this meditation on natural conversation as heterogeneous intercourse. Might those yuppie Wisconsin ducks have a legitimate queer birthright after all, and might there be a respectable material foundation to my sexual pleasure in mitochondria respiratory enzymes? Using Lynn Margulis and Dorion Sagan's *Origins of Sex: Three Billion Years of Genetic Recombination* (1986) as my guide, I will tell a very different concluding story from Cantor's version of the human genome project or corporate biotechnology's harvest of Darwinism.

As elsewhere, biology in my narrative is also a rich field of metaphors for ethno-specific cultural and political questions. My bag-lady version of Margulis and Sagan's authoritative account of the promiscuous origins of cells that have organelles[8] is about metaphor-work. Doing such work is part of my vocation to prepare for my job at the *Reader's Digest* after the revolution. I think this kind of metaphor-work could tell us something interesting about the metaphor-tools "we" (who?) might need for a usable theory of the subject at the end of the second Christian millennium.

Consider, then, the text given us by the existence, in the hindgut of a modern Australian termite, of the creature named *Mixotricha paradoxa,* a mixed-up, paradoxical, microscopic bit of "hair" (*trichos*). This little filamentous creature makes a mockery of the notion of the bounded, defended, singular self out to protect its genetic investments. The problem that our text presents is simple: what constitutes *M. paradoxa*? Where does the protist[9] stop and somebody else start in that insect's teeming hindgut? And what does this paradoxical individuality tell us about beginnings? Finally, how might such forms of life help us imagine a usable language?

M. paradoxa is a nucleated microbe with several distinct internal and external prokaryotic symbionts, including two kinds of motile spirochetes, which live in various degrees of structural and functional integration. All the associated creatures live in a kind of obligatory confederacy. From Margulis and Sagan's "symbiogenetic" point of view, this kind of confederacy is fundamental to life's history. Such associations probably arose repeatedly. The ties often involved genetic exchanges, or recombinations, that in turn had a history dating back to the earliest bacteria that had to survive the gene-damaging environment of ultraviolet light before there was an oxygen atmosphere to shield them.

> That genetic recombination began as a part of an enormous health delivery system to ancient DNA molecules is quite evident. Once healthy recombinants were produced, they retained the ability to recombine genes from different sources. As long as selection acted on the recombinants, selection pressure would retain the mechanism of re-combination as well. (Margulis and Sagan 1986, 60)

I like the idea of gene exchange as a kind of prophylaxis against sunburn. It puts the heliotropic West into perspective.

Protists like *M. paradoxa* seem to show in mid-stream the ubiquitous, life-changing association events that brought motile, oxygen-using or photosynthetic bacteria into other cells, perhaps originally on an opportunistic hunt for a nutritious meal or a secure medium for their metabolic transactions. But some predators settled down inside their prey and struck up quite a conversation. Mitochondria, those oxygen-using organelles with the interesting respiratory enzymes integrated into membrane structures, probably joined what are now modern cells in this way.

> With the elapse of time, the internal enemies of the prey evolved into microbial guests, and, finally, supportive adopted relatives. Because of a wealth of molecular biological and biochemical evidence supporting these models, the mitochondria of today are best seen as descendents of cells that evolved within other cells. (Margulis and Sagan 1986, 71)

The story of heterogeneous associations at various levels of integration repeated itself many times at many scales.

> Clones of eukaryotic cells in the form of animals, plants, fungi, and protoctists seem to share a symbiotic history . . . From an evolutionary point of view, the first eukaryotes were loose confederacies of bacteria that, with continuing integration, became recognizable as protists, unicellular eukaryotic cells . . . The earliest protists were likely to have been most like bacterial communities . . . At first each autopoietic [self-maintaining] community member replicated its DNA, divided, and remained in contact with other members in a fairly informal manner. *Informal* here refers to the number of partners in these confederacies: they varied. (Margolis and Sagan 1986, 72)

Indeed, they varied. So, speaking as a multicellular, eukaryotic, bilaterally symmetrical confederacy, a fish, in short, I want to learn to strike up interesting intercourse with possible subjects about livable worlds. In nineteenth-century bourgeois U.S. law, such sexually suspect doings were called criminal conversation. Mitchison's spacewoman understood: "Although, of course, I longed in the normal human way for exploration, I found my first world oddly disconcerting . . ."

NOTES

This essay is a meditation on three works: *Darwin's Metaphor: Nature's Place in Victorian Culture,* by Robert M. Young (Cambridge: Cambridge University Press, 1985); *Humans and Other Animals: Beyond the Boundaries of Anthropology,* by Barbara Noske (London: Pluto, 1989); and *Memoirs of a Spacewoman,* by Naomi Mitchison (London: The Women's Press, 1976 [1962]).

1. See King 1994.

2. Here I borrow from the wonderful project of the journal *Public Culture,* Bulletin of the Center for Transnational Cultural Studies, at the University of Pennsylvania. In my opinion, this journal embodies the best impulses of cultural studies. It is available from The University Museum, University of Pennsylvania, Philadelphia, PA 19104, USA.

3. See Keller 1990.

4. In his preface to the 1985 reprint of his essays, Young gives his justification for not dealing with the language of the pseudo-universal "man" in his revisions: "I cannot resolve the question of gender in these essays: 'man's place in nature' was the rhetoric of the period, and 'he' had characteristic resonances which it would be anachronistic to expunge, and this set the style" (xvii). I disagree, not with Young's decision to keep "man" and "he," but with the absence of sustained discussion of precisely what difference the "characteristic resonances" and "style" made to nineteenth-century discourse and to Young's discourse. Feminist demands are not to expunge offensive material but to require precise analysis of how the unmarked categories work—and how we continue to inherit the trouble. That analysis could not proceed if the problem were made harder to see by covering up "man" with a euphemistic and anachronistic "human." Some of Young's most important discussions, for example, in the essay on "Malthus and the evolutionists," originally published in 1969, before recent feminist theory could have made a difference, by the mid-1980s merited at least a footnote on how feminist analyses require the restructuring of historical understanding of the debates about natural theology, human perfection, and evolution. Minimally, Malthus's argument against Godwin's version of future human perfection through the complete transcendence of need, especially sex, and Malthus's doctrine on the private ownership of women and children in the institution of marriage were intrinsic to the establishment of a constitutively self-invisible masculinist discourse in natural theology.

Similarly, in "Natural Theology, Victorian Periodicals, and the Fragmentation of a Common Context," I waited for some discussion of how the processes of specialization and publication fundamentally restructured the gender fabric of the practice of evolutionary biology. The 1985 postscript to that essay might have been a place to say something about how feminist theory makes one rethink the issues of "common context" and "fragmentation." I also think Young should have revised some of his notes, especially for "The Historiographic and Ideological Contexts of the Nineteenth-century Debate on Man's Place in Nature," themselves a real treasure for which I remain in his debt politically and professionally, to take better account of feminist theory in the field. It is because his notes are otherwise so exhaustive that I am critical of the very thin attention to feminist reformulations of science studies debates (see note 174.2 on p. 273; here would have been an opportunity).

Robert Young's notes helped train me in the history of science; that's why I am disappointed in this aspect of his revisions for the 1985 book. The unexamined *commitment* to masculinism in the chief texts of the history of science to which Young reacted at Cambridge remained present in too much of the radical science movement and its literatures. The same *commitment to* masculinism is evident in the canonized texts of the current social studies of science orthodoxy, e.g., Shapin and Schaffer, *The Leviathan and the Air-Pump,* and Latour, *Science in Action.* The trouble must not be allowed to persist in the movement to address science *as* culture, in which Young is a creative leader.

5. I am indebted here to MacKinnon 1982.

6. Here I rely heavily on Carby 1987, and Spillers 1987.

7. To my mind, on this subject as elsewhere in her interesting and rich book, Noske makes sweeping generalizations and does not ask carefully enough how her claims should be limited or modified. Her discussion of the history of "objectifying" Western science is particularly stereotypical in this regard. Other discussions, like those about the history of primate behavioral studies, are much better. But these issues are quibbles in relation to the fundamental and synthetic project of her book, which remains unique in green (environmentalist), red (socialist), purple (feminist), and ultraviolet (scientific) literatures. Noske's book is firmly located in critical conversation with social movements and with natural and social sciences on the tricky problem of anthropocentrism.

8. Such cells are called eukaryotes; they have a membrane-bound nucleus and other differentiated internal structures. Prokaryotes, or bacteria, do not have a nucleus to house their genetic material, but keep their DNA naked in the cell.

9. A protist is a single-celled, eukaryotic micro-organism such as the familiar amoeba. Plants, animals, and fungi descended from such beginnings.

REFERENCES

Carby, Hazel. 1987. *Reconstructing Womanhood.* New York: Oxford University Press.

Hearne, Vicki. 1986. *Adam's Task Calling Animals by Name.* New York: Knopf.

Keller, Evelyn Fox. 1990. "From Secrets of Life to Secrets of Death." In Mary Jacobus, E. F. Keller, and Sally Shuttleworth, eds., *Body/Politics: Women and the Discourses of Science,* 177–91. New York: Routledge.

King, Katie. 1994. *Theory in Its Feminist Travels: Conversations in U.S. Women's Movements.* Bloomington: Indiana University Press.

Latour, Bruno. *Science in Action.* Cambridge, Mass.: Harvard University Press, 1987.

LeGuin, Ursula. 1989. "The Carrier-Bag Theory of Fiction." In D. du Pont, ed., *Women of Vision,* 1–11. New York: St. Martin's.

MacKinnon, Catharine. 1982. "Feminism, Marxism, Method, and the State: An Agenda for Theory." *Signs* 7.3: 515–44.

Margulis, L., and D. Sagan. 1986. *Origins of Sex: Three Billion Years of Genetic Recombination.* New Haven, Conn.: Yale University Press.

Mitchison, Naomi. 1976 [1962]. *Memoirs of a Spacewoman.* London: The Women's Press.

Noske, Barbara. 1989. *Humans and Other Animals: Beyond the Boundaries of Anthropology.* London: Pluto.

Shapin, Steve, and Simon Schaffer. *The Leviathan and the Air-Pump.* Princeton, N.J.: Princeton University Press, 1985.

Spillers, Hortense. 1987. "Mama's Baby, Papa's Maybe: An American Grammar Book." *Diacritics* 17.2: 65–81.

Young, Robert M. 1985. *Darwin's Metaphor: Nature's Place in Victorian Culture.* Cambridge: Cambridge University Press.

———. 1973. "The Historiographic and Ideological Contexts of the Nineteenth-century Debate on Man's Place in Nature." In Mikuláš Teich and Robert Young, eds., *Changing Perspectives in the History of Science: Essays in Honour of Joseph Needham.* London: Heinemann Educational.

6

VISCOUS POROSITY: WITNESSING KATRINA

Nancy Tuana

The events of August 29, 2005, have left a lasting impact on the citizens of the United States. Seeing through the eye of a Category Four hurricane has resulted in multiple destabilizations. Levees have been breached, a historic city devastated, climate change rendered not simply believable, but palpable,[1] and the face of suffering given a complexion that revealed to a shocked nation the plight of the poor and the racism that is woven into our economic structures.

As I considered the news reports of the various impacts of Katrina and thought about the city of New Orleans, I knew that I was witnessing afresh the reasons why I have, for the last two decades, been advocating that feminists—no, *all* theorists—embrace an interactionist ontology.[2] And I knew that I had to rewrite my essay for this volume, for the events unfolding in the wake of Katrina provided a trenchant illustration of the importance of embracing such an ontology and its concomitant epistemology. For in witnessing Katrina, the urgency of embracing an ontology that *rematerializes the social and takes seriously the agency of the natural* is rendered apparent.

In the course of this analysis, I will employ the conceptual metaphor of viscous porosity as a means to better understand the rich interactions between beings through which subjects are constituted out of relationality. I will demonstrate that while an interactionist ontology eschews the type of unity and continuity celebrated in traditional Western metaphysics, viscous porosity helps us understand an interactionist attention to the processes of becoming in which unity is dynamic and always interactive and agency is diffusely enacted in complex networks of relations.

Medicine, the natural sciences, and engineering are designed to provide us with knowledge about the natural world. The social sciences and humanities are designed to provide us with knowledge of the social world. While the actual workings of knowledge production in these areas are far from simple, given that various institutions that are linked to these disciplines are often committed to the maintenance of ignorance as well as to the acquisition of knowledge,[3] even this realization ignores an important gap in knowledge. As the phenomenon of Katrina's devastation has taught us all too well, the knowledge that is too often missing and is often desperately needed is at the intersection between things and people, between feats of engineering and social structures, between experiences and bodies.

In part, the problem arises from questionable ontological divisions separating the natural from the humanly constructed, the biological from the cultural, genes from their environments, the material from the semiotic.[4] We can make divisions between the biological and the social, as we feminists did with sex and gender, but what we soon discovered is that the divisions are both permeable and shifting, while at the same time deeply entrenched in bodies and practices. In "Re-Fusing Nature/Nurture" (1983) and "Fleshing Gender, Sexing the Body" (1996), I urged feminists to abandon the sex/gender dichotomy, arguing both that the nature/culture dualism that it rested on was flawed and that its use—though perhaps liberatory at a particular historical moment—was perpetuating the conceptual framework out of which sexist as well as racist practices have emerged. I argued that bodies, and sexes, are neither fixed nor inert, but fluid and emergent.

Seeing through the eyes of a Category Four hurricane impressed upon me the viscous porosity of the categories "natural," "human-made," "social," "biological." In this essay I will argue that we must attend to this porosity and to the in-between of the complex interrelations from which phenomena emerge. As I have in other publications, I will argue for an interactionist account that shifts the debates from "realism" vs. "social constructivism" to *emergent interplay,* which precludes a sharp divide between the biological and the cultural. Given an interactionist ontology, what exists are "not things made but things in the making" (James 1958, 263),[5] and differences are fluid, evolving, and contextual. Donna Haraway's invocation of "material-semiotic" (1997) is kin to this ontology, as is Andrew Pickering's notion of a "dance of agency" (1995).

Seeing through the eye of Katrina transformed an essay that was focused on women's embodiment to the embodiment of levees, hurricanes, and swamps as well as the embodiment of the women and men of New Orleans. It is thus, at the surface, a less obviously feminist materialism that I reflect in this essay, but I would argue that at the core of this essay is the centrality of an interactionist ontology as the lens through which we must be feminists and do our feminism. And it is from this perspective that I argue that feminist work must re-embrace the richly interdisciplinary origins of women's studies scholarship, for it is only through erasing the dichotomies that have been erected between the natural and the social, including the natural and the social sciences as well as the arts and the humanities, that we can craft a material feminism.

ON WHAT IS: INTERACTIONISM

Realism is a prevalent philosophical as well as "commonsense" commitment. While there are numerous philosophically nuanced accounts of realism, common tenets include both existence and independence. A realist is one who not only accepts the existence of various objects and phenomena but sees those entities as independent of human beliefs, conceptual schemes, linguistic practices, and social structures. In the commonsense terms of John Searle's *The Construction of Social Reality,* external realism is the position that "the world (or alternatively, reality or the universe) exists independently of our representations of it" (1995, 150). Searle certainly allows for entities that exist *because of* human beliefs and practices; indeed, he is known to wave about a dollar bill as a paradigmatic example. But he argues that a significant portion of what exists are mind-, culture-, language-, perception-independent entities and processes. Realism, then, is the belief that what exists is both *prior to* and *independent of* human interactions.

Versions of social constructivism have been central to many feminist analyses. Various phenomena—gender, sexuality, ability, cognitive authority—once taken to be "natural" phenomena, have been studied by feminists and shown to be socially constructed. These phenomena are fully *real* in the sense that they affect lives and have economic, social, and psychological effects, but they are not *independent* of human interactions. Indeed, they are emergent from them.

I have argued that feminists must avoid the divide of realism vs. social constructivism, for neither framework is adequate (Tuana 2001). Both are embedded in a problematic nature/culture schism that does not do justice to the complexity of interactions of phenomena. Interactionism enables us to dissolve the divisions between these two poles and transform the terms of the debate.

Interactionism acknowledges both the agency of materiality and the porosity of entities. What I have termed "interactionism" has been inspired by a Whiteheadean process metaphysic (Tuana 1983) where the basic units of existence are phenomena (rather than physical objects) that are emergent from interactions. Donna Haraway's concept of material-semiotic arose from the same Whiteheadean foundation (see Haraway 1997).[6] Interactionism is a metaphysic that removes any hard-and-fast divide between nature and culture, while at the same time troubling the division between realism and social constructivism. As I have argued elsewhere: "The world is neither 'fabricated' in the sense of created out of human cultural practices, nor is its existence independent of human interactions of a multitude of forms, including cultural." Interactionism posits "a world of complex phenomena in dynamic relationality" (2001, 238–39).

Interactionism begins with the recognition that our biological theories, not to mention other accounts of interactions between organisms and environments, too often retain a division between nature (sometimes translated as gene) and environments (be they natural or social). Despite acknowledging an interweaving of genetic and environmental factors, such accounts retain an additive model that maintains an ontological divide between the two. Such a move simply changes the question from "Which traits are due to innate factors and which to environmental factors?" to "To what extent is the trait in question due to innate factors and to what extent to environmental factors?" But the nature/culture divide remains intact.

Interactionism acknowledges the robust porosity between phenomena that destabilizes any effort to finalize a nature/culture divide. We can, and often need, to make distinctions between such poles, but it is crucial not to see these distinctions as "natural kinds" or to read them as reflecting a dualism. Adequate distinctions can be made, even distinctions between "nature" and "culture," but they are made for a particular purpose and at a particular time. In other words, we do not simply "read" such distinctions from nature, *but take epistemic responsibility*[7] *for the distinctions we employ.* As Lorraine Code as so persuasively argued, we cannot separate epistemic analysis from ethical analysis. To know well, we must be responsive to the differences articulating themselves in our experiences and practices, along with being attentive to how the distinctions we embrace, in part, construct our experiences, as well as how these distinctions are enacted in social practices, how they enable as well as limit possibilities and for whom, what they conceal as well as what they reveal, and so on. Knowledge practices themselves often involve articulations of differences, but with an interactionist understanding of these differences being fluid, unfolding, and situated, epistemic responsibility requires this enhanced responsiveness. "Knowing well is a matter both of moral-political and of epistemic concern" (Code 1991, 72).

ON WHAT IS: KATRINA

Look at Katrina. Katrina is a natural phenomenon that is what it is in part because of human social structures and practices. Seeing through the eye of Katrina reveals no hard-and-fast divide between natural and social; rather, they are seamlessly swept together in its counterclockwise rotation. Katrina came into being because of a concatenation of phenomena—low pressure areas, warm ocean waters, and perhaps swirling in that classic cyclone pattern are the phenomena of deforestation and industrialization. There is now general scientific consensus that some degree of climate change is inevitable, and the vast majority of scientists argue that the signs of anthropogenic climate change are visible—melting glaciers, rising coastlines (Oreskes 2005).

But what of Katrina? A hurricane pulls its strength from the heat of the ocean surface waters. Katrina swirled into a Category Five hurricane thanks to surface waters in the Gulf of Mexico that were two degrees warmer than normal for the time of year.[8] Does it make sense to say that the warmer water or Katrina's power were socially produced, rendering Katrina a non-natural phenomenon? No, but the problem is with the question. We cannot sift through and separate what is "natural" from what is "human-induced," and the problem here is not simply epistemic. There is scientific consensus that carbon dioxide and other greenhouse gases are raising the temperature of the Earth's atmosphere. These "natural phenomena" are the result of human activities such as fossil fuel combustion and deforestation. But these activities themselves are fueled by social beliefs and structures. In the United States we have hammered home a solid belief that economic success and independence is determined in part by access to and consumption of goods. The average household sports two vehicles, with the number of minivans and SUVs significantly rising since 1990.[9] Current projections indicate that without severe reduction in these emissions, warming will increase from 2.5°F to 10.4°F, causing serious weather-related changes that pose grave threats to biodiversity.

Katrina, then, is emblematic of the viscous porosity between humans and our environment, between social practices and natural phenomena. My point is that there is no sharp ontological divide here, but rather a complex interaction of phenomena. This does not mean that we cannot attempt to determine the extent to which human factors increased the intensity of a hurricane or some other weather-related phenomena. Indeed, issues of distributive justice may require that such a distinction be made in order to determine how to apportion responsibility across nations for harm from human-induced climate change as may be done if we adopt a "polluter-pays" principle of responsibility. Again, distinctions can be made, which is why I employ the phrase "viscous porosity" rather than "fluidity." *Viscosity* is neither fluid nor solid, but intermediate between them. Attention to the *porosity* of interactions helps to undermine the notion that distinctions, as important as they might be in particular contexts, signify a natural or unchanging boundary, a natural kind. At the same time, "viscosity" retains an emphasis on resistance to changing form, thereby a more helpful image than "fluidity," which is too likely to promote a notion of open possibilities and to overlook sites of resistance and opposition or attention to the complex ways in which material agency is often involved in interactions, including, but not limited to, human agency. To weave flesh onto these theoretical bones, let us turn to New Orleans.

ON WHAT IS: NEW ORLEANS

While it began with Katrina, attention quickly shifted to New Orleans. And if we do the same, the viability of interactionism will be further illustrated. Remember also that my intention in this essay is to argue for a return to an enriched commitment to interdisciplinarity by feminists and all theorists, for we cannot understand or live responsibly in the world we are of and in without doing so. A thesis that weaves through this essay is the importance of understanding material agency, namely, the importance of re-materializing the social as well as understanding material agency—the human as well as the more than human.

New Orleans is a city surrounded by water: the Gulf of Mexico, the Mississippi, and Lake Pontchartrain. It is a city built on land that is an average of six feet below sea level, though there are points at which the land is a staggering ten feet below sea level. New Orleans is a city that emerged out of complex interactions. Much of the city lies below the level of the river that helped to create it. The Mississippi and its coursing into the gulf was the transit by which wealth in the form of cotton, sugar, grain, and other goods was naturally carried from the North to the South, to the city that became New Orleans. This water carried wealth, but given the particulars of the land, it also carried death. Flooding has been a commonplace of the city of New Orleans, not to mention the illnesses the swampy land bred, and efforts to control the water were equally commonplace.

A city is a complex material-semiotic interaction, and New Orleans rests at the heart of multiple interactions. Consider the levees, which have emerged from the interaction of social and material forces. The city sits on the banks of the Mississippi, where sediment from the river had created areas of elevated land called "natural levees." New Orleans' earliest buildings sat on top of these levees, but as the population grew, houses were built farther inland at lower elevations. To create usable land, water had to be pumped out of the area, which in turn caused the ground to sink even lower. *The levees transform the local geology and hydrology, and are in turn shaped by them. But the local geology and hydrology also emerge from complex social vectors.* Without the U.S. Army Corp of Engineers, which has been building levees along the Mississippi River for two centuries, neither New Orleans nor the Mississippi would be what they are today.

But before turning to the extensive levee system that makes New Orleans what it is today, it is important to understand that not all the reclaimed land of the area was crafted through engineering technologies. I pick this complex interaction as a reminder, a caution to avoid positing an Edenic time before colonialization and industrialization and against the persistent myth of passive indigenous peoples who simply lived in but did not transform "nature." The peoples who lived in the area that was to become New Orleans actively shaped its land. The land was rich in resources, including shellfish, which was such a prevalent food source that shell middens or debris mounds accumulated. From these emerged a new ecozone in the marsh, a clear material-semiotic interaction. The middens contributed to the emergence of significantly different plants and distributions of plants in the marshes as well as providing the dry land needed for human habitation (see Kidder 2000). Indeed, the cypress trees that are the hallmark of the eastern marshes took root because of the middens, as did the oak trees that lent their name to the islands. And it was the economic promise of these oak stands that, in the eighteenth century, attracted colonists. These same middens would be the literal foundation of building in New Orleans as the contents of middens were used to create the material of houses or the lime that plastered the walls of the buildings of the emerging city.

As is often the case, human agency, though not always intention, is knit together with more-than-human agency. Human consumption and refuse practices resulted in material-semiotic interactions that altered flora habitats, which in turn altered human interests. Material-semiotic. The point is that material agency in its heterogeneous forms, including irreducibly diverse forms of distinctively human agency, interact in complex ways. Agency in all these instances emerges out of such interactions; it is not antecedent to them. Our epistemic practices must thus be attuned to this manifold agency and emergent interplay, which means we cannot be epistemically responsible and divide the humanities from the sciences, or the study of culture from the study of nature.

We often view nature as subdued through technology, the story of human agency affecting the natural order. But we forget to reverse the interaction for the Mississippi and Katrina—and those shell middens have agency too, an agency that influences the so-called natural and social order. And as we make pragmatic divisions between what is natural and what is social, as I have here, it behooves us to remember the viscous porosity between these phenomena, a porosity that undermines any effort to make an ontological division into kinds—natural and cultural—where the edges are clean and the interactions at best additive.

Go back to the levees. The levee system has been shaped by numerous forces—technology, economics, weather, sedimentation patterns, the Mississippi River, to name a few. A 1947 hurricane that caused 100 million dollars in damage gave rise to hurricane protection levees along Lake Pontchartrain's south shore. Another deadly hurricane in 1965 caused the Orleans Levee Board to raise existing levees to a height of 12 feet. We knew that those levees and floodwalls were not designed to provide protection from a Category Four or Five hurricane storm damage. Numerous studies that had been conducted had concluded that a hurricane of this force could result in levee breaches that would put the city underwater. Even a 2001 FEMA report (the Federal Emergency Management Agency at the Department of Homeland Security) warned that a hurricane flood of New Orleans was one of three most likely disasters to strike the United States in the near future.[10]

But levees and flood walls are expensive. *New Orleans CityBusiness* reported in June of 2005 that federal funding for the U.S. Army Corp of Engineers projects in New Orleans would be reduced by $71.2 million, shelving a study to determine ways to protect the region from a Category Five hurricane. State Senator Mary Landriew was quoted as saying that the Bush administration was not making the Corps of Engineers funding a priority. Katrina is shifting those priorities in unpredictable ways.

Part of the psychology of living in New Orleans, a city in which there are points at which cargo boats on the river are sailing on water levels significantly *higher* than street level, is believing that human agency will win out over other forms of material agency. That belief was not warranted, but it made living below sea level palatable. One had only to read the numerous scientific studies produced by the Army Corps of Engineers that provided computer simulations predicting the devastation. But denial is a powerful force. Even President Bush and Michael Chertoff, Secretary of the U.S. Department of Homeland Security, practiced it. In an interview with Diane Sawyers on *Good Morning America* on September 1, 2005, Bush claimed that he did not think that anyone could have anticipated the breach of the levees. And Chertoff justified the slow disaster response rate as being due to what he called the "second catastrophe," namely the breach of the levees "really [catching] everybody by surprise."[11] Denial indeed functions in complex ways.

One need not practice this type of denial to live below sea level. Approximately 27 percent of the Netherlands is below sea level, an area that supports over 60 percent of the country's population of almost sixteen million people. After a serious flood in 1953, the Netherlands inaugurated the Delta Commission to set up a system of dykes, dams, and other structures that are built to provide flood safety at a far higher storm level than the New Orleans system. While no technology is foolproof, the confidence of New Orleanians prior to Katrina had to be based either on denial or on ignorance, whereas the confidence of Netherlanders has a more solid foundation. This is not to say that there is no denial at work even in the Netherlands, for to wall off major sea arms means destroying ecosystems and losing coastline (almost 400 miles of coastline in this case). Living below sea level can be done, but it requires what Andrew Pickering calls a "dance of agency" between the human agents—the engineers—and the nonhuman agents—the sea.[12]

ON WHAT IS: PLASTIC FLESH

The dance of agency between human and nonhuman agents also happens at a more intimate level. The boundaries between our flesh and the flesh of the world we are of and in is porous. While that porosity is what allows us to flourish—as we breathe in the oxygen we need to survive and metabolize the nutrients out of which our flesh emerges—this porosity often does not discriminate against that which can kill us. We cannot survive without water and food, but their viscous porosity often binds itself to strange and toxic bedfellows.

Katrina's wake left New Orleans flooded with what headlines called a "toxic soup." There are five superfund toxic waste sites in and around New Orleans, all of which were compromised by Katrina's flooding. There are even more superfund sites in Louisiana and Mississippi that were in the path of Katrina's wake. These sites contain a range of contaminants, but the most common are barium, which can damage the heart, liver, and kidney; polycyclic aromatic hydrocarbons, which are carcinogens and can impair immune systems; and benzene, which causes cancer and damage to bone marrow. As I type these words, most official reports indicate that the sites have not been damaged, but there are unofficial reports of disturbed caps at some sites and general worries that floodwaters seeping into contaminated soil may be spreading toxic chemicals or leaching them into groundwater.

While Katrina may have compounded the problem, any effort to witness Katrina cannot ignore the fact that toxic wastes have been a long-standing concern in New Orleans. More than 130 petroleum and chemical plants dot the Mississippi River from Baton Rouge to New

Orleans. According to Barbara Allen, "the chemical industry in Louisiana annually reports the equivalent of sixteen thousand pounds of hazardous waste for every citizen in the state," the equivalent of "12.5% of all hazardous waste reported nationally" (2003, 1). While there are many types of industries clustered along this corridor, a region which has come to be known as "cancer alley," I will focus on the plastics industry to provide an illustration of a complex material-semiotic interaction, an interaction that permeates flesh.

Gerald Markowitz and David Rosner, in *Deceit and Denial: The Deadly Politics of Industrial Pollution,* trace material-semiotic factors that led to the U.S. plastics industry relocating many of its plants to the South, and in particular to the region known as cancer alley. Markowitz and Rosner argue that understanding the reasons for these moves requires numerous perspectives—from the geography of Louisiana to the psychology of Louisiana's legislature—again the importance of addressing questions through an interdisciplinary lens. The Mississippi and the port in New Orleans provided transportation options. Louisiana's salt deposits provided a resource needed for plastics production. Louisiana's governmental structure promised fewer environmental regulations, and its seeming acceptance of corruption suggested a "flexibility" the industries found attractive.[13] The plastics factories settled in, as did the pollution of their products.

Polyvinyl chloride (PVC) is an inexpensive and, when combined with plasticizers, a highly malleable material that has a manifold of uses. Medical equipment, coke bottles, children's toys, food wraps, siding for houses, credit cards, water pipes—even the chairs we sit on and floors we walk on—came to be made of it. Look around you at home and at work; you are likely to be surrounded by it. The complex material-semiotic interactions that resulted from PVC replacing materials like glass, wood, and metal are a complex and interesting story, but not the one that interests me here. For this commonly found substance has not only transformed our lives, it has transformed our flesh. That is the interaction that interests me here.

There is a viscous porosity of flesh—my flesh and the flesh of the world. This porosity is a hinge through which we are of and in the world. I refer to it as viscous, for there are membranes that effect the interactions. These membranes are of various types—skin and flesh, prejudgments and symbolic imaginaries, habits and embodiments. They serve as the mediators of interaction. My interest in the story of PVC has to do with skin and flesh.

PVCs are produced by running an electrical current through salty brine in the presence of a catalyst, which is sometimes mercury. A series of interactions occur at the molecular level from which chlorine, sodium hydroxide, and hydrogen are produced. And when the catalyst is mercury, there is mercury released, perhaps as emissions. But that is another story of interactions. The chlorine is then mixed with carbon to form ethylene dichloride, from which vinyl chloride monomer is synthesized. This is polymerized to create PVC, which is often made softer and more flexible by additions of plasticizers, typically phthalates.

There are numerous studies linking cancer threats to PVC production. Studies of workers in industries that produce PVC have shown significantly increased mortality from cancer deaths, including lung cancer, angiosarcoma (liver cancer), and leukemia. One source of the problem may be the plasticizers. Phthalates have been shown to be endocrine disruptors, mimicking hormonal action in animal studies. Studies of the effects of vinyl chloride, polyvinyl chloride, and phthalates have documented damage to liver (Wong et al. 2002), kidneys (Maltoni and Lefemine 1975), lungs (Mastrangelo et al. 2003, Suzuki 1981), and brain (Tabershaw and Gaffey 1974, Wong et al. 1991). They are both genotoxic and carcinogenic, causing a wide spectrum of tumors in various animal species. The plastics industry continues to insist that humans are exposed to such small amounts of phthalates that they pose no significant risk.

The viscous porosity of entities and the interactions out of which phenomena emerge are well illustrated by this example. Beginning at the molecular level, we know that phthalates and vinyl chloride affects, in the human and also in nonhuman animal bodies, a complex interaction that can result in cancer. Workers inhale PVC dust, and those who live by incinerators inhale it as plastics are burned.[14] The viscous porosity of our bodies and that of PVC allow for an exchange of molecules, where PVC and phthalates pass through the porosity of skin and flesh, particularly the mucosal linings of our intestines and our lungs. Plastic becomes flesh.

The molecules that mix with our flesh are endocrine disrupters that mimic, enhance, or inhibit a hormonal action. They function as chemical messengers, traveling through our blood until they hit an appropriate target—a lung, our liver. When such a molecule hits such an organ, it interacts with a receptor, which "recognizes" the molecule as a hormonal component. It then either passes through the membrane into the cell to interact with the DNA or RNA of the cell to either turn on or turn off a genetic process, or it releases a molecule that is part of the receptor that does the same thing. That interaction can lead to cancer.

Young children are at greater risk. Their organs and nervous system are still developing during the first year of life. Their ability to metabolize, detoxify, and excrete toxins is often less developed than that of adults, and their nervous systems are less capable of repairing damage. The viscous porosity of breast milk has been the subject of attention of the ecologist Sandra Steingraber. "When it comes to the production, use, and disposal of PVC, the breasts of breast-feeding mothers are the tailpipe," writes Steingraber (1999, 363), for of all human foods, breast milk is the most contaminated. Burning PVC creates dioxin, a known human carcinogen. It is lipophilic, concentrated in fat, so breast milk concentrates the levels of dioxin and other toxic residues. As Steingraber explains,

> This is why a breast-fed infant receives its so-called "safe" lifetime limit of dioxin in the first six months of drinking breast milk. Study after study also shows that the concentration of carcinogens in human breast milk declines steadily as nursing continues. Thus the protective effect of breast feeding on the mother appears to be a direct result of downloading a lifelong burden of carcinogens from her breasts into the tiny body of her infant. (1999, 363)

Plastic flesh.

The viscous porosity of bodies belies any effort to identify a "natural" divide between nature/culture. When I drink coke out of a plastic bottle, I have been taught to think of myself as a natural being and the bottle as a cultural artifact, a product of technology. The bottle is made of naturally occurring materials but is constructed by humans to be a different material or structure than what occurs in nature. Now incinerate that bottle and breathe deeply. The components of the bottle have an agency that transforms that naturally occurring flesh of my body into a different material or structure than what occurs in nature. The parts of the plastic become as much a part of my flesh as parts of the coke that I drank. Once the molecular interaction occurs, there is no divide between nature/culture, natural/artificial. These distinctions, while at times useful, are metaphysically problematic, for there are important migrations between and across these divides that can be occluded by efforts to posit a dualism.

I pointed to Haraway's figure of OncoMouse™ in my earlier work as emblematic of a culturally constructed natural being, a site where the nature/culture divide dissolves (Haraway 1997, Tuana 2001). But the bodies of the plastics industry workers—indeed, my body, your body—are similarly emblematic of a divide that is richly porous, and one that we ignore only at our own peril. OncoMouse™ is a transgenic research mouse, which has been materially refigured by technology to contain an oncogene, a transplanted, human tumor–producing gene, the gene that produces breast cancer. While her material reconfiguration was intentional, it reflects the flesh of workers in the plastics factories along that stretch of the Mississippi dubbed cancer alley. The cancers that emerged from their flesh were also the results of material-semiotic interactions: industries choosing Louisiana because of corrupt politicians (Markowitz and Rosner 2002); the complex interactions of endocrine disruptors; industries like Dow and B. F. Goodrich suppressing and misrepresenting data (Sass, Castleman, and Wallinga 2005); the complex ways the products used to create plastics leach into groundwater, contaminate soil, and become part of the flesh of the food that we eat; the process by which chemical industry employees and consultants serve as external peer reviewers of EPA assessments of the risks of vinyl chloride (Sass, Castleman, and Wallinga 2005); the practices we use to "dispose" of PVC, including incineration, which releases toxins to air and soil, to name a few. We do not need a transgenic animal to make us aware of the porosity of distinctions we make between nature and culture, or to remind us of the robust interrelationality of material agency.

This example also illuminates the significance, the urgency, of rematerializing the social in all its meanings. The plastics industries have the material resources to lobby Congress and ensure that their representatives serve as reviewers of EPA studies. And we can trace the interaction of poverty as we map the location of industries and the neighborhoods of the poor and recognize that health disparities are not due only to inequitable access to health care, but to environmental racism and classism. Political failures to address the environmental hazards of plastics have left their signature on the flesh of many bodies, but the bodies of industry workers who toil in the plastics factories or the garbage incinerators and the bodies of those who live in the path of their pollutants have disproportionately suffered the negative effects of this material-semiotic interaction.

WITNESSING KATRINA: MATERIALIZING IGNORANCE

Poverty leaves its effect in the bodies and psyches of those it touches. This material-semiotic interaction should come as no surprise to anyone. Grow up without proper nutrition, and physiological development will be affected. Grow up without educational resources, and cognitive development will be affected. Grow up living the effects of institutionalized racism, and trust in those institutions will be affected.

But the poverty that Katrina forced us to witness came as a "shock" to the nation as it watched news coverage of Katrina's wake. This serves as an interesting lens for considering some of the ways that ignorance is materialized, and the various institutions and motives that have a stake in the production and maintenance of ignorance. Consider just a few representative headlines and news reports:

> "Katrina Pushes Issues of Race and Poverty at Bush" (*Washington Post*, September 15). "Katrina Uncovers Poverty States Away" (*The Guardian*, Detroit, Mich., October 18).

> In the last twenty years, nothing has put grinding American poverty on display like Hurricane Katrina. The powerful Gulf Coast storm ripped the lid off an issue many Americans liked to think was behind us.
>
> The stark images from New Orleans and the Gulf proved it isn't. Two weeks after Katrina hit—and under the glare of world shock and dismay—President Bush stood in the French Quarter, acknowledged "deep, persistent poverty" with "a history in racial discrimination," and promised "bold action." (Ashbrook 2005)

This ignorance and the wrenching out of ignorance caused by the news coverage of Katrina were discussed in *Newsweek*'s September 19 issue:

> It takes a hurricane. It takes a catastrophe like Katrina to strip away the old evasions, hypocrisies and not-so-benign neglect. It takes the sight of the United States with a big black eye—visible around the world—to help the rest of us begin to see again. For the moment, at least, Americans are ready to fix their restless gaze on enduring problems of poverty, race and class that have escaped their attention. Does this mean a new war on poverty? No, especially with Katrina's gargantuan price tag. But this disaster may offer a chance to start a skirmish, or at least make Washington think harder about why part of the richest country on earth looks like the Third World. (Alter 2005)

That some U.S. citizens were shocked by the poverty they witnessed provides additional support for what Charles Mills called an epistemology of ignorance.[15] "On matters related to race, the Racial Contract prescribes for its signatories an inverted epistemology, an epistemology of ignorance, a particular pattern of localized and global cognitive dysfunctions (which are psychologically and socially functional), producing the ironic outcome that whites will in general be unable to understand the world they themselves have made" (1997, 18). If we are to fully understand the complex practices of knowledge production and the variety of factors that account for why something is known, we must also understand the practices that account for *not* knowing, that is, for our *lack* of knowledge about a phenomenon. Epistemic responsibility requires that we attempt to understand the interactions that result in the poverty that is woven into the lives of so many in New Orleans, or any major U.S. city, *being well-known, but ignored or rationalized.*

In New Orleans, as with other U.S. cities, poverty and racism interact. Sixty-seven percent of New Orleans' residents are black, and about half of them are poor. According to the 1999 Census, 27.9 percent of people in New Orleans live below the poverty line. In New Orleans, 38 percent of children live in poverty compared to 17 percent average in the United States. And those children are likely to be black. In Louisiana, 44 percent of black children live in poor families, while 9 percent of white children live in poor families. Just to get a sense of what it means, materially, to be poor, the federal poverty level is $16,090 for a family of three and $19,350 for a family of four.

Katrina interacted with poverty in relatively predictable ways. The poor are less likely to be able to evacuate. They are less likely to have the cash needed to leave and to live elsewhere. And when displaced, as thousands of New Orleanians have been, they have fewer marketable skills, financial resources to cushion them, and so forth, and hence fewer options. The interactions we saw on the news were mainly material—people dying in nursing homes or crowded into a dark, hot stadium with few resources. But Katrina also stirred up psychic interactions. For example, many Lower Ninth Ward residents who were interviewed by *The NewStandard* (October 17, 2005) said "they believed the levees had been intentionally destroyed—either by dynamite, barges or neglect—in order to divert flood waters from richer neighborhoods" (Azulay 2005) and attributed this belief to the memory that the government blew up a levee in 1927 to save parts of New Orleans at the expense of poorer areas.

During a devastating flood in 1927, a decision was made to have the U.S. Army Corps of Engineers dynamite a section of the levee. The Poydras levee at Caernarvon was dynamited, flooding the St. Bernard Parish wetlands, home of a relatively poor, working class community of farmers, fishers, and trappers.[16] While those displaced by this action were promised compensation, the city's Reparation Committee enacted rules that would result in far less monetary compensation than residents deemed appropriate. According to Gary Gomez, this led to "resentment against the 'rich neighbor' that had singled out their lands for sacrifice [that] lingered for decades" (2000, 120).

Seventy-eight years later, the memory of the bombing of the levee intersected in complex ways with memories of overt and legally sanctioned racism and segregation, memories and lived experiences of environmental racism (Allen 2003), and the like, which gave rise to a plausible suspicion that the government would once again sacrifice a levee in a black neighborhood to protect a white neighborhood. As explained by *Washington Post* reporter Eugene Robinson in a September 18 interview on *Meet the Press,*

> I was stunned in New Orleans at how many black New Orleanians would tell me with real conviction that somehow the levee breaks had been engineered in order to save the French Quarter and the Garden District at the expense of the Lower Ninth Ward, which is almost all black. You know, I don't for a minute think the Corps of Engineers or the city of New Orleans would be clever enough to do that at this point. But these are not wild-eyed people. These are reasonable, sober people who really believe that. And that tells you something about our racial divide in New Orleans.

When institutions prove themselves time and time again to be untrustworthy, it shifts the burden of proof, and "reasonable and sober people" will believe that poverty and race were again the fulcrum of unjust actions. Grow up living the effects of institutionalized racism and trust in those institutions will be affected.

The dance of agency to which Pickering urges us to attend can only be seen and understood if we understand the rich interactions between organisms and environments in all their complexities. Katrina, herself an interaction between what we have labeled the "social" and the "natural," flooded us with thousands of interactions—just a few of which I've attempted to document here. What caught our attention on the nightly news—those of us who were not in New Orleans, that is—was the heartrending impact of being poor and being in the middle of a disaster. Witnessing children and adults, the firm and the infirm, struggling to stay afloat, at first literally, and later regarding finding adequate food, water, shelter, we watched a complex interaction between social structures—class, governmental emergency reactions, and so forth—and thousands of humans and nonhuman animals.

The U.S. poverty rate of about 13 percent is the highest in the developed world and twice as high as the rate in other industrialized countries. Feminists and other theorists have developed careful investigations of the complex of interactions—material, social, psychic—that keep these figures so high.[17] But what was equally surprising about Katrina is that while it "blew the roof off" of efforts to ignore poverty, it had no comparable impact on our social understanding of the material interactions of disability. Materializing ignorance.

CNN's "Death and Despair" showed graphic pictures of New Orleans after the storm. Despite pictures of victims of nursing homes and the numerous pictures of dead people in wheelchairs making the face of disability painfully visible, *it was not seen* amidst the storm. While headlines screamed the impact of poverty and of race on those who could not evacuate New Orleans, no headlines decried the plight of those with a disability, a far greater number of whom live below poverty than any other group of individuals and whose ability to evacuate is limited not only by financial materiality but may also be affected by their embodied materiality. As hard as it is for someone with limited financial resources to evacuate, that difficulty increases exponentially if the individual with limited financial resources has limited physical mobility.

Poverty and disability are strongly linked, and in both directions. Disability can link to poverty if the disabled individual is denied access to economic opportunities and if appropriate accommodations are not made. The U.S. Census Survey of Income and Program Participation showed that 28 percent of adults ages 25 to 64 with a severe disability lived in poverty, compared with 8.3 percent for the general population of adults aged 25 to 64. Poverty can also be a cause of disability. Inequitable access to health care, dangerous living conditions, environmental racism and classism, and malnutrition can all lead to disability. Data derived from the National Health Interview Survey, which was conducted by the National Center for Health Statistics, indicated a 1 percent increase in the rate of childhood disability between 1983 and 1996, with the increase due to children living in poverty.

The 2000 Census reported 23 percent of New Orleanians as having a disability. That is 23 percent of 484,000 people. Add to this the number of individuals who were seriously ill when the hurricane struck or who needed medications to stay well, medications that were made inaccessible by the storm, and you have a clearer answer to why so many people did not, no, could not, evacuate New Orleans. Some people were not physically able to move or be moved. Materiality.

But while the U.S. news reports responded to Katrina by decrying the impact of poverty on the lives of U.S. citizens, few even noted the impact of disability, despite its "visibility" all around them. Michael Bérubé explained:

> But even as we watched the stunning spectacle of people dying of starvation and thirst in the streets of an American city that seemed to have been abandoned by every form of government, I was struck time and again at the fact that while race had become "visible," disability had not—even though we were watching the deaths of so many people with disabilities. . . . It is not that their disabilities were invisible; paradoxically, it was quite the contrary. Who among us can forget that iconic image of the dead woman in the wheelchair outside the Superdome, covered only in a blanket? That might well have been the very symbol of Katrina's devastation in New Orleans, the wheelchair—not the woman, who was not visible, but the wheelchair itself. For if you used a wheelchair, and you lived in New Orleans in late August, you were very likely subject to something I will not hesitate to call terror. (2005)

As politicians decried individuals who "refused" to evacuate New Orleans, they rendered invisible the large number of people who could not leave.

In this section I have tried to gesture at just a few of the forms of ignorance that circulated in the eye of Katrina. Its devastation gave witness to poverty and lingering racism, and to the power of ignorance.

VISCOUS POROSITY: WHAT MIGHT YET BE

So what is at stake? The separation of nature and culture has impoverished our knowledge practices. We posit a reasonably predictable natural world and a far less law-governed social realm. The natural sciences emerged from this model of the natural, divorced from the social. The humanities and the social sciences have focused on the social divorced from the natural—representations, meanings, and institutions. But the world in which we live cannot be divided in this way into two neat and tidy piles. In the words of Andrew Pickering, we live "in the thick of things" (2001). Witnessing the world through the eyes of Katrina reveals that the social and the natural, nature and culture, the real and the constructed, are not dualisms we can responsibly embrace. In more ways than I can demarcate in this essay, it is the *interaction* between them that is the world that we know and are of.

Interactionism. It is easier to posit an ontology than to practice it. It is easy to point out that dividing up the academy between the natural sciences oriented toward studying the natural apart from the social and the humanities and social sciences oriented toward studying the social apart from the natural is a stultifying idea. But despite years of efforts geared at cultivating and practicing interdisciplinarity, we seem at a loss of how to proceed. There are various reasons for this. The academy, granting agencies, and publishing houses all contribute to this separation. But effective interdisciplinary research is difficult and time-consuming. For those of us who are women's studies scholars and have battled to be taken seriously in institutions that do not value interdisciplinary work, perhaps it is no surprise that our scholarship has become increasingly disciplinary.

My witnessing of Katrina is a call to transform feminist theory and practice by abandoning all traces of ontological divides between nature and culture. It is a plea to better understand our being in the world. The viscous porosity I have asked you to attend to involves recognizing the interaction of nature-culture, genes-environment in all phenomena, not just the phenomena of sex or of race. As important as it is to make the case that categories of race or distinctions between sex and gender are actually reinforcing sexist and racist practices and impeding efforts to truly understand these phenomena, our efforts are more likely to be ineffectual if we treat race or sex as somehow different than other phenomena, even unintentionally by only attending to them. Nature/culture is a problematic ontology—not just for the human world, but for what is, as well as what might yet be.

Attention to the viscous porosity of phenomena provides a Copernican revolution that will serve to protect our work against the charge of biological essentialism. Interactionism not only allows but compels us to speak of the biological aspects of phenomena without importing the mistaken notion that this biological component exists somehow independent of, or prior to, cultures and environments. It serves as witness to the materiality of the social and the agency of the natural.

NOTES

My work on this paper has been greatly enriched by very helpful comments from Stacy Alaimo, Vincent Colapietro, and Susan Hekman.

1. *Time*'s cover story on October 3, 2005, was "Are We Making Hurricanes Worse? The Impact of Global Warming; The Cost of Coastal Development" (Kluger 2005).

2. My first foray into developing this ontology concerned the sex/gender distinction, which I first attempted to trouble from an ontological perspective in 1983 in my essay "Re-Fusing Nature/Nurture." More recent versions of this ontology have been the subject of "Fleshing Gender, Sexing the Body" (1996) and of "Material Locations" (2001).

3. For an overview of aspects of epistemologies, see my "Speculum of Ignorance" (forthcoming).

4. Each of these divisions, and others, have significance in different domains and in different disciplines. While a longer study would be needed to trace the similarities and divisions of these divides, at this point I can only urge the reader to consider how such divisions have functioned in different historical periods and in different contexts.

5. In using the term "interaction" I also hope to create a bridge to the pragmatist tradition of John Dewey, for the notion of interaction was a central tenet of his thesis that logic is naturalistic, not in the sense of being *reducible* to natural objects, but as emergent from the interactions of intra-organic and extra-organic energies, where no sharp divide is created between the biological and the cultural.

6. Karen Barad's attention to phenomena as material-discursive is another iteration of this thesis, although she traces the genesis of her position to the work of Neils Bohr, a genealogy that helps to account for her attention to measurement in the context of scientific practice. She argues for a form of realism that she labels "agential realism" (Barad 1996).

7. Code coined this phrase in her book of the same name, *Epistemic Responsibility,* but has over the years refined and developed this concept significantly. See, in particular, Code 1991 and forthcoming.

8. NOAA reported in 2000 that ocean waters had warmed to a depth of two miles in five years. These findings were reported in *Science* (Levitus et al. 2000). The scientists who reported these findings argued that the world ocean warming is probably caused by a combination of natural variability and human-induced effects.

9. Energy Information Administration, "Household Vehicles Energy Use: Latest Data and Trends," http://www.eia.doe.gov/.

10. The other two disasters were an earthquake in California and a terrorist strike in Manhattan.

11. "Well, I think if you look at what actually happened, I remember on Tuesday morning picking up newspapers and I saw headlines, 'New Orleans Dodged The Bullet,' because if you recall the storm moved to the east and then continued on and appeared to pass with considerable damage but nothing worse. It was on Tuesday that the levee—may have been overnight Monday to Tuesday—that the levee started to break. And it was midday Tuesday that I became aware of the fact that there was no possibility of plugging the gap and that essentially the lake was going to start to drain into the city. I think that second catastrophe really caught everybody by surprise. In fact, I think that's one of the reasons people didn't continue to leave after the hurricane had passed initially. So this was clearly an unprecedented catastrophe. And I think it caused a tremendous dislocation in the response effort and, in fact, in our ability to get materials to people." Michael Chertoff in a *Meet the Press* interview with Tim Russert, September 4, 2005. http://www.msnbc.msn.com/id/9179790/.

12. Pickering's *The Mangle of Practice* provides a helpful model of the dance of material agency, in which agency is often, but not always, human agency. His more recent work (see, e.g., "Asian Eels and Global Warming") extends this work to develop what he calls a posthumanist alternative to realism/social constructivism that emphasizes the coupled becomings of humanity and the environment, arguing that traditional disciplines necessarily obscure such "heterogeneous assemblages" (2005, 34).

13. Markowitz and Rosner (2002) point to the corruption of Louisiana's governor Huey Long as well as to a series of elected officials who were convicted of felonies and to a general lack of governmental oversight and potential for bribery.

14. There are other potential sources of this interaction: leaching from plastics into foods when foods are stored in plastic or food is microwaved in plastic containers, groundwater contamination, eating the flesh of animals who have been exposed through their food or water, among others.

15. Epistemologies of ignorance are extensively developed in Tuana and Sullivan 2006 and Sullivan and Tuana 2006.

16. For additional information on this event, see Barry 1998. This is also discussed in Gomez 2000.

17. See, for example, Amott 1993; Rank 2004; Ward 1990.

REFERENCES

Allen, Barbara. 2003. *Uneasy Alchemy: Citizens and Experts in Louisiana's Chemical Corridor Disputes.* Cambridge: MIT Press.

Alter, Jonathan. 2005. "The Other American." *Newsweek,* September 19.

Amott, Teresa. 1993. *Caught in the Crisis: Women and the U.S. Economy.* New York: Monthly Review Press.

Ashbrook, Tom. 2005. "Post-Katrina Anti-Poverty Agenda." *On Point,* October 18, 2005.

Azulay, Jessica. 2005. "Some Neighborhoods Rebuilt, But Part of Lower 9th Remains Off-limits." *NewStandard,* October 17, 2005, http://newstandard news.net.

Barad, Karen. 1996. "Meeting the Universe Halfway: Realism and Social Constructivism without Contradiction." In *Feminism, Science and the Philosophy of Science,* ed. Jack Nelson and Lynn Hankinson Nelson. Dordrecht: Kluwer.

Barry, John. 1998. *Rising Tide: The Great Mississippi Flood of 1927 and How It Changed America.* New York: Simon and Schuster.

Bérubé, Michael. 2005. "Disability and Disasters." Paper read to the Pennsylvania Association of Rehabilitation Facilities, September 28, 2005 (portions of which are reproduced on his blog at http://www.michaelberube.com/index.php).

Code, Lorraine. 1987. *Epistemic Responsibility.* Hanover, N.H.: University Press of New England.

———. 1991. *What Can She Know? Feminist Theory and the Construction of Knowledge.* Ithaca, N.Y.: Cornell University Press

———. 2006. *Ecological Thinking: The Politics of Epistemic Location.* New York: Oxford University Press.

Colton, Craig E. 2005. *An Unnatural Metropolis: Wrestling New Orleans from Nature.* Baton Rouge: Louisiana State University Press.

Gomez, Gay M. 2000. "Perspective, Power, and Priorities: New Orleans and the Mississippi River Flood of 1927." In *Transforming New Orleans and Its Environs: Centuries of Change,* ed. Craig E. Colton. Pittsburgh: University of Pittsburgh Press.

Haraway, Donna. 1997. *Modest_Witness@Second_Millennium.FemaleMan©_Meets_OncoMouse™: Feminism and Technoscience.* New York: Routledge.

James, William. 1958. *Essays in Radical Empiricism: A Plural Universe.* New York: Longmans, Green.

Kidder, Tristram R. 2000. "Making the City Inevitable: Native Americans and the Geography of New Orleans." In *Transforming New Orleans and Its Environs: Centuries of Change,* ed. Craig E. Colton. Pittsburgh: University of Pittsburgh Press.

Kluger, Jeffrey. 2005. "Global Warming: The Culprit? Evidence Mounts that Human Activity Is Helping Fuel These Monster Hurricanes." *Time,* October 3, 2005.

Levitus, Sydney, John I. Antonov, Timothy P. Boyer, and Cathy Stephens. 2000. "Warming of the World Ocean." *Science* 24 (March): vol. 287, no. 5461: 2225–29.

Maltoni, C., and G. Lefemine. 1975. "Carcinogenicity Bioassays of Vinyl Chloride: Current Results." *Annals of the New York Academy of Science* 246: 195–218.

Markowitz, Gerald, and David Rosner. 2002. *Deceit and Denial: The Deadly Politics of Industrial Pollution.* Berkeley: University of California Press.

Mastrangelo, G., U. Fedeli, El Fadda, G. Milan, A. Turato, and S. Pavanello. 2003. "Lung Cancer Risk in Workers Exposed to Poly(Vinyl Chloride) Dust: A Nested Case-Referent Study." *Occupational and Environmental Medicine* 60: 423–28.

Mills, Charles S. 1997. *The Racial Contract.* Ithaca, N.Y.: Cornell University Press.

New Orleans CityBusiness. 2005. "Contractors Feel Squeeze from Federal Budget." June 13.

Oreskes, Naomi. 2004. "Beyond the Ivory Tower: The Scientific Consensus on Climate Change." *Science* 3 (December): vol. 306, no. 5702: 1686.

Pickering, Andrew. 1995. *The Mangle of Practice: Time, Agency, and Science.* Chicago: University of Chicago Press.

———. 2005. "Asian Eels and Global Warming: A Posthumanist Perspective on Society and the Environment." *Ethics and the Environment* 10.2: 29–43.

———. 2001. "In the Thick of Things." Keynote address for Taking Nature Seriously conference, University of Oregon, February.

Rank, Mark Robert. 2004. *One Nation, Underprivileged: Why American Poverty Affects Us All.* Oxford: Oxford University Press.

Robinson, Eugene. 2005. Interview Transcript. *Meet the Press.* September 18, 2005. NBC, http://www.msnbc.msn.com/id/9327333/.

Sass, Jennifer Beth, Barry Castleman, and David Wallinga. 2005. "Vinyl Chloride: A Case Study of Data Suppression and Misrepresentation." *Environmental Health Perspectives* 113.7: 809–812.

Searle, John R. 1995. *The Construction of Social Reality.* New York: Free Press.

Steingraber, Sandra. 1999. "Why the Precautionary Principle? A Meditation on Polyvinyl Chloride (PVC) and the Breasts of Mothers." In *Protecting Public Health and the Environment: Implementing the Precautionary Principle,* ed. Carolyn Raffensperger and Joel Tickner. Washington, D.C.: Island Press.

Sullivan, Shannon, and Nancy Tuana. 2006. *Race and Epistemologies of Ignorance.* Albany: SUNY Press.

Suzuki, Yasunosuke. 1981. "Neoplastic and Nonneoplastic Effects of Vinyl Chloride in Mouse Lung." *Environmental Health Perspectives* 41: 31–52.

Tabershaw, I. R., and W. R. Gaffey. 1974. "Mortality Study of Workers in the Manufacture of Vinyl Chloride and Its Polymers." *Journal of Occupational Medicine* 16.8: 509–518.

Tuana, Nancy. 1983. "Re-fusing Nature/Nurture." *Hypatia,* published as a special issue of *Women's Studies International Forum* 6.6: 45–56.

———. 1996. "Fleshing Gender, Sexing the Body: Refiguring the Sex Gender Distinction." *Spindel Conference Proceedings, Southern Journal of Philosophy* 35: 53–71.

———. 2001. "Material Locations: An Interactionist Alternative to Realism/Social Constructivism." In *Engendering Rationalities,* ed. Nancy Tuana and Sandi Morgen. Bloomington: Indiana University Press.

———. 2006. "The Speculum of Ignorance: The Women's Health Movement and Epistemologies of Ignorance." *Hypatia: A Journal of Feminist Philosophy* 21.3: 1–19.

Tuana, Nancy, and Shannon Sullivan. 2006. *Feminist Epistemologies of Ignorance. Hypatia* special issue.

Ward, Kathryn. 1990. *Women Workers and Global Restructuring.* Ithaca, N.Y.: Cornell University Press.

Wong, O., M. D. Whorton, D. E. Foliart, and D. Ragland. 1991. "An Industry-Wide Epidemiologic Study of Vinyl Chloride Workers, 1942–1982." *American Journal of Industrial Medicine* 20.3: 317–334.

Wong, R. H., P. C. Chen, C. L. Du, J. D. Wang, and T. J. Cheng. 2002. "An Increased Standardised Mortality Ratio for Liver Cancer among Polyvinyl Chloride Workers in Taiwan." *Occupational and Environmental Medicine* 59: 405–409.

7

NATURAL CONVERS(AT)IONS: OR, WHAT IF CULTURE WAS REALLY NATURE ALL ALONG?

Vicki Kirby

THE LINGUISTIC TURN—CULTURE TAKES PRECEDENCE

The "linguistic turn" in postmodern and poststructural criticism has had a major impact on the landscape of the humanities and social sciences and the way we conceive and communicate our various concerns. Words such as "text," "writing," "inscription," "discourse," "language," "code," "representation," and so on are now part of the vernacular in critical discussion. Indeed, over the years the textualizing of objects and methodologies has generated new interdisciplinary formations across the academy and transformed the content, approach, and even the justifications for research. On the political front we have seen similar shifts in the practices, modes of argumentation, and even the alliances and strategies that once identified particular social movements and struggles for equity. And all this because the material self-evidence of initial conditions or first causes, those stable analytical parameters that allow us to identify a problem and then debate what needs to be done to correct it, has suffered a significant assault. Although in a very real sense political contestation has always debated first principles, once the substantive difference between nature and culture, or temporal priority and causal directionality is disestablished, we enter a very different zone of political possibility.

The following meditation will revisit what has surely been a truism for cultural criticism, namely, the need to interrogate the nature/culture division and the entire conceptual apparatus that rests upon it. Although one might be forgiven for assuming that the insights we can glean from such an examination have been exhausted, the aim of this essay is to illuminate the more counterintuitive and surprising aspects of this problematic that could open new and unusual avenues for critical attention. Why they are routinely overlooked is a curious phenomenon in itself, because the evidence I want to bring to the discussion is neither hidden nor missing, but is patently manifest. For this reason we will give some consideration to why these particular provocations have been elided, and perhaps more profoundly, we will ask why their very possibility should prove so unthinkable.

This analysis will draw on one of the genetic markers of a certain style of feminist and cultural criticism, namely, the critique of Cartesian thought and the political inflections that pivot around its binary logic. Theorists of gender, sexuality, and race, for example, have found that Nature/the body is routinely conflated with woman, the feminine, the primordial, with unruly passion and "the dark continent"—all signs of a primitive deficiency that requires a more rational and evolved presence (the masculine/whiteness/heterosexuality/culture and civilization) to control and direct its unruly potential. The value of this work is not in dispute here; indeed, in a very real sense this paper will try to extend the more intricate and productive aspects of its insights. Nevertheless, the immediate task is to understand why, on closer inspection, the strategies for overturning the automatic denigration of Nature and the battery of devaluations associated with it have remained wedded to its repetition.

Since this is a big claim, it is best approached in small steps, steps that will retrace our commitments to some foundational building blocks. Let's begin with the problem of binary oppositions in order to understand why this logic might enable Cartesianism as well as the arguments in cultural criticism that strive to overturn it. For example, it is somewhat routine within critical discourse to diagnose binary oppositions as if they are pathological symptoms: conceptual errors that are enduring, insidious, and whose effects can normalize political inequity. However, if the remedial treatment for such symptoms is to replace these binary errors with non-binary correctives, then surely we are caught in something of a quandary. In other words, if every maneuver to escape binary logic effectively reinstates it in a more subtle way, then perhaps we need a more careful examination of what we are actually dealing with.

To take just one facet of the binarity riddle, we might consider whether the difference that renders entities distinct and autonomous is a true reflection of their actual independence and separateness. This seems like a straightforward question, yet one of the insights in semiology is that when we identify something and attribute it with its very own meaning and properties, we arrive at this determination through an entangled knot of associations. The co-responding resonances that animate language and perception actually determine (some might say produce) particularity, and this is why certain poststructural accounts of identity formation argue that context, an external difference, is also constitutively and operationally interior to the identity it seems to surround. However, if we commit to the notion of difference as an internal ingredient in identity formation rather than an external "in-between" identity, should we then conclude that different identities must be inseparable rather than autonomous? The real curiosity appears at this juncture: we are now unable to hold on to the difference between separability and inseparability, between one identity and another, because we have just conceded that the effective difference within all binary oppositions, including this one, is profoundly compromised.[1]

As discussions of the Cartesian mind/body (nature/culture) division so often illustrate, the more counterintuitive and potentially productive dimensions of the binary puzzle that query the very makeup of the categories can often disappear in the diagnostics of critique. Because instead of acknowledging that the very stuff of the body and the processes that purportedly separate thought from carnality are now something of a mystery, the essence of these "components" and their connections can be taken for granted. There is little risk in most contemporary criticism, for example, of attributing agency and intelligent inventiveness (culture) to the capacities of flesh and matter (nature). In sum, nature is deemed to be thought-less, and political interventions into Cartesian logic are much more likely to preserve this assumption by expanding the category "culture" to include whatever it is defined against. If the myriad manifestations of nature are actually mediations or re-presentations, that is, second order signs of cultural invention, then nature, as such, is absent.

Although these analytical maneuvers represent crucial points of entry into the more fascinating implications of this problematic, it becomes clear that both Cartesianism and its critique are entirely committed to the difference between nature and culture, presence and absence, and matter and form. Arguing that we remain indebted to the materiality of the body, that we are always attached to it and never independent of it, that both women and men are equally corporeal, or that none of us can *properly* be identified with nature's primordial insufficiency if this determination is a political (cultural) one, doesn't in any way dislodge the premise of Cartesianism. In all of these arguments it goes without saying that nature/the body/materiality preexists culture/intellect/abstraction, and furthermore, that the thinking self is not an articulation of matter's intentions. Given this, what we will need to keep at the forefront of this meditation is whether the conventional sense of difference as something that divides identities from each other—materiality *from* abstraction—or similarly, something that joins materiality *to* abstraction (because we still assume in this case that two different things are connected), can adequately acknowledge the riddle of identity.[2]

But let's return to the nature/culture division to consider how this particular example of identity that presumes opposition is commonly explained in cultural and feminist theoretical writings. In the main, it is now axiomatic to eschew naturalizing arguments for several reasons. First, and perhaps most importantly, they are regarded as inherently conservative. And compared with the cacophony of cultural explanations that exemplify contestation, movement, and change, it follows that natural determinations will seem like a prescriptive return to something from the past, something undeniable and immutable. In the former case, when we explain our thoughts and actions as cultural products and effects, we are also emphasizing that we are active agents in our political destinies. By embracing the notion of natural cause and determination, however, we run the risk of reducing what seems so special about the human condition to evolutionary happenstance, or nature's caprice. In a very real sense, then, it is the essential nature of human be-ing that is at stake in these debates.

The assumption that the threat of nature can be put aside in some way has been justified theoretically by the linguistic turn itself, which promotes the belief that culture is an enclosed system of significations that affords us no immediate access to nature at all. According to this view and as already noted above, cultural webs of interpretation, which include linguistic and even perceptual frames of legibility, are intricately enmeshed and cross-referenced, and this raft of mediations stands between any direct experience or knowledge of nature's raw facticity. Consequently, the difference between cultural and natural facts is impossible to adjudicate, and this is why we inevitably confuse cultural constructions of nature with "Nature itself."

WHEN SCIENTIFIC OBJECTS TURN INTO LANGUAGE

A clear illustration of the view that it is in the nature of culture to misrecognize culture as nature is evident in the following example. In an interview with Judith Butler, whose work is well known for its analytical commitment to cultural constructionism, I took the opportunity to ask if the organizing trope in her work, namely, language, discourse—textuality—had been too narrowly conceived. My question was inspired by medical and scientific research that claims to investigate the brute reality of material objects and processes: why does the essential nature of these scientific objects also appear to be textual? Within the sciences, the stuff of the body appears as codes, signs, signatures, language systems, and mathematical algorithms. In the cognitive sciences, for example, it seems that explanations of neural-net behavior, or how neurones learn new material (become different), parallels Ferdinand de Saussure's explication of the peculiar resonances of the language system.[3] Other useful comparisons have been made between the communicative structures of biological languages and the language theories of Charles Sanders Peirce.[4] And Jacques Derrida acknowledged that the puzzle of language was just as evident in the biological sciences as it was in literature and philosophy.[5] Even the layperson is increasingly aware that biological information in general, from genetic structures to the translation capacities of our immune system, shares some workable comparison with natural languages. But what are these languages, these biological grammars that seem to be the communicative stuff of life?

Admittedly, we don't tend to think of signs as *substantively* or ontologically material. But what prevents us from doing so? With such considerations in mind, I directed the following question to Butler: "There is a serious suggestion that 'life itself' is creative encryption. Does your understanding of language and discourse extend to the workings of biological codes and their apparent intelligence?" (Breen et al. 2001, 13). On this last point, I was thinking of the code-cracking and encryption capacities of bacteria as they decipher the chemistry of antibiotic data and reinvent themselves accordingly. Aren't these language skills?

Butler's response is a form of admonition, a reminder that language is circumscribed, that its author and reader is human, and that the human endeavor to capture a world "out there" through cultural signs will always be a failed project. To this end, she warns:

> There are models according to which we might try to understand biology, and models by which we might try to understand how genes function. And in some cases the models are taken to be inherent to the phenomena that is being explained. Thus, Fox-Keller has argued that certain computer models used to explain gene sequencing in the fruit fly have recently come to be accepted as intrinsic to the gene itself. I worry that a notion like "biological code," on the face of it, runs the risk of that sort of conflation. I am sure that encryption can be used as a metaphor or model by which to understand biological processes, especially cell reproduction, but do we then make the move to render what is useful as an explanatory model into the ontology of biology itself? This worries me, especially when it is mechanistic models which lay discursive claims on biological life. What if life exceeds the model? When does the discourse claim to become the very life it purports to explain? I am not sure it is possible to say "life itself" is creative encryption unless we make the mistake of thinking that the model is the ontology of life. Indeed, we might need to think first about the relation of any definition of life to life itself, and whether it must, by virtue of its very task, fail. (Breen et al. 2001, 13)

Butler is understandably vigilant about the seductive slide that conflates representations, models, and signs that substitute for material objects, with the objects themselves. In other words, although it is inevitable that we will misrecognize one in the other, Butler cautions against committing to the error. When dealing with scientific objects, the transparent self-evidence of reality is even more persuasive, but even here we are encouraged to remember that these objects are actually literary—textual, or encoded forms of language—and to this extent, if they can only emerge through cultural manufacture, then their reality and truth is attenuated, or even illusional.

Although this argument is certainly persuasive, especially against the sort of hard-edged empiricist and positivist scientific claims that give little consideration to the vagaries of interpretation, there are lingering problems nevertheless. If we contextualize Butler's intervention in terms of the political legacy of binarity mentioned earlier, she effectively challenges the devaluation of nature (the feminine, matter, the origin) by arguing that these significations are cultural ascriptions with no essential truth. If the economy of valuation can be analyzed, contested, and redistributed (because this is the operational definition of culture), then the question of nature is *entirely* displaced: put simply, it can have no frame of reference that isn't properly cultural. Indeed, even the concept/word "nature" is misleading because it evokes meanings, prejudices, and even perceptions that are learned and therefore inherently historical/cultural.

To accept that we are bound within the enclosure of culture is to commit to a raft of related assumptions, and although there is certainly some interpretive play in what we make of them, it might be helpful to register something of their broad outline here. The most important is the assertion that humanness is profoundly unnatural. The abstracting technology of language, intelligence, and creative invention is separated from the body of the material world, indeed, from the material body of human animality. Ironically, given the initial concern to question the separation of nature from culture within Cartesianism, the sense that human identity is somehow secured and enclosed against a more primordial and inhuman "outside" (which must include the subject's own corporeal being!) recuperates the Cartesian problematic, but this time without question. Given this, it is not surprising that cultural arguments that relentlessly interrogate the autonomy and integrity of identity formation fall mute when it comes to the question of how culture conceives and authenticates its own special properties and self-sufficiency. If we translate the separation of culture from nature into the mind/body split, it seems that the Cartesian subject can admit that s/he has a body (that *attaches* to the self), and yet s/he is somehow able to sustain the belief that *s/he is not this body.* This denial is necessary because to contest the latter and all its possible consequences would at least suggest that it might be in the nature of the biological body to argue, to reinvent, and rewrite itself—to cogitate.

Neither Descartes, nor any cultural critic who draws analytical purchase from some version of the linguistic turn, would deny that human identity incorporates two quite different systems of endeavor. Not many would dispute the presence of a biological reality that is quite different from culture and that we imperfectly try to comprehend. But surely, if we were without our skin and we could witness the body's otherwise invisible processes as we chat to each other, read a presentation aloud, type away at our computers, or negotiate an intense exchange with someone we care about, we might be forced to acknowledge that perhaps the meat of the body *is* thinking material. If it is in the nature of biology to be cultural—and clearly, what we mean by "cultural" is intelligent, capable of interpreting, analyzing, reflecting, and creatively reinventing—then what is this need to exclude such processes of interrogation from the ontology of life? The difference between ideality and matter, models and what they purportedly represent, or signs of life and life itself, is certainly difficult to separate here. However, it is important to emphasize that this confusing implication can't be corrected in the way that Butler attempts to do. Although her work underlines why there will always be confusion, she explains this blurring of object and interpretation as an inevitable mistake that derives from the human condition and the hermetic enclosure of the interpretive enterprise, or mind itself.

ENTANGLING THE QUESTION OF LANGUAGE/SYSTEM

Two different considerations arise at this juncture that assist in pushing the problematic forward instead of reiterating the normative frame of reference that is increasingly routine in cultural criticism. In passing, we might note that in a very different field of inquiry the implication between concepts (ideality) and things (materiality) in quantum theory is so profound that it undermines our understanding of their respective difference. Space re-forms as phenomena turn out to be specific and local as well as general and ubiquitous. And similarly, the temporal differences that separate past, present, and future appear to be synchronized when thought experiments can anticipate what will have already taken place: remarkably, the results of these experiments are retrospectively actualized and empirically verifiable.[6] Is the weirdness of this evidence rendered explicable because it reflects the epistemological intertextualities—the crisscrossings of metaphors and models whose cultural origins have little if anything to do with the actualities of the universe at large? Or is there a more worldly form of intertextual referencing in these scientific results that collapse concept (model) and thing, and disperse authorship, identity, and causality?

To underline the counterintuitive complexities in this question, we need to appreciate why the description of the thought experiment that can retrospectively anticipate and materialize what will already have taken place, can inadvertently ignore the mysterious sense of entanglement in this "event's" operational possibility. There is a temporal configuration in the above description's narrative order that preserves the logic of causal separation and the presumption that there are different moments in time, different places in space, and a very real difference between thought and material reality. To suggest that one affects the other in a way that renders them inseparable doesn't confound the nature of their difference (respective identities) so much as it emphasizes that these differences are joined, or connected in some way. In the first instance, we interpret "inseparability" to mean that human agency and intention produced a change in the nature of reality and that this is proof of some mysterious connection between them. The very same logic would allow us to reverse the direction of this causal explanation to suggest that some agential force in the universe directed humans to conduct an experiment whose results the world had already anticipated. However, neither of these explanations captures the space/time entanglement at work here, even though this last reversal begins to trouble the properties that we tend to attribute to these different identities (human and nonhuman) and the relational asymmetries that affirm the difference in their properties, capacities, and timings.

If we consider these implications more rigorously, then significance and substance, thought and matter, human agency and material objectivity, must be consubstantial. But what does this actually mean, and can we do anything interesting with such a wild assertion? Of course, the linguist Ferdinand de Saussure said something very similar about the consubstantiality of semiological entanglement, just as Judith Butler's more contemporary interpretation of his argument insists that signification matters and that ideation can real-ize. In other words, many of the most important interventions in cultural criticism that condense differences together seem to mimic such counterintuitive assertions. Our question is whether these insights only relate to the peculiar attributes of culture. To return to the question of scientific modeling, must we assume that these models are interpretive illusions produced by humans to mirror a world that can't be accessed? Because if they are mere illusions and the world is not present *in* them, then how can they possess the extraordinary capacity (as we see in the case of quantum relations) to anticipate verifiable outcomes whose pragmatic results heralded contemporary advances in computer and electronic technologies?

It seems that the little steps by which we retraced our way to certain foundational commitments about binarity and the nature of language very quickly turned into the most puzzling quandaries about the nature of life and the mysteries of the universe! And while the complexities of scientific theory surely exceed our disciplinary expertise, the discussion above has made the appeal to an "absolute outside" of anything, whether the discipline of physics, or theories of textual interpretation, for that matter, considerably more fuzzy. For this reason, and in the spirit of a more meditative style of inquiry, perhaps we can at least risk the suggestion that if the quantum conflation of *thesis* with/in *physis* has general purchase, then we should not read the most complex aspects of poststructuralism as pure *thesis*. The most counterintuitive arguments about the superposition of matter and ideation, concept and object; all of the close analytical criticism that discovers systems of referral and relationality *within* identity/the individual; the peculiar space/time condensations that we confront in Freud's notion of memory or *nachträglichkeit* (deferred action); or the "intra-actions"[7] of Derridean *différance* and its counterintuitive implications—need we assume that such insights are purely "cultural" because the world itself, in its enduring insistence, simply couldn't be that dynamically involved and alien to ordinary common sense?

But let's stick to something more straightforward that will test the conventional interpretation of cultural constructionism just as effectively by showing that a precritical understanding of reference as something self-evident in nature is inadequately countered by theories of the referent as a cultural artifact. The question is disarmingly simple, so simple that one has to wonder why such questions are so rarely asked within the disciplinary protocols of cultural criticism; namely, can the rampant culturalism that understands the mediations of language as a purely cultural technology, a technology that *cannot* have any substantial purchase because it remains enclosed against itself, explain how computational models, bio-grams of skin prints, blood evidence, genetic signatures, pollen chemistries, and insect life cycles (all data that present as languages)—how can this cacophony of differences possess *any* possibility of predictive reference? As we are well aware from forensic investigation techniques, data is indicative. From global networks of information that bring geology, biology, psychology, entomology, cryptography, and even the very personal street-smarts of a particular observing investigator into conversation and convergence, a referent is thrown up. The most obvious question that this intricate process raises is—how?

QUANTUM IMPLICATIONS AND THE PRACTICE OF CRITIQUE

The reluctance of postmodern styles of criticism to actively consider how scientific models of nature work at all (even when imperfectly, but certainly when we witness their extraordinary predictive accuracy) has led many to discount the productive energy in these theories without appreciating what they can actually offer. Bruno Latour, for example, a sociologist and historian of science, pours vitriol upon those "gloating" cultural constructivists whose smug self-enclosure attributes all agency and articulation to a brain in a vat (1999, 8). With considerable irritation, he rails against the idea that anyone could celebrate musing blindly about a world that can no longer be accessed from the confines of a linguistic prison-house. To paraphrase his position, such arguments descend further and further into the same dark and spiraling curves of the same hell that is Cartesianism—"We have not moved an inch" (1999, 8).

As a prominent figure in the field of Science Studies,[8] a field that draws much of its analytical energy from Cultural Studies, Latour is in an awkward position: he has to marry what he sees as the intrinsic value of empirical research in the sciences with his own discipline's attention to the subjective, historical, and cultural inflections of knowledge production. The way he does this is to refuse reality an "ahistorical, isolated, inhuman, cold, objective existence" (1999, 15). Accordingly, he shifts his attention from objects and claims to objectivity, to the messy business of scientific practice, or science-in-the-making. Although this may seem like a sociological version of cultural analysis that leaves the terms of the debate intact, unlike conventional postmodern approaches, Latour's approach doesn't emphasize the vagaries of subjectivism and the relative illusiveness of truth. Such a claim would reiterate Butler's position—that an essential and natural truth is veiled behind culture's misguided attempts to represent it. Instead, Latour effectively redefines "the social" in a more comprehensive way—as a confluence of forces and associations, a collective assembly of human *and* nonhuman interactions that together produce social facts with referential leverage. In clarifying this notion of a more "realistic realism" that refuses the divide between nature and culture, Latour draws on the contributions of actor-network theory (ANT)[9] to explain how this works. Preferring Michel Serres's notion of "quasi-object" rather than "object," Latour explains:

> real quasi-objects do not have the characteristic of being things out there, passive and boring, waiting to be unveiled. Things become active, and the collective becomes made of things—circulating things—which do not have the characteristics they have in the realist argument. So these hybrids (quasi-objects) start resembling what our world is made of. It is not that there are a few hybrids; it is that there are *only* hybrids. . . . actor-network and quasi-object are exactly the same word. (1993b, 261 and 262)

One of the most important aspects of Latour's intervention is this suggestion that nonhumans must be accommodated within the fabric of society and our understanding of agency and intentionality reconceived accordingly. This means that actors no longer appear as fixed entities, for they are like "nodes" that emerge within circulating flows of force—the agential fields of networked intentionality (1993b, 261). Because words that evoke the passivity of thingness are usually alien to the active descriptions of human intention and vice versa, Latour acknowledges that the words he uses to conjure the mix of this "realistic realism" are imperfect:

> Every word is good if it can be used to cross the boundary between people and things. . . . The whole notion of actor-network theory is not a very well packaged argument, but the rule is simple: do not use culture, the content of science, or discourse as the cause of the phenomenon. So the vocabulary of actor-network theory is voluntarily poor. It is not a metalanguage, but an infralanguage. Its core principle is not to limit a priori who or which are the actors and their properties. (1993b, 263)

How this network of "distributed agency" that involves human and nonhuman "actants" can actually function and communicate its collective energies is especially fascinating to Latour, who responds by calling for a new philosophy of reference. We might consider the example of forensic investigation mentioned earlier as a good illustration of this network's pragmatic interplay because it has the capacity to produce nodes of reference, or evidence, that *effectively* correspond. Latour underlines that the resulting *dispositif* is not a purely human achievement, and he captures the exquisite mystery of its communicative conversions in the simple question—"How do we pack the world into words?" (1999, 24).

The question's disarming challenge is powerfully evoked in "Circulating Reference: Sampling the Soil in the Amazon Forest" (1999), an essay that conveys the sheer wonder of how empirical field research into the physical densities of biological and geological material can transubstantiate into the sort of representational abstractions that we consult in books. The puzzle of reference that Latour is grappling with must accommodate immutability as well as comparative endurance. As he muses, "if I can manage to grasp this *invariant,* this *je ne sais quoi,* I believe, I will have understood scientific reference" (1999, 36). However, his dilemma is that the staying power of this referent persists despite its constant metamorphosis. Science requires "a reversible route that makes it possible to retrace one's footsteps as needed"—from scholarly writings, graphs, and mathematical measurements we can verify someone's findings and repeat their observations in exactly the same place and under the same conditions:

> Across the variation of matters/forms, scientists forge a pathway. Reduction, compression, marking, continuity, reversibility, standardization, compatibility with text and numbers. . . . No step—except one—[which concerns the accurate documentation of soil color in this particular study] resembles the one that precedes it, yet in the end, when I read the field report, I am indeed holding in my hands the forest of Boa Vista. A text truly speaks of the world. How can resemblance result from this rarely described series of exotic and miniscule transformations obsessively nested into one another so as to keep something constant? (1999, 61)

We will recall that Latour eschews the postmodern solipsism of cultural constructionism because it concedes no place to nature at all. Indeed, the difference between nature and culture, world and interpretation, is regarded as so enormous that the abyss is unbridgeable. However, in the networks of information noted above, Latour discovers negotiable pathways that turn this incommensurable gap into a more manageable series of stepping stones. Instead of a yawning gulf between nature and culture, we shuttle across little bridges of translation and transfer—passages of metamorphosis where the communication between matter and form is mutually enabled. In Latour's reconception, the articulation of the referent is actively produced from both sides (nature *and* culture, matter *and* form), and this joint enterprise encourages us to embrace the notion that nature is articulate, communicative—and, in a very real sense—intentional.

Given the postmodern conflation of culture with language, agency, intention, and human subjectivity, it is a welcome intervention that muddles these rigid alignments and forces us to rethink the content of the terms and the more general puzzle of relationality/communication. But is this what Latour is really encouraging us to do here? Is the identity of matter, for example, or the ontology of nature, something to be pondered and reviewed, or has Latour assumed that what constitutes the stuff of nature is more or less self-evident and that this difference should be added to culture's input? Latour is certainly pressing us to question this frame of reference, but has he inadvertently introduced a limit to his own inquiry?

Before we continue, it is important to note that the practice of doing critique involves close encounters with another person's way of thinking, with their intellectual commitments and even the temperament and personal idiosyncrasies that animate their writing style. How we manage the intimacy of these exercises, especially when the aim of our analysis might be to discount that position and take our distance from it, already rehearses this difficult question about identity formation and the implications of relationality. Both Butler and Latour have specifically acknowledged that one of the most pressing issues in political analysis today is the question of critique—how to engage others more generously through interconnection, how to avoid the more murderous maneuvers of dialectical reasoning that negate another's position as wrong in order to affirm our own position as right—as *the* one (and only) position.[10] If we want to address the question of nature or materiality in a way that doesn't presume that materiality can be either added to, or subtracted from, something that it isn't (culture, ideation), then how we identify our own position vis-à-vis another's will need to anticipate this particular problem.

Keeping this last consideration at the forefront of what I'm trying to do in this essay, I want to emphasize that I share Butler's conviction that there is "no outside of language." My justification for wanting to *naturalize* language and its productive energies rests on considering how strange this "inside" of language might be. It could be likened to the way physicists negotiate the spatial demarcation of what is inside or outside the universe: what seems outside is actually another aspect of the inside, an answer that also "explains" why the expansion of the universe is described as an expansion into itself. There are suggestive reconfigurations of how we conceive space in these statements, and it is something of this implicate order, this in-habiting, that I am trying to encourage here. For this reason I am persuaded that by studying the workings of language we are not merely looking at a *model* of the world's "intra-actions" that, by dint of being detached from the world's palpable reality, will inevitably prove mistaken. For it seems quite possible that we may be investigating and witnessing an instantiation of a more general articulation and involvement whose collective expression . . . *we are.* In sum, the provocation I am offering, albeit in sketchy fashion and without the many caveats that its apparent simplicity betrays, might be to interpret "there is no outside of language" as "there is no outside of Nature." What do I forfeit in doing this, and more importantly, what might I gain?

This interpretation recuperates what is axiomatic for Butler's argument, namely, that "there is no outside of language"—we are agreed, yet in a way that affirms Latour's conviction that nature is articulate, that there is no radical disconnection between nature and culture, and that agency is a distributed, implicated eco-logy with no central, organizing origin. Since the conventional bifurcations and political asymmetries that provoke both thinkers to action are now happily awry, is there a way to suggest that despite our differences we share an uncanny alliance?

To recapitulate, it is clear that Butler is vigilant about the dangers of naturalizing arguments because she is convinced, as thoroughly as any conservative, unfortunately, that nature is *pre*-scriptive. It is quite unthinkable to even suggest that nature is, already, all of those mutating, complex plasticities that culture's corrective would animate it with. But what of Latour? Could Latour embrace my suggestion as a permutation of his own, especially in light of his stated concerns about the agonistics of critique and the need to forge more intimate modes of engagement? After all, it is Latour who comments, "Critique as a repertoire is over. It has run out of steam entirely, and now the whole question is, 'how can we be critical, not by distance but by proximity?' " (2004b).

Indeed—how to do it? The inclusiveness of Latour's "assembly of assemblies," that revamped parliament of distributed utterance where human *and* nonhuman discourse in concert to produce referential meaning sounds promising.[11] But things get weird once "this everything" of a system's communion, its communication, is naturalized; that is, once you insist that nature reads, writes, articulates *itself.* Clearly, "the human" has no privileged position as scribe if nature is, and always was, a self-recording. And yet we needn't fear, as Latour does, that this admission displaces and disregards the wonder of human history and the veritable din of its discord. If "to naturalize" means that we deny such things, then it's time to reconsider, as Latour invites us to do, the very nature of nature.

Latour's struggle to marry the movement and contingency of construction with some workable sense of reality is surely realized in the distributed agency, the *dispositif,* of nature's manifest literacy. However, Latour's insistence that the reader of the world must remain human completely qualifies the meaning of both distribution and agency. For instance, his exasperated rants against socio-biology, deconstruction, and science fundamentalism warn us that the "danger" in these approaches is their "mutual ideal" to reach "what has not been built at all by any human hand" (2003, 41). Even assuming this were the case, why is this so reprehensible, and isn't Latour at this point uncannily Butlerian in defending the world's need for a human amanuensis?

At this point, what is most wild and wonderful in the irreverence of Latour's work needs to be remembered, because it is Latour who evokes the provocation of consubstantiality that invites us to rethink identity's Cartesian framework of temporal and spatial coordinates, coordinates that discover individuated identities that preexist their actions; causes that are straightforwardly different, and prior to, the effects they engender; or more straightforwardly, individuals (of whatever sort) that preexist their networked encounter. To allow the implications of consubstantiality to work its mystery is to enter a counterintuitive realm where identities might be conceived as emergent "mutualities"—"collectivities" that are not mere aggregates. In his various clarifications of "network" and "actor," Latour explains that nets are inseparable from the act that traces them, and that this act of tracing isn't done by an actor that is external to the network that reveals them. In other words, all "parts" of this *dispositif* are a sort of synchronous assemblage/emergence. We are reminded here of Michel Foucault's attempt to reconceptualize the *dispositif* of power as a ubiquitous and generative force, one that doesn't seize upon a body that preexists it.[12]

My understanding of this phenomenon is that actants materialize in the distributed agency of this tracing, and if they don't preexist this mediation, they will always be *inherently* hybrid. Latour makes much of this appeal to hybridity, yet the implicated scenography that *evolves* these identities is stripped of all magic if we understand hybridity as a composite of *both* "human" *and* "nonhuman." Latour helps me here, when in a different context he describes his impatience with the complacency that informs this simple notion—"both." The context in this particular case is the way a critical sociology can be downright stupid in its management of metaphysical quandaries. To the question, "Is constructed reality constructed or real?" Latour notes the "mildly blasé smile" that greets the answer "both," an answer that shows no appreciation that identity and relationality are questions to be considered and not facts to be assumed. Latour lets fire:

> How I despise this little "both" that obtains so cheaply a veneer of depth that passes nonetheless for the ultimate critical spirit. Never was critique less critical than when accepting as an obvious answer what should be, on the contrary, a source of utter bewilderment. (2003, 35–36)

This reminds us of Latour's provocation mentioned above, "how to be critical by proximity," achieved, perhaps, by making yourself at home in the very logic of your opponent's argument and showing how the direction of that argument can comprehend a very different set of implications. The strategy illustrates the inherent potential, the open-ended and "intermediating" insinuations that in-form all positions/identities and trouble their definitive separation and even their inherent constitution. Latour's emphasis on the hybrid nature of identity and his awareness that recourse to a notion of conjunction, or aggregation, is inadequate to this complexity, must surely beg the question of how the respective identities of the human and nonhuman are kept apart. Why, for example, does nature require a human scribe to represent itself, to mediate or translate its identity?

When we posit a natural object, a plant, for example, we don't assume that it is unified and undifferentiated: on the contrary, this one thing is internally divided from itself, a communicating network of cellular mediations and chemical parsings. It is a functioning laboratory, a technological apparatus whose intricate operations are finely elaborated—an "intermediate" node that communicates its ecological significance in a way that incorporates and blurs the outside with/in the inside. Given this, why is it so difficult to concede that nature already makes logical alignments that enable it to refer productively to itself, to organize itself so that it can be understood . . . by itself? If we return to Latour's explanation of circulating reference as a mutual "construction" of human *and* nonhuman in the soil study, it is clear that the soil offers itself as the material origin or object *for* study. Locked in at one end of a continuum, nature needs to be cultivated, cultured, and coaxed to reveal its secrets. Its lessons are educed by something that, inasmuch as it has the capacity to reveal and encode, cannot be a natural operation by definition. For Latour, then, nature is not itself a laboratory, an experimental, communicative enterprise.

I could conclude the argument by suggesting that nature doesn't require human literary skills to write its complexity into comprehensible format. But if I did this, I'd actually be reiterating the premise of Latour's position all over again by dividing "human" from "nonhuman": those "nonhumans" simply don't need us . . . don't be so pompous in assuming that they do! But perhaps there is a position that can affirm the human, *with* Latour, and even with a sociobiological twist that will address Latour's concerns about such "science fundamentalists" and allow their work to challenge us and not simply define our value against their foolishness.

My suggestion is to try a more counterintuitive gambit, namely, to generalize the assumed capacities of humanness in a way that makes us wonder about their content—after all, what do we really mean by agency, distributed or otherwise, or by intentionality and literacy? For example, why condemn the sociobiologist E. O. Wilson because he sees humanity reflected in the behavior of ants, in their animal husbandry and finessed horticultural skills, in the political complexities of their caste system, their slaving behaviors, the adaptive ministrations of their nursery regimes, their language and culture? When we explain this social complexity as an anthropomorphic projection whose comparison diminishes what is specific to human be-ing, we automatically secure the difference of our identity *against* the insect (nature) and reiterate that agrarian cultivation and animal husbandry (culture) first appeared with Neolithic peoples. We hang on to such assumptions by insisting that natural "smarts," clear evidence of engineering intelligence, social complexity, ciphering skills, and evolutionary innovation are just programs, the mere expression of instinctual behaviors. It is understandable why both Butler and Latour, for that matter, would reject the suggestion that human subjectivity, self-consciousness, and agency are "mere" programs. But what is a program if it can rewrite itself? Certainly not *pre*-scriptive? Surely, the point isn't to take away the complexity that culture seems to bring to nature but to radically reconceptualize nature "altogether."

The distributed agency of a "human nature" would "act, or communicate, at a distance." This quantum puzzle is actively embraced in "Circulating Reference," where Latour ponders how soil samples taken from the Brazilian savanna can maintain ontological constancy through the variety of instrumental translations, representations, and transformations they undergo—from soil, crumbling between the researchers' fingers, to its final recordings on many sheets of paper. Latour assures us that "here it is no longer a question of reduction [of the soil into words and graphs] but of transubstantiation" (1999, 54). Transubstantiation is a religious term, and yet one that could just as well be applied to quantum phenomena. It certainly evokes an abyssal crossing; however, this is not the gulf between nature and culture that Butler finds insurmountable, nor is it the gulf between nature and culture across which Latour discovers many bridges of cooperation. This radical disjunction/inseparability is comprehensive—a fault line that runs throughout all of human nature. It articulates the nonlocal within the local, nature within culture, and human within nonhuman. The superposition of these differences means that any identity is articulated with and by all others—consubstantiality and Latour's transubstantiation are one and the same. This is a comprehensive process, a process of comprehension, a material reality.

What happens if nature is neither lacking nor primordial, but rather a plenitude of possibilities, a cacophony of convers(at)ion? Indeed, what if it is that same force field of articulation, reinvention, and frisson that we are used to calling—"Culture"? Should feminism reject the conflation of "woman" with "Nature," or instead, take it as an opportunity to consider the question of origins and identity more rigorously?

NOTES

1. For a detailed discussion of this puzzle in regard to the identity of the sign, see Kirby 1997.

2. Jacques Derrida's early work on the logic of the supplement is especially pertinent here. See Derrida 1984.

3. See Elizabeth A. Wilson (1998, 189–98).

4. Jesper Hoffmeyer (1993) provides a good example of this.

5. Although the point is made in passing in *of Grammatology* (1984, 9), Derrida specifically addresses this connection in a series of seminars on the Nobel Prize winner François Jacob, who worked on the language of RNA. To date, the seminars remain unpublished.

6. Experiments undertaken by Alain Aspect and, more recently, Nicolus Grisin have confirmed that non-locality is a general property of the universe. Consequently, if any "event" in the universe is inseparable from another, any part inseparable from the whole, then the local is articulated through the universal and vice versa. This rather extraordinary suggestion compromises spatial divisions and temporal differences: the notion of individuated events *in* time or *in* space is imploded. For a helpful introduction to this field of inquiry, see Nadeau and Kafatos 2001.

7. Just as Derrida conceived the neologism *différance* to complicate the meaning of difference, so Karen Barad has coined the term "intra-action" to evoke an involvement that is inadequately accommodated by the term "interaction." For an elaboration of this way of thinking, see Barad 2006.

8. Science Studies, like any disciplinary formation, is not a uniform set of assumptions but an evolving argument between its various practitioners and those who engage their writings. It should be noted that feminists working within the sciences have played a prominent part in establishing Science Studies as a specific

field of interest, whether intentionally or not, and like Latour, they have brought a certain respect for scientific practices and epistemologies into dialogue with the sorts of cultural criticism that investigates the political agendas that inform them. For many critics such as Latour, cultural criticism and scientific research need not be positioned in an agonistic way. Prominent thinkers who originally hail from the sciences and retain an interest in the value of its specificity include Donna Haraway, Anne Fausto-Sterling, Karen Barad, Evelyn Fox Keller, and Susan Oyama.

9. Although Latour's enthusiasm for the value of ANT has faded in more recent writings, his work continues to tease out the many questions it raises. For an early example of this style of thinking, see Latour 1993a. Other notable thinkers in the field of Actor Network Theory include Michael Callon, John Law, M. Lynch, Steve Woolgar, and S. L. Star.

10. See Judith Butler (2001) and Bruno Latour (2004a).

11. See Latour 1993a.

12. This is well illustrated by the problematic of sexuality. See Foucault 1980.

REFERENCES

Barad, Karen. 2007. *Meeting the Universe Halfway: Quantum Physics and the Entanglement of Matter and Meaning.* Durham, N.C.: Duke University Press.

Breen, Margaret Soenser, et al. 2001. "'There Is a Person Here': An Interview with Judith Butler." *International Journal of Sexuality and Gender Studies* 6.1/2: 7–23.

Butler, Judith. 2001. "What Is Critique? An Essay on Foucault's Virtue." In *The Political,* ed. David Ingram, 212–26. Oxford: Blackwell.

Derrida, Jacques. 1984. *Of Grammatology.* Trans. Gayatri Chakravorty Spivak. Baltimore: Johns Hopkins University Press.

Foucault, Michel. 1980. *The History of Sexuality.* Vol. 1: *An Introduction.* Trans. Robert Hurley. New York: Vintage Books.

Hoffmeyer, Jesper. 1993. *Signs of Meaning in the Universe.* Trans. B. J. Haveland. Bloomington: Indiana University Press.

Kirby, Vicki. 1997. *Telling Flesh: The Substance of the Corporeal.* London: Routledge.

Latour, Bruno. 1993a. *We Have Never Been Modern.* Trans. Catherine Porter. Cambridge: Harvard University Press.

———, with T. Hugh Crawford. 1993b. "An Interview with Bruno Latour." *Configurations: Journal of Literature, Science and Technology* 1.2: 247–68.

———. 1999. "Circulating Reference: Sampling the Soil in the Amazon Forest." In *Pandora's Hope: Essays on the Reality of Science Studies,* 24–79. Cambridge: Harvard University Press.

———. 2003. "The Promises of Constructivism." In *Chasing Technoscience: Matrix for Materiality,* ed. Don Ihde and Evan Selinger, 27–46. Bloomington: Indiana University Press.

———. 2004a. "Why Has Critique Run out of Steam? From Matters of Fact to Matters of Concern." *Critical Inquiry* 30.2: 225–48.

———, with Maria J. Prieto and Elise S. Youn. 2004b. "Interview with Bruno Latour: Decoding the Collective Experiment," July 5. *agglutinations.com.* http://agglutinations.com/archives/000040.html.

Nadeau, Robert, and Menas Kafatos. 2001. *The Non-Local Universe: The New Physics and Matters of the Mind.* Oxford: Oxford University Press.

Wilson, Elizabeth A. 1998. *Neural Geographies: Feminism and the Microstructure of Cognition.* New York: Routledge.

8

TRANS-CORPOREAL FEMINISMS AND THE ETHICAL SPACE OF NATURE

Stacy Alaimo

Despite the tremendous outpouring of scholarship on "the body" in feminist theory and cultural studies and the simultaneous outpouring of environmental philosophy, criticism, and cultural studies, these two streams of scholarship rarely intermingle. Although there are notable exceptions, by and large two isolated conversations have evolved—conversations that would be complicated and enriched by collisions and convergences. Most feminist analyses of the body, in particular, sever their topic from the topos of "nature." Indeed, from an environmentalist-feminist standpoint, one of the most unfortunate legacies of poststructuralist and postmodern feminism has been the accelerated "flight from nature" fueled by rigid commitments to social constructionism and the determination to rout out all vestiges of essentialism. Nature, charged as an accessory to essentialism, has served as feminism's abject—that which, by being expelled from the "I," serves to define the "I" (Kristeva 1982, 1–4). This by now conventional move epitomizes one of the central contentions of this collection: that the predominant trend in the last few decades of feminist theory has been to diminish the significance of materiality. Predominant paradigms do not deny the material existence of the body, of course, but they do tend to focus exclusively on how various bodies have been discursively produced, which casts the body as passive, plastic matter. As Elizabeth A. Wilson puts it, "the body at the center of these projects is curiously abiological—its social, cultural, experiential, or psychical construction having been posited against or beyond any putative biological claims"

(1998, 15). Bracketing the biological body, and thereby severing its evolutionary, historical, and ongoing interconnections with the material world, may not be ethically, politically, or theoretically desirable.

Fortunately, there are other options. One would be that feminism take root in the very realm that has so long served as the abject. I would like to propose that we inhabit what I'm calling "trans-corporeality"—the time-space where human corporeality, in all its material fleshiness, is inseparable from "nature" or "environment." Trans-corporeality, as a theoretical site, is a place where corporeal theories and environmental theories meet and mingle in productive ways. Furthermore, the movement across human corporeality and nonhuman nature necessitates rich, complex modes of analysis that travel through the entangled territories of material and discursive, natural and cultural, biological and textual.

Crucial ethical and political possibilities emerge from this literal "contact zone" between human corporeality and more-than-human nature. Imagining human corporeality as trans-corporeality, in which the human is always intermeshed with the more-than-human world, underlines the extent to which the corporeal substance of the human is ultimately inseparable from "the environment." It makes it difficult to pose nature as a mere background for the exploits of the human,[1] since "nature" is always as close as one's own skin. Indeed, thinking across bodies may catalyze the recognition that the "environment," which is too often imagined as inert, empty space or as a "resource" for human use, is, in fact, a world of fleshy beings, with their own needs, claims, and actions. By emphasizing the movement across bodies, trans-corporeality reveals the interchanges and interconnections between human corporeality and the more-than-human. But by underscoring that "trans" indicates movement across different sites, trans-corporeality opens up an epistemological "space" that acknowledges the often unpredictable and unwanted actions of human bodies, nonhuman creatures, ecological systems, chemical agents, and other actors. Emphasizing the material interconnections of human corporeality with the more-than-human world, and at the same time acknowledging that material agency necessitates more capacious epistemologies, allows us to forge ethical and political positions that can contend with numerous late-twentieth-century/early-twenty-first-century realities in which "human" and "environment" can by no means be considered as separate: environmental health, environmental justice, the traffic in toxins, and genetic engineering, to name a few.

FEMINIST THEORY'S FLIGHT FROM NATURE

Nature, as a philosophical concept, a potent ideological node, and a cultural repository of norms and moralism, has long been waged against women, people of color, indigenous peoples, queers, and the lower classes. Paradoxically, women, the working class, tribal peoples, and people of color have been denigrated because of their supposed "proximity" to nature, even as queers have been castigated for being "unnatural." The contradictory, ubiquitous, and historically varied meanings of "nature" have made it a crucial site for various feminist social struggles, including feminist anarchism, socialism, birth control, racial equality, and lesbianism. In *Undomesticated Ground: Recasting Nature as Feminist Space* (2000), I argue that because "woman" has long been defined in Western thought as a being mired in "nature" and thus outside the domain of human transcendence, rationality, subjectivity, and agency, most feminist theory has worked to disentangle "woman" from "nature." From the writings of Simone de Beauvoir, to Sherry Ortner, Juliet Mitchell, Gayle Rubin, and Monique Wittig, most feminist theory transports "woman" from the category of nature to the realm of culture. Working within rather than against predominant dualisms, many important feminist arguments and concepts necessitate a rigid opposition between nature and culture. For example, feminist theory's most revolutionary concept—the concept of gender as distinct from biological sex—is predicated on a sharp opposition between nature and culture. Moreover, while it would be difficult to overestimate the explanatory and polemical force of feminist theories of social construction, such theories are haunted by the pernicious notions of nature that propel them. Thrust aside, completely removed from culture, this nature—the repository of essentialism and stasis—nonetheless remains dangerously intact (Alaimo 2000, 4–14). Rather than fleeing from this debased nature, associated with corporeality, mindlessness, and passivity, it would be more productive for feminist theory to undertake the transformation of gendered dualisms—nature, culture, body, mind, object, subject, resource, agency, and others—that have been cultivated to denigrate and silence certain groups of human as well as nonhuman life.

In a strange twist on feminist claims that women are created by culture, not nature, a diverse range of North American women writers, activists, and theorists, from the early nineteenth century to the present—including Catherine Sedgwick, Mary Wilkins Freeman, Sarah Orne Jewett, the Darwinian feminists Antoinette Brown Blackwell and Eliza Burt Gamble, Mary Austin, the Marxist-feminist theorists Mary Inman and Rebecca Pitts, Octavia Butler, Marian Engel, and Jane Rule—have turned toward nature as a habitat for feminist subjects. Their formulations condemn the *social* "manufacturing" of women as "unnatural" and imagine nature, not as the ground of essentialism, but as a habitat for gender-minimizing, sometimes queer, often nascent poststructuralist feminisms. Darwinian feminist Antoinette Brown Blackwell, in her 1875 *The Sexes Throughout Nature,* for example, turns to the "inorganic world" to undermine the cultural significance of sexual difference, arguing that "these elements and these forces [of sexual difference] are continually changing sides, entering into indefinite rearrangements in conjunction with other forces. Thus what might be distinguished as masculine in one case, would become feminine in the next" (1875, 44). In her striking formulation, matter, which is forever transforming, exposes the rigidity of sexual oppositions within culture. Similarly, the early-twentieth-century writer Mary Austin imagines the desert as an undomesticated ground for feminist subjects, a lawless place where the landmarks fail, gender unravels, and meanings come undone. This rich and innovative group of feminist writers demonstrate not only that it is possible to imagine nature in such a way that it is unrecognizable as the ground of essentialism, but that the project of radically redefining nature has long been at the heart of a range of feminist social struggles.[2]

Human corporeality, especially female corporeality, has been so strongly associated with nature in Western thought that it is not surprising that feminism has been haunted not only by the specter of nature as the repository of essentialism, but by, as Lynda Birke puts it, "the ghost of biology" (1999, 44). She charges that the "underlying assumption that some aspects of 'biology' are fixed becomes itself the grand narrative (albeit implicit) from which feminist and other social theorists are trying to escape" (1999, 44). Nancy Tuana, noting the recent resurgence of popular belief in racial and sexual determinism, charges that "we feminists have been epistemically irresponsible in leaving in place a fixed, essential, material basis for human nature, a basis which renders biological determinism meaningful" (1996, 57). Only by directly engaging with matter itself can feminism do as Tuana advocates: render biological determinism "nonsense." For instance, rather than bracketing the biological body, Birke insists upon the need to understand the biological body as "changing and changeable, as *transformable*" (1999, 45). Cells "constantly renew themselves," bone "is always remodeling," and "bodily interiors" "constantly react to change inside or out, and act upon the world" (1999, 45).

Even with these few sparse examples, it is clear that the notion of "biology as destiny," which has long haunted feminism, depends on a very particular—if not peculiar—notion of biology that can certainly be displaced by other models. Since biology, like nature, has long been drafted to serve as the armory for racist, sexist, and heterosexist norms, it is crucial that feminists invoke a counter-biology to aid our struggles. For example, Myra J. Hird, in "Naturally Queer," offers an abundance of biological examples that make heterosexism seem, well, unnatural. "The *vast* majority of cells in the human body are intersex"; "most of the organisms in four out of the five kingdoms do not require sex for reproduction," and, marvelously, the schizophyllum "has more than 28,000 sexes." She concludes by arguing that "we may no longer be certain that it is nature that remains static and culture that evinces limitless malleability" (2004, 85–86, 88). If this biology sounds queer, all the better. As a "situated knowledge" (Haraway 1991), this queer biology contests not only the content and the ramifications of normative hetero-biology, but its claim to objectivity and neutrality.

Perhaps the only way to truly oust the twin ghosts of biology and nature is, paradoxically, to endow them with flesh, to allow them to materialize more fully, and to fully attend to their precise materializations.

THE MATERIAL TURN IN FEMINIST THEORY

Wondering whether it makes her a "survivor or a traitor of the age of (post)structuralism," Teresa de Lauretis, in the recent *Critical Inquiry* symposium devoted to "The Future of Criticism," boldly suggests that

> now may be a time for the human sciences to reopen the questions of subjectivity, materiality, discursivity, knowledge, to reflect on the post of posthumanity. It is a time to break the piggy bank of saved conceptual schemata and reinstall uncertainty in all theoretical applications, starting with the primacy of the cultural and its many "turns": linguistic, discursive, performative, therapeutic, ethical, you name it. (2004, 368)

What has been most notably excluded by the "primacy of the cultural" and the turn toward the linguistic and the discursive is the "stuff" of matter. However, scholars within three areas of feminist theory—feminist corporeal theory, environmental feminism, and feminist science studies—have all been working to conceptualize innovative understandings of the material world. The most intriguing work is that which is informed by poststructuralism, social construction, and cultural studies but that pushes against the edges of those very paradigms; those writers who have been immersed within the cosmos of the "linguistic turn," yet are turning toward the extra-discursive, or extra-linguistic realm. Theorists such as Donna Haraway, Vicki Kirby, Elizabeth Wilson, and Karen Barad have extended the paradigms of poststructuralism, postmodernism, and cultural studies in ways that can more productively account for the agency, "thought," and dynamics of bodies and natures. None of these theorists deny the profound significance of culture, history, and discourse; yet, even as they take social construction seriously, by insisting that culture profoundly shapes what we experience, see, and know, they ask how nonhuman nature or the human body can "talk back," resist, or otherwise affect its cultural construction. The most daunting aspect of such a project is to radically rethink materiality, the very "stuff" of bodies and natures. Some feminist theorists, such as Moira Gatens, Claire Colebrook, and Elizabeth Bray, have embraced the work of Spinoza and Deleuze as countertraditions to the linguistic turn. Others have reread theorists at the heart of poststructuralism—for example, Derrida (Vicky Kirby and Elizabeth Wilson), Michel Foucault (Ladelle McWhorter and Karen Barad), Judith Butler (Karen Barad)—and have extended their paradigms into the material realm. Together, these theorists, as well as some others, constitute the "material turn" in feminist theory, a wave of feminist theory that is taking matter seriously.

Theorists such as Barad mark a decisive departure in recent feminist theory, which has branded any movement toward materiality as "essentialist." Susan Bordo tells a disturbing tale, for example, of having been ostracized at a feminist theory conference for having uttered the word "material" (1998, 88)—despite the fact that her rich, complex analyses never underestimate the power of social and political forces. Although material feminisms take matter seriously, they can hardly be labeled essentialist since they radically recast the very foundations of essentialism. They do not appeal to a nature or human body that exists prior to discourse, but they work to understand materiality as co-constituted by various forms of power and knowledge, some of these being more or less "cultural," and some more or less "natural," though such distinctions have become increasingly problematic. Indeed, even as I use these terms I am struck by their impossibility, since most material feminisms jumble the nature-culture opposition.

Such radical rethinkings of the material are difficult to sustain within an overwhelmingly discursively oriented theoretical cosmos. For example, Donna Haraway's provocative and influential figure of the cyborg (1991), which uproots the founding dualisms of Western thought, including the nature/culture opposition, has been celebrated in most feminist theory and cultural studies as a figure that blurs the boundary between humans and technology—but, significantly, in this latest "flight from nature," the cyborg is rarely embraced as an amalgamation of "human" and "nature." (Perhaps this is why Haraway has distanced herself from this celebrated figure and turned to canines in her most recent work.[3]) Thus, feminist cultural studies, profoundly influenced by theories of social and discursive construction, have embraced the cyborg as a social and technological *construct,* significantly, but have ignored, for the most part, the *matter* of the cyborg, a materiality that is as biological as it is technological, both fleshy and wired, since the cyborg encourages human "kinship with animals" as well as with machines (Haraway 1991, 154). Most disturbingly, the pervasive recoding of the cyborg as technological but not biological resembles a sort of neo(super)Humanism, in which the (Wo)Man/Machine finally transcends nature. Yet Haraway's writing, as well as that of other material-feminist theorists, demonstrates that it is possible to radically reconceive materiality precisely by extending, reconfiguring, and working through many of the theoretical models of the linguistic turn.

The material turn in feminist theory casts matter as, variously, material-semiotic, inter-corporeal, performative, agential, even literate. Whereas discursively oriented studies of human corporeality confine themselves to the corporeal bounds of the human, material feminisms open out the question of the human by considering models of extension, interconnection, exchange, and unraveling. Even though many of the theories that I will discuss focus neither on nature nor on environmentalism, their reconceptualization of materiality, and especially of the interchanges between human corporeality and the more-than-human world, bear great significance for environmental philosophy. And crossing back in the opposite direction, many of the ongoing debates in environmental philosophy regarding the agency of nature and the possibility for more capacious epistemologies bear significance for emerging models of materiality in feminist theory.

AGENCY WITHOUT SUBJECTS

One of the most significant and thorny questions that arises from a radical reconsideration of matter is the question of agency. If we are to understand nature as something other than as a passive resource for the exploits of Man, and if we are to understand the human body as something other than a blank slate awaiting the inscription of culture, we must reconceptualize bodies and natures in ways that recognize their actions. Lynda Birke contends that it is crucial for feminists to "insist on more complex, nuanced ways of interpreting biological processes." She advocates that feminists "rename nature through complexity and transformation" in order to "challenge persistent dualisms" that feed the dualisms of gender (1999, 48). The concept of the agency of biological bodies is crucial for understanding biological entities as complex and ever-transforming. Birke argues, for example, that "internal organs and tissues" can be said to "perform," and, more broadly, that biological bodies are neither passive nor mechanistically determined, but instead exhibit "*active* response to change and contingency" (1999, 45).

Environmental philosophy and science studies offer rich and revealing discussions of agency that may be beneficial for corporeal theorists to consider. How to conceive of nature's agency (in ways that are neither anthropomorphic, nor reductive, nor silly-seeming) has been a central problem for the dismantling of discourses that define nature as a *terra nullius,* an empty ground, evacuated of all that culture would claim for its own self-definition. It is difficult, however, to imagine what agency would look like in an other-than-human sense. How is it possible to understand agency without a subject, actions without actors? How can we rethink matter as activity rather than passive substance?

Carolyn Merchant has long insisted upon the need for environmental historians to account for the agency of nature. In *Ecological Revolutions: Nature, Gender, and Science in New England* (1989) she "reasserts the idea of nature as historical actor"—an actor that may very well challenge the discursive constructions through which it is understood (7). Merchant places both humans and nonhuman nature on the historical stage: "The relation between humans and the nonhuman world is thus reciprocal. Humans adapt to nature's environmental conditions; but when humans alter their surroundings, nature responds through ecological changes" (1989, 8). A robust understanding of the agency of nonhuman nature not only enriches historical understanding but also catalyzes an environmental ethics of partnership. In *Earthcare: Women and the Environment* (1996) Merchant brings together chaos theory, which sees nature as "disorderly order," and "postclassical, postmodern science," which is a "science of limited knowledge, or the primacy of process over parts, and of imbedded contexts within complex, open ecological systems." She urges us to envision nature as a "free autonomous actor" that we should respect as an equal partner deserving political representation (1996, 221). Merchant presents an environmental ethics that is compelling and understandable—if only nations, communities, and individuals would embrace a partnership ethic!

Merchant mounts an indisputable case for the agency of nature—citing floods, hurricanes, and other events. She also places humans and nature on an equal footing, describing nature as a "free, autonomous actor," "just as humans are free autonomous agents" (1996, 221). While this model encourages egalitarian relations between humans and nature, the conception of the "free autonomous actor" may not be sustainable. The autonomous actor suggests a distinct, humanist subject who is not entangled with or constituted by discourses, creatures, ecological systems, or biochemistry. Even though Merchant's model promotes the ethical ideal of considering nature as a sovereign entity rather than a resource for unbridled consumption, it is difficult to imagine nature—or humans, for that matter—as either free or autonomous, ultimately. Thus, the partnership ethic may isolate nonhuman nature from humans by forwarding a notion of autonomy that cannot flourish within models of interdependency, ecological systems, or environmental health.

Conceptions of nonhuman agency need not be predicated upon a humanist model of the free individual. In fact, some poststructuralist models of subjectivity may offer more fruitful ways to conceptualize nature's agency. The subject in Judith Butler's "Contingent Foundations" (1992), for example, bears some resemblance to various actors who populate the more-than-human world. In Butler's formulation, the subject is certainly not "its own point of departure." Instead, agency results precisely from the way in which the subject is produced by "matrices of power and discourse" (1992, 9). This discursive model of subjectivity is akin to an ecological model in which various nonhuman creatures act within complex systems and are interlaced with their "environment," which is never a background, but instead, the ground of their being that they, in turn, affect and transform. Notwithstanding these intriguing parallels, Butler's conception of agency would need to be substantially recast in order to make sense for nonhuman creatures, since she describes the exercise of agency as a "purposive and significant reconfiguration of cultural and political relations" (1992, 12). The work of Ladelle McWhorter and Karen Barad, however, allows us to thoroughly rethink material agency in ways that make sense for that which is not human.

In her book *Bodies and Pleasures: Foucault and the Politics of Sexual Normalization*, Ladelle McWhorter boldly conducts a genealogy of her own body, which includes accounts of "becoming white" as well as that of "becoming dirt." McWhorter came to regard dirt quite differently while attempting to grow her own tomatoes. She notes that her change in perspective was an "amazing shift," since most "people treat dirt as nothing more than the place where plants happen to be, like a kind of platform that plants stand on, or in. . . . Dirt is inactive. Inert. Nobody pays much attention to dirt" (1999, 165). McWhorter, however, grants dirt a great deal of philosophical attention. Her account, in fact, puts forth a striking model of agency without subjects. After noting that dirt "has no integrity," she explains how it still acts:

> Dirt isn't a particular, identifiable thing. And yet it acts. It aggregates, and depending upon how it aggregates in a particular place, how it arranges itself around various sizes of empty space, it creates a complex water and air filtration system the rhythms of which both help to create more dirt from exposed stone and also to support the microscopic life necessary for turning dead organic matter back into dirt. Dirt perpetuates itself. (1999, 166)

Dirt demonstrates an agency without agents, a foundational, perpetual becoming that happens without will or intention or delineation. In fact, dirt, a rather indiscrete substance, is necessary for the emergence of less diffuse life forms: "Whatever discreteness, integrity, and identity living things may have, it all comes from the activity of that undifferentiated, much maligned stuff we call dirt" (1999, 167).

Thinking through the agency of dirt with McWhorter's poetic narrative demands a reconceptualization of agency itself. Neither humanist models of reasonable subjects nor psychoanalytic models of unreasonable subjects will do. Instead, we must thoroughly rethink the very nature of agency along the lines of Donna Haraway's trickster coyote, which acknowledges "the world as a witty agent" with an "independent sense of humor" (1991, 199). Whereas Haraway's work is replete with such compelling figures as the cyborg, primate, trickster coyote, OncoMouse, and canine, all of which reconceptualize agency in more-than-human terms, Barad's work puts forth a more abstract reconceptualization of material agency that emerges from physics. Barad's theory, in which "agency is not an attribute" but a " 'doing'/'being' in its intra-activity" (2003, 826), helps makes sense of McWhorter's dirt—or, from another perspective, it is the dirt that makes Barad's theory a bit more clear. In "Posthumanist Performativity: Toward an Understanding of How Matter Comes to Matter," Barad offers an "elaboration of Performativity—a materialist, naturalist, and posthumanist elaboration—that allows matter its due as an active participant in the world's becoming, in its ongoing 'intra-activity.' "[4] Transporting the ideas of Niels Bohr to feminist theory, she constructs a notion of "agential realism" in which agency "is cut loose from its traditional humanist orbit":

> Agency is not aligned with human intentionality or subjectivity. Nor does it merely entail resignification or other specific kinds of moves within a social geometry of antihumanism. Agency is a matter of intra-acting; it is an enactment, not something that someone or something has. . . . Agency is not an attribute whatsoever—it is "doing"/"being" in its intra-activity. (2003, 826)

Barad's account of Bohr's "intra-activity," as opposed to interactivity, rejects an ontology whereby "things" precede their relations. Instead, "relata" (as opposed to discrete "things") "do not preexist relations; rather, relata-within-phenomena emerge through specific intra-actions" (2003, 815). Barad's agential realism, which rejects representationalism in favor of a material-discursive form of performativity, "circumvents the problem of different materialities." Thus, "there is no mystery about how the materiality of language could possibly affect (through whatever mechanism and to any degree whatsoever) the materiality of the body" (1998, 108). Barad formulates an utterly comprehen-
terly compelling model of materiality, specifically, of material

For our purposes here, it is important to note that one of the reasons Barad's theory offers such a far-reaching and potent reconceptualization of materiality is that it does not sever nature from culture, human from nonhuman. In fact, Barad critiques Butler's theory of materiality because it is restricted to human bodies, in particular, to their surfaces (1998, 107). She also states that materiality "is explicitly not nature-outside-of-culture" (1998, 109). Barad's ontology, which renders distinctions between "nature" and "culture" nonsensical, is a major intervention in feminist and cultural theory. Even as I find her onto-epistemology extraordinarily valuable for feminist and environmentalist philosophy, I think that such radical reconceptualizations will not take root very quickly, and thus it is still useful to consider the different implications of endowing human bodies and nonhuman natures with agency. Acknowledging the agency of the more-than-human world is crucial for environmental ethics because it challenges the prevalent practice of "thingification" (in Barad's terms), which, in this case, means the reduction of lively, emergent, intra-acting phenomena into passive, distinct resources for human use and control. Moreover, acknowledging the agency of all that is not human affirms the need for places—urban, suburban, and especially "wilderness"—in which the "doing/being" of creatures, ecological systems, and other nondiscrete life forms can flourish. In fact, one of the most fundamental values of environmental ethics—the value of the "wild"—can be understood as a kind of material agency. Wildness may well be defined as nature's ongoing, material-semiotic intra-actions—actions that may well surprise, annoy, terrify, or baffle humans, but that nonetheless are valued by environmentalists as the very stuff of life itself.

An environmental ethic of wildness, as vast as it is, however, may not provide a suitable habitat for the material agency of the human body. While desire, especially sexual desire, can be readily celebrated as a form of material agency, when one's own body baffles, annoys, disappoints, or falls ill, such actions are rarely valued. As Susan Wendell contends, the celebratory tone of most feminist writing about the body signals the failure to fully confront the "experience of the negative body" (1996, 167). Disability studies works to account for a different sort of corporeal agency—bodies that resist the processes of normalization, or refuse to act, or act in ways that may be undesirable to those who inhabit them or to others. Yet even as Wendell argues that people who inhabit disabled bodies, chronically ill bodies, or bodies in pain have good reason to desire the transcendence of the corporeal and to practice "strategies of disengagement," the very obdurateness of the disabled body itself insists upon a recognition of corporeal agency. As Wendell puts it, "the body may have a complex life of its own, much of which we cannot interpret" (1996, 175). In short, the agency of the body demands an acceptance of unpredictability and not-quite-knowing.

Chronic illnesses, such as lupus or rheumatoid arthritis, present a tangible example of the "negative" agency of corporeality, since the actual symptoms, as well as their severity, can vary from day to day and even within the course of the same day. Pain moves. A knee suddenly doesn't work. The sun kindles a flaming headache. Furthermore, since auto-immune diseases are affected by countless known, suspected, and unknown factors—such as stress, diet, or the weather—they illustrate Barad's sense of material agency as "'doing'/'being' in its intra-activity," in which myriad forces are constantly in play. While one no doubt would appreciate a full and complete understanding of this particular medical condition, even the combined information from physicians, medical research, support groups, and the experiential data of one's own body will not result in some sort of crystalline understanding, since there are many (how many?) forces continually intra-acting.

Without diminishing the specificity of living as a chronically ill person, there is obviously a sense in which all embodied beings experience corporeal agencies, be they positive, negative, or neutral. Acknowledging that one's body has its own forces, which are interlinked and continually intra-acting with wider material as well as social, economic, psychological, and cultural forces, can not only be useful but may also be ethical. In the most obvious sense, if one cannot presume to master one's own body, which has "its" own forces, many of which can never fully be comprehended, even with the help of medical knowledge and technologies, one cannot presume to master the rest of the world, which is forever intra-acting in inconceivably complex ways.

JUST BEYOND REACH: EPISTEMOLOGICAL SPACE AS ETHICAL SPACE

Feminist epistemology and environmental philosophy have long recognized the ethical impact of epistemological paradigms and practices. There is no space here to sketch out the intersections between these two fields, but we may note two salient examples of environmental feminist theory that encourage more cautious and capacious ways of knowing—ways of knowing that do not foreclose the actions, significance, and value of the more-than-human world. Donna Haraway, in "Situated Knowledges: The Science Question in Feminism and the Privilege of the Partial Perspective," offers a compelling epistemological model which requires that "the object of knowledge be pictured as an actor and agent, not a screen or ground or a resource, never finally as a slave to the master that closes off the dialectic in his unique agency and authorship of 'objective knowledge'" (1991, 198). Haraway uses a spatial metaphor to describe this stance: "Feminist objectivity *makes room* for surprises and ironies at the heart of all knowledge production; we are not in charge of the world" (1991, 199, emphasis added). We may imagine, perhaps, that the trickster coyote needs some sort of space, or habitat, to thrive.

Likewise, Catriona Sandilands uses some spatial metaphors to describe her "radical democratic vision that includes nature, not as positive, human-constructed presence, but as enigmatic, active Other" (1999, 181). She contends that "the best kind of human language around the space of unrepresentable nature is a democratic and politicized one that validates partiality and multiplicity and that can never claim to 'get it right'" (1999, 181). Epistemological "space" becomes ethical in environmental philosophy and feminist theory because it repels presumptions of human mastery that would reduce the stuff of life to mere "resources" for human consumption. Epistemological space needs to be contiguous space—it is always as close as our own skin—and yet it offers ample room for the more-than-human world to act, and, more to the point, to intra-act, in surprising ways. Allowing a space-time for unexpected material intra-actions, be they the actions of hawks nesting in high-rises or the effects of genetically modified plants on bees, butterflies, or human populations, is one way of understanding an ethics that embraces the wild, even as it is wary of wilderness paradigms that divide humans from nature and erase the presence of indigenous peoples.

Interestingly, some avenues of approach to "the" body, or even one's own body, sometimes echo wilderness imaginings of nature as an external, foreign, unknown, and perhaps unknowable space. As the poet and novelist Linda Hogan puts it in her memoir, *The Woman Who Watches Over the World:* "In the world of matter what is valuable lives, in much the same way, as in dreams, beneath the ground, just outside of human sight, sometimes just a bit beyond reach" (2001, 137). Hogan's musings imagine the interior of her own body as an unfamiliar space where she would like to "journey":

> Sometimes I see the dress of muscle and flesh worn by these bones, and wonder why I can't heal myself, why I can't change the body clothing as some believe, and let the bones be free, why I can't journey into the matter of my own body and touch the organs, loosen the ligaments where they hold things together, like the body Vesalius found, the network, the tangle not existing at the base of this human brain that sets us apart from animals who have so much grace. But the interior, the vital force, slips through all our hands, even with our own bodies. (2001, 191)

The passage begins with the repetition of "why I can't," which serves to complicate conventional notions of subjectivity—the "I" severed from the body is far less omniscient and omnipotent than it would like to be. The next sentence poses an alternative, a more constrained epistemology in which the image of "all our hands" suggests ways of knowing that are more corporeal and communal, and that recognize the elusive agency of natural forces. Significantly, the "I" here is no longer the subject of the sentence, but instead it is "the interior, the vital force" who acts, by "slip[ping] through all our hands."

Hogan's poetic account traces an internal journey that ends with a community of hands, reaching outwards. The space the "vital force" traverses is a trans-corporeal one, linking corporeal interiority with the more-than-human life processes. This trans-corporeal space may help us to imagine an epistemological time-space in which, because they are always acting and being acted upon, human bodies and non-human natures transform, unfold, and thereby resist categorization, complete knowledge, and mastery. As Moira Gatens explains, the

> Spinozist account of the body is of a productive and creative body which cannot be definitively "known" since it is not identical with itself across time. The body does not have a "truth" or a "true" nature since it is a process and its meaning and capacities will vary according to its context. . . . These limits and capacities can only be revealed by the on-going interactions of the body and its environment. (1996, 57)

These "ongoing interactions of the body and its environment" demand knowledge practices that emerge from the multiple entanglements of inter- and intra-connected being/doing/knowings. A material, trans-corporeal ethics would turn from the disembodied values and ideals of bounded individuals toward an attention to situated, evolving practices that have far-reaching and often unforeseen consequences for multiple peoples, species, and ecologies. Trans-corporeal, material ethics takes place in a "post-human" space, as described by Andrew Pickering: "a space in which the human actors are still there but now are inextricably entangled with the nonhuman, no longer at the center of the action and calling the shots. The world makes us in one and the same process as we make the world" (1995, 26).

MAPS OF TRANSIT

One way to map this post-human space is to focus on the traffic between bodies and natures. What are some of the routes from human corporeality to the flesh of the other-than-human and back again? How are both terms transformed by the recognition of their interconnection? What ethical or political positions emerge from the movement across human and more-than-human flesh?

Perhaps the most palpable example of trans-corporeality is that of food, whereby plants or animals become the substance of the human. While eating may seem a straightforward activity, peculiar material agencies may reveal themselves during the route from dirt to mouth.

Ladelle McWhorter tells how her quest to grow a real, flavorful tomato ends not only with a "high regard for dirt," as we have seen, but with a sense of kinship to this degraded substance. Munching on a bag of Doritos, she is about to toss the crumbs in her composting trench but stops:

> "Nope," I thought, "can't feed that crap to my dirt." I threw the crumbs in the trash and reached for that one last chip. It was halfway to my mouth before I was struck by what I'd just said. I looked out the kitchen window at my garden, my trenches, my dirt, and then my gaze turned downward toward my Dorito-stained hand. Dirt and flesh. Suddenly it occurred to me that, for all their differences, these two things I was looking at were cousins—not close cousins, but cousins, several deviations once removed. I haven't purchased a bag of Doritos since. (1999, 167)

As that last Dorito hangs—in mid-air—the epiphanic narrative surrounds it with a humorous recognition that this precarious sense of kinship between dirt and flesh may not only elevate dirt to the status of family member, but in this case, elevates the very substance of the self into something worthy of proper care and feeding. A queer, green, ethical family, indeed. We can trace the literal route though which dirt becomes flesh, via the tomato, a synecdoche for all plant and most animal foods that ultimately arise from the dirt, but McWhorter herself doesn't belabor that point, perhaps because dwelling on food, rather than the very matrix of life, serves up nature as an ingestible morsel. True, we are transformed by the food we consume (as the film *Supersize Me* will attest), but for the most part the model of incorporation emphasizes the outline of the human—food disappears into the human body, which remains solidly bounded.

In their revealing article "Incorporating Nature," Margaret FitzSimmons and David Goodman argue for a model of "incorporation" "as metaphor and as process—as a useful way of bringing nature into the body of social theory and, more literally, into the body of living organisms, including ourselves" (1998, 194). FitzSimmons and Goodman's complex model, which accounts for the agency of nature as well as social, economic, and political forces, promotes the notion of incorporation "to capture the relational materiality of ecologies and bodies that characterizes agro-food networks" (1998, 216). While this formulation provides an illuminating way of thinking through the productions of nature-culture, ultimately, the production of food is a rather one-sided affair, for the model of incorporation is only one bite away from capitalist consumption. Although McWhorter begins with a simple desire for a tomato, her scenario moves in the opposite direction, extending her own flesh to the dirt, rather than merely incorporating the fruits of the dirt into herself. McWhorter's Foucauldian analysis of corporeality, which for most of the book concerns not ecological issues but the regulatory regimes of sexual identity, reaches into the ground, becoming a thoroughgoing redefinition of the stuff of matter.

Drawing upon Spinoza rather than Foucault, Moria Gatens similarly describes human bodies that open out into the more-than-human world. The identity of the human body "can never be viewed as a final or finished product as in the case of the Cartesian automaton, since it is a body that is in constant interchange with its environment. The human body is radically open to its surroundings and can be composed, recomposed and decomposed by other bodies" (1996, 110). Whereas in a model of incorporation, the human self remains the selfsame, in Gatens's reading of Spinoza, the human body is never static because its interactions with other bodies always alter it. Gatens explains that these "'encounters' with other bodies are good or bad depending on whether they aid or harm our characteristic constitution" (1996, 110). Oddly, Spinoza's understanding of the body seems particularly akin to some twenty-first-century models of corporeality such as that of the environmental health movement, which warns that particular "interchange[s] with [the] environment" may result in disease, illness, and death. Indeed, the many protests against genetically modified (GM) foods demonstrate that these foods may not be benignly incorporated into the human body. GM foods may well have unintended health effects on humans or other creatures that science may not discover for decades.

While the gastronomical relations between earth and stomach offer a rather digestible example of trans-corporeal transit, Vicki Kirby presents a counterintuitive account of how human corporeality opens out onto the more-than-human world. In her brilliant book *Telling Flesh: The Substance of the Corporeal,* Kirby presents a provocative reading of Jacques Derrida's famous dictum, "There is no outside of text." She contends: "It is as if the very tissue of substance, the ground of Being, is this mutable intertext—a 'writing' that both circumscribes and exceeds the conventional divisions of nature and culture" (1997, 61). In fact, Kirby opens up the possibility "that nature scribbles or that flesh reads": "For if nature is literate, then the question 'What is language'—or more scandalously, 'Who reads?'—fractures the Cartesian subject to its very foundation" (1997, 127). Kirby extends the poststructuralist model of textuality to such a degree that its most basic terms are radically rewritten:

> What I am trying to conjure here is some "sense" that word and flesh are utterly implicated, not because "flesh" is actually a word that mediates the fact of what is being referred to, but because the entity of a word, the identity of a sign, the system of language, and the domain of culture—none of these are autonomously enclosed upon themselves. Rather they are all emergent *within* a force field of differentiations that has no exteriority in any final sense. (1997, 127)

Kirby's critique transforms poststructuralism into a truly posthumanist horizon as it refuses to delineate the human, the cultural, or the linguistic against a background of mute matter. Nature, culture, bodies, texts—all unravel into a limitless "force field of differentiation." For McWhorter, Gatens, and Kirby, that which had been exclusive to the Human opens out into a wider realm in which the substance of human corporeality—and in Kirby's case, even human linguistic systems—is not ultimately separable from that which it is difficult not to call "nature." These theorists can be read as a sort of postscript to feminism's many invocations of nature as an undomesticated—literally, non-domestic—space. For the walls of domestic enclosure that would separate human from nature and define the human as such are nowhere to be found, as human corporeality and textuality effortlessly extend into the more-than-human-world. Word, flesh, and dirt are no longer discrete.

From the standpoint of environmental ethics, it may be dangerous to make comparisons between human corporeality and nonhuman nature, since in some ways this replicates the very dualisms at the root of the problem. Nature, to put it bluntly, is populated with myriad nonhuman minds as well as matter; it does not make sense to equate the many self-directed, lively, communicative, "cultural" beings with the supposedly inert "stuff" of matter. Val Plumwood, for example, makes the compelling argument that to combat the persistent nature/culture, body/mind dualisms of Western culture we must "reconceive of ourselves as more animal and embodied, more 'natural,' and that we reconceive of nature as more mindlike than in Cartesian conceptions" (1993, 124). Similarly, even though Carolyn Merchant notes that one of the reasons women become activists is "because their bodies, or the bodies of those with whom they have a caring relationship, are threatened by toxic or radioactive substances," she does not emphasize corporeality as a connection between human and nonhuman, preferring instead, as we have seen, to "elevate" nature to the status of a political "subject" (1996, xviii).

I agree with Plumwood that it is essential for environmental politics, practices, and ethics to continually articulate compelling understandings of the "mindlike" aspects of nature—such as the languages of dolphins or bees, or the cultures of elephants and chimps—things that people have gone to great lengths to deny. I would suggest, however, that dwelling within trans-corporeal space, where "body" and "nature" are comprised of the same material, which has been constituted, simultaneously, by the forces of evolution, natural and human history, political inequities, cultural contestations, biological and chemical processes, and other factors too numerous to list, renders rigid distinctions between "mind" and "matter" impossibly simplistic. Thus, by recasting the terms of the debate, something as unlikely a candidate for glory as dirt may be understood as an agent, rather than as (solely) the ground for the action of something else. Although this may sound like a mere philosophical exercise, and in some ways it is, contemporary material realities and practices may propel this philosophical rethinking, since it has become more and more difficult to separate "human" from "nature." As Haraway so presciently predicted with her cyborg manifesto, in the early twenty-first century the dichotomies between mind and matter, culture and nature, are no longer stable moorings. Examples abound. Here's one: the recent cascade of psychopharmaceuticals, most notably the (in)famous popularity of Prozac, make it impossible to consider the human mind, emotions, psyche, or "spirit" as something distinct from biochemistry and neuro-networks.[5]

Yet even as it becomes more difficult for humans to indulge in delusions of grandeur that place us far above a base nature, that does not mean, from an environmentalist perspective, that we should forward notions of trans-corporeal space that are, by definition, somewhat anthropocentric, since this space may be imagined as that which surrounds the human. More specifically, it may be dangerous, from an environmentalist perspective, to dwell within the interface between human and nature, since that is the very site of environmental devastation wrought by (over)consumption, dumping, and trampling. In short, it may still be best to embrace environmental ideals of wilderness, or the respect for the "sovereignty" of nature (as Plumwood puts it), both of which work to establish boundaries that would protect nature from human exploitation and degradation. Even as the wilderness ideal has become unsustainable, both because of its pernicious ideological legacy of erasing the presence of indigenous peoples and because it promotes a devaluation of the various "natures" that most of us actually inhabit,[6] the survival of many species depends on creating more areas in which wild creatures and ecosystems can flourish. Some of these places may include humans involved in sustainable subsistence practices. I think, however, that it is possible to argue both for the value of places in which nonhuman creatures are sovereign or wild and human impact is minimal and, at the same time, to reconceptualize various routes of connection to that seemingly distant space. For the nonhuman bodies that inhabit wild areas are riddled with the same toxins as our own human bodies, since these toxins reach everywhere, carried by water, air, and the tissues of living, traveling creatures. Trans-corporeality, in that sense, need not be limited to the area contiguous with the human, but may instead offer a path of connection from one's own embodied existence to the survival of nonhuman creatures.

The need to cultivate a tangible sense of connection to "nature" in order to encourage an environmentalist ethos is underscored by the pervasive sense of disconnection that casts "environmental issues" as containable, distant, dismissible topics. Witness, for example, the right-wing denial of global warming, or the blasé use of dangerous pesticides and herbicides at home (the attitude may be offhand, but the poison isn't). Observe, as well, the flood of horror movies that begin with the threat of some boundary-crossing creature, only to conclude with a triumphant human transcendence from nature.[7] Yet the sense of kinship, connection, and unraveling between dirt and flesh, word and world, needs to be accompanied by capacious epistemologies that allow for the unfolding of innumerable material intra-actions. Interestingly, the need for actual wilderness areas, which grant various creatures the space to thrive, parallels the need for epistemological space, which insists that the material world continually intra-acts in ways that are too complex to be predicted in advance. The "material world" here includes human actions and intra-actions, along with the intra-actions of man-made substances, all of which intra-act with natural creatures, forces, and ecological systems as well as with the bodies of humans. The maps of transit between human corporeality and nonhuman nature are infinite. But even a few sketches suggest that political and ethical interests usually seen as separate are inextricably linked by the substantial transit across bodies and natures.

THE TRANS-CORPOREAL TIME-SPACE OF TOXIC BODIES

Pickering, in *The Mangle of Practice: Time, Agency, and Science,* describes scientists as "human agents in a field of material agency which they struggle to capture in machines." He argues that "human and material agency are reciprocally and emergently intertwined in this struggle. Their contours emerge in the temporality of practice" (1995, 21). Time, then, fosters a kind of "space" for the actions, or agency, of the material world to reveal itself. Just as Pickering's mangle of (scientific) practice captures nature's agency by observing how it unfolds in time, trans-corporeal ethics acknowledge a time-space for the workings of human and nonhuman bodies. The space-time of trans-corporeality is a place of both pleasure and danger—the pleasures of desire, surprise, interconnection, and lively emergence as well as the dangers of pain, toxicity, disability, and death.

Unfortunately, we have neither the space nor the time to examine pleasure here. Instead, we will turn toward one particularly potent site for examining the ethical space of trans-corporeality: toxic bodies. Certainly, all bodies, human and otherwise, are, to greater or lesser degrees, toxic at this point in history. Even those humans and animals who reside far from the most polluted zones still harbor a chemical stew in their blood and their tissues, as the oft-cited example of contaminated Inuit breast milk will attest. Since the same chemical substance may poison the workers who produce it, the neighborhood in which it is produced, and the plants and animals who end up consuming it, the traffic in toxins reveals the interconnections between various movements, such as those of environmental health, occupational health, labor movements, environmental justice, environmentalism, ecological medicine, disability rights, green living, anti-globalization, consumer rights, and child welfare. The traffic in toxins may, in fact, render it nearly impossible for humans to imagine that their own health and welfare is disconnected from that of the rest of the planet or to imagine that it is possible to protect "nature" by merely creating separate, distinct areas in which "it" is "preserved." In other words, the ethical space of trans-corporeality is never an elsewhere but is always already here, in whatever compromised, ever-catalyzing form. Greenpeace, an environmental organization known for its innovative tactics, recently launched a campaign against mercury that encouraged people to send in a sample of their own hair to be tested for mercury contamination. Such an action renders one's own corporeal connection to global environmental campaigns quite palpable, especially since Greenpeace, in turn, informed each participant of the level of mercury in his or her body, explained the significance of that number in terms of possible health effects, and discussed how to minimize mercury exposure through both dietary and political means. To take another example, tracing the traffic in toxins may allow us to notice that carcinogenic chemicals are produced by some of the same companies that sell chemotherapy drugs. This may be a useful thing to notice.

On a larger scale, it is useful to consider that it is probably not possible, even in the "foreseeable(?) future," to predict the staggeringly vast number of chemical interactions that may occur as a result of the "*billions* of pounds of toxic chemicals being routinely emitted" in the United States alone (Steingraber 1997, 102). The problem is not only that, as Sandra Steingraber informs us, "two-thirds of the most widely used chemicals have still not gone through basic carcinogenicity tests," but that far less is known about how various chemical combinations inter- and intra-act in bodies and "environments" (1997, 281, 258). Steingraber advocates the "precautionary principle," which states, in part, that

> [w]hen an activity raises threats of harm to human health or the environment, precautionary measures should be taken even if some cause and effect relations are not fully established scientifically. In this context, the proponent of an activity, rather than the public, should bear the burden of proof. (1997, 284)

From the perspective of all of us inhabitants of toxic, trans-corporeal, material places, the "precautionary principle" may well epitomize the notion of epistemological space as ethical space, as it emerges from a scientific and political understanding of the enormity of the effects of material agencies that humans can never quite chart and can certainly never master. The precautionary principle serves as a practical, commonsensical procedural map as well as an embodiment of an inter-corporeal, as well as trans-corporeal ethic that emerges from more constrained, more responsible epistemologies.

To turn back to feminist theory, thinking through toxic bodies allows us to reimagine human corporeality, and materiality itself, not as a utopian or romantic substance existing prior to social inscription, but as something that always bears the trace of history, social position, region, and the uneven distribution of risk. Indeed, as Sandra Steingraber puts it, comparing the composition of the human body to the rings on a tree, "our bodies, too, are living scrolls of sorts. What is written there—inside the fibers of our cells and chromosomes—is a record of our exposure to environmental contaminants" (1997, 236). Toxic bodies are produced and reproduced, simultaneously, by science, industrialized culture, agribusiness, capitalist consumerism, and other forces. Toxic bodies are certainly not essentialist, since they are volatile, emergent, and continually evolving, in and of "themselves," but also as they encounter different sorts of chemicals as they move from neighborhoods or jobs, or as they otherwise encounter various products or pollutants. These bodies are certainly post-Humanist, not merely because their borders are exceedingly leaky, but because even one's own putatively "individual" experience and understanding of one's body is mediated by science, medicine, epidemiology, and the swirl of subcultures, organizations, Web sites, and magazines devoted to exposing dangers and cultivating alternative and oppositional practices and pleasures.

Although they are not something to celebrate, toxic bodies may help lead feminist theory out of the false dilemma of having to choose between a romanticized valorization of bodies and natures or an anti-essentialist flight from the grounds of our being. As a particularly vivid example of trans-corporeal space, toxic bodies insist that environmentalism, human health, and social justice cannot be severed. They encourage us to imagine ourselves in constant interchange with the "environment," and, paradoxically perhaps, to imagine an epistemological space that allows for both the unpredictable becomings of other creatures and the limits of human knowledge.

NOTES

1. See Val Plumwood (1993) for an analysis of the "backgrounding" of both women and nature.

2. See Alaimo 2000 for more on how American women writers and theorists have transformed particular conceptions of nature for various political ends.

3. Haraway explains that the cyborg was designed to do "feminist work in Reagan's Star Wars times of the mid-1980s," but by "the end of the millennium, cyborgs could no longer do the work of a proper herding dog to gather up the threads needed for critical inquiry" (2003, 4). Substituting canines for cyborgs, Haraway insists that dogs are "fleshly material-semiotic presences," not just "surrogates for theory" (2003, 5).

4. This article is reprinted in this collection.

5. See Elizabeth A. Wilson's work in this volume and elsewhere.

6. See William Cronon, "The Trouble with Wilderness; or, Getting Back to the Wrong Nature" (1996).

7. See Alaimo 2001 and 1997.

References

Alaimo, Stacy. 1997. "Endangered Humans? Wired Bodies and the Human Wilds." *Camera Obscura* 40–41: 227–44.

———. 2000. *Undomesticated Ground: Recasting Nature as Feminist Space.* Ithaca, N.Y.: Cornell University Press.

———. 2001. "Discomforting Creatures: Monstrous Natures in Recent Films." In *Beyond Nature Writing,* ed. Karla Armbruster and Kathleen Wallace, 279–96. Charlottesville: University of Virginia Press.

Barad, Karen. 1998. "Getting Real: Technoscientific Practices and the Materialization of Reality." *differences* 10.2: 87–128.

———. 2003. "Posthumanist Performativity: Toward an Understanding of How Matter Comes to Matter." *Signs* 28.3: 801–31.

Birke, Lynda. 1999. "Bodies and Biology." In *Feminist Theory and the Body: Reader,* ed. Janet Price and Margrit Shildrick, 42–49. New York: Routledge.

Bordo, Susan. 1998. "Bringing Body to Theory." In *Body and Flesh: A Philosophical Reader,* ed. Donna Welton, 84–97. Malden: Blackwell.

Brown Blackwell, Antoinette. 1875. *The Sexes Throughout Nature.* New York: G. P. Putnam's Sons.

Butler, Judith. 1992. "Contingent Foundations: Feminism and the Question of 'Postmodernism.'" In *Feminists Theorize the Political,* ed. Judith Butler and Joan W. Scott, 1–21. New York: Routledge.

Cronon, William. 1996. "The Trouble with Wilderness; or, Getting Back to the Wrong Nature." In *Uncommon Ground: Rethinking the Human Place in Nature,* ed. William Cronon. New York: Norton.

De Lauretis, Teresa. 2004. "Statement Due." *Critical Inquiry* 30.2: 365–68.

FitzSimmons, Margaret, and David Goodman. 1998. "Incorporating Nature: Environmental Narratives and the Reproduction of Food." In *Remaking Reality: Nature at the Millennium,* ed. Bruce Braun and Noel Castree. London: Routledge.

Gatens, Moira. 1996. *Imaginary Bodies: Ethics, Power and Corporeality.* New York: Routledge.

Haraway, Donna J. 1991. *Simians, Cyborgs, and Women: The Reinvention of Nature.* New York: Routledge.

———. 2003. *Companion Species Manifesto: Dogs, People, and Significant Otherness.* Chicago: Prickly Paradigm Press.

Hird, Myra J. 2004. "Naturally Queer." *Feminist Theory* 5.1: 85–89.

Hogan, Linda. 2001. *The Woman Who Watches Over the World: A Native Memoir.* New York: W. W. Norton.

Kirby, Vicki. 1997. *Telling Flesh: The Substance of the Corporeal.* New York: Routledge.

Kristeva, Julia. 1982. *Powers of Horror: An Essay on Abjection.* Trans. Leon S. Roudiez. New York: Columbia University Press.

McWhorter, Ladelle. 1999. *Bodies and Pleasures: Foucault and the Politics of Sexual Normalization.* Bloomington: Indiana University Press.

Merchant, Carolyn. 1989. *Ecological Revolutions: Nature, Gender, and Science in New England.* Chapel Hill: University of North Carolina Press.

———. 1996. *Earthcare: Women and the Environment.* New York: Routledge.
Pickering, Andrew. 1995. *The Mangle of Practice: Time, Agency, and Science.* Chicago: University of Chicago Press.
Plumwood, Val. 1993. *Feminism and the Mastery of Nature.* New York: Routledge.
Sandilands, Catriona. 1999. *The Good-Natured Feminist: Ecofeminism and the Quest for Democracy.* Minneapolis: University of Minnesota Press.
Steingraber, Sandra. 1997. *Living Downstream: A Scientist's Personal Investigation of Cancer and the Environment.* New York: Vintage.
Tuana, Nancy. 1996. "Fleshing Gender, Sexing the Body: Refiguring the Sex/Gender Distinction." *Southern Journal of Philosophy* 35 (Supplement): 53–71.
Wendell, Susan. 1996. *The Rejected Body: Feminist Philosophical Reflections on Disability.* New York: Routledge.
Wilson, Elizabeth. 1998. *Neural Geographies: Feminism and the Microstructure of Cognition.* New York: Routledge.

9

LANDSCAPE, MEMORY, AND FORGETTING: THINKING THROUGH (MY MOTHER'S) BODY AND PLACE

Catriona Mortimer-Sandilands

December 12, 2004

I have just arrived at the Royal Jubilee Hospital, having driven here with my father immediately after my arrival in Victoria from Toronto. My mother is inside this building; she has been here for two weeks as an inpatient undergoing a battery of tests to determine, exactly, what's wrong with her. Apparently she had very low blood volume, which—given that they can't actually find a logical cause, even after several invasions culminating in a colonoscopy—suggests a bleeding ulcer that has now healed. She has received liters of blood. According to my father, she looks a great deal better than she did even last time I saw her in the fall.

But since she came to the hospital, she has been extremely confused about where and when she is, and who the people are around her. Admittedly, she spent a lot of that time in a temporary bed in the ER, surrounded by the most disturbing hospital noises possible, 24 hours a day—no real sleep there. And admittedly, my mother has never in her life acquiesced to the idea that she might be sick and probably has no idea what to do with being a patient, let alone with being surrounded by (other) sick people with their particular needs, noises, sounds, smells. But I am afraid of what I am going to find as I follow my father along the surgical green corridor toward my mother's ward bed. I am afraid that she won't recognize me. In anticipation, I rehearse the recent history of our interactions and find in it ample evidence of memory loss, confusion, odd fragments of retrospection inserted into conversations about something else, and most of all, those slightly blank stares that suggest that she may be here but she is really somewhere else entirely.

Dad and I arrive at her bed. To my great relief, she seems to recognize me, but at the same moment she thanks me for coming to visit her today. I can't quite explain what is wrong about that gesture—the visit, the "today," the sense that I had been there yesterday, the feeling that I might have been another hospital volunteer, the absence of recognition that I had just arrived from 5,000 kilometers away—but something was quite profoundly wrong. Yes, Mum has had moments of confusion for some months, years even, a sort of withdrawal from the demands of daily cycles of reality, clearly a part of the very gradual process in which she has abdicated from the necessity of making meaning with other people in the same way that she has divested herself of the responsibility for driving, cooking, shopping, reading. Yes, Mum has had lapses of word-memory, but these are almost as old as my memory of her—and not much worse than my own. Today's confusion and withdrawal seems quite different. It feels like she has a world of her own making, and I have punctured it, uncomfortably forcing her out into the cold, pressing her to touch a reality—my reality—of which she no longer has much need.

She is passive. She is docile. (My mother is neither of these things.) She is not quite aware of the relationship between the "now" and the moments that preceded or are to follow. My father leaves her a note, in his unmistakable handwriting, telling her in large letters that he loves her, that we will be back the following morning, that she shouldn't worry. Without it, she might panic during the night. The thing that worries me the most, oddly, is the fact that she has eaten all the butterscotch pudding that was served with her hospital meal. The mother that I knew hated pudding, hated butterscotch, hated the bland, sweet flavors that she associated with all of the worst of North American TV culture. My father tells me that he has had to hide the pudding on her hospital trays every evening or she won't eat the rest of her dinner.

December 15

I am sitting in a meeting room just off the ward, surrounded by an occupational therapist, a psychologist, a social worker, and two other women whose titles and roles are not entirely obvious, even if they are clearly familiar with my mother's recent condition. We are talking about the process through which my mother will return home and the care arrangements that will kick in once she gets there. The OT is talking about lifting chairs, toileting assistance, mobility aids; the psychologist is talking about my mother's less-than-stellar performance on several tests of her mental competence; the social worker is talking about 24-hour home care. My father is also present, but I think he is even more overwhelmed and frightened than I am by this new reality; he lets me do the talking.

All eyes turn to the door as the gerontologist enters the meeting, late. She sits down, talks about different causes of dementia, talks about my mother's various physical and cognitive tests, talks about thyroid levels and acetylcholine and CT scans. She is sympathetic but clearly not interested in hearing about butterscotch pudding. She says the word I have been dreading: Alzheimer's.

BODY, LANDSCAPE, MEMORY

In a recent exchange in the journal *Environmental Ethics,* David Abram and Ted Toadvine engage in a spirited debate about questions of sensuousness, perception, reflection, writing, memory, and landscape. Focused on their conflicting interpretations of Abram's popular book *The Spell of the Sensuous* (1996), and eventually resting on their divergent readings of Merleau-Ponty's *Phenomenology of Perception* (1962),[1] Toadvine and Abram each attempt to address a set of ontological questions that are, I think, foundational for environmental philosophy: How can we understand the human body as a particular site of perceptions of, and interactions with, the more-than-human world? How can we describe the relationship between body and mind, or between experience and reflection, in organizing human experiences of the environment? And—crucially for a feminist inquiry, if not always for Abram and Toadvine—how is this relationship historical and social, in that embodied perception and reflection take particular forms in the midst of the technological and discursive (i.e., power) relations in which they cannot help but be situated?

Abram's argument in *The Spell of the Sensuous* is provocative. It rests, I think, on two important phenomenological premises. First, and in contradistinction to the majority of current environmental wisdom, Abram locates both human ontology and ethical possibility in the body's experiential and sensuous relationships to the world. Although he is not the first to point out the importance of this kind of trajectory for environmental philosophy (see Evernden 1985), he argues clearly, for example, that one cannot conceive of an environmental ethics simply as a question of mind, as if one can simply, reasonably, choose to live one's body differently. Second, and perhaps more foundationally, Abram understands that *all meaning* includes a perceptual dimension and that perception itself is a quality of the relationship between body and world, necessarily a dynamic product of relationship, experience, influence. As he puts it in his rejoinder to Toadvine, "the simplest event of sensory perception is already an instance of an organism receiving an echo of itself from the world—an interaction with the world from which one returns to oneself changed, refracted somewhat, and through which the world is also reflected, returned to itself afresh" (2005, 172).

The problem for Toadvine is not so much Abram's basic eco-phenomenological position that all human thought has a basis in perceptual relations to the world and that environmental philosophy must thus attend to the material, sensual, bodily nature of these relations—and not just to reason and reflection, as is often the case—en route to any kind of ecological transformation.[2] Rather, the problem for Toadvine lies in Abram's reading of environmental history, and particularly in what he sees as the latter's move to *reverse* the Western priority of reason and reflection over perception and experience by castigating the advent of literacy and "alphabetical thinking" as the source of human alienation from the richness of our perceptual experiences. For Abram, the acquisition of writing has, historically, eroded the ability of literate cultures to *recognize* the basis of conscious thought in the perception of the world in the way that oral cultures continue to do:

> In the absence of a formalized writing system, it would seem that human cultures spontaneously find a ready echo of their own vitality in

> the manifold life of the sensuous surroundings; their direct sensory participation with those surroundings discloses a cosmos that is everywhere animate, a breathing landscape that speaks in a myriad of voices. (2005, 176)

For Toadvine, Abram's argument demonizes reflection and consciousness as modes of thought that are an "ill-fated consequence of our appropriation of the phonetic alphabet" and "a challenge to and a break with our perceptual reciprocity rather than . . . an elaboration or recapitulation of this reciprocity" (Toadvine 2005, 161). Mental self-reflexiveness is, in this argument, a short-circuiting of sensual appreciation; the ability to write transfers our attention from the other to the sign; and the page substitutes, solipsistically, for the more-than-human world as source of meaning. Thus to Toadvine, Abram is advocating a (conscious!) return to perception (and thus a move away from reflection as part of the *problem*) as the embodied basis of an environmental ethics; in so doing, Abram "implies that the problem of solipsism, and, in fact, any problem of separation between self and other, is eliminated once we rediscover this sensual level of contact" (2005, 165).

Abram sees his own argument a bit differently. Where Toadvine sees Abram rejecting reflection in favor of perception, and literacy in favor of animism, Abram argues that reflection, engendered by attention to alphabetic scribbles on a page is, in fact, a historically specific *mode* of animism: "Only by transferring the synaesthetic magic of our senses away from the many-voiced earth to the marks inscribed on a sheet of papyrus could we make these marks—these ostensibly inanimate bits of ink—begin to speak" (Abram 2005, 176). The problem for Abram, here, is not the existence of alphabetic reflection as much as it is its hegemony. Clarifying his emphasis in *The Spell of the Sensuous,* he writes in response to Toadvine that "written letters, *and the multiple technologies made possible by the printed word,* have today usurped much of the evocative power that once resided, for us, in the depths of the surrounding terrain" (2005, 177; emphasis in original). Thus the necessary move for environmental ethics, as Abram sees it, is more about redeploying than rejecting reflection. Eco-phenomenology in particular, given its concern "with the careful *description* of the way things present themselves to our awareness" (2005, 188; emphasis in original) should begin to write *to*, rather than simply *about*, rivers, trees, and other actors in the more-than-human world, thus moving writing away from rational solipsism and into ecopoetics (on which there is much more to say, but that is a topic for a different essay).[3]

In the midst of this debate, there is a fascinating germ concerning the relations among body, mind, and landscape. If we understand symbolic reflection and sensual perception as specific embodied practices that are not only physically but *historically* located—enabled differently in the context of different technologies, social relations, and interactions with the more-than-human world—then it becomes possible to investigate the *specific* physical and historical conditions in which these practices unfold, and unfold in relation to one another.[4] Abram takes us partway toward this view in his argument that oral cultures develop collective meaning and memory by inscribing their stories on the landscape, rather than on paper: "Each part of the topography evokes a part of some tale that quietly resounds in one's awareness. *The land, in other words, is the primary mnemonic, or memory-trigger, for recalling the ancestral stories*" (2005, 177; emphasis in original).

If we replace the sweeping statement about the essential nature of orality and landscape (and the Edenic sense of an ecology lost in the wake of literacy, which Toadvine is right to criticize) with a set of questions about the specific relations in which different forms of thought support, and are supported by, different perceptual relations to landscape (not to mention different landscapes), then we arrive at a useful interrogative tool with which to question the complex relationships between modes of thought and modes of embodied interaction with the more-than-human world. It is no longer (if it was ever) a question of challenging the detachment of mind from body, thinking from perception, or reason from nature; on this view, it is a question of asking *how* particular modes of thought are located in embodied experience, of *how* both symbolic reflection and sensuous perception are phenomenally organized in particular techno-historical relationships between human bodies and others.

I recognize that my account does no particular justice to Merleau-Ponty (who, as Toadvine points out, has argued that reflective knowledge is a "sublimation" of incarnation and not its opposite), and is also a considerable distillation of both Abram's and Toadvine's eco-phenomenological positions. Nonetheless, I will now move on to the more specific question animating this paper, and more precisely the role my mother plays in prompting me to ask questions about the different ways that symbolic reflection and perceptual experience might find, in particular historical and social contexts, expression and support in the sensuous experience of the more-than-human world. To be less cryptic: The more I come to know about Alzheimer's disease, the more carefully I am led to consider the social, and indeed deeply personal, ways in which embodiment is intertwined with relationships between and among reflection, perceptual experience, and landscape. Against those phenomenological accounts that emphasize a relatively universal human perception of the world (including both Abram and Toadvine, despite the former's emphasis on the historical transformations wrought by writing), Alzheimer's shows the deep particularity of experiencing and reflecting bodies in their relations to place; *with* phenomenology, however, Alzheimer's demonstrates the ways in which reflection is supported by perception, and in which both are located in interactions with place. In particular, in Alzheimer's disease the question of *memory* ties together bodies and landscapes in ways that reveal the inextricable connection between physicality and reflection and also the ways in which different types of memory combine to enable (or not) socially sanctioned and culturally meaningful interactions with the more-than-human world.

Most accounts of Alzheimer's disease focus on brain structure and function. In general, the accepted (if profoundly uncertain) medical narrative is that Alzheimer's disease is characterized by an abundance of "plaques and tangles," which are, respectively, deposits of beta-amyloid (a protein fragment that builds up in the space between nerve cells) and fibers of tau (another protein that builds up inside cells; Alzheimer's Association 2006, 11). Although nobody seems certain about the cause of Alzheimer's (do plaques cause tangles? do tangles cause plaques? does something else cause them both?), what is also generally accepted is that most people develop plaques and tangles as they age, that people who have Alzheimer's develop a lot more than people who don't, and that these complex deposits of protein in and around brain nerve cells disrupt communication between and among cells in addition to diminishing cellular function itself; ultimately "it's the destruction and death of nerve cells that causes the memory failure, personality changes, problems in carrying out daily activities and other symptoms of Alzheimer's disease" (2006, 11). Firm diagnosis is as elusive as a clear causal explanation; the only way of knowing for certain that a person has Alzheimer's is through a brain biopsy, generally only performed postmortem.

What is particularly interesting about Alzheimer's disease is that it always starts in the same region of the brain, the hippocampus, which David Shenk, more poetically than most, describes as "a curved, two-inch-long, peapod-like structure in the brain's temporal lobes" (2001, 37). The hippocampus is key to the creation of long-term memories (which can be either episodic, what we remember doing, or semantic, what we know); it seems to be the place in the brain (and we know so little about the brain that "seems" is a necessary qualifier) where short-term memory is converted into long-term, the middle part of the longer remembering process that takes us all the way from sense perception to abstraction and recall. What happens to people with Alzheimer's is that, say, the memory of "leaving the car keys in the bathroom isn't so much *lost* as it was never actually *formed*" (Shenk 2001, 47; emphases in original). Older memories (both episodic and semantic) persist long after new information can't be remembered. (One remembers what keys are, and possibly even where this particular set was ground, even if one can't remember where they were five minutes ago.) And muscle memory, or procedural or kinesthetic memory, persists even longer for the person with Alzheimer's; it is created differently (specifically, through physical repetition), and stored in an entirely different region of the brain. One can dance beautifully with a beloved partner that one now no longer recognizes even faintly.

Memory of *all* kinds is, however, physical. As Shenk puts it, "memory, like consciousness itself, isn't a thing that can be isolated or extracted, but a living process, a vast and dynamic interaction of neural synapses involved in . . . a temporary constellation of activity. Each specific memory is a unique network of neurons from different regions of the brain coordinating with one another" (2001, 51). A memory traces an electro-chemical pathway from neuron to neuron (called an engram); no two memories follow the same path, and the more often a particular route is followed, the more chemically sensitive particular neurons become to one another. I find this idea quite extraordinarily beautiful: in the act of remembering something, the world is, quite literally, written into our brain structure. And memory allows the body to greet the world with greater physical ease the more often we have a particular sensory experience. Far from a reductionist account that would discard consciousness in favor of brain structure, this account is of a meeting between embodied mind and active world that must include not only physical experience but social relationships, not only sensory data but the interaction between any given sense-moment and what has gone before. (Indeed, a dominant social relationship would be, literally, more clearly inscribed in the brain and more amenable to a strong memory: hegemony is physical.) Histories are uniquely embodied.

More robust memories are less susceptible to disintegration. That is part of the reason why studies have tended to show that people with more education generally develop Alzheimer's later in life (though one can also imagine questions of nutrition and environmental contamination playing a role—not that the Alzheimer's research industry has seriously pursued the possibility of an environmental cause). That is also why people who do crossword puzzles tend to fare better than others (although my mother was a brilliant crossword puzzler; my parents used to do the terribly hard cryptic ones from the British papers that my aunt used to send in packets several times a year). In an odd way, then, Abram turns out to be partly correct, in this view, about the debilitating effects of alphabetic technologies; as lists and encyclopedias and databases take the place of individual memorization (in other words, as memory becomes more collective and less experiential), the brain simply doesn't get exercised as much. Although I don't think anyone would consider that Alzheimer's is a trade-off for literacy or reflective consciousness (it is fair to say that it is a product of industrial societies in which health care helps people to live long enough to develop it), it is interesting to note that human beings are the only creatures that "naturally" suffer from Alzheimer's. (Several species, including cats, dogs, bears, lemurs, and polar bears are, however, known to have some form of senile dementia, and similar proteins appear to be at work in the brain in all of them; Shenk 2001, 179.)

What these accounts of hippocampus and engram and plaque and tangle fail to emphasize, however, despite the glorious physicality of their view, is that memory does not reside solely in the brain. As Abram and Toadvine both argue, in their own ways, perceptual and reflective thought converge in remembrance; and remembrance—the act of bringing experience to reflection and/or tissue, the act of embodying an act or object or place or concept in some portion of the brain or another—is not solely a question of the remembering subject. Both the written page and the storied landscape are warehouses of memory that are external to the individual body; although the act of reading a page and that of walking through a range of sacred hills might be different, both in terms of the portion of the brain involved and in terms of the relationship to place engendered in the act, the fact remains that the act of remembering involves a recognition of a relationship between the body/mind and the external world that is not only determined by internal forces. The experience of memory is thus always already social, technological, and physical in that the conditions of the relationship between brain and object cannot help but be located in a complex range of conditions that offer the subject to the experience, and experience to the subject.

For a person with Alzheimer's, the diminution of the hippocampus does not eradicate memory: it eradicates the ability to create, from the immediate world, a new pathway that leads, eventually, into narrative or semantic longevity. Kinesthetic memory is the last thing to go; one can remember the physical acts involved in walking through a landscape in the absence of recognizing the landscape itself, naming it, telling it to others. This does not mean that there is no memory; it means that the kinds of memory that are valued and understood in the context of current social relationships of coherent, narrative self (not to mention language) are undermined, rendered impossible in the same moment that the memories that are very much present to the person—the familiarity of what it feels like to walk, to touch, even to dance—are read as irrelevant, primitive, part of a diminished self that has moved away from rational comprehension and expression.

Stories about Alzheimer's brains tell us a great deal about the progression of a disease, about the gradual and eventually complete obliteration of areas of mind, rather like an electrical blackout that progressively shuts off parts of a power grid, leaving the world dark, without communicative connection between place and place. But such stories, in their valuation of reflection over perception and cognitive over kinesthetic memory, and in their blindness to the fact that memory does not, in fact, reside solely in the body, do not necessarily serve the needs of the person with Alzheimer's well. What, for example, would it look like to attend to the parts of memory that persist once episodic and then semantic memories fail? Could one offer familiarity, not in the name or even the face, but in the touch or motion? Is there a bodily rhythm of a person's being that could be echoed in assessing and assisting memory, rather than diagnostic drills about dates and events and signs to which even the most rational person might not be able to respond correctly? Phenomenology suggests that there are perceptual relations that cradle reflective ones, that there are bodily experiences that engender specific possibilities for symbolic reflection, that the symbolic is one realm of modes of thinking with complex relations to the perceptual. Is it that great a step to suggest that memory resides in the body, and in the brain, and in the landscape, in different ways in different sets of circumstances?

June 19, 2005

My mother has been, for about three months now, walking a lot. At first, although she is clearly much better than she was in December (a fact that I gratefully, if probably reductively, attribute to her thyroid medication),

I was very nervous about this turn of events. Not only did she insist on using a walker, even around the house, as recently as March (she actively resisted going for a walk with us on Easter weekend), but she still hasn't demonstrated that she is entirely capable of such acts as recognizing people, dates, and current events. None of her other ordinary skills have returned: she still hasn't learned how to work the "new" stove (my parents have had it for two years); she regularly forgets common words for things, inserting "so to speak" when she uses a wildly imprecise term for an object, as if she cleverly intended the metaphor (at least she knows that she is forgetting, and compensating); and despite her stated intentions about the stack of Christmas cards beside her chair, she hasn't corresponded with a single one of her family or close friends (for my mother, this is a noticeable gap). Having heard, perhaps, one too many stories of Alzheimer's "wanderers," I worry that she will go out for a walk and find herself lost, not because she hasn't been where she finds herself a thousand times (they have lived on Ten Mile Point for more than fifty years, so the walks can indeed be counted in thousands), but because she no longer has the ability to recognize the place as familiar. I am a long way away, even if I come back regularly to check in; my father simply can't walk well enough to go with her. So she walks by herself, and I have to hope that, after fifty years, people know where she belongs even if she doesn't.

But despite my paranoia, the walking appears to be doing her good. Not only is she physically more robust than she has been in a long time—before the hospital, before the paleness of last summer that we now think was about the bleeding ulcer—but she has something to talk about, has found a restored engagement with her surroundings that is not only grasping her attention but supporting her conversation. She speaks about her interactions with dogs and people; she comments on the changes to the flowers, building construction sites, and weather conditions that differentiate the one day's walk from the next. She is able to describe the present tense of her walking, as opposed to the reflective and sometimes nostalgic past of much of the rest of her lived world: her mother (who died in 1988, probably with Alzheimer's); her days in the WRENs (she was, perhaps ironically, a decoder in the top-secret Ultra project); a driving trip to the Carmel Valley with my father long before I was born.

So we have bought her, among other things, simple, decent walking shoes (blue) that she will certainly wear immediately, and a bright, stylish, short raincoat (yellow) that she might not, for her eightieth birthday. For her birthday dinner, she has asked for salmon, which, last visit, she completely refused to eat ("You know I have never liked fish"). I am relieved by the return to her older preference but also frustrated: her new reality doesn't include remembering that her taste did change, and she seems to think I am making up a story about it in order to be argumentative ("You know I have always liked salmon"). Needless to say, the containers of butterscotch pudding that I bought on sale in December are still in the fridge, untouched.

My mother takes Diltiazem, Altace, and Furosemide for high blood pressure, Synthroid for thyroid, and one baby aspirin every day. The gerontologist had encouraged us to try her on Aricept, which (I now know) helps about half of all people in the early stages of Alzheimer's by increasing the brain's supply of acetylcholine (a neurotransmitter that is deficient in people with Alzheimer's—researchers don't seem to know why, but they do know that it's a symptom, not a cause). We said we would wait until her thyroid levels had balanced out (it generally takes three months), at which point we would know where we were really starting; thyroid imbalance is one of the major curable causes of dementia. Given her considerable improvement since December, we have not proceeded with the Aricept (yet). Other than that, there's not much we can do. Except encourage her to walk.

LANDSCAPE, REMEMBERING, FORGETTING

Jane Urquhart's novel *A Map of Glass* begins with an arresting knot of perception, reflection, and landscape: "He is an older man walking in winter. And he knows this" (2005, 1). The man, we discover later, is Andrew Woodman, a historical geographer whose life passion has been to trace the multiple ways in which the landscape of Prince Edward County, Ontario, is etched with the traces of history, particularly that of his own family: His great-great-grandfather, Joseph, was instrumental in the early-nineteenth-century eradication of the southern Great Lakes forests for the shipbuilding industry; his grandfather,

Maurice, profited grandly from his participation in a massive barley monoculture of the late nineteenth century and in so doing completely destroyed the soil; his great-grandfather, Branwell, lost everything as he watched the resulting sand drift over his small hotel, eventually burying all traces of the structure and leaving only stories to remind the world of his hand-painted frescoes, his wife Marie's much-used Kitchen Queen cookstove.

At the start of the novel, however, we know none of this: Andrew Woodman has lost his name, lost his family, lost language; he is aware simply that he is older, that he is walking through the snow toward an island (we come to know that it is Timber Island, the place of his great-great-grandfather's home and empire) and that the place will be familiar: "Even now, though the word for island has gone, he believes he is walking toward a known place. He has a map of the shoreline in his brain; its docks and rundown wooden buildings, a few trees grown in the last century. Does he have the word for trees? Sometimes yes, but mostly no. He is better with landforms" (2005, 1). As he walks, he encounters "an unusually cluttered form" in his path: " 'a fence,' he once would have called it . . . but now he knows it only as something that has not grown out of the earth, something that is impeding his progress. . . . He does not remember what to do with a fence, how to get over it, through it, past it, but his body makes a decision to run, to charge headlong into the confusion" (2005, 2). Having successfully hurdled the fence to fall into the soft snow on the other side, he continues to walk, without the word for island, to "*the place where water touches all around*. . . . Often he bumps against trees, but this does not worry him because he knows they are meant to be there, and will remain after he has passed by them. . . . While he is among the pines, an image of an enormous raft made of timber floats through his imagination" (2005, 3; emphasis in original). But neither sense nor imagination is sufficient. He falls asleep in the snow, and just before he dies, he is overwhelmed by one last memory: that he has lost everything, that "the whole unnamed world is so beautiful to him now that he is aware that he has left behind vast, unremembered territories, certain faces, and a full orchestra of sounds that he has loved" (2005, 4).

In Andrew and throughout the interlaced stories that support the narrative, Jane Urquhart is very clear that memory does not only reside in the mind, but rather in the complex interrelations among bodies, minds, and landscapes. The novel centers on Sylvia Bradley, a middle-aged woman with an unspecified and unnamed "condition" (probably a form of autism) that makes her particularly reflective, particularly apt to transform even the tiniest perceptual sensation into consciousness, and to remember such sensations vividly and viscerally. She lives the physical, sensuous world in almost unbearable thickness; every fragment of the world carries in it the possibility of her undivided attention, and thus she is easily overwhelmed. In response, she has learned to calm herself with (willed?) absences from social reality or with concentrated attention to the familiar objects and places of her everyday life in the home in which she grew up. She counts things. Sylvia loves both certainty and the idea of certainty: "the trees, their reliability, the fact that they had always been there on the boundaries of fields or along the edges of roads" (2005, 37). Indeed, her sense of her own consistency is confirmed by the persistence of things, by the persistence of history and memory in things, and by the persistence of *her* history within a very constrained geography. She volunteers at the local museum, finds herself in the world of objects and histories; and their familiarity softens the constant potential onslaught of sensate attention:

> She knew the three-pronged ladders leaning against trees in autumn orchards, the arrival at barn doors of wagons filled with hay, the winter sleighs, the suppers held on draped tables out of doors in summer, the feuds over boundary lines, politics, family property, the arrival of the first motor car, the first telephone, the departure of young men for wars, the funeral processions departing from front parlours. (2005, 37)

Completely out of character—or, at least, completely out of the pathologized character that has been imposed upon her by her parents and, later, by her kind, paternalistic doctor-husband, Malcolm—Sylvia takes a train journey to Toronto to find Jerome McNaughton, the young artist who, during a solitary residency in an old sail loft on Timber Island, found Andrew Woodman's frozen body. Sylvia does not offer the word "lover" in reference to Andrew until much later, but it is immediately clear from the glimpses of their relationship that we see through her thoughts and words to Jerome that there is a passionate physical relationship between them and that, for Sylvia at least, the relationship is both corporeally and emotionally transformative. Andrew's sense of obligation to be a historical geographer, to pay "careful attention to the landscape, to its present and to the past embedded in its present" (2005, 77), has led him to Sylvia, who, in her absolute identification with the place that is both her present and his past, seems almost a sexual confirmation of his "dynastic necessity" (2005, 77) to know the land. Sylvia, on the other hand, finds in Andrew an unprecedented possibility for newness. Sexuality and love enter into her life in a small cabin, and despite Andrew's volatility (he eventually leaves her, only to return seven years later as he is beginning his journey into Alzheimer's): "The love they had made was barren, had resulted in no quickening, no quickening at all except this newborn capacity of hers to see things the way they really are, that and the ability to feel pain" (2005, 136). Sylvia remains in place, but the place is opened up to a new layer of existence engendered in her body: "Until Andrew opened the door of the world for her, the physicality of the past was mostly brought toward her by objects stored by relics inside her family home" (2005, 117).[5]

There are several overlapping stories of memory in the novel, including Jerome's traumatic recollections of his alcoholic father sparked by his conversations with Sylvia, and an extended middle story focused on great-grandfather Branwell Woodman and his sister Annabelle, both artists (Branwell paints frescoes of landscapes when he is not running his hotel; Annabelle prefers burning ships and keeps a "splinter book" of pasted object-fragments from her past). Particularly in this historical section—which is revealed to us at the same time as Jerome through Andrew's heavy green leather notebooks—we get a sense of the ecological quality of the body-memory-landscape relations that tendril through the characters' lives. As noted earlier, two large-scale transformations were wrought partly by Woodman: the deforestation of the Great Lakes for shipbuilding, and then the transformation of a part of Prince Edward County to sand dunes as a consequence of both deforestation and a subsequent barley monoculture. Branwell's wife (and Annabelle's friend) Marie fades and eventually dies as their hotel is gradually, inevitably covered over by the dunes; "she is being depleted, along with the soil" (2005, 251). Branwell watches as her flower beds disappear, "what seems to be a complete erasure of everything he had worked for and everything he had loved" (2005, 278). This destruction obliterates not only the artifacts of his life but the fact of his life itself: "It was as if he was living in the bottom half of an hourglass in which, as the days passed, he was being buried alive" (2005, 278). He searches for objects that will restore Marie to him—the rosary that carries her touch, the cookstove in which she had prepared her famous pastries—but the memory, increasingly unsupported by this new place, is more and more difficult. And so he leaves, no longer a relevant creature in this new, desert landscape.

The landscape, in other words, is a site of forgetting as well as remembering; the sand that drifts over everything is, both metaphorically and literally, a physical break in memory, a step in the process of the erasure of presence from history. For Branwell, the environmental erasure of the traces of his and Marie's life is a destruction of the bodily relations in which the memory of his life is carried. Branwell goes on to paint more frescoes and to raise his grandson T. J., Andrew's father, in the cabin that is later to become the site of Sylvia's sensory "quickening." But the frescoes are covered over by layers of wallpaper that also stand for the ecological transformation of the landscape (they are added as someone else's inn becomes a highway restaurant becomes a heritage building becomes a rooming house). Ultimately, the only memories that persist are the ones for which Andrew has, carefully and archaeologically, searched and which Sylvia, Jerome, and the reader now carry through Andrew's notebooks. As Sylvia tells Jerome, "Andrew thought he *was* the history that his forebears created, he felt responsible for that history, I think, and for those people. They are my responsibility now" (2005, 75; emphasis in original).

Over a century after the sand dunes erased Branwell's hotel, Sylvia writes as a conclusion to Andrew's notebooks that "all of life is an exercise in forgetting" (2005, 367). The complex set of body-landscape-memory relations portrayed in the novel is every bit as much about forgetting as it is about remembering: "Think of how our childhood fades as we walk into adulthood, how it recedes and diminishes like the view of a coastline from a deck of an oceanliner" (2005, 367). At one level, of course, one must forget in order to have meaning: if we were to remember everything with equal weight (which is always Sylvia's potential), we would not be able "to form general impressions, and from there useful judgments" (Shenk 2001, 57). At another level, however, change also requires forgetting. As much as relations between bodies and landscapes are enabled by remembering, they also change in the transformation of the present into the past, in which some pieces remain standing and others are buried in the sand. Maps are a good metaphor for this process; they trace particular flights of memory through a landscape (and facilitate the further physical and conceptual apprehension of the landscape through that flight), but, as the title of the novel suggests, they are inevitably "of glass." Here, of course, there are two meanings: a map of glass can be a representation *of* a fragile landscape, or it can be the substance of the map itself.[6] The double movement here signals the complex relationships among body, memory, and place; remembering and forgetting are a constant process, and that process occurs in our minds, in our bodies, and in the world that surrounds us.

Andrew Woodman's opening voyage into the landscape leads to his death because he has forgotten the landscape and also because the landscape has forgotten him. But that voyage is not, in many respects, atypical. Alzheimer's disease is an extension of the process of forgetting through which all human beings pass in their relations to people, places, their own minds and bodies. It is a speeding-up of that process of historical transformation through which generations, even societies also pass. To say so is not to undermine the pain of having, or living with, Alzheimer's. As Sylvia writes, the forgetting that is an inevitable part of change "is not as terrible as being forgotten by the man you love while he is breathing the same air, while he is standing in the same room. He has forgotten you and yet some part of him remembers that he should touch you, and he does this, but as he moves against you he no longer speaks your name as he plunges his hands into your hair because he has forgotten your name" (2005, 368). But in the midst of that terror, Alzheimer's disease underscores the embodiment of all memory and the inevitable involvement of place in the physical, cognitive, emotional, and social acts of remembering and forgetting.

I noted earlier that Abram takes us partway: landscape is an embodiment of stories. What he has failed to emphasize, and what I think Urquhart demonstrates so eloquently, is that this process clearly continues despite the advent of alphabetic technologies. To be sure, one can speak of the historical transformations to phenomenal experiences wrought by particular technologies; to be sure (and I have not, perhaps, sufficiently emphasized this dimension[7]), one must also speak of the particular power relations—race, gender, class—in which bodies and landscapes remember and forget (one wonders what would have happened to Sylvia were she not a white woman in a rural, middle-class household at the dawn of the twenty-first century). But the fact that landscape continues to embody, support, and create memory suggests a far less apocalyptic scenario than the one Abram envisions. We have not, whether or not we would like to think so in our societal and philosophical obsession with mind, lost all traces of the environmental physicality of our memories. The question is: How can we cultivate an awareness of and respect for this process through our environmental philosophies and activisms?

April 22, 2006

My mother is still walking. She still wears the blue shoes we gave her, but the yellow raincoat languishes in the closet. I am not sure if she doesn't like it or if she simply has no use for it, given that she prefers not to walk in the rain (which, in Victoria, means that she didn't walk all that much from November to March). The day we arrived, I made us all a rather nice French dish involving fresh and smoked salmon and mashed potatoes. I hadn't seen her ask for seconds of anything in a long time, and I am very pleased that

I served her something she so obviously liked. I think now that I am so invested in what she will/will not eat partly because food is one of the few things left that I can give her that gives her real pleasure (flowers, I have discovered, are another). It's not just that I am worried about the specter of butterscotch because it signals that there is something unusual, probably negative, going on in her brain; it's also that it means I can no longer rely on the ways I have known her pleasure (and displeasure) for most of my forty-one years. (That I am fixating on food is hardly surprising, I suppose: need, desire, and gendered social conditioning form a tight and tangled ball in the middle of every plate I serve.)

My mother actually seems happy. Although I find, at this moment, that I stand with Dylan Thomas on the "do not go gentle into that good night" side of the fence, I also have to recognize that she is not terribly uncomfortable with her withdrawal from the world. Now, unlike that awful time in the hospital, she seems to be in control of the degree to which she wants to participate in everyone else's reality. One of the people Shenk met in his research observed: "Once the idea is lost, everything is lost and I have nothing to do but wander around trying to figure out what it was that was so important earlier. You have to learn to be satisfied with what comes to you" (2001, 43). I see a lot of that kind of acceptance in my mother. In fact, although I was frustrated with it when I saw it happening ten years ago, I think she learned to find pleasure in the present for its own sake, rather than struggle to make it more closely resemble the past, long before this most recent chain of events.

My mother's lack of emotional volatility, in fact, leads me sometimes to think that she may not have Alzheimer's at all (it is an early symptom). Although I know that it is highly likely that she does, and that she is just at a much earlier stage than the gerontologist had thought, I am still quite astounded at the transformation that has taken place in her since she returned home, since she started walking, since the place of her daily life has come to occupy so much more of her attention in the wake of her attachment to social, political, literary, or other cognitive activities. She spends a lot of time looking (her eyesight is terrible, but that doesn't stop her), especially while she walks; she spends a lot of time in the pleasure of the sensuous present, noticing that the pink rhododendron is almost out, that there is one last tulip that the deer didn't eat (she didn't, however, notice that her beloved chocolate lily under the oak tree did not come up at all this year). It is almost as if she is allowing her surroundings to hold the thoughts that she can't manage by herself; sort of like a real, physical memory-palace, the places of my mother's life, and her kinesthetic memories and sensual relationships to these places—places in which she finds her own traces almost constantly—serve as a substitute for her withering hippocampus. Like a stroke victim who re-learns speech by developing a different part of her brain, my mother seems to have re-learned herself by diverting her process of remembrance beyond the confines of her own body and into a world that has long carried, and continues to carry, her traces and memories.[8]

I am sure that the gerontologist would be even less interested in this theory than she was in butterscotch pudding. And I am also sure that once my mother begins to falter in her recognition of where she is (that recognition may be partly physical, but is also about the ability to transform sensory experiences from consciousness into long-term history and abstract concept[9]*), we will enter a new and frightening stage in which her beloved home-landscape is as unfamiliar to her as the hospital was (that is, assuming that the landscape itself doesn't become so transformed in the meantime that she couldn't recognize it even with all her faculties intact—not entirely out of the range of possibility). But we're not there yet.*

NOTES

1. There is an extensive literature that brings phenomenology to environmental philosophy, and this paper will not address the many debates that emerge from their resulting meeting. For a different feminist version of the conversation, see Bigwood 1993. Despite its problems (e.g., a deeply troubling articulation of embodiment with maternity with "home"), Bigwood's *Earth Muse* attempts to formulate a feminist eco-phenomenology that is attentive not only to the experiential qualities of bodies in landscapes but to the power relations in which both experiences and landscapes are located.

2. Toadvine, beginning from a similar sense of convergence between phenomenology and ecology, actually advances a very interesting position that rests on Merleau-Ponty's later and unfinished text *The Visible and the Invisible* (1968), in which he describes the human body as a site of reversibility, the simultaneous experience of perceiving and being perceived, and thus constituted *as* world by the other (which is also an act of sensory alienation in which the one thing I cannot perceive is the me that is perceived). Feminist scholars have both deployed and criticized this view of bodies; see, most famously, Luce Irigaray (1993), who

shows (among other things) that Merleau-Ponty's sensing body is, problematically, always already individuated (and male).

3. There are, of course, many writers of both feminist and environmentalist hues who demonstrate, with more focus and nuance than Abram, the fact that not all modes of writing and speaking are created equal. As many literary critics have noted, poetry, for example, has the potential to disrupt the transparency of signification—its solipsism, or in Abram's terms, the illusion behind the magic of its animism—by reminding the reader/listener of the disjuncture between word and world. As Don McKay (2001) reminds us, this is how metaphors work: the is/is not relationship on which they hinge is a constant reminder of the fact that the world defies linguistic grasp. McKay, importantly, also reminds us of the physicality of poetry: as an act of writing with the listening folded in, the nature-poem attempts to embody exactly Merleau-Ponty's perceptual interface, here, in speaking and being spoken to in the same moment. In light of this subtle argument, Abram's castigation of the alphabet seems a rather blunt instrument.

4. As should be apparent, part of my desire in this paper is to draw on both phenomenological and social constructivist accounts of nature and embodiment to work toward an interrogative practice that includes the insights of both. Once again, I am not alone in this endeavor among feminists. Despite the fact that she is often (incorrectly) held up as an example of the disembodied limits of social constructivism, Judith Butler (e.g., 1993) has made huge inroads into understanding gender and embodiment as simultaneously and complexly material and social.

5. The question of Sylvia's "condition" is left unsolved in the novel. On the one hand, her husband makes it clear that Sylvia's love affair with Andrew must have been an imaginary one, as her illness could not possibly allow her to sustain an intimate, physical relationship with anyone (Malcolm has never touched Sylvia). Sylvia has clearly internalized her diagnosis, speaking of "people like me" who are "supposed to have next to no attention span" (134), but she has also clearly reflected on both diagnosis and attribution process and finds them inadequate to describe her. She knows *how* she is, but the diagnosis clearly tells her nothing about what or who. Indeed, she demonstrates her refusal of this knowledge by noting that Andrew and her friend Julie (Jerome agrees) either don't know about or don't "believe in" her condition. What we have, here, is an interesting reflection on the nature of Sylvia's "unusual" perception: she is aware, as part of her conscious daily existence (which ends up being similar to Andrew's), of the importance of objects and places as embodiments of memory and history; and the phenomenal richness of this view is completely at odds with the instrumental rationality, the forgetting, of parents, doctor, and modernity in general (she certainly understands herself as an anachronism).

6. It is also a metaphor for the nature of memory itself. In a dream, Jerome "was looking at Smithson's [artwork] *A Map of Broken Glass*. Each shard reflected something he remembered about his father" (145).

7. For a brilliant account of the (disciplinary and other) effects of power on the experienced body, see McWhorter 1999; for a more specific account of the

disciplinary power relations embodied in dominant versions of environmental politics, see Sandilands 2004.

8. Shenk recounts the fascinating story of William de Koonig, who continued to paint prolifically (and had considerable critical success, despite debates about whether his work could be counted as "art" once he lost the capacity for self-reflection) long after he developed dementia (probably Alzheimer's) and lost his ability to manage his own affairs or remember his daily routines. Koonig was, crucially for Shenk, a very physical painter rather than a highly conceptual one; his art-making was about "the moment—the thrust and parry of the brush, from the 'excavation' of his emotional state" (Larson in Shenk 2001, 202).

9. There is, in fact, a particular region of the hippocampus responsible for creating body maps from visual perception.

REFERENCES

Abram, David. 1996. *The Spell of the Sensuous: Perception and Language in a More-Than-Human World.* New York: Pantheon Books.

———. 2005. "Between the Body and the Breathing Earth: A Reply to Ted Toadvine." *Environmental Ethics* 27.2 (Summer): 171–90.

Alzheimer's Association. 2006. *Basics of Alzheimer's Disease: What It Is and What You Can Do.* Available online at www.alz.org.

Bigwood, Carol. 1993. *Earth Muse: Feminism, Nature, and Art.* Philadelphia: Temple University Press.

Butler, Judith. 1994. *Bodies That Matter: On the Discursive Limits of "Sex."* New York: Routledge.

Evernden, Neil. 1985. *The Natural Alien: Humankind and Environment.* Toronto: University of Toronto Press.

Irigaray, Luce. 1993. *An Ethics of Sexual Difference.* Trans. Carolyn Burke and Gillian C. Gill. Ithaca, N.Y.: Cornell University Press.

McKay, Don. 2001. *Vis-à-Vis: Field Notes on Poetry and Wilderness.* Wolfville, N.S.: Gaspereau Press.

McWhorter, Ladelle. 1999. *Bodies and Pleasures: Foucault and the Politics of Sexual Normalization.* Bloomington: Indiana University Press.

Merleau-Ponty, Maurice. 1962. *Phenomenology of Perception.* Trans. Colin Smith. New York: Routledge.

———. 1968. *The Visible and the Invisible.* Ed. Claude Lefort. Trans. Alphonso Lingis. Evanston, Ill.: Northwestern University Press.

Sandilands, Catriona. 2004. "Eco Homo: Queering the Ecological Body Politic." *Social Philosophy Today* 19: 17–39.

Shenk, David. 2001. *The Forgetting: Alzheimer's: Portrait of an Epidemic.* New York: Doubleday.

Toadvine, Ted. 2005. "Limits of the Flesh: The Role of Reflection in David Abram's Ecophenomenology." *Environmental Ethics* 27.2 (Summer): 155–70.

Urquhart, Jane. 2005. *A Map of Glass.* Toronto: McClelland and Stewart.

PART 3. MATERIAL BODIES

10

DISABILITY EXPERIENCE ON TRIAL

Tobin Siebers

On May 17, 2004, the fiftieth anniversary of *Brown v. Board of Education,* the U.S. Supreme Court delivered, in *Tennessee v. Lane,* another ruling with far-reaching implications for civil rights. The Court ruled unexpectedly and by a narrow margin that states not making courtrooms and legal services physically accessible to people with disabilities could be sued for damages under Title II of the Americans with Disabilities Act (ADA). George Lane, the plaintiff and a wheelchair user, told how he was summoned to the Polk County Tennessee Courthouse on a minor traffic charge and had to crawl up two flights of stairs to the courtroom as the judge and other court employees stood at the top of the stairs and laughed at him. "On a pain scale from 1 to 10," he later explained, "it was way past 10" (for details of the case, see Cohen 2004). When his case was not heard in the morning session, Lane was told to return following lunch for the afternoon session. When he refused to crawl up the two flights of stairs a second time, he was arrested for failing to appear and jailed. A second plaintiff, Beverly Jones, who works as a court reporter, joined the suit, claiming that she had to turn down work in twenty-three Tennessee courthouses because they were not accessible to her wheelchair. Once, in a courthouse without an accessible bathroom, the judge had to pick her up and place her on the toilet. Another time, a court employee carrying her to the next floor slipped and dropped her on the stairs.

Every indication was that the Supreme Court would find for the state of Tennessee, since the Court has favored states' rights in general and had ruled only three years before that states are immune from employment suits based on disability discrimination, regardless of the evidence in the case.[1] Why did the justices rule against the states in *Tennessee v. Lane*? Did the interest of the Court in the legal process give the case a different slant? Was it the compelling nature of the personal testimony? What did the justices learn from the experience of the disabled plaintiffs that they did not know before?

The focus on experience is not arbitrary to the ruling but required by the ADA itself. Any application of Title II of the ADA necessitates that it be "judged with reference to the historical experience which it reflects" (Syllabus, *Tennessee v. Lane,* 2). The justices note at the beginning of the majority decision that "Congress enacted Title II against a backdrop of pervasive unequal treatment of persons with disabilities in the administration of state services and programs, including systematic deprivations of fundamental rights" (Syllabus, *Tennessee v. Lane,* 3). More importantly, they affirm that Title II is "an appropriate response to this history and pattern of unequal treatment" and set out to demonstrate that the pattern of disability discrimination continues to this day (Syllabus, *Tennessee v. Lane,* 3). *Tenessee v. Lane* itself takes as one of its primary tasks the documentation of disability experience required for the application of Title II; the ruling catalogues experience after experience of disability discrimination for the purpose of proving that the U.S. legal system excludes people with disabilities.

By attending to the testimony of disabled plaintiffs, however, the justices may be guilty of relying on an evidentiary notion of experience. Using experience as evidence, Joan Scott claims, in an essay that now defines the dominant theoretical position on experience in historical and cultural studies, "weakens the critical thrust of histories of difference" by remaining within "the frame of orthodox history," naturalizes the "difference" and "identities" of those whose experience is being documented, and "reproduces rather than contests given ideological systems" (Scott 1991, 777–78).[2] Even when used to create alternative histories or to correct prevailing misinterpretations, according to Scott, experience becomes, if given the status of evidence, merely another brick in the foundationalist discourse of history; and she attacks feminist and cultural historians for backsliding into foundationalism when they argue for the need to rewrite history on the basis of the experiences of women, people of color, and victims of class discrimination. "It is not individuals who have experience," she concludes, "but subjects who are constituted through experience" (1991, 779). Apparently, because it is socially constructed, individual experience may serve neither as origin of explanation nor as authoritative evidence about what is known (1991, 780).

The value of experience is on trial for both Scott and the Supreme Court, but they have entirely different ideas about it. It may be worth asking for a moment about the political shape of this difference. The disability community was surprised and pleased when the conservative Court suspended its attack on the ADA in *Tennessee v. Lane* and recognized both the existence of disability discrimination and the judiciary's prior endorsement of it. We witnessed an orthodox Court apparently led out of orthodoxy by the power of disability experience. Scott's attack on the use of experience as evidence also stands against orthodoxy. She does not want to see historians of difference entangled in orthodox epistemologies to establish their emancipatory goals, although it is not clear that her critique of experience is ultimately compatible with these goals.

One of the legacies of poststructuralism is the desire for absolute critique, one in which the ability to turn critique against itself is valued above all others and critique as such is defined as a process of subtraction in which knowledge claims have fewer and fewer foundations on which to base themselves. The argument has always been that the more radical and absolute the critique, the greater its potential for emancipation, but the proof for this argument is less and less apparent. The question arises whether the desire for absolute critique always serves politically progressive goals. Is the banishment of experience, for example, radical or reactionary? I argue here that disability experience has the potential both to augment social critique and to advance emancipatory political goals. More importantly, it is my hope that the knowledge given by disability experience might renew the incentive to reclaim and to re-theorize other experiences of minority identity, despite the argument by Scott and others that they have no critical value.[3]

We are at a curious moment in history. Is this the last moment when we might reduce emancipatory thinking to orthodoxy in the name of critique without being thought to serve orthodoxy?[4] From now on, it might be better to keep in mind the political implications of our arguments and to put them in the service of both critique and emancipation.

DISCRIMINATION BY DESIGN

Jean-François Lyotard (1988) defines the *différend* as a situation in which victims are denied the means to demonstrate that they have been wronged. The wronged are doubly victimized because they have both suffered injustice and been deprived of the means to argue their case. It is ironic that Scott's critique of experience posits a *différend* that even the Supreme Court justices with their orthodox tendencies cannot accept. They interpret Lane's experience, not as evidence about his life in isolation, but as evidence establishing a pattern of injustice affecting many people, thereby giving them the opportunity to demonstrate the wrongs against them and to give voice to their suffering. Perhaps more significant, Justice Souter indicted the U.S. legal system itself in the history of discrimination against people with disabilities, calling the decision in *Tennessee v. Lane* a "welcome step away from the judiciary's prior endorsement of blunt instruments imposing legal handicaps" and inviting the judiciary to critique its previous support of discriminatory behavior (Souter concurring, 2).

It is nevertheless important to realize that Scott and the Court share some ideas about what experience is, even though they disagree about its evidentiary value. The justices take seriously, as does Scott, that experience is socially constructed. They trace the basis for Lane's discrimination, as Scott might, to a "history and pattern of unequal treatment" rather than attributing it to a natural cause such as the biological inferiority of disabled people. Unlike Scott, the justices do not believe that experience is threatened by its social construction as a basis for knowledge claims. In fact, they find that the built environment is socially constructed and reasonably conclude that it has been constructed in the wrong way for disabled bodies and minds. Notice that it is not Lane's personal suffering per se that sways the Court. The fact that the judge laughs when Lane crawls up the stairs to his hearing is reprehensible but not evidence for the rightness of his discrimination suit. Rather, it is the fact that Lane's experience is representative of discriminatory behavior writ large. Lane experiences discrimination on the basis of his identity as a disabled person, and this discrimination toward a member of a class is demonstrated most clearly by the blueprint of the Polk County Courthouse itself. The physical inaccessibility of the building is a social fact readable by everyone from the Supreme Court justices and Lane to those who made him an object of ridicule, and when this inaccessibility represents a widespread feature of many other buildings, as it does, then one may rightfully conclude that prejudices against disabled people are at work in the architecture of society itself. The majority decision and the amicus briefs strive to render obvious this blueprint of society's prejudice against people with disabilities, exposing what Justice Stevens calls the "pattern of disability discrimination" (*Tennessee v. Lane,* 15). This pattern of discriminatory behavior includes "hearing impaired prisoners who normally express themselves by using sign language . . . shackled at their hearings making such communication impossible," "a blind witness . . . denied access to information at his hearings because he could not see the documents," "a double amputee forced to crawl around the floor of jail," "criminalizing the marriage of persons with mental disabilities," and deaf and blind persons "categorically excluded from jury service" (*American Bar Association as Amicus Curaie,* 13 n. 16, 13 n. 11, 13 n. 8, 14 n. 1).

In a country of the blind, the architecture, technology, language use, and social organization would be other than ours. In a country of the mobility impaired, staircases would be nonexistent, and concepts of distance would not imitate our own. In a country of the deaf, technology would leave the hands free for signing, and there would be no need to shout across a noisy room. Disability provides a vivid illustration that experience is socially constructed, but it exposes just as vividly that the identities created by experience also contribute to a representational system whose examination may result in verifiable knowledge claims about our society. When a disabled body enters any construction, social or physical, a deconstruction occurs, a deconstruction that reveals the lines of force, the blueprint, of the social rendering of the building as surely as its physical rendering. Constructions are built with certain social bodies in mind, and when a different body appears, the lack of fit reveals the ideological assumptions controlling the space. The presence of a wheelchair at the Polk County Courthouse exposes a set of social facts about the building. We may reduce these facts to an ideology, but this should not prevent us from understanding that what is revealed has an objective social location. We witness the social location of disability identity in a verifiable way.

In general, the social construction of identity is displayed when forbidden bodies and minds enter spaces. When Rosa Parks sat in the front of the bus, for example, a social construction of African American identity in our society was displayed. "Identities are indexical entities," according to Linda Alcoff, and "real *within* a given location" (2000, 337). Social identities may be constructed, but they are also "real," and because they are real, they are entirely open to political critique and transformation, as *Tennessee v. Lane* demonstrates. The Court's opinion recognizes people with disabilities as a minority identity suffering from unequal treatment under the law and thereby empowers them to gather as a group, both to force changes in the inaccessible environment and to increase their participation in public life.

Groups are constituted as minorities in two ways: by patterns of discriminatory treatment of them, and by their awareness of these patterns. Minority groups must have, according to Dworkin and Dworkin, "identifiability, differential power, differential and pejorative treatment occasioned by the power differential, and group awareness facilitated by the differential treatment" (1976, viii; see also Albrecht 1992, 79). Subjects are both formed by experience and have an awareness of the formative nature of their experience—and when this experience is both negative and different, the subject's identity takes on a minority cast. To refuse to recognize these aspects of identity formation is to fail to understand that experience is always socially constructed and that our most valuable knowledge concerns verification of a social construction's given features. The belief seems to be that oppression will end as soon as minority identities vanish, but without a theory that can verify how social identities are embodied in lived experience, how they become real, it is not clear that we can understand what oppression actually is and how it works.[5]

Here is the primary difference between poststructuralist and realist accounts of minority identity. Poststructuralists often discount the knowledge claims of minority identities because they hold that identities are little more than socially constructed fictions.[6] Philosophical realists recognize both the social construction of identity and that identities constitute theories of knowledge—sometimes right, sometimes wrong, sometimes indifferent—about the world in which we live. Realism defines objects of knowledge not as natural entities but as social facts that exist in human society as part of a causal network.[7] In other words, realists take the cognitive value of social constructions seriously, viewing them as points of departure for further research into the status of knowledge claims. They understand that social knowledge comprises a dense network of social facts where teasing out one fact summons others for the simple reason that each fact is mediated by others—and not always in predictable ways. Knowledge, for realists, defines precisely the verifiability of a social construction in meaning as referenced by other meanings. There are few cases that exemplify this theory of knowledge better than the disability experience. It demonstrates both the social construction of experience and the political promise arising from the knowledge that experience is constructed. The experiences of people with disabilities help to clarify the fact that identities may contain legitimate claims to knowledge, and this knowledge, once verified, is a valuable weapon against the oppression of minority people.

THE SEX OF ARCHITECTURE

Poststructuralist theory has difficulty with both suffering and sex.[8] It often eschews suffering as a weakness of identity politics and uses sexual behavior as a prop to enrich its analysis of gender and sexual orientation. Scott's argument about experience would seem to be a case in point. Scott has little patience for the idea that gays and lesbians might constitute themselves as a minority identity facing a history of painful discrimination, and even though Samuel Delany's *The Motion of Light in Water* (2004) is manifestly about sexual experience, sexual practices have no place in her analysis of the book. Sexual behavior is an important factor in the way that our identities and experiences in the world are constructed, but it is often set aside in favor of activities more easily associated with the public sphere. The bedroom does not seem as paradigmatic as the courtroom when one considers the social construction of experience and the ways in which this construction discriminates against various people. Disability law, for example, has had only minor success ensuring the accessibility of public buildings. *Tennessee v. Lane* is significant precisely because it makes such a crucial and unexpected intervention in the legislation of accessibility for public state buildings. This minor success looks like a major success, however, when considered in the context of private residences, since no law exists to compel individuals to make single-family dwellings accessible to differently-abled people.[9] The chance of a law promoting accessibility for intimate sexual behavior is even more remote.

And yet there is such a thing as the sex of architecture, and it affects the sexual practices allowed by various spaces and the artifacts in them. Sex may seem a private activity, but it is wholly public insofar as it is subject to social prejudices and ideologies and takes place in a built environment designed according to public and ideal conceptions of the human body. Significantly, *Tennessee v. Lane* documents a variety of public and legal practices discriminating against the sexual practices and reproductive rights of disabled people. Justice Stevens emphasizes laws barring the marriage of people with disabilities in the majority opinion, and Justice Souter builds on the emphasis when concurring by attacking the involuntary sterilization of people with mental disabilities and citing some of the most egregious examples in the law, including Oliver Wendell Holmes's opinion: "It is better for all the world, if instead of waiting to execute degenerate offspring for crime, or to let them starve for their imbecility, society can prevent those who are manifestly unfit from continuing their kind. . . . Three generations of imbeciles are enough" (Souter concurring, 1–2). In short, the Court does not set aside sex in its consideration of disability discrimination but asserts the relevance of sexual experience as evidence of unequal treatment under the law.

The idea that sexuality is socially constructed usually refers to concepts of gender or sexual orientation rather than to sexual practices. Homophobia and sexism tend facilely to confuse identities with sexual practices, and maintaining a separation between identity and sexual practices has been one way to resist these prejudices. Consequently, sexual existence seems marginal to the argument about social construction, and people with disabilities, of course, are often marginal to the way that experience—sexual or other—is conceived. Nancy Mairs makes this point with great clarity, reorienting at the same time the critical concept of the margin away from its ableist tendencies and insisting on the right of people with disabilities to assert a sexual component of their identities. She complains that modern theory always conceives of marginality in terms of power relations between one group of people and another. "It is never taken to mean," she claims, "that those on the margin occupy a physical space literally outside the field of vision of those in the center" (Mairs 1996, 59).

The centrality of experience in arguments about social construction preserves the presupposition that individuals have access to the centers of social and public existence. Experience is nearly always described in spatial metaphors, referring either to how experience positions and encloses the subject or to how the subject acts as a receptacle for experiences, storing them in the mind or unconscious. Rarely, if ever, do these spatial metaphors include considerations of access. Similarly, many discussions of gender and sexual orientation assume that people have the opportunity and ability to explore sexual identities and emotions, but this is not the case for many disabled people. Samuel Delany's coming to consciousness about gay political identity, for example, takes place in a labyrinthine, badly lit building with multiple floors. Other notable episodes in his sexual education occur in subway lavatories and truck parks—not the most accessible venues.[10] Mairs stresses the fact that she and other disabled people live elsewhere: "over here, on the edge, out of bounds, beneath your notice" (1996, 59). There are people with disabilities who never enter the spaces that cultural theorists associate with the defining social experiences of modernity, and when they do manage to occupy these spaces, they fall outside the awareness of many people.

Disability activists and theorists are beginning slowly to take up the problem of sexual access. Their focus extends from public venues concerned with sexual and reproductive health, such as hospitals and doctors' offices, to private spaces where sex manuals, products, devices, and assistance are used to create new sexual environments better suited to people with disabilities. In "Sex and the Gimpy Girl," Mairs provides an unforgettable illustration of the reproductive care that women with disabilities are liable to receive:

> I had scheduled a Pap smear at a clinic new to me, on the eighth floor of the hospital at the center of the Arizona Health Sciences Center. In this building, I can't reach higher than "3" on the elevator buttons, so I must make sure someone else gets on with me. When I arrived at the clinic, the doors weren't automated: another wait till some other woman came along. The counter was too high for me to reach the sign-in sheet—so high, in fact, that I couldn't see the receptionist to ask for help. After a thirty-five minute wait, a nurse escorted me into a windowless cubicle with a standard examining table, although I had specified when booking the appointment that I required a model that can be lowered and tilted.
>
> "I can't use that," I said.
>
> "You can't?" She sounded skeptical and slightly aggrieved.
>
> "No, my legs are too weak to climb up. That's why I use a wheelchair." (1999, 44)

Mairs goes on to recount a sexual history full of dismissals of her erotic feelings and contradictory advice about her reproductive health. Doctors do not want her to have sex or children, and she contrasts her experience with that of nondisabled women for whom doctors muster an "arsenal of scopes and dyes and hormones and catheters" to increase sexual attractiveness and fertility (1999, 48). As a disabled woman, Mairs has as much difficulty fitting into the medical conception of woman as she does into her doctor's examining room. Disabled women supposedly have no reason to reproduce and no reason to have sex:

> When it comes to sexuality in the disabled, dismissal is apt to turn into outright repression. Made uncomfortable, even to the point of excruciation, by the thought of maimed bodies (or, for that matter, minds) engaged in erotic fantasy or action, many deny the very possibility by ascribing to them the "innocence" of the very young. . . . Perhaps this disgust and denial stem, as the sociobiologists would probably have it, from the fact that such bodies are clearly less than ideal vehicles for the propagation of the species. Whatever its origin, the repulsion lies buried so deeply in consciousness as to *seem* natural rather than constructed. As a result, even someone with the best intentions in the world may fail to see a disabled woman whole. The parents of a congenitally disabled daughter may rear her to believe that she will never enter into a sexually intimate relationship like the one that they enjoy themselves, withhold information about reproductive inevitabilities like menstruation, perhaps punish her for the sexual acting out that adolescence brings. Those responsible for her health may "forget" that she requires reproductive care or provide it in a manner so cursory that she is left baffled and ashamed. (1999, 50)

In contrast to the reception of disabled people at the center of the modern experience is their experience on the margins where some of them are trying to create a safe space for sexual activity and expression. Mairs notes playfully in her memoir, *Waist-High in the World,* that she considered calling the book "Cock-High in the World," because she is not opposed to giving a nuzzle or two when the opportunity presents itself (1996, 54). A small shift in the ethics of personal assistantship may be moving in the direction of greater sexual access, as some personal attendants accept that part of their job includes helping their disabled employers make love and have sex. Education is paramount to understand what disabled bodies can and cannot do and how to overcome the feelings of disgust associated with the erotic body. Personal attendants, for example, are trained to overcome feelings of disgust when cleaning up excrement, but they are often repulsed by the idea of cleaning up semen or vaginal discharge. Specialized sexual aids may be designed for disabled bodies, explains Cory Silverberg, who retrofits sex toys with tongue toggles for people with limited use of their hands: "You have to look at what a person can do. If they don't have fine motor control, they may be able to press themselves against a vibrator. There are vibrators you can put on the hand, and they can masturbate that way, if they can press their hands against their body. If they can't use their hands at all, they may be able to lie beside a vibrator" (cited by Stoner 2004). Significantly, as in universal design, where innovations in architecture and product design for nondisabled society often evolve out of a disability context, some of the newest and most significant inventions in sexual products have been developed by people with disabilities. For example, Goswell Duncan, president of his local chapter of the National Spinal Cord Injury Foundation, invented and first put into production the silicone dildo (Kaufman, Silverberg, and Odette 2003, 271). It is a considerable improvement over other models because it is soft, pliable, easy to clean, and retains body heat.

Other people with disabilities are claiming the right to sexual accessibility based on different conceptions of the erotic body and a variety of gender and sexed identities. These emerging sexual identities have at least two significant characteristics. First, they represent disability, not as a defect that needs to be overcome to have sex, but as a mode of being that enhances sexual activities and pleasure. Second, they give to sexuality a political dimension that redefines people with disabilities as sexual citizens.[11] It is crucial to understand that sexual citizenship does not translate merely into being able to express sexuality in public—a charge always levied against sexual minorities—but to the right to break free of the unequal treatment of minority sexualities and to increase accessibility for sexual expression. In the case of disabled people, the right to sexual access has particular stakes. Some specific demands include access to information about sexuality, freedom of intimate association in institutions and care facilities, demedicalization of disabled sexuality, addressing sexual needs and desires as part of health care, re-professionalization of caregivers and medical professionals to recognize not deny sexuality, and privacy on demand. The rights of sexual access change the conditions of enablement for sexual expression, giving support to the sexual needs and desires of disabled people.

Despite the fact that people with disabilities are usually assumed to be asexual, their sexual practices seem on first hearing outlandish or kinky, exposing that limited expectations about the relationship of bodies to other bodies determine the choreography of sexual life and its spaces. For example, the question that everyone wanted answered (and still does) about Chang and Eng, "the original Siamese twins," is how they had sex with their two wives. Did everyone do it together, or did the twins take turns with each wife? Chang and Eng had custom chairs installed for their body in the parlor but nothing designed for the bedroom, and the bedroom today remains an inhospitable space for people with different bodies or for those who need help from personal attendants.[12] A recent study guide for a video about sexuality after spinal cord injury illustrates not only the physical obstacles to sexual fulfillment but also the social obstacles confronting the idea of disability sex. Here is a description of one scene: "Lynn is straddling Mark while he is undressing her. He takes off her panties with the use of his mouth and teeth" (Tepper 1997, 198). Lynn and Mark are having sex, so their actions are meant to be erotic, but removing your partner's panties with your teeth means something different when you are paralyzed and have no use of your arms. People who view the film need to be prepared, the study guide explains, about the meaning of the acts they will witness. Illiteracy about the minds and bodies of disabled people drapes their sexual practices in deviance and perversion. My point, however, is not to celebrate the presumption of deviance as a special resource for eroticism. Only a greater illiteracy about disability than what we have currently would assume that the marginality of disabled sexual practices is in itself a viable resource for pleasure.

A familiar idea of recent cultural theory describes excluded people and ideas as representing a constitutive outside—an uncanny space on the margins possessing the power either to determine the character of modern existence or to invert it, thereby serving as an explicit critique of the center and a resource for transgressive happiness. Michel Foucault (1984), for instance, refers to these outside places as "heterotopias"—places external to all places, even though they may be possible to locate in reality. Hospitals, prisons, cemeteries, fairgrounds, freak shows, vacation villages, brothels, imperial colonies, and cheap motels define some heterotopic spaces of free-flowing difference and desire. The heterotopia par excellence for Foucault is the ship—a floating piece of space, a place without a place, existing by itself, enclosed in itself, and yet given over to the infinity of the sea and unbounded freedom of movement—vying from port to port in quest of treasure and sexual delight. Heterotopias are spaces of sexual desire by virtue of their difference, marking places where those in power go to express forbidden desires or where the powerless are held and branded as deviant. The conception of these spaces, however, relies on the idea that a free-wheeling mobility exists between the center and margin, that the center in fact requires for its very existence the others at the margin, and that in this sense the margin is the true center. People with disabilities living on the margins have a different experience. Their experience demonstrates that society is constructed without their access in mind and with little thought of visiting the places left to them. Theirs are not heteroclite and mobile spaces of transgression, fancy, or revolution but places with real-world qualities where human beings want to experience pleasure, creativity, knowledge, and recognition—basic needs often ignored and unsupported when it comes to the disability experience.[13]

Prejudices against disability are extremely difficult to overcome because they are built into the environment. Even if one could wave a magic wand and improve everyone's attitudes about disability, the built environment would still remain as a survival of discrimination and an impenetrable barrier to the participation of people with disabilities. For those who doubt the existence of disability discrimination, the built environment should stand as living proof of the social exclusion of the disabled, but attitudes sometimes prove to be as rigid to change as concrete walls, wooden staircases, and cobblestone walkways. When George Lane crawled up the stairs of the Polk County Courthouse the first time and refused to crawl up a second time, he sent a message to the highest court in the land—a courtroom that disabled people have not always been able to reach—about the value of disability experience as evidence, and the Court used that evidence to rewrite history, this time in favor of both critique and emancipation.

NOTES

I wish to express my gratitude to audiences at the School of Criticism and Theory at Cornell University and the First Draft Club at the University of Michigan.

1. In *Board of Trustees of Univ. of Ala. v. Garrett* (2001), the Court ruled that the Eleventh Amendment bars private money damages for state violations of ADA Title I, which prohibits employment discrimination against the disabled.

2. Scott prefers the use of discourse theory for writing alternative histories

to gathering the evidence of experience. However, if the problem with experience is its constructed state, resorting to discourse does not present an advantage because discourse is no less socially constructed.

3. Emblematic of a second-wave re-theorization of minority identity and experience is Moya, *Learning from Experience* (2002).

4. Bruno Latour (2004), for example, tracks how radical constructivist critique has been turned to reactionary ends and stresses the importance of embracing realist alternatives for progressive political results.

5. On the realism of lived embodiment as a point of departure for social change, see Siebers (2001, 748–50).

6. While it is dangerous to speak of poststructuralism in general, the position on identity claims argued by social constructionists in the poststructuralist tradition seems uniform. They tend to attack minority and identity politics as either exclusionary or the product of a history of oppression that should be eschewed. In addition to Scott, for examples of those who discount political claims made on behalf of oppressed identities, see Brown (1995, 70–72) and Butler (1997, 104). For an extended analysis of the rejection of minority identity claims by social constructionists, see Alcoff (2000) and Siebers (2001, 738–42; 2006).

7. For a basic exposition of realist theory, see Moya and Hames-García 2000, especially in this context the response by Wilkerson (2000) to Scott's critique of Delany. On the realist implications of feminism, see the work of Linda Martín Alcoff (2000, 2005).

8. Mario Perniola offers an argument complementary to mine, claiming that sexuality and suffering "constitute great challenges for postmodernism" because they "relate to the body understood as something given" (2004, 32).

9. The concept of "visitability," the application of which has not been widespread, extends accessibility to private housing beyond the needs of renters or property owners, while the Fair Housing Amendment of 1988 mandates basic architectural access in new multifamily housing, although its enforcement has been weak. No law currently requires accessibility to single-family dwellings. For an overview, see "Laws on Disability Access to Housing" (2004). On the importance of making private residences accessible, see Siebers (2006).

10. My point is not to criticize Delany, who maintains a laudable openness to people with disabilities throughout his memoir. Two episodes are worth mentioning in particular. In one episode he is mistaken for a mute, mentally disabled man, pushed into a backroom, and awkwardly raped, after which he wonders "if this was what happened to the mute or simple-minded wandering New York" (2004, 140). In the second episode, he meets a man in a subway lavatory whose penis has its tip cut off and does not withdraw from the sexual encounter: "He came very fast. I wanted to talk with him afterward, but he zipped up once we were finished and hurried away. I never saw him again, although I looked for him" (2004, 188).

11. For a discussion of sexual or intimate citizenship, see Plummer (2003) and Weeks (1998). O'Toole (2000), O'Toole and Doe (2002), and Tepper (1999) track the impact of new modes of sexual being and demands for sexual access for the disabled. In one remarkable development, O'Toole and Doe report that disabled mothers have come together to initiate a new sexual culture that teaches disabled

children to love and to care for their bodies. The main strategy is to pass on positive sexual values to children and to teach them how to resist negative stereotypes about disabled sexuality. A consensus statement by 614 women from 80 countries captures the essence of their philosophy: "We want a disability sexual culture focused on our entitlement to pleasure and love, understanding the advantages of possessing bodies and functions different when compared to women's majority culture" (2002, 99).

12. I am indebted to the discussion of Chang and Eng's sexuality by Cynthia Wu (2004).

13. See Johnson (2003) for an unfanciful description of disability on the margins.

REFERENCES

Albrecht, Gary. 1992. *The Disability Business: Rehabilitation in America.* Newbury Park, Calif.: Sage.

Alcoff, Linda Martín. 2000. "Who's Afraid of Identity Politics?" In *Reclaiming Identity: Realist Theory and the Predicament of Postmodernism,* ed. Paula M. L. Moya and Michael R. Hames-García, 312–44. Berkeley: University of California Press.

———. 2006. *Visible Identities: Race, Gender, and the Self.* New York: Oxford University Press.

Board of Trustees of Univ. of Ala. v. Garrett. 2001. 531 U.S. 356, 1–17.

Brief for the American Bar Association as Amicus Curaie Supporting Respondents. 2003. No. 02-1667, 1–25.

Brown, Wendy. 1995. *States of Injury: Power and Freedom in Late Modernity.* Princeton, N.J.: Princeton University Press.

Butler, Judith. 1997. *The Psychic Life of Power: Theories in Subjection.* Stanford, Calif.: Stanford University Press.

Cohen, Adam. 2004. "Editorial: Can Disabled People Be Forced to Crawl Up the Courthouse Steps?" *New York Times,* January 11, sec. 4, 14.

Delany, Samuel R. 2004. *The Motion of Light in Water: Sex and Science Fiction in the East Village.* 1988; rev. ed. Minneapolis: University of Minnesota Press.

Dworkin, A., and R. Dworkin. 1976. *The Minority Report.* New York: Praeger.

Foucault, Michel. 1984. "Des Espaces autres." *Architecture, Mouvement, Continuité* 5 (October): 46–49.

Johnson, Harriet McBryde. 2003. "The Disability Gulag." *New York Times Magazine,* 23 November, 58–64.

Kaufman, Miriam, M.D., Cory Silverberg, and Fran Odette, eds. 2003. *The Ultimate Guide to Sex and Disability.* San Francisco: Cleis.

Latour, Bruno. 2004. "Why Has Critique Run out of Steam? From Matters of Fact to Matters of Concern." *Critical Inquiry* 30.2: 225–48.

"Laws on Disability Access to Housing: A Summary." 2004. http://www.concretechange.org/laws_overview.htm (accessed Nov. 11, 2006).

Lyotard, Jean-François. 1988. *The Differend: Phrases in Dispute.* Trans. Georges Van Den Abbeele. Minneapolis: University of Minnesota Press.

Mairs, Nancy. 1996. *Waist-High in the World: A Life Among the Nondisabled.* Boston, Mass.: Beacon.

———. 1999. "Sex and the Gimpy Girl." *River Teeth* 1.1: 44–51.

Moya, Paula M. L. 2002. *Learning from Experience: Minority Identities, Multicultural Struggles.* Berkeley: University of California Press.

Moya, Paula M. L., and Michael R. Hames-García, eds. 2000. *Reclaiming Identity: Realist Theory and the Predicament of Postmodernism.* Berkeley: University of California Press.

O'Toole, Joan Corbett. 2000. "The View from Below: Developing a Knowledge Base About an Unknown Population." *Sexuality and Disability* 18.3: 207–24.

———, and Tanis Doe. 2002. "Sexuality and Disabled Parents with Disabled Children." *Sexuality and Disability* 20.1: 89–101.

Perniola, Mario. 2004. *Art and Its Shadow.* Trans. Massimo Verdicchio. New York: Continuum.

Plummer, Kenneth. 2003. *Intimate Citizenship: Private Decisions and Public Dialogues.* Seattle: University of Washington Press.

Scott, Joan W. 1991. "The Evidence of Experience." *Critical Inquiry* 17: 773–97.

Siebers, Tobin. 2001. "Disability in Theory: From Social Constructionism to the New Realism of the Body." *American Literary History* 13.4: 737–54.

———. 2006. "Disability Studies and the Future of Identity Politics." In *Identity Politics Reconsidered,* ed. Linda Martín Alcoff et al., 10–30. New York: Palgrave-MacMillan.

State of Tennessee v. George V. Lane et al. 2004. 541 U.S.

Stoner, Kyle. 1999. "Sex and Disability: Whose Job Should It Be to Help Disabled People Make Love?" *Eye,* August 12, 1999, http://www.eye.net/eye/issue/issue_08.112.99/news/sex.html (accessed June 2004).

Tepper, Mitchell S. 1997. "Discussion Guide for the Sexually Explicit Educational Video *Sexuality Reborn: Sexuality Following Spinal Cord Injury.*" *Sexuality and Disability* 15.3: 183–99.

Weeks, Jeffrey. 1998. "The Sexual Citizen." *Theory, Culture, and Society* 15.3–4: 35–52.

Wilkerson, William S. 2000. "Is There Something You Need to Tell Me? Coming Out and the Ambiguity of Experience." In *Reclaiming Identity: Realist Theory and the Predicament of Postmodernism,* ed. Paula M. L. Moya and Michael R. Hames-García, 251–78. Berkeley: University of California Press.

Wu, Cynthia. 2004. "'The Mystery of Their Union': Cross-Cultural Legacies of the Original Siamese Twins." Ph.D. diss., University of Michigan.

11

HOW REAL IS RACE?

Michael Hames-García

> (a) The state shall not classify any individual by race, ethnicity, color or national origin. . . .
> (g) Nothing in this section shall prevent law enforcement officers . . . from describing particular persons in otherwise lawful ways. Neither . . . the legislature nor any statewide agency shall require law enforcement officers to maintain records that track individuals on the basis of said classifications . . .
>
> —*The Racial Privacy Initiative,* submitted to the California Attorney General, September 28, 2001

A quick read of Ward Connolly's Racial Privacy Initiative (which would have eliminated California's use of race as a means of classification) reveals much about the contradictions in public discourse about race. Among other things, it explicitly provided for the retention of racial profiling on the part of the police while freeing police departments from having to keep track of the race of the people they arrested or detained. The ballot measure, promoted using liberal, antiracist rhetoric, would have frustrated all attempts to demonstrate discriminatory patterns of surveillance, arrest, or harassment by police. Race clearly matters, and yet throughout its history as a concept, its elaboration has been buttressed by biological fictions that have not held up to scientific scrutiny. In this essay, I explore some of the contradictions between social and biological conceptions of the reality of race and suggest that what is needed now is creative experimentation with racial identities, rather than their abandonment.

Few would deny that social identity has become a primary means for political action within liberal democracy. Many, however, bemoan this fact, and "identity politics" has become a pejorative, frequently denoting at best an unproductive approach to social change. Within the academy, a strong body of work has emerged that opposes identity—especially racial identity. While numerous alternatives exist, a deep suspicion of racial identity has been a highly influential position (even outside the academy, as demonstrated by the Racial Privacy Initiative).[1] In this essay, I argue both that racial identities can be useful, productive, and transformative, and that their progressive political potential can benefit from a substantive account of their material reality. If social identities, including race, make a significant difference for how people live their lives, for what kinds of experiences they are likely to have, and for how they are treated by others, surely progressive political struggle would benefit from a substantive account of what makes identities matter and how they might be addressed. Instead, however, some theorists have sought to make racial identities go away, largely by arguing that they should, rather than by addressing the material conditions giving rise to and resulting from them. I would like to begin, therefore, by considering two examples of antirealist views of social identity and race that see them as obstacles to transformative politics and as lacking substantial "real" referents in the world.

RACIAL IDENTITY AS PROBLEM RATHER THAN SOLUTION

There are two major approaches to arguments against race and identity. The first sees any invocation of collective identity other than class identity as a divisive impediment to radical transformational social struggle. The second singles out racial identity specifically as founded on a biological fiction and therefore as an invalid category of social analysis. These two positions are not mutually exclusive, and critics often invoke them simultaneously. By way of illustration, I have tried to emphasize each approach in the writings of two influential scholars, both of whom have risen to prominence in part because of their rejection of social identities, including racial identity.

The first, more general indictment of (racial) identity emerges in political theorist Wendy Brown's book *States of Injury,* which paints a pessimistic picture of identity politics. According to Brown, identity politics either commits itself to the preservation of class inequality or becomes caught up in an unproductive cycle of blame and resentment. Both outcomes circumvent radical, progressive transformation of society. Brown thus charges identity politics with seeking merely to get a place at the table, followed by a piece of the pie, and motivated by resentment at being excluded from society (1995, 54). She asks, "To what extent do identity politics require a standard internal to existing society against which to pitch their claims, a standard that not only preserves capitalism from critique, but sustains the invisibility and inarticulateness of class—*not accidentally, but endemically*? Could we have stumbled upon one reason why class is invariably named but rarely theorized or developed in the multiculturalist mantra, 'race, class, gender, sexuality'?" (1995, 61). In Brown's account, identity politics is "a protest against exclusion" that seeks inclusion into (what turns out to be) a fictional communal ideal rather than seeking transformation of society; identity politics thereby reinforces that fictional ideal and its various exclusions (1995, 65).[2] According to Brown's insistently psychological account of identity, identity politics seeks revenge for exclusion (1995, 64).[3] Participants in identity politics remain trapped, according to Brown, by their inability to get over the past (described variously as "a past injury" or a "history of suffering"), and they therefore locate a reason for that history in the present. Basing their identity on a past injury generates "an ethicizing politics . . . of recrimination that seeks to avenge the hurt even while it reaffirms it" and that cannot offer a "future—for itself or others—that triumphs over this pain" (1995, 74).

Conceding that one cannot simply do away with identity, however, Brown *does* offer a cure for what ails identity politics in the form of two suggestions. The first is something along the lines of a truth and reconciliation committee that would allow people to tell their pain, to be heard without seeking revenge, without asking for anything in the present to address the past (since to do so would inscribe the past in the present).[4] Next, she suggests that we speak and read identity politics less in terms of "I am" and more in terms of "I want this for us," thus shifting emphasis away from an affirmation of identity in the present toward a focus on wants, needs, desires, and the future (1995, 75).

Brown's account of identity politics, however, is deliberately ahistorical and antimaterialist, and she casts her critique in abstract, general terms, implying that hers is an account of any kind of politics predicated on the affirmation of an identity. Her critique would be damning, except that she only offers a single example of identity politics in her chapter (an anti-discrimination ordinance in her local town), eschewing consideration of the *social movements* that have become the dominant expression of identity politics. While her criticism of identity politics might be valid for some examples of contemporary U.S. identity-based movements, it would require a significant amount of historical and ethnographic data to determine that it is true of all, or even most, of these movements. Such data is simply absent.

Ultimately, since Brown's work remains unengaged with the history of identity politics, even in the United States, I think she misses many of the ways in which that history demonstrates the complex relationships that are possible among the affirmation of identity, the histories of oppression, and the articulation of freer, more egalitarian futures. Furthermore, identity-based political movements have often pursued socially transformative futures in more complex ways than even Brown's shift from "I am" to "I want this for us" can account for. Brown narrowly figures the origins of identity politics in a psychological need for recognition, rather than in material, historical, and economic injustice, and understands identity politics as only seeking *recognition* within an unreconstructed social order. Consequently, she offers a solution that is itself linguistic, rather than material, leaving unaddressed the material concerns that give identity its political salience to begin with. Rather than radical social transformation (something she criticizes identity politics for being unable to invoke), her solution amounts essentially to a change in political language.[5]

My objections to Brown's work do not entail a complete rejection of her ideas. Rather, it seems to me that she too narrowly circumscribes her conception of identity politics. Furthermore, she does not sufficiently acknowledge the limits of that conception (giving her work the tone of a definitive take on all that identity politics is). Finally, she does all of this without empirical support, without any substantive engagement with (or even reference to) the long history of identity-based political struggles. An examination of this long history would reveal that a goal of inclusion is often compatible with a goal of radical social transformation. Furthermore, many kinds of identity politics (from many versions of nationalism to Lesbian separatism) quite simply do not seek inclusion. While some of *these* movements might turn out to inscribe a past in the present and to fail to move beyond affirmation of identity, this empirical question requires careful consideration of each social movement. It is not something that one can settle in advance of the facts.

Another opponent of identity, literary critic Walter Benn Michaels, offers some similar objections to Brown's but adds the more specific claim that race is an unjustifiable category of social classification. He puts his specific claim about race most sharply in a 1997 article:

> To the extent that both of the projects—celebrating race and abolishing it—depend upon a conception of race as a social fact, I want to argue that neither can succeed. We cannot think of race as a social fact, like slavery or . . . like class. . . . I will argue that race is not like class, that it neither happens nor can be made to unhappen. And despite those who wish to "respect and preserve" rather than abolish race, I will argue it makes no more sense to respect racial difference than it does to try to abolish it. . . . [O]ur actual racial practices . . . however "antiessentialist," can be understood only as the expression of our commitment to the idea that race is *not* a social construction, and I want to insist that if we give up that commitment, we must give up the idea of race altogether. Either race is an essence or there is no such thing as race. (1997, 125)

Michaels notes that for critical race theorists, "the claim that there are no races in nature—that race is a social construction—is not meant to deny that there is such a thing as race; it is meant to give us a better account of what race is" (1997, 132–33). That is, social constructionists about race, rather than arguing that race is merely a fiction, argue that it exists, only not as a natural or biological given outside of or before cultural meanings. For Michaels, however, race is either a biological fact or a biological fiction; it is neither a structural location within an economic system like class nor a mesh of cultural practices like ethnicity. In fact, biology is typically the defining element in modern distinctions between race and ethnicity.[6]

Since race turns out to be irreducible to simple, physical criteria (e.g., skin color, descent, or genetic distance), Michaels concludes that social constructionists must believe that race is a consequence of what one does, an expression of behaviors.[7] Here is where the (dis)analogy to class becomes important. While Michaels agrees that social classes exist, even though classes are not "natural," he denies that the same reasoning could apply to race (that it could be not a natural fact and nonetheless real). Class (in the Marxian sense in which Michaels is using it) is a function of what someone does (that is, working or owning), not who the person is according to society or that person's self-definition. It is a purely structural social location. In contrast, Michaels believes that race is "irreducible to action" because it is possible for someone to act in a way incompatible with her or his race. If a black person can "act white" without thereby becoming white, or a white person can "act black" without becoming black, in other words, then race must be a part of one's being rather than a consequence of one's actions (1997, 134–40). Michaels levies his attack most successfully, therefore, against those who appear to define race as strictly cultural rather than biological, since an account of race that refuses biological criteria cannot adequately explain the persistence of physical features for determining racial identity. He goes further, however, and denies the possibility of a gray, "blurry" definition of race as something complexly arising out of the interactions of biology and culture. Michaels insists that the "identity that is irreducible to action is essential, not socially constructed, and the identity that is identical to action is not really an identity—it's just the name of the action: worker, capitalist. If, then, we do not believe in racial identity as an essence, we cannot believe in racial identity as a social construction and we ought to give up the idea of racial identity altogether—we should . . . deny that there are such things as Jews, or blacks, or whites" (1997, 142).[8]

Among the problems with Michaels's position, therefore, is its reductivism. He bases his argument on the conviction that race must have only one meaning and only one determinate factor. Race, like most social concepts, however, means many different things and is not reducible to neat, orderly categories. As I have argued elsewhere, social identities, including race, have blurry boundaries, change over time and from place to place, and produce ambiguities and indeterminacies (Hames-García 2000, esp. 110–11). Like Michaels, I would agree that race is reducible neither to behavior nor to genes, nor is it exclusively a function of physiognomy. Race is not the same thing, in other words, as culture, class, nation, or color. The fact that something is not easily defined, that it contains exceptions, ambiguities, and indeterminate boundaries, however, does not mean that it does not exist or that it makes no sense to speak of it (Wittgenstein 1967, I, §66).

In making his general case against identity, Michaels's ultimate goal is to replace political discussions of being with debates over beliefs. He characterizes proponents of identity politics as claiming that "the things you do and the beliefs you hold can be justified by a description of who you are" (2004, 10). Like Brown, however, he assumes rather than demonstrates that this claim is the basis of identity-based political movements. If, however, Michaels's statement were to read that the things one does and the beliefs one holds can be *explained,* in part, through a description of who one is and what one has experienced, then I think it would be a more accurate sense of the thinking behind much identity politics. Of course, in this formulation it is hard for me to see how Michaels's arguments provide a basis for opposition. After all, what *else* might lead a person to hold particular beliefs *other than her or his experiences* (see Wilkerson 2000, 272–75)? This claim need not reduce all that a person is to race, gender, class, sexuality, ability, and so on. Furthermore, the claim that identity contributes to a person's beliefs need not imply that all people with similar identities will hold the same beliefs. Consider famed communist Angela Davis, who grew up middle-class, black, female, and intellectually gifted in Birmingham, Alabama; and famed anticommunist Condoleezza Rice, who grew up middle-class, black, female, and intellectually gifted in Birmingham, Alabama, a mere ten years later. The fact that they hold diametrically opposed political beliefs does not mean that their identities as black women had nothing to do with how they came to hold those beliefs. To argue otherwise would seem to border on obstinacy, or else to suggest that social identities cannot hold any significance unless they are absolutely bounded, uniform, deterministic, and foundational.

Studies of race show it to be a powerful concept that has transformed repeatedly over the past five centuries. It is also unlikely to go away any time soon. Rather than dismissing it, I believe that critical theorists should ask what the possibilities are for its further reinvention and how those possibilities might promote progressive social change. In a similar vein, Nobel laureate Toni Morrison writes,

> For three hundred years black Americans insisted that "race" was no usefully distinguishing factor in human relationships. During those same three centuries every academic discipline . . . insisted "race" was the determining factor in human development. When blacks discovered they had shaped or become a culturally formed race, and that it had specific and revered difference, suddenly they were told there is no such thing as "race," biological or cultural, that matters and that genuinely intellectual exchange cannot accommodate it. . . . It always seemed to me that the people who invented the hierarchy of "race" when it was convenient for them ought not to be the ones to explain it away, now that it does not suit their purposes for it to exist. (2000, 26)

Morrison's words might cause one to ask what critics have to gain by discounting identity and race. What interests do polemics against race and identity serve?[9]

Of course, scholars of race can glean important insights from critics like Brown and Michaels. One might see Brown's work as an important caution against versions of identity politics that fall too easily into a liberal democratic framework without questioning the reproduction of economic inequality as well as against those versions that fall into divisiveness and navel gazing. Similarly, one might generously read Michaels's work as a caution against an overinvestment in racial language. Theorists and activists should not retain the language of race simply because we are attached to it, trying to make it do the work of culture, ethnicity, and class.[10] One should also be on guard against the lingering elements of nineteenth-century scientific racism in contemporary racial discourse as well as against the collective tendency of the

U.S. Left to conflate race with class and culture. I think that Michaels is wrong, however, in thinking that, because people often conflate race with these other concepts, it does not describe any social reality at all. Race need be neither an account of absolute, naturally given biological difference, nor a conflation of ways of acting with social categories in order to be real. Rather than seriously ask what race means, whether or not it is useful, whether or not it actually obfuscates economic exploitation, and whether or not it is real with reference to its developments in material contexts, Michaels, like Brown, opts for abstract, theoretical answers intended to transcend time and space. What race means and describes (or attempts to describe) in different times, places, and contexts is an empirical question that I shall consider in this essay. My own approach is undeniably a theoretical one, but since my argument has of necessity to be both theoretical and empirical, I will draw on the empirical research of others.

THE POWER OF RACE AND THE COLONIALITY OF POWER

One of the most influential empirical and theoretical thinkers about identity in recent years is sociologist Manuel Castells, who offers a wide-ranging account of the new form of global social organization that he believes has quickly replaced both the industrial capitalist and state socialist forms of society at the end of the twentieth century. What he calls "the network society" is a pervasive global system characterized by "the globalization of strategically decisive economic activities," "the flexibility and instability of work, and the individualization of labor," dispersed forms of organization and media, and the pervasion of ideology through the most fundamental categories of life (1997, 1). Within the network society, collective identity movements have gained significance as the most powerful counterpoint to globalization. For Castells, identity-based political movements encompass not only "proactive movements, aiming at transforming human relationships at their most fundamental level, such as feminism and environmentalism," but also "reactive movements that build trenches of resistance on behalf of . . . the fundamental categories of millennial existence now threatened" by "techno-economic forces and transformative social movements," for example, God, nation, family, and so on (1997, 2).

Drawing from a broad array of examples, Castells argues for a three-part typology of collective identity: legitimizing identities, resistance identities, and project identities (1997, 8). *Legitimizing identity* arises through formal and informal, but "official," institutions, such as the church, voting, schools, corporate media, and so on. Legitimizing identities, such as "the citizen" or U.S. middle-class identity, ultimately serve to reinforce and legitimate existing social structures of control and domination. *Resistance identities* come into existence through actions by people who have suffered oppression, exclusion, or domination; they reject the norms of society and affirm opposing norms. *Project identities* attempt to redefine a group's position and role in society, but unlike resistance identities, they expand outward in the pursuit of radical transformation of society as a whole. His typology is overlapping: some movements begin as resistance identities and later become project or legitimizing identities, or a mixture of some or all of the above.

Castells's account of project identities makes accessible a whole range of possibilities that are foreclosed by Brown's account, and raises serious challenges to Michaels's nostalgia for (allegedly) purely belief-based, as opposed to identity-based, political movements. According to Castells, project identity becomes part of a larger process of reinventing and reordering society. While the process of creating a project identity might begin through the affirmation of a denigrated identity, it has the potential to expand "toward the transformation of society as the prolongation of this project of identity, as in the . . . example of a post-patriarchal society, liberating women, men, and children, through the realization of women's identity" (1997, 10). While project identities need not necessarily be politically progressive, Castells believes that they are, in the contemporary era, *necessary* for social change (1997, 11). Castells does acknowledge that most contemporary identities do not become project identities, remaining caught in a reactive posture (1997, 65). However, despite the bad odds, identity remains the best hope for transforming the current global network society into a better and more humane world.

Given the power of Castells's account, it is important to examine how he understands the prospects for race as a project identity. However, before turning to Castells's consideration of racial identity in the contemporary period, I want to briefly retrace some of the long history of race as a social category. In particular, I would like to turn to historical sociologist and world-systems theorist Aníbal Quijano's account of the origin and significance of race. I do so both because world-systems theory has proven to be among the most powerful models for analyzing historical change on a global scale and because Quijano has been at the forefront of using that model to understand race. His use of world-systems theory offers a much longer and wider sense of the origins of race than do accounts of race that take nineteenth-century scientific racism and legal classifications as the definitive examples of racial thinking.

For Quijano, race emerges in the sixteenth century, alongside a complex and global (re)organization of power around three interrelated and inseparable factors: "coloniality," capitalism, and Eurocentrism. The development of the concept of race is essential to explaining how these factors are mutually constitutive:

> What is termed globalization is the culmination of a process that began with the constitution of America [the "discovery of the Americas"] and colonial/modern Eurocentered capitalism as a new global power. One of the fundamental axes of this model of power is the social classification of the world's population around the idea of race, a mental construction that expresses the basic experience of colonial domination and pervades the more important dimensions of global power, including its specific rationality: Eurocentrism. The racial axis has a colonial origin and character, but it has proven to be more durable and stable than the colonialism in whose matrix it was established. Therefore, the model of power that is globally hegemonic today presupposes an element of coloniality. (Quijano 2000, 533)

Two things about race are crucial for Quijano. First, its origin supposed the existence of biological differences from which followed a natural hierarchy among superior and inferior groups. Second, race enabled (and was enabled by) new social and economic relations; racial identities thus became "constitutive" of unequal roles, locations, beliefs, and practices (2000, 534). Thus, according to Quijano, race, in its origin, was a web of beliefs that served to legitimate domination, to naturalize inequality so that people accepted it as inevitable and eternal rather than contingent and produced. In the process, the ideology of race "encroached on" the ideology of gender domination, mutating and transforming it (2000, 545–56).[11]

According to Quijano, race came into existence (separately from ethnicity or nation) as a marker of inherited, "natural," and hierarchically ranked differences in temperament, morality, intellectual ability, and aptitude for cultural and scientific achievement among populations. These supposed differences justified the naturalization of social relations of domination. Race emerged both as a justification of social domination and as a basic way of assigning places within the labor market (2000, 538). Race divided the world into inferior and superior populations, which then legitimated a racial division of labor. (Thus, wage labor was restricted to whites, while the racial order assigned nonwhites to serfdom and slavery.) Quijano writes, "In this way, both race and the division of labor remained structurally linked and mutually reinforcing, in spite of the fact that neither of them were necessarily dependent on the other in order to exist or change" (2000, 536).[12] The independence of race from the division of labor is significant for its continuing effects (the "coloniality of power").

Concurrent to the consolidation of a Eurocentered world economic system was the Eurocentrification of knowledge, culture, and history. The classification according to race of the world's population, in other words, came to have intense epistemic and cultural effects.[13] *Eurocentrism,* for Quijano, names the cognitive and cultural dimension of the new model of global power dominant since the sixteenth century. It entails both the imposition of a "racial, colonial, and negative" identity on non-Europeans and the classification of their culture as "naturally" inferior and historically antecedent to Europe (as premodern or primitive) (2000, 551, 552). The well-discussed, linked dualisms of modern Western thought are but one enduring legacy of the coloniality of power: reason/body, culture/nature, superior/inferior, male/female, white/black, north/south. The seventeenth-century separation of the body from the mind and the identification of the body with nature (and femaleness, Indian-ness, and blackness) made possible, according to Quijano, the scientific racism of the nineteenth century (2000, 555).[14]

It is worth noting that both Castells and Quijano cast race in almost exclusively negative terms.[15] After a lengthy consideration of the importance of race (in terms of oppression and discrimination) for African Americans, Castells finally holds that the concept of race (which he here conflates with ethnicity) can only take on significant communal meaning as it combines with broader categories (gender, nation, religion, class, and so on) (1997, 53, 59, 65):[16]

> Ethnicity does not provide the basis for communal heavens in the network society, because it is based on primary bonds that lose significance, when cut from their historical context, as a basis for reconstruction of meaning in a world of flows and networks. . . . Ethnic materials are integrated into cultural communes that are more powerful, and more broadly defined than ethnicity, such as religion or nationalism, as statements of cultural autonomy in a world of symbols. . . . Race matters, but it hardly constructs meaning any longer. (1997, 59)

The primary basis for this striking claim (striking because Castells does not make the same claim about nationality or religion) lies in the growing class polarization of blacks in the United States. In the case of race, Castells concludes that the fracturing of identity in one example prevents it from being a source of meaning in all cases (while the fracturing of some national identities does not preclude the cohesion of some other national identities for Castells). However, he offers his own counterexample of a racial project identity, although he does not frame it as such. I will return to this counterexample in my concluding section.

IS IT REAL? IS IT *REALLY* REAL?

Given Quijano's account of race, there are obviously good reasons why one might want to argue against its biological reality—perhaps even more so in the wake of nineteenth- and twentieth-century versions of scientific racism. Yet as Castells notes, with a nod to Cornel West, "race matters a lot" (1997, 57). Determining what that mattering consists of, then, becomes a crucial task. If one understands race, as

Quijano implies, as different from culture, ethnicity, class, or nation, then I suggest that the claim that race is real could mean at least three different things: (1) Race has a material-economic reality in the immediate effects and legacies of racism. (2) Race has a social and psychological reality as an existing system of beliefs and attitudes with material effects (this would include certain epistemic effects on the production and acquisition of knowledge). (3) Race exists in a physical or biological form, as bodily matter.

If we think of *race* as merely shorthand to reference the effects of racial classification and racism in contemporary society, then it is hard to deny its reality (although some might). Castells cites a host of studies on the impoverishment and imprisonment of blacks in the United States (1997, 53–55). As criminologist Coramae Richey Mann notes, "Racial minority suspects disproportionately become defendants [in court] and as defendants are disproportionately sent to prison or disproportionately executed" (1993, 219). A massive study of the death penalty in Georgia by criminologists David Baldus, Charles Pulaski, and George Woodworth (1983) found that defendants were four times more likely to receive a death sentence for killing white victims than for killing black victims. Moreover, blacks convicted of killing whites were twenty-two times more likely to receive a death sentence than blacks convicted of killing blacks. The study found race to be much more influential than more than two hundred other possible factors that influence sentencing (including various kinds and degrees of aggravation and motivation, whether victims were police officers or very young or female, and whether the defendant had a prior record) (1983, 689–95, 707–10). It is difficult to understand the disproportionate treatment of racial minorities in the United States as anything other than an effect and legacy of racism. Even politically conservative arguments that poverty and disadvantage are the result of cultural traits are dependent on racial thinking insofar as they identify the problem as the culture of poor blacks, Latinas/os, and Native Americans but not of poor whites. Black poverty, in other words, becomes a consequence of being black, while white poverty simply results from being poor. At the very least, race is important for understanding, explaining, and addressing the effects of contemporary and historical racism.[17]

The next way in which race might matter is as a set of beliefs with material effects. Put another way, do ideas about race influence how people think and act? In recent years, social psychologists have offered startling answers to this question. In 1995, Claude Steele and Joshua Aronson conducted a study in which researchers gave black and white Stanford undergraduates difficult exams measuring advanced English language skills. When researchers told test-takers that the exam was diagnostic of verbal ability, blacks performed about half as well as whites. When the same exam was given and test-takers were told that it was not diagnostic of ability but merely a way to study how people solve problems, blacks and whites performed roughly equivalent (Steele, Spencer, and Aronson 2002, 382–84; Steele and Aronson 1995). Another group of researchers was able to produce similar results in the domain of physical performance, having black and white college athletes play ten holes of golf in a laboratory course. When athletes were told that the goal was to measure "natural athletic ability," the blacks outperformed the whites significantly; when they were told that the test measured "sport strategic intelligence," the outcome was the opposite (Steele, Spencer, and Aronson 2002, 386; Stone et al., 1999). Thus, setting aside the question of whether racism (intentional or structural) currently exists, it is clear that race as a set of ideas exists and has significant material effects not only on people's thinking but also on their performance in a wide variety of mental and physical tasks. Furthermore, these effects are not arbitrary but rather have clear connections to the long history of Eurocentrism and evaluative hierarchies recounted by Quijano (white/black, mind/body, and so on).

Perhaps the most controversial meaning of the claim that race matters (or that race is real) would be the suggestion that race has, as a basis, biological or physical causal structures that result in the social differences one finds between contemporary, socially defined racial groups. Among the problems with this claim, as I have just laid it out, is the assumed separability of biology and culture. Furthermore, it risks playing into historical and commonsense racist thinking. Paleontologist and historian of science Stephen Jay Gould, among others, has meticulously documented the abuses of nineteenth-century scientific racism as an attempt to legitimate socially defined racial classifications and their attendant social inequality in terms of biological differences (for example, the idea that brain size or intellectual capacity has a direct connection to skin color) (Gould 1996, esp. 26–36; Harding, ed. 1993; Hubbard and Wald 1999, 13–38). More recently, evolutionary biologist Joseph L. Graves Jr. (2004) has compiled a range of scientific and social data to argue that contemporary categories of socially defined races are usually unhelpful, and often harmful, for attempting to understand sexual behavior, health and medicine, athletics, and intelligence. While he also looks at considerations like bone density and muscle mass, the main targets of Graves's argument are genetic explanations for social differences. He observes that humanity as a species has come into existence very recently, in evolutionary terms. The even more recent dispersal of human populations geographically and the relatively short time populations have spent in geographical isolation have not been sufficient for the development of different geographical races as the term is applied to other species. In other words, by contrast to many other mammals, humans are remarkably alike when it comes to our genes.[18] Furthermore, with regard to supposed racial genetic predisposition for disease, Graves shows that our current, socially defined races obscure the actual genetic commonalities and differences of various populations. Genes for sickle cells, for example, while prevalent in people from western Africa, the Mediterranean and Middle East, and India, are uncommon among people from eastern Africa. Similarly, while much has been made of a supposedly genetic predisposition among African Americans for high blood pressure, Nigerians have far lower rates of high blood pressure than do U.S. whites (the difference between Nigerians and U.S. whites being more than double the difference between U.S. whites and U.S. blacks) (2004, 226). As Graves observes, "Geographical distance does not necessarily equal genetic distance. In fact, assuming that two people are genetically different because they look like they came from different parts of the world can be really dangerous for their health. . . . [b]ecause things like people's blood type or their ability to accept transplanted organs are dictated by how genetically close they are, not necessarily by where their ancestors came from geographically" (2004, 8).[19]

There are, then, good reasons to be skeptical about attempts to link biology and race—especially given such familiar examples of racial biological determinism as Richard J. Herrnstein and Charles Murray's resoundingly refuted book *The Bell Curve.*[20] However, I think there are important reasons not to eliminate all consideration of biology and the body from our discussions of race, provided we understand biology as mutually constituted with culture and as significantly less determinate than it is often taken to be. In particular, I would like to suggest that an important dimension of what race is and how it functions results from the interaction of social ideologies of race with visible human difference. This dimension is lost if scholars are unable to consider the physical matter of race. While such outward differences as skin color, hair texture, or eye shape may hold little or no meaning for our biological functioning as organisms or for our innate capacities, they are crucial, in Western societies, for our social functioning.[21]

It helps to understand the physical or natural as something that is not simply given or inert, passive, and acted upon by culture. Theoretical physicist Karen Barad suggests that an adequate social theory of the body needs to account for "*how the body's materiality*—for example, its anatomy and physiology—and *other material forces actively matter to the processes of materialization*" (2003, 809; emphasis in the original). Drawing from the quantum theory of Niels Bohr, her view of bodies seeks to reject the separation between observer and object, and therefore also that between society/culture/ideology and matter. If one understands the world as fundamentally a big soup of inseparable processes, with indeterminate boundaries that are constantly in flux (which is easiest to do at the quantum level of atoms, particles, and waves), then one can begin to see the degree of mutual constitution at stake among observers and objects. Both the "observer" (which would include theoretical assumptions as well as instruments used to observe and measure) and the "observed matter" interact (or, as Barad insists, "intra-act") in order to produce an event or phenomenon. Both observer and matter are "agential." The observer is therefore not neutral in Barad's account, nor is matter passive: "The world is a dynamic process of intra-activity in the ongoing reconfiguring of locally determinate causal structures with determinate boundaries, properties, meanings, and patterns of marks on bodies" (2003, 817). Agency is then a process through which the causal intra-action of different parts of the world produces intelligible phenomena. As Bohr notes, indeterminacy is particularly salient in the study of quantum phenomena, such that accounting for an event requires a thorough description "of all relevant features of the experimental arrangement" (Bohr 1963, 4; cited in Barad 2001, 82–83).

Extrapolating Barad's and Bohr's ideas to the realm of social theory, I would argue that indeterminacy and mutual constitution are equally as characteristic of social, political, and historical phenomena as they are of quantum phenomena. In considering race, most biological reductionists tend to eschew histories of racism as relevant features, while most attempts to debunk scientific racism tend to discount the importance of biologically superficial physical differences for understanding the reality of race. As Barad cautions, however, "explanations of various phenomena and events that do not take account of material, as well as discursive, constraints will fail to provide empirically adequate accounts (not any story will do)" (2001, 88). Furthermore, the temptation to eliminate race as a category of analysis in favor of culture, ethnicity, or class, while well intentioned, can fail precisely by not accounting for the active role of otherwise superficial physical differences, as well as customs of assigning meaning to family descent, in shaping racial formations.

Unless we accept the causal role of matter in the formation of racial meanings and phenomena, our theories of society will be unable to explain how and why people experience race as they do. To put it bluntly, how can I understand my ease at hailing a taxicab in New York City or Washington, D.C., in the face of countless stories from black friends about having to walk forty blocks without having one stop? Along similar lines, a 1991 study by Verna Keith and Cedric Herring found that while African Americans identified as "very light" earned 80 percent of the average income for U.S. whites in 1980, "very black" African Americans earned 53 percent—with the incomes of "light brown," "medium brown," and "dark brown" African Americans forming a downward-sloping curve between the two extremes (1991).[22] In the latter case, at least two possible explanations are imaginable, both of which point to the intra-actions of raced bodies and social ideologies of race. The first possibility is that, because of biological racism, darker-skinned blacks face greater discrimination than their lighter-skinned peers, resulting in both inherited and acquired income differences. The second possibility is that, given that skin color in Keith and Herring's data set was self-reported, the respondents to the survey from which their data comes saw their own bodies as darker or lighter in relation to their economic and social status. These two explanations are certainly not mutually exclusive, and both suggest the continuing effects of the racial division of labor that Quijano sees emerging in the sixteenth century. In either case, I want to note that a theory of race that does not account for the intra-action of culture and body is inadequate to explain the data. Some of the social psychology studies discussed above also suggest the importance of considering the active participation of bodies in racial meanings. Steele, Spencer, and Aronson note, for example, that when a verbal ability test was given to black and white college students and described as culturally fair, whites did not outperform blacks. When it was presented as a normal diagnostic test, however, whites outperformed blacks—and blacks (while not reporting more anxiety than the white students) had "dramatically" higher blood pressure levels (2002, 400–401).[23] The biological body is not inert matter in the face of racial ideologies.

Race is a phenomenon that emerges through the intra-action of a number of things, including human phenotypic differences such as eye and nose shape, skin tone, hair texture, and so on. These differences become salient in the ongoing process of racial formation. They become meaningful as components in the intra-active phenomenon of race, which in turn varies across time and space. Thus, the significance of those bodily differences changes and is not always even present when the concept of race emerges. One cannot fully explain certain racial phenomena, however, without reference to human bodies. Attempts to reconfigure race solely as culture or as legal fiction fall into absurdity if they cannot consider the significant role of bodily difference in the "whitening" of European immigrants in the United States (or the uneven ability of different Mexican Americans to "become" white).[24] Whiteness may not only result from a lack of melanin, but it certainly helps to be light-skinned in order to qualify as white. Studies on the ambiguity of the category of whiteness, in fact, support the link between skin tone and social whiteness. After all, ambiguity about who qualified as white in the United States did not affect immigrants from Nigeria or Sweden. The very fact that U.S. case law determining the boundaries of racial identity focuses overwhelmingly on Asians, Middle Easterners, Latinas/os, and people of mixed-race descent shows the extent to which physical appearance is a causal, if not always determinate, factor in the materialization of race in the United States (Haney López 1998).

Bodies do not have inherent meanings. Yet, given the physical properties of bodies and the historical sediment of their intra-actions with ideologies and politico-economic practices, one cannot attach just any meaning to any body. In other words, the body is something more than an inert, passive object on which ideology inscribes meaning, but rather it is an agential reality with its own causal role in making meaning. A black person, for example, cannot become white simply through discursive feats, because her or his body's production of melanin is an inseparable component in racial production. In addition, race is not just color, although in some times and places color becomes not merely an indispensable but a determinate component of race. Race is a produced, intra-active phenomenon, involving the modern/colonial gender system (itself a phenomenon with many intra-acting components), individual bodily differences and histories of family descent, as well as social ideologies and practices (including those of courts, legislatures, and police/prisons). It consequently varies and changes across time and space. That in the contemporary United States two people with very light pigmentation and known sub-Saharan African ancestry can be considered black, while in contemporary Brazil a brother and sister with different complexions but the same ancestry might be considered of different races, does not mean that race does not exist. Rather, such differences indicate that the social phenomenon of race emerges differently because of intra-actions among history, economics, law, and human bodily differences in contemporary U.S. and Brazilian societies.

IS IT ALL BAD? RACIAL IDENTITY PROJECTS

Given the more than three centuries of racial thinking that preceded the rise of scientific racism in the nineteenth century, it seems odd to insist that race need inherently be reducible to the biological classifications of that period. It seems considerably less odd to insist that race is an inherently oppressive construction that legitimizes social inequality, domination, and exploitation (that is, to assert that *race* equals *racism*). Thus, it is relatively easy to understand race as a social location that one finds oneself placed in by racial classifications, given the substantial empirical data on the effects of social ideologies of race. It is harder to defend race as a self-consciously chosen standpoint necessary to antiracist struggle.[25] It is particularly hard given the persistent characterization of race as a negative construction, one that has had the effects on the construction of knowledge described by Quijano and others.[26] In the remainder of this essay, I would like to suggest that the creative elaboration of racial standpoints is not just compatible with, but necessary for, radical social transformation.

An increasing number of scholars have argued that identity is an indispensable theoretical construct shaping one's cognitive access to the world. Whether this access is more or less clear is an empirical question, but its answer does not make socially constructed identities any more or less real. Furthermore, it is through active social struggle (or the elaboration of project identity) that one can both transform the world and generate new knowledge about what the world is and what it might become. One might then understand some project identities as the elaboration of a standpoint from a social location in order to act in the world in such a way that that social location is forever altered. It is often difficult (even, or perhaps particularly, for those who are oppressed by one) to imagine an imposed, negative identity as a resource of hope and transformation.[27]

I want to briefly offer two examples of racial project identities by way of conclusion to this essay. Performance scholar Carrie Sandahl recounts one example of the potential for progressive racial project identity in her analysis of black and blind performance artist Lynn Manning's *Weights*. Of particular centrality to her analysis of Manning's performance piece is his departure from the traditional "overcoming" narrative of disability, in which "disability experience becomes a generalized metaphor for psychological adjustment" (Sandahl 2004, 584). According to this traditional narrative (a narrative with no shortage of similarities to Brown's prescription for identity politics), a newly disabled person is first devastated by her or his disability and eventually learns to transcend it and achieve a wiser, happier state because of the effort of overcoming (Siebers 2004, 13–16). The pivotal point when *Weights* departs from the overcoming narrative occurs when Manning regains consciousness after being shot and learns that he has lost his sight. At this moment, he recalls, "something akin to joy surges through me" (Sandahl 2004, 588). While his doctors see his response as "abnormal," Manning is not so much happy to be blind as he is happy to be blind and still alive. However, later he does begin to revel in his blindness. As Sandahl notes, "what Manning learns could only be known through the biological configuration of his new body, or what [Paula] Moya calls the 'causal constraints' of the natural world. He discovers new dimensions, or new truths, about what he thought he had known. It would take a phenomenological experience with blindness to make these discoveries" (2004, 591).

For Sandahl, what is significant about Manning's response to becoming blind is that it provides him with an "interpretive framework" for understanding the world around him. Drawing from the insights of the approach to identity laid out in the anthology *Reclaiming Identity,* Sandahl argues that Manning's interpretive framework, rather than impeding objective knowledge about the world, makes it possible.[28] In order to obtain knowledge about the world from a blind person's standpoint, Manning must embrace his blindness and revel in his disability, rather than seeking to eliminate or to overcome it. The project that Sandahl brings out in Manning's work, furthermore, is a manifold one. He must take the knowledge he has about what it means to be black and what it means to be blind and integrate the two standpoints. His integration of disability and black identities calls forth a further reimagining of social struggles and categories, transforming the very elaboration of project identities. The materiality of Manning's dark-skinned and blind body (his social location) is relevant, but not determinate. Rather, it is one of the agential factors in the emergent phenomenon of his blind man, black man standpoint. As Sandahl notes in conclusion, "Manning's performance makes clear that we need to spend more time exploring what disability *is* and *can be,* along with what blackness *is* and *can be,* in as many variations as possible" (2004, 602). It is not coincidental that Sandahl's analysis addresses both race and disability. Disability activists and disability studies have been at the forefront of developing proactive identity projects. While emphasizing the constructed nature of reality, some of the leading scholars in disability studies have also pointed to the persistence of concrete physical bodies that are irreducible to "culture" (understood as separate from, rather than mutually constitutive with, nature).[29]

The project of reveling in minority identity, as literary theorist Satya Mohanty argues, is necessary, not simply for the well-being of minorities, and not simply for its own sake, as if all identity projects lead naturally to progressive social change (Moya and Hames-García 2000, 60–64, 186–87, 313–15). Rather, it is often by exploring identities and fostering communal resistance that one can reveal the social conflicts produced by modernity and coloniality and begin to recognize possibilities that might lead to better ethical knowledge and progressive social change. Of course, one can more easily grant the importance of embracing gender or cultural identity, which appear to have ready referents beyond oppression, exploitation, and domination, than does racial identity. In this light, however, it is worth noting Castells's account of the Zapatistas in Chiapas, Mexico. Castells finds it remarkable that the Zapatista identity formation is historically unprecedented, insofar as the indigenous communities of Chiapas have been separated by ethnic and linguistic differences for centuries. Thus, "it does not seem that the defense of ethnic identity was a dominant element in the movement" because a "new Indian identity was constructed through their struggle and came to include various ethnic groups" (1997, 77, 78).[30] Although Castells earlier claims to discount racial identity, it is hard to imagine what the Zapatistas' "new Indian identity" can be if not a racial identity. It is neither ethnicity, nor culture, nor nation, nor language. Their "new" racial identity, in turn, does not make sense (as Castells notes) apart from the five hundred years of struggle against the coloniality of power (as described by Quijano). Yet Quijano too describes race in purely negative terms, as a "mental construction" that is mapped onto (passive) bodies and populations in order to naturalize social difference and a hierarchy of value, knowledge, and labor. What makes the Zapatistas' racial identity "new," however, is precisely the fact that it is not completely dependent for meaning on how race has taken shape within the coloniality of power. While Eurocentrism is the epistemic standpoint that emerges from the birth of the colonial/modern world system, Zapatismo has emerged in the late twentieth century as a self-conscious Indian standpoint seeking to criticize and transform that world system (Mignolo 2002, 245). As a critical standpoint, it is not committed to retaining racial categories and hierarchies as they currently exist, but its birth in an analysis of a racially specific social location is undeniable in the First Declaration from the Lacandon Jungle: "We are the product of five hundred years of struggle" (Marcos et al., 1995, 51). Theirs is a radical, unprecedented, and transformational racial identity project that aims to creatively reimagine the possibilities of existence, not for Indians alone, but for all people.

We need creative racial identity projects more than we need philosophical arguments against race. Race is no more or less a fiction than nation or ethnicity, and it is just as unlikely to go away. One cannot easily dismiss it as "only cultural" or "just ideological" because it emerges from the intra-action of history, culture, economics, and material human bodies. It has played a constitutive role in shaping the modern world, and it continues to shape people's most intimate and unconscious behaviors. Furthermore, racial hierarchies and biological determinist assumptions about racial difference will not evaporate without a significant reorganization of economic, political, and cultural relations at the personal and societal levels as well as an accounting for how different bodies intra-act with racial categories and ideas. That reorganization, in turn, must come in part from racial identity projects that do not simply reaffirm what race is and has been, but rather, seek a transformation of race into something new.

There have been and continue to be many attempts at transforming racial identities, including that of the Zapatistas. Other creative and transformational racial identity projects include the Harlem Renaissance, the Negritude movement, Pan-Africanism, Pan-Indigenism, and the contemporary formations of Asian American and Chicana/o identities.[31] While internally heterogeneous and often imperfect, these projects have begun *recently* (recently, that is, given that the present racial order took over five hundred years to come about) to imagine what race might be beyond a means for oppression and exploitation. It is only by encouraging these and other project identities to flourish that we will be able to find possibilities for a more egalitarian future.

NOTES

I would like to thank Ernesto Martínez and Paula Moya for their invaluable comments on earlier drafts of this essay. Stacy Alaimo and Susan Hekman also gave me marvelous feedback that has strengthened the essay. I would also like to thank Rosemarie Garland Thomson, Satya Mohanty, Carrie Sandahl, and Tobin Siebers for conversations around several parts of this essay that originated as part of a Future of Minority Studies Project symposium on "Disability Studies and the Realist Theory of Identity."

1. The work on identity (and related questions like subjectivity and agency) is vast. In addition to the works I take up in this essay, examples of the anti-identitarian position include Butler 1990; Gilroy 2001; Gitlin 1995; Hobsbawm 1996; Rorty 1998; Žižek 1998. Many recent theorists, however, have addressed the question of identity with a new seriousness, taking to heart criticisms of identity while exploring better formulations of it. See, among others, Alcoff 2006; Alcoff et al. 2006; Moya 2002; Moya and Hames-García 2000. Another recent productive overview of the question of identity is Hekman 2004.

2. Others articulate similar criticisms of identity politics (Aronson 1995; Hobsbawm 1996). For some responses, see Alcoff 2006, 20–46; Hames-García 2004, 249–54; Kelley 1997, 103–24.

3. For Brown, oppression might be material, but identity is a psychological response to oppression, and an unproductive psychological response at that:

> Revenge as a "reaction," a substitute for the capacity to act, produces identity as both bound to the history that produced it and as a reproach to the present which embodies that history. The will that "took to hurting" in its own impotence against its past becomes (in the form of an identity whose very existence is due to heightened consciousness of the immovability of its "it was," its history of subordination) a will that makes not only a psychological but a political practice of revenge, a practice that reiterates the existence of an identity whose present past is one of insistently unredeemable injury. This past cannot be redeemed *unless* the identity ceases to be invested in it, and it cannot cease to be invested in it without giving up its identity as such, thus giving up its

economy of avenging and at the same time perpetuating its hurt. (Brown 1995, 73)

4. Brown writes, "For if I am right about the problematic of pain installed at the heart of many contemporary contradictory demands for political recognition, all that such pain may long for—more than revenge—is the chance to be heard into a certain release, recognized into self-overcoming, incited into possibilities for triumphing over, and hence losing, itself" (1995, 74–75).

5. "The replacement—even the admixture—of the language of 'being' with 'wanting' would seek to exploit politically a recovery of the more expansive moments in the genealogy of identity formation. . . . How might democratic discourse itself be invigorated by such a shift from ontological claims to these kinds of more expressly political ones . . . ?" (Brown 1995, 76).

6. While common descent is often central to defining both *race* and *ethnicity, race* typically carries with it more of an exclusive association with biologically inherited physical and mental traits (especially after the nineteenth century). By contrast, *ethnicity* always includes—and has increasingly come to be limited to—cultural inheritance (e.g., cuisine, customs, music, and folklore). Thus, Irish Americans, Russian Jews, Inuits, and Navajos might all be definable ethnic groups, but in the contemporary United States, the first two would be racially white, and the last two, racially Native American. Furthermore, a Romanian infant adoptee in the United States would likely be raised both ethnically American and racially white, while Korean adoptees to white parents regularly grow up to think of themselves and to be perceived by others as ethnically American and racially Asian (Shiao, Tuan, and Rienzi 2004).

7. I discuss some of the problems with simple biological definitions of race later in this essay. See Gould 1996; Graves 2004.

8. For a much more cautious consideration of the proposal to simply stop talking about race, which she calls "eliminativism," as well as the many practical barriers to it posed by the social reality of race, see Zack 1998, 16–17.

9. Gutiérrez-Jones suggests an alignment between Michaels's rejection of collective identity and a larger "angry white male" cultural backlash in the United States in the 1990s (2001, 48–65). Other scholarly criticisms of Michaels's work on race include Taylor 2004 and Elam forthcoming.

10. See note 6 above.

11. A longer study might consider the significance of emerging conceptions of gender, sexuality, sin, and perversion for the development of the modern/colonial racial regime outlined by Quijano. For a useful and full discussion of Quijano's thought, the coloniality of power, and the role of gender and heterosexuality in its development, see Lugones 2007. Other scholars have explored the mutual constitution of gender, race, and sexuality in the eighteenth, nineteenth, and early twentieth centuries (see, e.g., McClintock 1995; Somerville 2000).

12. Quijano's view marks a decisive change from earlier theorists like Eric Wolf, who sees race as essentially subordinate to the division of labor and as not having a structural independence (Wolf 1997, 380–81).

13. In the first place, they [Europeans] expropriated the cultural discoveries of the colonized peoples most apt for the development of

> capitalism to the profit of the European center. Second, they repressed as much as possible the colonized forms of knowledge production, the models of the production of meaning, their symbolic universe, the model of expression and of objectification and subjectivity. . . . Third, in different ways in each case, they forced the colonized to learn the dominant culture in any way that would be useful to the reproduction of domination. . . . All of those turbulent processes involved a long period of the colonization of cognitive perspectives, modes of producing and giving meaning, the results of material existence, the imaginary, the universe of intersubjective relations with the world: in short, the culture. (Quijano 2000, 541)

See also Amin 1989; Dussel 1996; Mignolo 1995; Mudimbe 1988; Said 1979.

14. See also Mignolo 2000, 114–16, 314–15.

15. Castells attempts to distinguish *race* as a source of oppression and discrimination, an externally imposed biological categorization, from *ethnicity* as "a source of meaning and identity" that comes closer to *nationality,* although without the key features of language and territory (1997, 53). He does not systematically distinguish between the two concepts in his book, however. Quijano, as noted above, distinguishes sharply between them.

16. I note Castells's slippage between *race* and *ethnicity* in note 15 above; see also note 6.

17. Even most critics of racial identity concede some version of this point (Michaels 2004, 164; Zack 1998, 44–45).

18. "The genetic distances in humans are statistically about ten times lower (2 percent) than the 20 percent average in other organisms, even when comparing the most geographically separated populations within modern humans. There is greater genetic variability found within one tribe of western African chimpanzees than exists in the entire human species!" (Graves 2004, 10).

19. See also Graves 2004, 103–36; and Hubbard and Wald 1999, 72–107.

20. For two of the many critiques of *The Bell Curve* that also address genetics, heredity, and intelligence more generally, see Graves 2004, 172–84; and Gould 1996, 34–36, 367–90.

21. Omi and Winant note that "although the concept of race invokes biologically based human characteristics . . . selection is always and necessarily a social and historical process" (1994, 55). While I agree with their general theorization of "racial formation," I find their understanding of matter to be passive rather than active or agential.

22. Telles discusses this study in comparison with data on complexion in Brazil (Telles 2004, 114–16). For a related study with regard to Chicanas/os, phenotype, and life chances, see Arce, Murguía, and Frisbie 1987. Goldsmith, Hamilton, and Darity (2006) have found slightly different data suggesting that, while lighter-skinned blacks are advantaged in labor markets in relation to more qualified, darker-skinned blacks, those identified as "medium-skinned" did not receive a significant preference from potential employers. Skin tone in this study was digitally manipulated rather than self-reported.

23. The details of the study are in Blascovich et al. 2001.

24. Michael Calderón-Zaks (2005) has recently explored the consequences for racial formation and whiteness theories of the fluctuating white and nonwhite status of Mexicans in the United States during the late nineteenth and early twentieth centuries.

25. I am here drawing on the distinction developed within feminist philosophy between standpoint and social location. *Social location* is the part of one's identity defined by laws, customs, and practices quite apart from one's individual sense of self. Racial social location is that which generally results in a person experiencing or not experiencing the direct effects of racism. *Standpoint* is a mediation, or interpretation, of social location. It generally reflects someone's decision to make a public and political issue of one's identity. It is identity as rearticulated in the pursuit of social transformation, and it is thoroughly bound up with one's individual and collective sense of self. For an overview of some of the debates around these issues, see Wylie 2003.

26. See, among others, the works cited in note 13 above.

27. Recently, the theoretical project of imaginatively and critically reconstructing identity has formed the undertaking of a multidisciplinary and multi-institution research project, The Future of Minority Studies. For more information, see Alcoff et al. 2006, 1–9. Also see the Web site www.fmsproject.cornell.edu.

28. For more on objectivity, see Moya and Hames-García 2000, 12–14, 39–41, 136–37, 200–202. See also Wylie 2003, 32–33.

29. Conversations with disability scholars have greatly informed my thinking about creative racial identity projects. One should also note the historical inseparability of race and (dis)ability in the development of ideas about different and hierarchically ranked bodies. See Baynton 2001; Garland Thomson 2002; Siebers 2006.

30. Here, unlike elsewhere, Castells seems to consider ethnicity as a separate category from race. See notes 6 and 15 above.

31. See, as well, Alcoff's consideration of recent formations of U.S. Latino identity (2006, 227–84).

REFERENCES

Alcoff, Linda Martín. 2006. *Visible Identities: Race, Gender, and the Self.* New York: Oxford University Press.

Alcoff, Linda Martín, et al. 2006. *Identity Politics Reconsidered.* New York: Palgrave.

Amin, Samir. 1989. *Eurocentrism.* Trans. Russell Moore. New York: Monthly Review Press.

Arce, Carlos H., Edward Murguía, and W. Parker Frisbie. 1987. "Phenotype and Life Chances among Chicanos." *Hispanic Journal of Behavioral Sciences* 9.1: 19–32.

Aronson, Ronald. 1995. *After Marxism.* New York: Guilford Press.

Baldus, David C., Charles Pulaksi, and George Woodworth. 1983. "Comparative Review of Death Sentences: An Empirical Study of the Georgia Experience." *Journal of Criminal Law and Criminology* 74.3 (Fall): 661–753.

Barad, Karen. 2001. "Re(con)figuring Space, Time, and Matter." In *Feminist Locations: Global and Local, Theory and Practice*, ed. Marianne DeKoven, 75–109. New Brunswick, N.J.: Rutgers University Press.

———. 2003. "Posthumanist Performativity: Toward an Understanding of How Matter Comes to Matter." *Signs* 28.3: 801–31.

Baynton, Douglas C. 2001. "Disability and the Justification of Inequality in American History." In *The New Disability History: American Perspectives*, ed. Paul K. Longmore and Lauri Umamsky, 33–57. New York: New York University Press.

Blascovich, Jim, et al. 2001. "African Americans and High Blood Pressure: The Role of Stereotype Threat." *Psychological Science* 12.3 (May): 225–29.

Bohr, Niels. 1963. "Quantum Physics and Philosophy: Causality and Complementarity." In *Essays 1958–1962 on Atomic Physics and Human Knowledge*, 1–7. New York: Interscience Publishers.

Brown, Wendy. 1995. *States of Injury: Power and Freedom in Late Modernity*. Princeton, N.J.: Princeton University Press.

Butler, Judith. 1990. *Gender Trouble: Feminism and the Subversion of Identity*. New York: Routledge.

Calderón-Zaks, Michael A. 2005. "Racial Formation and Chicanos: Some Critical Points." Paper presented at the *Pacific Coast Council on Latin American Studies Conference* (Loyola Marymount University). Los Angeles, November 3–5.

Castells, Manuel. 1997. *The Power of Identity*. Vol. II of *The Information Age: Economy, Society, and Culture*. Malden, Mass.: Blackwell.

Dussel, Enrique. 1996. *The Underside of Modernity: Apel, Ricoeur, Taylor and the Philosophy of Liberation*. Ed. Eduardo Mendieta. Atlantic Highlands, N.J.: Humanities Press.

Elam, Michele. Forthcoming. *Mixtries: Mixed Race in the New Millennium*. Stanford, Calif.: Stanford University Press.

Garland-Thomson, Rosemarie. 2002. "Integrating Disability, Transforming Feminist Theory." *NWSA Journal* 14.3 (Fall): 1–32.

Gilroy, Paul. 2001. *Against Race: Imagining Political Culture beyond the Color Line*. Cambridge, Mass.: Harvard University Press.

Gitlin, Todd. 1995. *The Twilight of Common Dreams: Why America Is Wracked by Culture Wars*. New York: Metropolitan Books.

Goldsmith, Arthur H., Darrick Hamilton, and William Darity Jr. 2006. "Shades of Discrimination: Skin Tone and Wages." *American Economic Review* 96.1 (May): 242–45.

Gould, Stephen Jay. 1996. *The Mismeasure of Man*. Rev. and exp. ed. New York: Norton.

Graves, Joseph L., Jr. 2004. *The Race Myth: Why We Pretend Race Exists in America*. New York: Dutton.

Gutiérrez-Jones, Carl. 2001. *Critical Race Narratives: A Study of Race, Rhetoric, and Injury*. New York: New York University Press.

Hames-García, Michael. 2000. "'Who Are Our Own People?' Challenges for the Theory of Social Identity." In Moya and Hames-García, *Reclaiming Identity: Realist Theory and the Predicament of Postmodernism*, 102–29. Berkeley: University of California Press.

———. 2004. *Fugitive Thought: Prison Movements, Race, and the Meaning of Justice.* Minneapolis: University of Minnesota Press.

Haney-López, Ian F. 1998. *White by Law: The Legal Construction of Race.* New York: New York University Press.

Harding, Sandra, ed. 1993. *The "Racial" Economy of Science: Toward a Democratic Future.* Bloomington: Indiana University Press.

Hekman, Susan. 2004. *Private Selves, Public Identities: Reconsidering Identity Politics.* University Park: Pennsylvania State University Press.

Herrnstein, Richard J., and Charles Murray. 1994. *The Bell Curve: Intelligence and Class Structure in American Life.* New York: Free Press.

Hobsbawm, Eric. 1996. "Identity Politics and the Left." *New Left Review* (May/June): 38–47.

Hubbard, Ruth, and Elijah Wald. 1999. *Exploding the Gene Myth: How Genetic Information Is Produced and Manipulated by Scientists, Physicians, Employers, Insurance Companies, Educators, and Law Enforcers.* Rev. ed. Boston: Beacon.

Keith, Verna, and Cedric Herring. 1991. "Skin Tone Stratification in the Black Community." *American Journal of Sociology* 97: 760–78.

Kelly, Robin D. G. 1997. *Yo' Mama's Disfunktional! Fighting the Culture Wars in Urban America.* Boston: Beacon.

Lugones, María. 2007. "Heterosexualism and the Colonial/Modern, Gender System." *Hypatia* 22.1 (Winter): 186–209.

Mann, Coramae Richey. 1993. *Unequal Justice: A Question of Color.* Bloomington: Indiana University Press.

Marcos, Subcomandante, and the Zapatista Army of National Liberation. 1995. *Shadows of Tender Fury: The Letters and Communiqués.* Trans. Frank Bardacke, Leslie López, and the Watsonville, California, Human Rights Committee. New York: Monthly Review Press.

McClintock, Anne. 1995. *Imperial Leather: Race, Gender, and Sexuality in the Colonial Contest.* New York: Routledge.

Michaels, Walter Benn. 1997. "Autobiography of an Ex-White Man: Why Race Is Not a Social Construction." *Transition* 73: 122–43.

———. 2004. *The Shape of the Signifier: 1967 to the End of History.* Princeton, N.J.: Princeton University Press.

Mignolo, Walter D. 1995. *The Darker Side of the Renaissance: Literacy, Territoriality, and Colonization.* Ann Arbor: University of Michigan Press.

———. 2000. *Local Histories/Global Designs: Coloniality, Subaltern Knowledges, and Border Thinking.* Princeton, N.J.: Princeton University Press.

———. 2002. "The Zapatistas' Theoretical Revolution: Its Historical, Ethical, and Political Consequences." *Review* 25.3: 245–75.

Morrison, Toni. 2000. "Unspeakable Things Unspoken: The Afro-American Presence in American Literature." *The Black Feminist Reader,* ed. Joy James and T. Denean Sharpley-Whiting, 24–56. Malden, Mass.: Blackwell.

Moya, Paula M. L. 2002. *Learning from Experience: Minority Identities, Multicultural Struggles.* Berkeley: University of California Press.

Moya, Paula M. L., and Michael Hames-García, eds. 2000. *Reclaiming Identity: Realist Theory and the Predicament of Postmodernism.* Berkeley: University of California Press.

Mudimbe, V. Y. 1988. *The Invention of Africa: Gnosis, Philosophy, and the Order of Knowledge.* Bloomington: Indiana University Press.

Omi, Michael, and Howard Winant. 1994. *Racial Formation in the United States: From the 1960s to the 1990s.* New York: Routledge.

Quijano, Aníbal. 2000. "Coloniality of Power, Eurocentrism, and Latin America." Trans. Michael Ennis. *Nepantla: Views from the South* 1.3: 533–80.

Rorty, Richard. 1998. *Achieving Our Country: Leftist Thought in Twentieth-Century America.* Cambridge, Mass.: Harvard University Press.

Said, Edward. 1979. *Orientalism.* New York: Vintage.

Sandahl, Carrie. 2004. "Black Man, Blind Man: Disability Identity Politics and Performance." *Theatre Journal* 56: 579–602.

Shiao, Jiannbin Lee, Mia Tuan, and Elizabeth Rienzi. 2004. "Shifting the Spotlight: Exploring Race and Culture in Korean-White Adoptive Families." *Race and Society* 7: 1–16.

Siebers, Tobin. 2004. "Disability as Masquerade." *Literature and Medicine* 23.1 (Spring): 1–22.

———. 2006. "Disability Studies and the Future of Identity Politics." In *Identity Politics Reconsidered,* ed. Linda Martín Alcoff et al. New York: Palgrave.

Somerville, Siobhan. 2000. *Queering the Color Line: Race and the Invention of Homosexuality in American Culture.* Durham, N.C.: Duke University Press.

Steele, Claude M., and Joshua Aronson. 1995. "Stereotype Threat and the Intellectual Test Performance of African Americans." *Journal of Personality and Social Psychology* 69.5 (November): 797–811.

Steele, Claude M., Steven J. Spencer, and Joshua Aronson. 2002. "Contending with Group Image: The Psychology of Stereotype and Social Identity Threat." *Advances in Experimental Social Psychology,* vol. 34, pp. 379–440. San Diego: Academic Press.

Stone, Jeff, et al. 1999. "Stereotype Threat Effects on Black and White Athletic Performance." *Journal of Personality and Social Psychology* 77.6 (December): 1213–27.

Taylor, Paul C. 2005. "Social Construction and Passing: Why Walter Benn Michaels Is Wrong." Presented at *The California Roundtable for Philosophy and Race.* University of San Francisco, September 24–26.

Telles, Edward E. 2004. *Race in Another America: The Significance of Skin Color in Brazil.* Princeton, N.J.: Princeton University Press.

Wilkerson, William S. 2000. "Is There Something You Need To Tell Me? Coming Out and the Ambiguity of Experience." In Moya and Hames-García, eds., *Reclaiming Identity: Realist Theory and the Predicament of Postmodernism,* 251–78. Berkeley: University of California Press.

Wittgenstein, Ludwig. 1967. *Philosophical Investigations.* Trans. G. E. M. Anscombe. New York: Macmillan.

Wolf, Eric R. 1997. *Europe and the People without History*, 2nd ed. Berkeley: University of California Press.

Wylie, Alison. 2003. "Why Standpoint Matters." In *Science and Other Cultures: Issues in Philosophies of Science and Technology*, ed. Robert Figueroa and Sandra Harding, 26–48. New York: Routledge.

Zack, Naomi. 1998. *Thinking about Race.* Belmont, Calif.: Wadsworth.

Žižek, Slavoj. 1998. "A Leftist Plea for 'Eurocentrism.'" *Critical Inquiry* 24: 988–1007.

12

FROM RACE/SEX/ETC. TO GLUCOSE, FEEDING TUBE, AND MOURNING: THE SHIFTING MATTER OF CHICANA FEMINISM

Suzanne Bost

> Illness granted me a set of experiences otherwise unobtainable. It liberated me from the routines which would have delivered me, unchallenged and unchanged, to discreet death. . . . The experience has also ratified my conviction that I, and therefore you, are unequivocally physical constructs, if spectacularly complicated ones.
>
> —Inga Clendinnen, *The Tiger's Eye*

When Gloria Anzaldúa and Cherríe Moraga first collaborated on *This Bridge Called My Back: Writings by Radical Women of Color* at the end of the 1970s, their primary concern was addressing the simultaneous oppressions experienced by women of color along the axes of race, class, sex, and sexuality. As they challenged the masculinist subject of Chicano nationalism, these writers turned to coalition building and editorial collaboration to locate themselves at the intersection of multiple sociopolitical identifications. Collections like *Bridge* shifted feminist criticism toward a greater sensitivity to the ways in which feminist identity politics traverse racial and sexual differences. One limitation of this critical focus is a myopic tendency to see identity only in terms of existing sociopolitical categories, especially race and sex, rather than imagining new ways of thinking about identity and new foundations for forming coalitions (like physical needs or shared environments that are not race- or sex-specific). Moreover, since this theoretical shift of twenty-five years ago, discussions of "race/sex/etc." are increasingly superficial: lists repeated by rote, apologies for failing to account for how heterogeneity might complicate an argument, and untheorized gestures toward inclusiveness that do not think critically about the messy corporeal, psychological, and political matter of race, sex, or the empty "etc."[1] Identity politics often protect their boundaries by *not* analyzing their interiors.

In "Speaking Secrets: Living Chicana Theory," Deena González critiques the ways in which Chicana feminist analyses of difference tend to study only the "boundaries or conflicts lying between majority or minority voices," presuming a united Chicana feminist voice and avoiding internal contradictions in order to combat marginalization (1998, 46–47). To challenge the reification of "Chicana feminist identity," she proposes "speaking secrets" about differences, posing transgender and transsexual personalities as a "counter-discourse to the entire issue of identification" (1998, 56). Yet the fluidity of "trans" is suppressed as these identities are politically mobilized, codified, and inscribed within sexual coalitions like "LGBT."

What if we thought about politics other than in terms of protecting identities? In *States of Injury,* Wendy Brown explains how "drawing upon the historically eclipsed meaning of disrupted and fragmented narratives of ethnicity, race, gender, sexuality, region, continent, or nation . . . permits a sense of situation—and often a sense of filiation or community—without requiring profound comprehension of the world in which we are situated" (1995, 35). In opposition to the nominal security of identity politics, she proposes that "our [political] spaces, while requiring some definition and protection, cannot be clean, sharply bounded, disembodied, or permanent: to engage postmodern modes of power *and* honor specifically feminist knowledges, they must be heterogeneous, roving, relatively noninstitutionalized, and democratic to the point of exhaustion" (1995, 50; emphasis in original).

I find just this sort of open-ended politics in the newest works of Anzaldúa and Moraga (1981), who parted ways (in terms of genres, publishers, and collaborative efforts) in the 1980s. After this parting, though, they both turned in different but equally material ways to the subject of Chicana feminism. Personal experiences of illness, pain, and medical treatment led both of them to an increasingly sharp focus on the body. Anzaldúa's 2002 essay makes clear that the diabetes that shaped her day-to-day existence also shaped her thinking and her politics. Moraga's writings about giving birth to a premature baby and living his early life with him in the neonatal intensive care unit shift the focus of her identity politics too. It is my contention that their (often ignored) autobiographical writings about their unraveling bodies explain the increasingly unbounded subject of their politics.

MRI scans, microscopes, and blood tests see the body beyond what we think of as identity. The "matter" that a medical lens reveals is in flux, unpredictable, and tremendously complex. The variously formed tissues of particular bodies unsettle any notion of shared femaleness, race, or even health itself.[2] This essay, then, will examine the shifting matter of bodies in Anzaldúa and Moraga's work, from illness and health care to death and mourning, to uncover what these corporeal boundary states have to offer in the place of identity politics. To shed light on this matter, I summon a variety of critical approaches: disability studies, postmodern feminism, queer theory, and cultural studies, as they intersect with Chicana/o Studies. Many critics (including, in some cases, myself) oppose using "white theory" for Chicana/o Studies. What I hope to reveal here is the falseness of the presumed opposition in this opposition. That is, Anzaldúa's and Moraga's stories are also queer, disabled, theoretical, and—to the degree that these multiple identifications are inseparable from the fragmentations, technologies, and circulations of postmodernity—postmodern.

I find the work of Linda Singer and Eve Sedgwick, both of whom studied the intersections of AIDS and postmodernity and both of whom turned increasingly to corporeal material when their own bodies developed cancer, particularly useful for this study. I regard the unexpected identifications and relationships forged by illness as an alternate foundation for politics: a foundation that is not exactly post-identity but that is no longer invested in the boundaries of identity. Sedgwick notes with ambivalence the surprising communities and dependencies that accompany AIDS diagnoses, leading sufferers "to entrust as many people as one possibly can with one's actual body and its needs, one's stories about its fate, one's dreams and one's sources of information or hypothesis about disease, cure, denial, and the state or institutional violence that are also invested in one's illness" (1993, 261). Just as illness changes the external and internal workings of a body, it also changes one's place in society, the nature of one's relationships, and the routes of one's movement.

I hope that applying disability studies to Chicana feminism will shed new light on subjects traditionally seen only through the lenses of race/sex/etc. Disability studies center on the ways in which certain bodies are ex-centric to social expectations, legal constructs, and cultural/sexual ideals. Like much early Chicana feminism, and like most of the contributions to *Bridge,* disability criticism is devoted to corporeal particularity and is frequently grounded in the actual bodies of its authors. Though this approach runs athwart of entrenched sociopolitical categories, there is a tension between corporeal particularity and the political content of disability. Disability activists have traditionally promoted a new identity category, "people with disabilities," by locating an additional axis of oppression that operates in analogous form to racism or sexism. In practical terms, locating a disabled subject has helped to identify the ways in which societies exclude people with disabilities and has helped to organize demands for rights around coherent "disadvantaged classes." But as with all identity-based movements, actual embodied people with disabilities strain against the content of their imagined political condensation. Perhaps this straining is even more dramatic with an identity category like "disability," which is used to describe both chronic and temporary, visible and invisible, mental and physical, as well as both genetic and trauma-induced conditions. In *Bending Over Backwards,* Lennard Davis suggests that this "malleable and shaky foundation" upon which disability politics has been built "can be the beginning of an entirely new way of thinking about identity categories" and the relationship between actual bodies and political movement (2002, 5).

In contrast to the corporeal center of disability studies, Linda Singer deliberately eschews her own (sick) body. At the beginning of her "Author's Introduction" to *Erotic Welfare: Sexual Politics in the Age of*

Epidemic, Singer invokes herself only as a series of unanswered questions: "Who am I and where am I in writing this . . . ? Why the first person to begin, when the question of identity is at stake? Am I the associate professor . . . ? Or am I the child who learned . . . ?" (1993, 25). This gesture establishes identity as a central problematic that eludes material solidity, maintaining the complexity of identity by maintaining its confinement to the speculative realm of theory.

Could we replicate this complexity without dodging the body? Judith Butler's introduction to *Erotic Welfare* self-consciously and somewhat guiltily locates the book within the context of Singer's cancer and her death, a contextualization necessary to explain the unfinished state of the manuscript but overtly in defiance of Singer's own inclination toward "broader, more conceptual, theoretical, abstract, visionary, speculative discourses on the relationship between sex, power, and philosophy" (1993, 25). In the second paragraph of the introduction, Butler states that "Linda Singer was against the personalist and confessional character of some work in women's studies" (1993, 1). This stylized erasure of Singer's body is palpable throughout *Erotic Welfare,* particularly in her final chapter on hospitalization, which is the only one in the book not to use the first person "I." Nonetheless, Butler says, in hyper-personal fashion, "I cannot write of this text without letting you, the reader, know something of the kind of person she was, from what struggle this work emerged, and how she took her illness as an occasion for intense speculation, radical critique, and a sympathetic connection with those who suffer from AIDS" (1993, 1). So when Butler then tells us about Singer's time in the hospital, particular treatments she resisted, and particular medical paraphernalia she required, it is, in good Butlerian fashion, a stylized and subversive performance that renders Butler and Singer both as actors (since actors put actual bodies "under erasure") in a drama about the parameters of feminist theory. "Linda Singer," as addressed in the introduction, acts out a compellingly staged role in resistance to the subjecting mechanisms of medicine, from her first dramatic admission to the hospital to her last words recalling that moment, according the circularity of such narratives.

As Anzaldúa and Moraga tell us about their own bodies, they are similarly embedded in political narratives, edited, despite the illusion of proximity created by graphic description. This strategy enables them to stage their ideas with matter. What I take from Singer is her commitment to post-identity politics, and I layer her provocative theoretical forms with the corporeal content of illness, racism, sexism, and homophobia theorized in Anzaldúa and Moraga. To quote Singer, again: "Is this juxtaposition of the noble claims and tropes of philosophy—truth, knowledge, logic, order—with the random movement of contagion between sweaty bodies itself a heresy . . . ?" (1993, 26). Anzaldúa and Moraga would not only answer "no" to this question but would deny any conceptual opposition between randomly moving, sweaty bodies and truth/knowledge/etc.

Sedgwick frames this question somewhat differently, with greater willingness to let bodies reform theory:

> As a general principle, I don't like the idea of "applying" theoretical models to particular situations or texts—it's always more interesting when the pressure of application goes in both directions—but all the same it's hard not to think of this continuing experience [cancer, surgery, chemotherapy, hair loss] as, among other things, an adventure in applied deconstruction. How could I have arrived at a more efficient demonstration of the supposed oppositions that structure an experience of the "self"? (1993, 12)

Unlike other examples that had presented themselves to her before, Sedgwick's own illness dissected identity, deconstructing oppositions between "the part and the whole," "safety and danger," "the natural and the technological" without centering any single axis of identity—unless illness, itself, counts as such an axis—as the defining component of this experience. With the open possibility of metastasis, cancer leaves the body in a "free-fall interpretative panic" (1993, 13). Of course, this is not to romanticize illness as a theoretical ideal. The tension Sedgwick maintains between theory and body keeps physical discomfort and the possibility of death always at the center. *Tendencies,* itself, oscillates between theories, bodies, and cultural artifacts; and the inclusion of two memorial pieces for friends who died of AIDS,

"Memorial for Craig Owens" and "White Glasses" (for Michael Lynch), disrupts any smooth theoretical narrative with the unsettling backdrop of death. Indeed, all four writers' work is juxtaposed with such a backdrop: AIDS for Moraga, Singer, and Sedgwick, and the authors' own deaths in the cases of Anzaldúa and Singer. This backdrop keeps the matter of illness situated on a continuum with death. In a sense, reading these writers is an act of mourning at the same time as it is an act of interpretation, theorization, and sentient experience.

The corporeal theories and the affect in Anzaldúa and Moraga's work are drawn from Mexican culture first. When they describe pain and illness, they also invoke ancient Mesoamerican sacrifice traditions that render corporeal boundary states (like pain, bleeding, and shape-shifting) sacred. Claiming cultural descent from the Aztecs is a common gesture in Chicano/a thought, but Anzaldúa and Moraga, unlike their Chicano nationalist predecessors, invoke not the Aztec warrior ideal but the fertility goddesses who also represent destruction, dismemberment, sexuality, and shape-shifting. In his comprehensive study of ancient Aztec medicine, Gonzalo Aguirre Beltrán writes about the interdependencies established in Aztec society based on religious beliefs and the communal organization of private life:

> *Esta relación de dependencia que responde a la ansiedad resultante de un sentimiento de desamparo, de una sensación de limitación de recursos, de falta de fortaleza y capacidad y que es una actitud de solicitación de ayuda, de apoyo y protección, tiñe todos los apartados de la medicina azteca.* [This relation of dependence corresponds to the anxiety resulting from a feeling of disempowerment, of a sensation of limited resources, of lack of strength and capacity and is an attitude of seeking help, support and protection, affects every aspect of Aztec medicine.] (Aguirre Beltrán 1963, 42–43)

Bodies signify differently in a culture that values communal interdependence and divine intervention more than individuals. Transgressing bodily boundaries, tattooing, piercing, bleeding, and shape-shifting were valued as keys to divinity, fertility, and expanded consciousness—perhaps because they visibly indicate humans' thin boundaries relative to each other and to the gods. Public rituals centered on puncturing bodies, letting out the sacred life force; priests often flayed the skins of sacrificial victims, passing these skins around and wearing them as symbols of regeneration.[3] Transfiguration through *nagualism* enabled humans to externalize their souls and to incarnate other beings. "Identity" must have been experienced as fluid and potentially shared rather than self-interested.[4] I submit this reverence for boundary-crossing as that which enabled Anzaldúa and Moraga to build Chicana feminist politics from the shifting ground of illness, health care, and mourning.[5] These understandings of ancient Mesoamerica provide a way out of the identity boundaries that trouble(d) Sedgwick and Singer.

Contemporary health care in the United States vehemently opposes material fluidity. Singer's *Erotic Welfare* studies the discourses of "contagion" that increasingly regulate bodies in the era of AIDS. In her argument, rather than caring for those who suffer from the disease, the dominant culture has instead focused on quarantine, dividing the population into the normal and the pathological, the healthy and the "high-risk." Vilifying the sick as the constitutive outside of a healthy society involves not paying attention to the content of sickness, drawing boundaries rather than healing, sorting us out to keep the queer and the ill away from the mythologized healthy family. Singer argues that this logic, derived from the sexual and cultural politics of AIDS, has inflected the regulation of all disease, indeed of all bodies, today:

> Conservative groups with a range of interests as diverse as those of Lyndon Larouche and Jerry Falwell have been able to exploit the anxiety operative in plague conditions as a basis for support not only for regulating the bodies of those in the high-risk groups, like gays and drug users, whose bodies are fetishized as vials of contagion and death, but also for controlling the process by which life is generated, in the form of a proposed constitutional amendment against abortion, limitation on support for sex education and contraception, and oppositions to the development of reproductive technologies. (1993, 31)

One of the primary questions I want to consider here is: can the regulatory boundaries drawn around women and "high-risk groups" be

Coatlicue, original photograph taken at the Museo Nacional de Antropología, México, D.F., 2005.

broken down by focusing on the material complexity of actual bodies? Studying the fluid matter of illness itself, in defiance of the medical and cultural discourses that demonize such matter, problematizes the identities and distinctions upon which such boundaries rest. By replacing the logic of contagion with caregiving and reshaping family as "out" Chicana dykes with open wounds and incurable diseases, Anzaldúa and Moraga bleed beyond the borders of identity. Drawing on the model of Coatlicue, Aztec goddess of creation *and* destruction, enables them to transcend oppositions, fusing birth and death, loving and mourning. With her serpent heads and her necklace of hands, skulls, and hearts, Coatlicue provides a model of corporeality that exceeds individual identity.

REREADING ANZALDÚA

Rereading Gloria Anzaldúa's *Borderlands* with the knowledge that she suffered from diabetes reframes her identity politics. I believe that diabetes informed the obsession with fluctuation and balance in her writings about *mestiza* identity formation: "I get dizzy and mentally foggy when I'm having a hypo. I lose my equilibrium and fall. Gastrointestinal reflex has me throwing up and having diarrhea. . . . Things like these change your image of yourself, your identity" (2000b, 289–90). The theoretical impulse of *mestiza* consciousness—synthesizing bloods and juggling differences—becomes concrete, imperative, and immediate with syringes and blood sugar levels. The content of diabetes breaks down the assumed fixity of a body and subjects it to outside intervention. Lynda Hall reads Anzaldúa through a lens of "ameliorography," claiming that the body of her work reflects "desires to heal the self" and "attempts to relieve personal pain as an 'othered' person" (Hall 2000, 113). Anzaldúa's illness complicates (modifies, internalizes) this designation of "otherness." Fear of having one's insides erupt in public imposes an otherness unlike that of racism or sexism. Otherness assumes binary opposition, often around singular identity categories. Since diabetes maps shared embodiment across assumed identities, Anzaldúa might have found herself dependent upon a white male physician, shunned by a *comadre,* or alienated from her own self—other to otherness.

The passage from Anzaldúa that Hall quotes to support her argument goes on to describe "making meaning of pain" as a suspended state of being rather than healing (Anzaldúa 2000b, 276). As Norma Alarcón suggests, in her privileging of "endless alterity," migration, and "parts that will never make her whole," Anzaldúa "risk[ed] the 'pathological condition' by representing the nonlinearity and the break with a developmental view of self-inscription" (Alarcón 2003, 362, 367). Though it might have made critics more comfortable, Anzaldúa's autobiographic body never assimilated to any identity categories (including that of the "other") or "developed" into healthy, static wholeness. Her embodiment was, like the borderlands itself, an "open wound" (Anzaldúa 1987, 3). In "now let us shift," she proposed a revolution in the way we think about identity, and this redefinition followed her acceptance of the effects of diabetes: "You've chosen to compose a new history and self. . . . Your ailing body is no longer a hindrance but an asset, witnessing pain, speaking to you, demanding touch. Es tu cuerpo que busca conocimiento; along with dreams your body's the royal road to consciousness" (2002, 558–59). Illness opens up new avenues of awareness and expands one's sense of embodiment, but this thinking was in Anzaldúa's work all along, in those seemingly abstract and mystical passages from *Borderlands* that most feminist critics seem to have avoided: "In our very flesh, (r)evolution works out the class of cultures. . . . *Nuestra alma el trabajo,* the opus, the great alchemical work; spiritual *mestizaje,* a 'morphogenesis,' an inevitable unfolding. We have become the quickening serpent movement" (1987, 81). This passage alludes to her theory of Coatlicue States, in which identities must continually dissolve and reform to keep consciousness from becoming stagnant. Coatlicue "devours" the self to allow for "evolution" and new "germination," "kicking a hole out of the old boundaries of the self and slipping under or over, dragging the old skin along, stumbling over it" (1987, 46–47, 49). The affect Anzaldúa draws from Coatlicue feels this painful fluidity as productive. The friction between this interpretation of sensation and modern medicine's assumption that health must be static, bounded, and anesthetized reflects the ways in which her work pushes against dominant thinking about embodiment.

The poems in *Borderlands* receive very little critical attention, but (or perhaps because) they are peopled with bodies, imagined and unimaginable, and their material discomforts. In her poem "*Cihuatlyotl,* Woman Alone," Anzaldúa describes her ambivalent relationship to Chicano identity politics in terms of dismemberment to reflect the difficulty of fitting embodied experience into constructed racial types:

> And as I grew you hacked away
> at the pieces of me that were different. . . .
> Oh, it was hard,
> *Raza* to cleave flesh from flesh I risked
> us both bleeding to death. . . .
> . . . there's no-
> thing more you can chop off or graft on me that
> will change my soul. I remain who I am, multiple
> and one of the herd, yet not of it. (1987, 173)

Even within a racially mixed identity like *la raza Chicana,* individual bodies always contain differences that exceed the *raza* ideal: "deviant" embodiments must be "hacked away," and missing "essential traits" must be grafted on. The personification of "*Raza*" in Anzaldúa's poem, a common address in Chicano nationalist writings, attributes agency to race itself, giving it hands with which to mold identities in order to solidify the nation. In the process of self-definition, *Raza* has amputated parts that are perhaps feminist, lesbian, or sick. Yet, Anzaldúa insists, where individual difference is censored by communal identity politics, she remains "multiple," apart, "on the ground of my own being" (1987, 173). The spacing in this poem emphasizes rupture. She inserts gaps both before and after "of me," making the phrase stand out from the line with individual visibility, independence, and integrity; but the speaker is both "of" and "not of" the herd. Sustaining this contradiction, as Anzaldúa does, breaks down the opposition between individual and community, identifying with *la raza* without relinquishing that which exceeds *la raza.*[6] "*Cihuatlyotl*" invests individual identity with contamination by others:

> I am fully formed carved
> by the hands of ancients, drenched with
> the stench of today's headlines. But my own
> hands whittle the final work me. (1987, 173)

Though she is "fully formed," being subject to "today's headlines," in the present tense, keeps her fully open to revision too. In Anzaldúa's earlier writings, then, the contradictions between identity politics and embodied individuality remain unresolved, in painful tension.

Fifteen years after *Borderlands,* in her essay "now let us shift," Anzaldúa broke more radically with the subjects of feminist and Chicano politics. She advocated the critical use of the spirit, the soul, and the body to form "less-structured thoughts, less-rigid categorizations," crossing beyond bodies and academic boundaries in order to exceed the status quo (2002, 568, 570). In my interpretation, these boundary crossings emerge not just from the Texas/Mexico borderlands where she grew up: they also reflect the experience of someone who is sick, who must continually submit her body to medical examinations, needles, and pharmaceuticals. A diabetic cannot maintain firm boundaries. Since her body needed the dominant culture's technology, Anzaldúa ultimately let go of traditional identity politics to form new kinds of couplings:

> At first la nueva historia resembles Shelley's Frankenstein monster—mismatched parts pieced together artificially—but soon the new rendition fuels your drive to seek alternative and emerging knowledges. . . . Beliefs and values from the wisdom of past spiritual traditions of diverse cultures coupled with current scientific knowledge is the basis of the new synthesis. (2002, 561)

Beyond the *mestiza* consciousness of *Borderlands,* this new synthesis belongs to the fourth stage of "el camino de conocimiento" [path/walk of consciousness] that she outlined in her final essay.

Ultimately, Anzaldúa proposed what she called "a new tribalism" as an alternative to identity politics. She begins with the familiar image of roots, but these roots are not metaphors for racial ancestry: "Your identity has roots you share with all people and other beings—spirit, feeling, and body make up a greater identity category. . . . The roots del árbol de la vida of all planetary beings are nature, soul, body" (2002, 560). Rather than taking identity as the groundwork for politics, this vision makes it impossible to separate individual identities, not just from each other but even from the world itself (trees, woods, and streams). If at times this proposal to "rethink yourself in more global-spiritual terms instead of conventional categories of color, class, career" seems to be hopelessly forging politics from ether, Anzaldúa consistently brings it back to bodily matter. Indeed, the power of what she proposes lies in its friction against existing material boundaries: "In this narrative national boundaries dividing us from the 'others' (nos/otras) are porous and the cracks between worlds serve as gateways" (2002, 561). Using the very material language of "pores" and "cracks," like the slash in "nos/otras," turns our attention to the actual places where "worlds" and "bodies" meet and the actual occasions that break the tissues of our boundaries. Diabetes forced Anzaldúa to accept identity that is "not contained by your skin," that "occurs by widening the psyche/body's borders" and uses "wounds as openings to become vulnerable and available (present) to others" (2002, 555, 571–72). The language of illness provides a metaphor for politics based on particular wounds and connections rather than universalizing identities.

MORAGA'S NEW *FAMILIA*

We can see the tension between universalized anatomy and particular embodiment in health care, yet hospitals are dedicated to deviations from "standard health," and caregivers are trained to locate, to understand, and to heal individuals' particular wounds. Encounters with sickness are encounters with difference. Cherríe Moraga notes the continual surprise and reconfiguration that accompanied the birth of her son, starting with the ease with which she became pregnant using a mason jar and a syringe. By taking in the baby's life, Moraga submitted her body to difference, culminating in two unexpected (and undesired) embodiments: carrying a son rather than a daughter, and giving birth at just 28 weeks of gestation. *Waiting in the Wings: Portrait of a Queer Motherhood* (1997), recounts the first three months of this "queer motherhood" spent in the neonatal intensive care unit as Rafael Angel struggled on the border between life and death. Unlike Singer's hidden hospitalized self, this narrative combines the author's original journal entries with commentary woven through at the time of publication, confessing her original feelings and later analyzing that journalistic self through critical lenses.

Although Moraga might have earlier perceived her lesbian Chicana self to be in opposition to the white/patriarchal/capitalist technologies of modern medicine, being forced into intimacy with doctors, nurses, tubes, and machines led her to re-conceive the material boundaries of her identity. Her baby's early life is intertwined with machines as his body's sustaining exo-skeleton changes from womb to incubator in the Intensive Care Nursery (ICN) after birth. The surface of the baby's isolette developed steam from his breathing (1997, 70). The contact between baby's breath and isolette, like the mother's milk flowing through the plastic tubes that feed the infant, crosses boundaries between body and plastic, mother and machine. Moraga senses a "seamless connection" between "those incubator walls and [her] milk-hard-breasted body" (1997, 57). She surrounds his incubator with healing stones and icons of the Virgin. This intimacy of life with machine further "queers" the "queer motherhood" Moraga narrates, unmooring maternity from female essence, "natural" reproduction, heterosexual intercourse, and mother-father families.[7]

As Moraga delineates Rafael Angel's queer family, she incorporates a racially and sexually heterogeneous community of Chicana/o activists, gay and lesbian writers, and a legacy of feminist thinkers into his spiritual parentage. The "making" of this "*familia* from scratch" involves more than birth. Moraga explains that "my own queer story of pregnancy, birth, and the first years of mothering" is a story of "struggle for survival/for life in the age of death/the age of AIDS" (1997, 14, 22). The parallelism in this description emphasizes how birth is experienced in tension with death, particularly in an age when (and in a city—San Francisco—where) living happens against the backdrop of AIDS. This narrative is thus intertwined with illness and impending death, not just the baby's but the death of César Chavez, memories of Audre Lorde's cancer and funeral, the deaths of Chicana dyke Myrtha Quintanales's mother and father, poets Ronnie Burke's and Tede Matthew's deaths from AIDS, the deaths of Moraga's uncle and the birth father's father, the aging of Moraga's parents, her partner's mother's gradual "crippling" by Parkinson's disease, and Moraga's own seemingly constant battles with pain, depression, anxiety, colds, flu, and allergies. Sickness and dying take up far more narrative space here than conception, pregnancy, and birth, so it is appropriate that most of the text is set in hospitals. "It is not the death that frightens so," she writes, "it is the slow humiliating dissolution of the body" (1997, 32–33). Rather than focusing on the endpoint of birth or death, this narrative is taken up by the processes of painful tissue reorganization and the "humiliating" erosion of self that both pregnancy and illness involve. Recalling Anzaldúa's Coatlicue States resignifies the sensation of this corporeal flux. During her pregnancy and new motherhood, Moraga was working on her play *The Hungry Woman: A Mexican Medea,* which recasts Medea's child killing through the lens of Coatlicue (for whom creation and destruction are intertwined) and her dismembered daughter, the moon goddess Coyolxauhqui (whose waning and waxing continually dismember and reconstitute her body in the heavens). This Aztec framework privileges embodiment that is fluid rather than "fixed" and supports Moraga's own pain and maternal ambivalence with a cultural history of pain and maternal ambivalence.

The centrality of destruction in Moraga's stories of motherhood is partially explained in an interview Rosemary Weatherston conducted with her shortly after Rafael Angel was born. Moraga links her "dangerous" decision to write a play about lesbian child killing to her preoccupation with "female wounding":

> I know that, as women, we have been deformed, by not being allowed full humanness. With this play [*The Hungry Woman*], I have picked one of the most taboo, antisocial acts a woman can commit as the essence of the plot. The only role women are given sanction for in society is motherhood, right? I mean, a good woman is a good mom. And so, what's the worst thing you can do against society, i.e., against patriarchy? Kill motherhood. The child killer is a greater aberration to society than is a dyke. (2000, 82)

This response suggests that one of the ways of freeing women from the "deformation" of patriarchy is by assaulting patriarchy's most treasured role for women: motherhood. In this context, both *The Hungry Woman* and *Waiting* can be read as a recasting of motherhood free from patriarchal (and Anglo-American) expectations. When she is ill during her pregnancy, Moraga writes that "this sickness es una limpieza," sweating out inherited stigmata to clear the way for creating new meaning (1997, 33). And her baby's premature birth to a circle of lesbian *familia* and "urgent latexed hands and plastic tubes and blinking monitors" does indeed resignify childbirth. Unlike the newborns placed on their mothers' stomachs "in the movies," Rafael Angel is "all wound," indio, hairy, "monkey," and unfathomably fragile in his "birdweight" (1997, 53, 54, 65). Moraga demystifies romantic icons of blissful motherhood and bouncing baby boys by pointing out the reciprocal wounding built within the medical process of childbirth and the contortions required to form racially and sexually ideal human beings.

In her book on Moraga, Yvonne Yarbro-Bejarano incisively interprets Moraga's work as "constantly tak[ing] apart the entire female body, recognizing how it has been appropriated and attempting to reclaim it" (2001, 5). Yarbro-Bejarano discusses this fragmentation in terms of resistance, as Moraga's attempt to sever the body from patriarchal/white/heterosexist norms and to reconstruct it "from the blueprint" of her own desire (2001, 7). In this argument, the poet deconstructs the body only in the context of possible healing, "with a vision of a new way to be whole" as a Chicana feminist lesbian (2001, 10). I find the opposite of this logic at work in *Waiting in the Wings.* Like Linda Singer, Moraga refuses to subject her son's body to institutionalized health, framing his life instead in the context of the communal "woman-wound that we spend our lives *trying* to heal" (1997, 33, emphasis added). As a baby, "He is all wound, and he is my son" (1997, 65). Though he does ultimately survive, his survival is a continual embodiment of death. She describes the first years of his life as "the road taken toward life . . . and death" (1997, 85). The sections written after bringing the baby home from the hospital continue to focus on illness. On his first visit to the sacred tree in Watsonville (where the image of the Virgin of Guadalupe appeared in 1992), the author's attention is consumed, not by her own son—who remains "unnoticed" under her rebozo—but on a six- or seven-year-old child in a tall stroller with "spaghetti legs," unable to walk: "And I am there in that mother's skin, as I pull Rafaelito into me, holding on for his dear life, his dear health. Knowing I could've been her. Still can" (1997, 89). The real possibility of disability structures Rafael's life. The mother's life, too, continues into the second year as "the haze of a prolonged and private illness, an acute exhaustion," fearing each time she lies down that she "may not rise up again" (1997, 105). If there is an order installed in the end of this narrative, continual disordering is its governing logic:

> Rafael Angel is a messenger of death, not in the negative sense of the word, but in that he brings the news of the cruel and sudden miracle of the cycle of our lives. I could write he is a messenger of life, but I know it is truer to acknowledge that my sometimes quiet sadness at the deepest moments of joy with my child has to do with this complete knowledge of impermanence. (1997, 127)

This ongoing dissolution, cruelty, and sudden change radiates from the baby to his entire *familia.*

The family bonds Moraga and her partner formed in the ICN show how physiological processes often matter more than the abstract sociopolitical categories assumed to shape human relations. As the baby opens his body to plastic tubes and surgical instruments, the mothers must open their own bodies to industrial detergent, hospital scents, and the claims others have on their baby's life: "Daily we have watched fear's venom pass through plastic tubes, in and out of open veins and miniature organs. I know fear's scent pressed into the industrial detergent of my baby's doll-sized sheets and blankets. We carry its odorless indifference home with us on our clothes, in our skin" (1997, 66). The cultures of queer *familia* and hospital infect each other through the spread of objects between them. As the hospital rooms are transformed by Moraga's kind of motherhood, so she too must take the technologies of the hospital into her home, her body, and her son's body: "Does he remember awakening at 3:00 AM under the hot glare of hospital lamps, no mama in sight, a sharp pain piercing his gut? I wonder where in his small body he has put all that suffering, what traces of it will reside in him as a grown man" (1997, 106). These boundary crossings gradually form a politics of openness rather than opposition. Though she initially "resent[s] these white male pediatrician-types with their nurse wives and seven kids 'bonding' their way into my Mexican psyche," she cannot expel their surgical interventions or her dependency on their medical knowledge. The hospital turns out to be more than a place of homophobic, patriarchal, and anglocentric norms. The staff of female caregivers—"Rose, Stacey, Bobbie, Sue, Gurline, Donna, Terry, and others whom we never met"—"watched [Rafael] throughout the night while we slept" and treated him as more than work. "Some of them have even come to love Rafa, thinking of him as 'their baby.'" Initially, Moraga is afraid of her dependence on these women, but in later reflection she reveals, "It is not our dependence on the nurses that I fear, so much as the loss of the connection. These women have become our family" (1997, 78). Moraga's mothering has incorporated the hospital caregivers' practices and attentions. The nurses' gifts and guidebooks go home with them in the car.

Moraga's new relationships do not just straddle a boundary between her queer *familia* and white doctors, resistance and institution. There is also Alex, who has sleeping limbs; Simone, who is blind; Freddy, who has Downs; and other "one- and two- and three-pound human animals with swollen brains and strokes and weak hearts and drug addictions and troubled families," "mirroring Rafa's own embattled state" (1997, 69). Mothers and fathers with whom Moraga would apparently have nothing in common outside the hospital share doctors, nurses, and machines with Rafa and Moraga in the ICN. The foundation for these new family connections is shared vulnerability, and the complexity of their differences and commonalities makes for incoherent boundaries. Singer describes the hospital as a punitive, exilic, threatening place where that which is "wrong" (or might go wrong, in the seemingly anomalous case of childbirth) is set apart from healthy society. Moraga's experience defies this opposition between health and sickness by making *familia* in the hospital, bilingually, queerly, against the backdrop of death, even when she herself is no longer "sick." She collapses the distinction between cultures and identities associated with the "norm" (health, motherhood, and family) and those associated with the "pathological" (illness, queerness, and eroded bodily boundaries).

By making AIDS central to her story, which is not necessarily a story about AIDS at all, Moraga invokes the epidemic culture Singer writes about, but by bringing queerness "in" and taking the hospital's healthcare tools "out" with her, she defies the quarantine of queer from healthy. Invoking AIDS also invokes its politicized "patient culture," which Singer claims resists "the isolation imposed by illness . . . [by] maintaining some sense of community and constituency," mobilizing illness as a political vehicle (1993, 105). As Butler characterizes Singer's experience with hospitalization as a cancer patient, Moraga, too, "brought a number of discourses into the medical circuit of discursive exchange, jamming the system, disrupting its regulatory rhythms, performing criticism until the end" (1993, 12).

LOVING ACROSS BORDERS

Rethinking identity through a body's connections to caregivers and prostheses is one of disability studies' most important theoretical contributions. Janet Price and Margrit Shildrick argue that disability troubles dominant thinking about identity, relationships, and difference, noting how people are led to reflect on their own vulnerabilities when they interact with the disabled. Writing of their own experiences with reciprocity in caregiving, they comment:

> What was uncovered during that acute period of Janet's illness [multiple sclerosis] was that, through the mutuality and reversibility of touch, we are in a continual process of mutual reconstitution of our embodied selves. Moreover, the instability of the disabled body is but an extreme instance of the instability of all bodies. (2002, 72)

Moraga's experiences in *Waiting* reveal that the ill and the disabled are not the only ones shaped by illness and disability. Resisting the taboo that keeps bodily processes private, and defying the cultural logic that "separation rather than contact figures the adult self" (2002, 71), Moraga shares her baby's vulnerability with an expansive *familia* of queers, Chicana/os, hospital staff, even readers. Public suffering demonstrates the susceptibility of all bodies; we are all, after all, only temporarily healthy.

In Singer's study, the "logic of contagion" posits that, in the wake of AIDS, "communication has become communicability; access is now figured as an occasion for transmission and contagion" (1993, 28). With circulation cut off to prevent the spread of disease, the politics of stigmatized subjects can only be figured through their exclusion, or, to recall Wendy Brown, their "states of injury." Disability studies must circulate differently, opening access and expanding the shape of health. Nancy Mairs mourns the "normals'" lack of injury—"I don't think it's the normals' own fault that they lack disabilities to deepen and complicate their understanding of the world"—and one of the more complicated understandings that she developed with MS is that "actively nurturing your fellow creatures . . . develops and disciplines that . . . part of the human psyche that transcends self-interest" (1996, 72, 78).

Corporeal fluctuation, mutuality, and suffering are radical to the ideals of Western modernity because they have been purged from healthy (i.e., self-interested) adult selfhood, bracketed from "safe" and "public" social interaction, and contained within the clinic or the lore of the ancients. What is radical about disability stories is not their opposition to the dominant but their challenge to those brackets, breaking down the opposition between "normal" and "disabled," between body and body. An ethics of care is based on crossing boundaries between individuals and recognizing dependence and vulnerability. In this way, it differs radically from identity politics, whose foundation is group solidarity. An ethics of care focuses on the particular needs of particular bodies, filtered through cultural value systems, power dynamics, sexualized embodiment, and access to resources, making for a far more material consideration of intersecting oppressions than race/sex/etc.[8]

From analysis of disability we have learned to understand the tenuousness of embodiment as well as the constructedness of medical norms and the social/topographical contexts that privilege these norms. But disability studies too is an identity-based field seeking equal access for a disenfranchised group. Much disability activism is based on visible assertions of difference that are also often visible assertions of political needs (for wheelchair access, for instance). In *The Rejected Body* (1996), Susan Wendell values the visibility of illness and disability "as either sources of knowledge or valuable ways of being," forcing us to think otherwise about our expectations for bodies. People with visible disabilities have a potential political impact, as "constant reminders of the inability of science and medicine to protect everyone from illness, disability, and death." Seeing disability paired with poverty, a female body, or dark skin could present an implicit critique of the (implicitly racist and sexist) capitalist medical system. In contrast are those whom Wendell terms "the 'disabled heroes,'" whose accommodations to dominant-culture norms and expectations "symbolize heroic control against all odds, and their public images comfort non-disabled people by reaffirming the possibility of overcoming the body" (1996, 63–64). Wendell's argument about the knowledge contained within disability is compelling, but she assumes that disability is a unique culture separated from "normal" by visible difference. It is difficult to draw this sort of boundary around an identity that is itself constantly changing—as with diabetes, multiple sclerosis, or postoperative recovery. Some identities are not always identical to themselves, are sometimes visibly disabled and sometimes *en*abled. The variable experiences of disability (both within and between disabled individuals) should force a recognition that bodies are not just different from others—as monolithic identities—but sometimes individual bodies, in themselves, are not recognizable as singular, stable, or categorizable entities. Anzaldúa extends her experience of transfiguration to all embodiment, destabilizing identity with the claim that "every seven years your body sheds its cells completely as it regenerates new cells" (2002, 562). Not only is it difficult to draw clear lines of identity around groups of bodies, but individual bodies in themselves do not fall consistently into the same patterns.[9]

What does the permeable and migratory politics of disability have to do with Chicana feminism, as such? I propose that, though the disabled subjects in Anzaldúa's and Moraga's recent works incorporate needs and movements beyond the boundaries of Chicana identity, they speak to the stated aims of Chicana feminism better than the corporeal nationalism of identity politics does. Even as they overflow the denotation of "Chicana feminism," their connotation is deeply Chicana and feminist: "feminist" in their search for agency with bodies that are permeable, fluid, and sexually specific, and "Chicana feminist" in their insistence on Mexican cultural lineage, racialized experience, and authority for politically disenfranchised subject positions. Indeed, as Chela Sandoval reminds us in a recent "Roundtable on the State of Chicano Studies," "Chicano/a (like the label feminist, Marxist, capitalist, socialist, and so on) is a *political* term," not just an identity (Davalos et al. 2002,

149; emphasis in original). (The number of Mexican Americans who reject the label "Chicano" or "Chicana" is evidence of this fact.) "Chicano/a," like "disabled," is a political affiliation of people who are heterogeneous in terms of their skin color, their class, their gender, their region, their language, and their generational distance from Mexico. After forty years of Chicana/o identity politics, this heterogeneity increasingly demands more open-ended filiation with shifting needs and concerns.

Recent shifts in Chicana feminism share an affinity with developments in postmodern feminism, but Moraga and Anzaldúa have not abandoned their own bodies' confessions as a source of feminist theorizing. Moreover, they have not abandoned race, sex, or class as material realities that determine day-to-day existence. (Indeed, experiences of illness are always mediated by race, sex, and class.) Rather, medical experiences forced them to focus on the body as sentient, ever-changing, always important, and highly vulnerable. This grounding in the sensory experience of contact with the world helps us to understand how race, sex, and class matter in actual situations. At the same time, the commonalities these authors find with others in oblique relation to the axes of race/sex/etc.—and their acceptance of bodies as fluid entities that are not always recognizable according to familiar frameworks—remind us that race, sex, and class are not horizons of experience, are not internally consistent, and are not always accurate markers of difference. We must then accept other corporeal aspects as equally important frameworks for political coalition-building.

I conclude with an analysis of one example of this new configuration for Chicana feminist politics beyond identity: the online altar, *Rest in Peace Gloria,* that has been constructed at http://gloria.chicanas.com, after Anzaldúa's death, from May to October 2004. The idea of an online altar itself reflects the "new synthesis" she proposed, fusing spirituality, feeling, and technology; and the altar bears some "Frankensteinian" attributes. From Moraga's opening letter to "Comadres, Compadres, Friends, and Estudiantes," telling them of Anzaldúa's death and inviting them to build their own altars, the online altar then grows beyond her control, a patchwork of unplanned gestures. Though submissions are moderated, they are not edited, forming an evolving cacophony of fragments, letters and prayers with their personal revelations, political differences, spelling errors, and typos. Some entries are raw, while others more closely resemble formal essays or polished poems. The contributors are male, female, and transgender. Though a majority self-identify as Chicana, they are also Cuban, Mexican, Guatemalan, Native American, white, Hawaiian, Chinese, Jewish/Southern Baptist, Sri Lankan/Eastern European, and racially unidentified. They are academics, students, activists, writers, editors, bookstore owners, farmworkers, travelers, and diabetics. Almost all of the entries include the cities from which they were written, spanning the globe.

In her entry, Irene Reti describes the altar as "waves of grief from all of you around the world," and Elga J. Martinez notes that, "Even after your death you are still building communities . . . look at us . . . from up there . . . how many are being connected through your passing away" (*Rest in Peace Gloria* 2004). Martinez goes on to outline movements for social justice that "always include people like you and I at the centre," but the altar itself defies putting any identity—any "like us"—at the center. Though all of these voices come together to mourn Gloria, the processes of this mourning are disordered and unregulated. Surprising things happen. Entries start cross-referencing each other, disputing each other. The tributes begin to intersect with other causes, other deaths, illnesses, writing projects, and career plans. Though they all come together for one cause, they come differently.

Though it is thoroughly decentered, the political content of the altar is implicitly feminist. The mourners, with all of their different investments in Anzaldúa's work, produce statements that are liberatory for women and others. Those who knew Anzaldúa through her feminism emphasize her "break with the hold that patriarchy had on our culture" (Sandra Benedet) and describe her as "a true inspirational role model para nosotras las 'Soldaderas de la Nueva Era' " (Marlene Chavez) (*Rest in Peace Gloria* 2004). But those who would not self-identify as a "*soldadera*" (female soldier) assume positions that are kin to feminism. It is remarkable how many describe Anzaldúa's politics as love, a gesture that runs against the "warrior" vision of a *soldadera* defending her territory. Beatriz Lopez-Flores eulogizes her as "a truly remarkable woman with the clarity of vision of a Dolores Huerta, the kindness of an internationalist that practiced her beliefs as a fighter for equality, love, and respect."[10] Erin Fairchild credits Anzaldúa for showing her that anti-oppression work "is life, it is necessary, it is beautiful, it is to have a heart larger and more fierce than any of the systems that would work to shatter our compassions." And Ellie Hernandez claims that *mestiza* consciousness "is really about transcendent love": Anzaldúa's "love of women of color, of poor working class women and of queers" (*Rest in Peace Gloria* 2004). These political practices are clearly drawn from Chicana feminism, but love, as a method, opens outward rather than shoring up the boundaries of one's identity. Love makes the self vulnerable and assumes that there is something to be gained from connection to another.

An anonymous biological male who "never enjoyed self-identifying as a 'man'" remembers Anzaldúa's Chicana feminist politics this way: "The problem, you wrote, is the system of ideologies that cleave apart our lives and bodies, that creates 'the other,' that demands we see everything in terms of irreconcilable opposites, that began the splitting of the world and is paving the highways of this path to world annihilation" (*Rest in Peace Gloria* 2004). The "other," in this account, is not clearly sexed; in fact, sex is part of the problem of this particular "othering." Though "woman" is the starting point for feminism, it does not have to be its horizon.[11] (Likewise, though Mesoamerican culture is the starting point for Anzaldúa's metaphysics, this metaphysics has porous horizons.) This anonymous entry (probably an interpretation of Anzaldúa's figure of the "Shadow-Beast") critiques any system that forces bodies into limiting frameworks and that splits materiality into binaries. Beyond Simone de Beauvoir's insights about otherness, the Shadow-Beast is unpredictable, transhuman, shadowing more than just sex or race. Anzaldúa calls it the "rebel in me," the projection of heterosexual males that falls into "nightmarish pieces," rather than simply raced or sexed forms. Like Coatlicue, with snakes for a head, it has "lidless serpent eyes," and one can see either "lust for power and destruction" or "tenderness" in its face (Anzaldúa 1987, 16–17, 20). The otherness of this creature embodies a simultaneity of political positions that accompanies the simultaneity of oppressions. This is not *just* a Chicana feminist insight, but it is that too.

Here I call upon Sedgwick's analysis of the AIDS quilt to understand the monumentalization of collective mourning. Sedgwick first optimistically reads the quilt as a patchwork coalition of heterogeneous identities and thus a militant gesture, defying the binaries imposed between straight and queer, sick and healthy: "Churned out of this mill of identities crossed by desires crossed by identifications is, it seems—or certainly seemed in October 1987—a fractured and *therefore* militant body of queer rebellion" (1993, 264–65). But then, after a paragraph break, she restarts, "But no one can really claim or own the relations of mourning," invoking the apolitical nostalgia and the homogenizing discourse of the Names Project. She concludes that the quilt is a "ravenously denuding, homogenizing, relentlessly anthropomorphizing and yet relentlessly disorienting abyssal voice" (1993, 265). This list of adjectives is very compelling. "Denuding" presents a vividly corporeal metaphor for the clash between supposedly private bodily states (love, illness, death, mourning) and public memorial, and most of the mourners at *Rest in Peace Gloria* are clearly aware of this denuding process. "Disorienting" seems to counteract "homogenizing," as the online altar provides a kaleidoscope of different feelings rather than a telescopic orientation. The adverb "ravenously" clearly captures the physical void and the insatiable longing of loss. But what is being (presumably wrongfully) "anthropomorphized" by the AIDS quilt? The absent victim, those who witness the quilt as it passes on display, or the quilt, itself? Does death transcend the corporeal?

One of the most striking aspects of the content of the mourning at *Rest in Peace* is its corporeal materiality, its "relentless anthropomorphizing" of Anzaldúa, of the mourners, and of electronic communication. In describing their tears, their own illnesses, their pains, their hands worn from work, their goose bumps, their body shapes and sizes, and their sexualities, the mourners at this site multiply corporeal markers beyond race/sex/etc. and unravel the boundaries between bodies to form a kaleidoscopic collective materiality. Anzaldúa's diabetes blends viscerally with that of Monica Dacumos's grandmother ("so strange and shocking to realize that she could be affected by such a mundane disease, just as my grandmother was, living a life that revolved around insulin shots and stubborn sugar binges"), then Dacumos's sister, mother, and, ultimately, "my own struggles with my body," inviting other mourners to find their own points of identification based on diets, sweat, spit, and "self-blame for not being disciplined enough, good enough, thin enough" (*Rest in Peace Gloria* 2004).

Online visitors scroll through the various mourners' stories and their various expressions of mourning in a way that becomes materially present in their own bodies. When I read it, I get chills. This materiality is particularly surprising, given the "virtual" medium and the fact that so many of the mourners never met Anzaldúa personally. "I never knew someone I didn't know personally could make such an important impact on my life," writes Bethany De Herrera-Schnering, and Raquel Evita Seidel feels "her hands on my life, albeit the distance physically" (*Rest in Peace Gloria* 2004). The extent to which these mourners *feel* Anzaldúa's absent body suggests that her lifework is still an "open wound" that bleeds into others (Anzaldúa 1987, 3). Alicia Gaspar de Alba writes: "Her passing is extremely personal and painful to me (as it is, I'm sure to many of us), and feels like a loss of a higher part of myself" (*Rest in Peace Gloria* 2004). Elsewhere, Inés Hernández-Ávila describes her grief as a gradual embodiment of Anzaldúa's absence: "My body is reluctantly registering in every cell that you are physically no longer with us" (quoted in Gonzales and Rodriquez 2004). It might seem like Anzaldúa's mourners are "followers," painfully straining against their foremother's body just as Anzaldúa strained against the collective politics of *la Raza,* but these tributes are thoroughly grounded in the diverse embodiments of a "new tribe": "Nothing is thrust out, the good the bad and the ugly, nothing rejected, nothing abandoned" (Anzaldúa 1987, 79).

In her Afterword to David Eng and David Kazanjian's edited collection, *Loss,* Judith Butler theorizes the sort of politics that emerges in the wake of death.[12] "Loss becomes condition and necessity for a certain sense of community," she writes, and pathos then "turns out to be oddly fecund, paradoxically productive" (2003, 468). I would pose this sense of community as a potential response to the defensive and strictly nominal subject of identity politics. Mourning is embedded in individual bodies and shared feelings. It is also, as Sedgwick says, "implacably inclusive" (1993, 265). The online altar, like the AIDS quilt, is open-ended, traveling, accessible (at least to those with computers). It invites reciprocal meditation about "injury" without requiring identification based on that injury. It forges a community that is not a community in any traditional sense. It maintains the friction between different identities, and this friction is one of the most palpable qualities of the Web site. Like disability, illness, and death, mourning by definition crosses boundaries. It lies *between* bodies, where one misses an other.

Of course, an altar is anomalous as a political gesture: its focus is more corporeal and emotional than most political movements, and one opens a memorial service to welcome the public in ways that one does not necessarily open a political meeting. One could interpret this altar as Sedgwick ultimately interpreted the AIDS quilt: as a backward-looking form that focuses all of its energy on a lost, static, iconic victim. Yet Anzaldúa's political subject opens up at the online altar through the unfurling list of different personal experiences, unique feelings, and embodied interpretations that reconstitute a variety of "Anzaldúas." The politics that emerges from such heterogeneity is based on difference rather than assumed consensus, allying schoolteachers, Christians, Jews, lesbians, straight women, and men, whether or not they perceive themselves to be allied. And these alliances produce new alliances, moving out toward the future. It is invigorating to read all of the unlikely connections that are forged by those who mourn Anzaldúa. The Rain and Thunder Collective of Oakland sent "support and strength and love and revolution" to all of the mourners at the site, while others prayed or dedicated their dissertations to Anzaldúa, forming a conceptually feminist network of care (*Rest in Peace Gloria* 2004).

Though these divergent methods might seem to jar against each other, they are consistent with Anzaldúa and Moraga's original impulse to embrace contradictions and to build bridges.[13] In *This Bridge Called My Back,* Moraga wrote: "We are women without a line. We are women who contradict each other. . . . For the women in this book, I will lay my body down for that [total] vision. *This Bridge Called My Back.* In the dream, I am always met at the river" (Anzaldúa and Moraga 1981, xix). Rather than assuming that differences lead to divisions, and rather than using bodies to undergird identity politics, this complicated vision uses bodies to reach out to others. A similarly counterintuitive passage in *Borderlands* opens Chicana feminist politics beyond Chicana identity: "We can no longer blame you, nor disown the white parts, the male parts, the pathological parts, the queer parts, the vulnerable parts. Here we are weaponless with open arms, with only our magic. Let's try it our way, the mestiza way, the Chicana way, the woman way" (Anzaldúa 1987, 88). If this is still "the Chicana way," it is because Anzaldúa and Moraga's particular bodies, beliefs, and homelands reach out with open arms rather than borders.

NOTES

1. "Race/sex/etc." reflects how class gets dropped out of many discussions of identity politics as well as how race and ethnicity, as well as sex and gender, become conflated.

2. "Medical consumerism" and "health management" have turned bodies into sites for capitalist exploitation, manipulation, and standardization. As David Morris writes, "Health (or an appearance of health) has become a prized commodity, as proudly displayed as a new SUV, while illness is an evil warded off with multivitamins and gym memberships" (2001, 59–60). In this context, all health is political, either an endorsement or a critique of the dominant culture's ideals, and the very materiality of health clarifies the stakes of assimilating one's body to such ideals.

3. See, for instance, Clendinnen (1991).

4. Susan Hekman argues that "without a coherent identity, actors cannot act; they require a stable sense of self to avoid the fragmentation and splintering that is the mark of insanity" (2004, 15). This is a logical assumption from the perspective of modern "Western" understandings of subjectivity and sanity. Drawing from ancient Mesoamerican understandings, however, enables Anzaldúa and Moraga to experience fluidity and self-fragmentation as expansions of their bodies and their states of consciousness.

5. Since the dominant view in the contemporary United States is that boundary crossing is a threat to security (both personal and national), Anzaldúa, in particular, has worked to resist this view. *Borderlands/La Frontera* begins with a number of images of boundary crossing as a political, intellectual, aesthetic, and humanitarian ideal. In opposition to the "unnatural" prohibitions installed at the U.S./Mexico border, Anzaldúa describes children innocently kicking their soccer ball across it; she watches the "silvered" and "marbled" ocean waves overwhelm the barbed wire fence dividing the two countries; and she theorizes the "third

country" of the borderlands as home to mixture, ambivalence, and transgression (1987, 1–4).

6. Elsewhere, Anzaldúa engenders this compromise within Chicana feminism: "In *nos/otras* we are them and they are us and we're contaminated by each other." "*Nos/otras*" reflects this "contamination" by splitting the plural feminine *we* down the middle—fragmenting the subject of Chicana feminism—and by using the slash simultaneously to divide and to fuse "us" and "them" (2000a, 11).

7. Many feminists decry artificial means of reproduction as a displacement of women's bodies by patriarchal science—as "the long-term triumph of the alchemists' dream of dominating nature through their self-inseminating, masturbatory practices"—but, as Rosi Braidotti notes, apparently monstrous fusions of mother and machine also help to transgress "the barriers between recognizable norms or definitions," to imagine "new ways of relating," to redefine "what we have learned to recognize as being the structure and the aims of human subjectivity in its relationship to difference, to the 'other' " (1994, 82, 88, 93, 94). The history of mechanized reproduction is intertwined with racism and misogyny, but these very technologies could be used to counter their own oppressive origins by re-conceiving motherhood apart from racist or misogynist norms. Medical technology can separate motherhood from domains that romanticize reproduction according to nationalistic, patriarchal, homophobic, or religiously governed ideals. Allowing technology into motherhood and motherhood into technology welcomes conceptual "otherness" into both, adding deliberate choices to motherhood and emotionally and corporeally grounded humanity to technology—a feminist gesture with the ability to redraw the boundaries that have circumscribed femininity, family, and motherhood.

8. A feminist ethics of care poses caregiving as an alternative to competition, dominance, differentiation, or other such frameworks through which interpersonal relationships are often negotiated. This idealization of caregiving has been criticized for romanticizing women's role as nurturers, for ignoring power dynamics, and for assuming a paternalistic stance toward those in need of care. Rosemarie Garland Thomson, for instance, explains that "the controversial feminist ethic of care has also been criticized by feminist disability scholars for undermining symmetrical, reciprocal relations among disabled and nondisabled women as well as for suggesting that care is the sole responsibility of women" (1997, 26). Margrit Shildrick, in contrast, theorizes caregiving as a mutual and dynamic undertaking that transforms both the caregiver and the receiver, requiring "the encounter *with* vulnerability to rest on an openness to the unpredictably strange and excessive, an openness that renders the self vulnerable" (2002, 78; emphasis in original).

9. Ana Castillo, who initially collaborated with Anzaldúa and Moraga in the 1980s, reaches a similar conclusion in *Massacre of the Dreamers* (1994), fusing the lessons of her *curandera* grandmother with science to outline a radical equality and interconnectedness of all things. If we make use of modern physics, she argues, "we instate a perception of life as being physically connected from atom to atom, no single part being more essential nor grander than the rest and that we are all vital to each other" (1994, 156). This claim substitutes the microscope for

the telescope as the tool for political examination, looking at bodies, not as individual members of a sociopolitical collectivity, but as a collectivity of atoms that continually interact with a changing environment. It is not just that Castillo opens the boundaries of bodies; she exposes the inherent instability of any boundary we could draw.

10. Dolores Huerta cofounded the United Farm Workers union with César Chavez and has been at the forefront of the Chicana/o civil rights movement since the 1960s.

11. See Butler (1992).

12. In *Loss,* Eng and Kazanjian theorize the productive potential of loss and the "new perspectives and new understandings" created by melancholia. Living with rupture and loss on a day-to-day basis can be both backward-looking and forward-looking, "rais[ing] the question of what makes a world of new objects, places, and ideals possible" (2003, 4). Walking around *missing* the ghosts of the past transforms the way we walk through the world.

13. One of the most oft-quoted passages in *Borderlands* states that "the new *mestiza* copes by developing a tolerance for contradictions, a tolerance for ambiguity" (Anzaldúa 1987, 79).

REFERENCES

Aguirre Beltrán, Gonzalo. 1963. *Medicina y Magia: El proceso de aculteración en la estructura colonial.* México, D.F.: Instituto Nacional Idigenista.

Alarcón, Norma. 2003. "Anzaldúa's *Frontera:* Inscribing Gynetics." In *Chicana Feminisms: A Critical Reader,* ed. Gabriela F. Arredondo et al., 354–69. Durham, N.C.: Duke University Press.

Anzaldúa, Gloria E. 1987. *Borderlands/La Frontera: The New Mestiza.* San Francisco: aunt lute.

———. 2000a. "Coming into Play: An Interview with Gloria Anzaldúa." Interview by Anne E. Reuman. *MELUS* 25.2: 3–45.

———. 2000b. *Interviews/Entrevistas,* ed. AnaLouise Keating. New York: Routledge.

———. 2002. "now let us shift . . . the path of conocimiento . . . inner work, public acts." In *This Bridge We Call Home: Radical Visions for Transformation,* ed. Gloria Anzaldúa and AnaLouise Keating, 540–78. New York: Routledge.

Anzaldúa, Gloria E., and Cherríe Moraga. 1981. *This Bridge Called My Back: Writings By Radical Women of Color.* New York: Kitchen Table: Women of Color Press.

Beauvoir, Simone de. 1953. *The Second Sex.* Trans. H. M. Parshley. New York: Knopf.

Braidotti, Rosi. 1994. *Nomadic Subjects: Embodiment and Sexual Difference in Contemporary Feminist Theory.* New York: Columbia University Press.

Brown, Wendy. 1995. *States of Injury: Power and Freedom in Late Modernity.* Princeton: Princeton University Press.

Butler, Judith. 1992. "Contingent Foundations: Feminism and the Question of 'Postmodernism.'" In *Feminists Theorize the Political,* ed. Judith Butler and Joan W. Scott, 3–21. New York: Routledge.

———. 1993. Editor's Introduction. In *Erotic Welfare: Sexual Theory and Politics in the Age of Epidemic,* ed. Judith Butler and Maureen MacGrogan. New York: Routledge.

———. 2003. "Afterword: After Loss, What Then?" In *Loss: The Politics of Mourning,* ed. David L. Eng and David Kazanjian, 467–73. Berkeley: University of California Press.

Castillo, Ana. 1994. *Massacre of the Dreamers: Essays on Xicanisma.* New York: Plume.

Clendinnen, Inga. 1991. *Aztecs: An Interpretation.* Cambridge: Cambridge University Press.

———. 2000. *Tiger's Eye: A Memoir.* New York: Scribner.

Davalos, Karen Mary, et al. 2002. "Roundtable on the State of Chicana/o Studies." *Aztlán* 27.2: 141–52.

Davis, Lennard. 2002. *Bending over Backwards: Disability, Dismodernism and Other Difficult Positions.* New York: New York University Press.

Eng, David L., and David Kazanjian. 2003. "Introduction: Mourning Remains." In *Loss: The Politics of Mourning,* ed. Eng and Kazanjian, 1–25. Berkeley: University of California Press.

González, Deena J. 1998. "Speaking Secrets: Living Chicana Theory." In *Living Chicana Theory,* ed. Carla Trujillo. Berkeley: Third Woman Press.

Gonzales, Patricia, and Roberto Rodriguez. 2004. *The Crossing of Gloria Anzaldúa.* http://www.uexpress.com.

Hall, Lynda. 2000. "Lorde, Anzaldúa, and Tropicana Performatively Embody the Written Self." *Auto/biography Studies* 15.1: 96–122.

Hekman, Susan J. 2004. *Private Selves, Public Identities: Reconsidering Identity Politics.* University Park: Pennsylvania State University Press.

Mairs, Nancy. 1996. *Waist High in the World: A Life Among the Nondisabled.* Boston: Beacon.

Moraga, Cherríe. 1997. *Waiting in the Wings: Portrait of a Queer Motherhood.* Ithaca: Firebrand.

———. 2000. "Queer Reservations; or, Art, Identity, and Politics in the 1990s." Interview by Rosemary Weatherston. In *Queer Frontiers: Millennial Geographies, Genders, and Generations,* ed. Joseph A. Boone et al., 64–83. Madison: University of Wisconsin Press.

———. 2001. *The Hungry Woman and Heart of the Earth.* Albuquerque: West End Press.

Morris, David B. 2001. "Narrative, Ethics, and Pain: Thinking *With* Stories." *Narrative* 9.1: 55–77.

Price, Janet, and Margrit Shildrick. 2002. "Bodies Together: Touch, Ethics, and Disability." In *Disability/Postmodernity: Embodying Disability Theory,* ed. Marian Corker and Tom Shakespeare, 62–75. London: Continuum.

Rest in Peace Gloria. 2004. http://gloria.chicanas.com.

Sedgwick, Eve. 1993. *Tendencies.* Durham, N.C.: Duke University Press.

Shildrick, Margrit. 2002. *Embodying the Monster: Encounters with the Vulnerable Self.* London: Sage.
Singer, Linda. 1993. *Erotic Welfare: Sexual Theory and Politics in the Age of Epidemic,* ed. Judith Butler and Maureen MacGrogan. New York: Routledge.
Thomson, Rosemarie Garland. 1997. *Extraordinary Bodies: Figuring Physical Disability in American Culture and Literature.* New York: Columbia University Press.
Wendell, Susan. 1996. *The Rejected Body: Feminist Philosophical Reflections on Disability.* New York: Routledge.
Yarbro-Bejarano, Yvonne. 2001. *The Wounded Heart: Writing on Cherríe Moraga.* Austin: University of Texas Press.

13

ORGANIC EMPATHY: FEMINISM, PSYCHOPHARMACEUTICALS, AND THE EMBODIMENT OF DEPRESSION

Elizabeth A. Wilson

Judith Kegan Gardiner opened her 1995 review of *Listening to Prozac*, *Talking Back to Prozac*, and *Prozac Nation* for the journal *Feminist Studies* with this anecdote:

> I recently attended an interdisciplinary feminist meeting that assumed a consensus about social constructionism and criticized scholarly work that was perceived as "essentialist," because it implied a biological basis for gender attributes. During meals and breaks, however, I heard a different story. Several women were taking Prozac or similar drugs for depression. Some of their children, who had been difficult, "underachieving," or disruptive in school, were also being medicated. These informal discussions centered on symptoms, side effects, and relief. They implied but did not discuss a view of personality as biochemically influenced. . . . The potential contradiction between such private solutions and the publicly avowed ideology of social constructionism was never voiced. (Gardiner 1995, 501–502)

Amongst other things, Gardiner's story is about the difficulties facing academic feminism as it tried to think about the relationship between personality and biochemistry. These difficulties had been greatly intensified by the dramatic changes to the psycho-cultural landscape that followed the release of Prozac into the U.S. market in 1989. More people than ever were taking antidepressant medications—not because the new SSRI and SNRI drugs are more effective as antidepressants (they are not), but because they seemed to have fewer adverse effects than the older medications.[1] People had become more aware of depression in themselves and in others, even though opinions differed—often sharply—as to whether the new drugs allowed previously unnoticed depressive conditions to be treated or whether they provoked an epidemic of unnecessary, pharmaceutically driven diagnoses of depression (Rose 2003). The widespread marketing and use of the SSRIs and SNRIs also gave new currency to biological theories of mood—particularly the hypothesis that depression was a consequence of low serotonin levels in the brain.

It is this latter transformation (an enthusiasm for thinking of depression in biochemical terms) that seems to have arrested feminist analysis of contemporary psychopharmaceutical events. As Gardiner's anecdote indicates, feminist research has been generated in an environment that is split off from biological data and theories. Accounts of cultural and psychic malleability have developed independently of biological data, and also—if we accept the veracity of Gardiner's story—independently of certain everyday experiences. Feminism has thought of biology more as a site of stasis and predetermination, and less as a source of variation, differentiation, and conversion (Wilson 2004b); and this has left academic feminism in a singularly ineffectual position for analyzing the new biochemical treatments of depressive states. Those feminists who have turned their attention to the new pharmaceutical treatments of depression often struggle to find critical purchase. Still allied with the anti-psychiatry movement of the 1960s and 1970s, these authors emphasize the cultural motivations for keeping women medicated, they are critical of the practices of pharmaceutical companies and the doctors that collude with them, and they remain dubious about the efficacy of pharmaceutical treatments for conditions they diagnose as essentially social in origin. In this register, Camilla Griggers's work (1997, 1998) has been paradigmatic.[2] Discussing Susanna Kaysen's autobiographical account of psychiatric institutionalization (*Girl Interrupted*), Griggers channels R. D. Laing's celebrated thesis in *Sanity, Madness and the Family:*

> One is hardly surprised that in Kaysen's family, the designated crazy is the disturbed daughter. The social limit of insanity, however, hardly ends with the family. Not only is the individuation of psychopathology within psychiatry a suppression system for the nervous system at large,

> but the oedipalization of the subject in psychoanalysis and psychotherapy, that is, the reduction of identity and meaning of the social subject to her familial history, is a suppression of group psychosis and general dysfunction in the socius. (Griggers 1998, 120)

In such a milieu, Griggers argues, psychopharmaceuticals reinforce cultural norms and suppress the capacity for change. Women, in particular, have been the target of these practices:

> Women are a large portion of the psychopharmacological market; most of those taking the antidepressant Prozac, for example, are women in their childbearing years. Because memory is emotional-state dependent, psychotropic intervention in and modulations of feminine affect produce at a neurobiological level a gendered chemical prosthetic subject whose repressed memories of the nervous system's circulating violences are the object of channeling, regulation, research, and development. (1998, 114)

It is not clear, however, that anti-psychiatry politics are immediately relevant to the post-Prozac environment. Most of the political and clinical agitation in anti-psychiatry was in relation to schizophrenia and institutionalized patients (Cooper 1967; Laing and Esterson 1964; Szasz 1961). SSRI and SNRI antidepressants are administered mostly in outpatient contexts (Rose 2003). In this sense, Kaysen's experience in 1967 of being institutionalized for depression is atypical of psychiatric interventions for depression since 1989. It is the spread of diagnoses of dysthymic depression outside the hospital and often beyond the reaches of the psychiatric profession (most antidepressant prescriptions in the U.S., UK, and Australia are written by general practitioners) that has fueled the extraordinary recent increase in antidepressant use.

Moreover, Griggers's condensation of psychopharmacology, psychiatry, neuroscience, psychotherapy, and psychoanalysis into a single monolithic entity—what elsewhere has been called the "psy sciences" (Rose 1998)—obscures rather than elucidates the nature of depressive events and their possible treatment. There are a number of important axiomatic differences between these knowledges: what is at stake conceptually differs considerably (e.g., is the mind neuronal activity? Is the mind libidinal? Is the mind built through dyadic patterns of attachment?), and their recommendations for treatment (pills vs. talk therapy) have been notoriously agonistic. Where Griggers sees epistemological collusion and the tyrannical deployment of power, I will argue for a more empathic orientation to the data: it is the moments of sympathy between these heterogeneous knowledges, I claim, that open up new avenues for political inquiry; new ways of using the data, theories, and commodities generated by these domains; and new ways of thinking about what the materials of feminist analysis could be.

In contrast to the academic literature, autobiographical feminist writing about being depressed and taking drugs like Prozac has had a fairly broad political and affective profile.[3] These authors describe hope and enthusiasm as well as anger and disillusionment. They can gravitate toward repair; their cooperation with pharmaceutical treatment waxes and wanes, as does their interest in psychotherapy. They express intense, mixed passions for their cultural milieu, their biochemistry, their doctors, family, friends, and themselves. What differentiates this genre of story from that of an earlier generation and from its academic kin is a curiosity about the role of pharmaceuticals in the treatment of depression and a willingness to engage more closely, more actively with the biological character of depressive states. Kate Millet's *The Loony-Bin Trip* (1990), which describes her struggles with manic-depression and lithium, is a useful point of contrast to these more recent feminist narratives. *The Loony-Bin Trip* is a defiant, stubborn, and angry text that explicitly aligns itself with anti-psychiatry. Published in 1990, it stands on the cusp of this transition from feminist politics under the influence of anti-psychiatry to feminist politics after Prozac. Jonathan Metzl's excellent analysis of the narrative constraints at work in post-Prozac feminism documents this change:

> The changes brought about by Prozac . . . allowed for a new telling of the woman's mental-illness narrative. Since the late nineteenth century, the genre had been marked by often-tortured relationships between women and the psychiatric establishment. . . . [However,] the women within these Prozac narratives would seem anything but stuck behind wallpaper or constrained by a civilization built by the fearful sons of psychoneurogentic mothers. Rather, they are engaged in the active creation of the terms of their illness and the active search for their own happiness. (2003, 174–76)

Metzl notes that Prozac usually failed these authors: it didn't magically restore self structure, nor did it provide sustained relief from social and psychological distress. Nonetheless, it is clear from Metzl's reading that the feminist politics of mental illness and pharmaceuticals changed after 1989. Psychopharmaceuticals are now less likely to be thought of as agents of coercion (as they had been by Millet); they have become one way—amongst others—through which the experience of depression can be explored and understood.

This essay argues for a more intimate engagement with biology in academic feminist writing on the politics of antidepressant use. The schism between politics and biology that has been foundational for contemporary critical research creates considerable difficulties for feminist analysis of psychopharmaceuticals. Social constructionism, in particular, has amplified a deep-seated distrust of biologically based argument. The success of social constructionism as the premier mode of feminist analysis in the social sciences in the 1990s can be attributed in large part to an axiomatic anti-biologism:

> Social constructionist theory is . . . centrally concerned with understanding how the language we use and the taken-for-granted categories we employ construct our experience in ways which we then reify as "natural," "universal" and "the way things have to be."
>
> A "weak" form of social constructionism is widely accepted across sociology and psychology and consists of little more than the claim that individuals cannot be adequately understood without looking at the social, historical and cultural context within which they are embedded. By contrast, the "strong" form of social constructionism profoundly unsettles both conventional and much feminist social science by proposing that social science categories (such as "the individual," "emotions," "sex" and, indeed, "scientific knowledge" itself) are social rather than natural products. (Kitzinger 2000, 451)

It is this preference in social constructionism for social explanations at the expense of natural explanations that has been the source of both its success and now, eventually, of its enervation. The separation between biology and politics that is emblematic of social constructionism has also become a defining trait of academic feminist research: more often than not, biology is thought to have consequences for politics, but the substrata themselves (e.g., neurons, genes, hormones) are not considered political material. It is familiar questions like "Are the brains of men and women different?" "Is IQ genetically inherited?" or "Do hormones control sexual preference?" that come to the fore (as though neurons, genes, and hormones stand before political events). More curious but no less political concerns, like the performativity of matter (Barad 2003) or the literacy of nature (Kirby 2003), have come less readily to a feminist audience. Jo-Ann Wallace, for example, is interested in the revitalizing effects that attention to biological detail may have for feminism. In the end, however, the nature of such an engagement with biology is disconcerting and unfamiliar. She hesitates:

> As it stands, the dizzying material and posthumanist world unveiled by feminist studies in the new "data of biology" seems both too small and too big, too intimate and too impersonal to imagine, and its implications for women remain unclear. . . . [T]he *ontological* consequences of new developments in neurobiology seem somewhat clearer at this point than the feminist or political consequences. (Wallace 2001, 38–39)

For Wallace, the analysis of biological data has missed its feminist mark: captivating as these new ontologies may be, they don't address tangible political concerns. It is my argument, however, that the analysis of biological matter is important, not so much because there are consequences that bear on feminism, but because biology itself is "as actively literate, numerate, and inventive as anything we might want to include within Culture" (Kirby 2003, 438). That is, the capacity for transformation—the sine qua non of politics as it is usually understood—is already native to biological substrata. We don't need to take politics to biology, or wait for biology to adjudicate over our political events (as if it were an unimpeachable authority); rather, we can explore the peculiar ways in which biological material writes, calculates, and fabricates. My interest lies less in the deconstruction of biology than in learning how biology itself deconstructs.[4] This shift in focus massively expands the bedrock of feminist analysis, and it changes what can count as political material or political action.

This essay will put pressure, then, on the commonplace feminist presumption that biology and politics are separate domains and that biology is a supplement (a dangerous adjunct) to politics. Feminism could be more curious about the biological substrata of depressive states; indeed, without conceptual interest in the vicissitudes of biology—how it invents, transforms, crafts, redistributes, incorporates, and bequeaths—feminists will remain perplexed by the character of psychopharmaceutical events. I will begin, then, with a focus on pharmacokinetic data: Where are antidepressant drugs absorbed in the body? How are they metabolized? What organs are involved in the circulation of these drugs? It is my wager that close, conceptually rigorous attention to biological detail will procure more dynamic (and more politically vibrant) accounts of depression and its treatment than we have hitherto suspected.[5]

PHARMACOKINETICS

Let me begin with a prosaic but important datum about the new antidepressant medications: they are all administered orally. That is, they are manufactured in tablet form, and they are swallowed.[6] While it is the case that most pharmaceuticals are administered orally (Kottke and Rudnic 2001), there is particular significance in the oral administration of antidepressants: there is an intimate connection between the gut and depression (Wilson 2004a, 2004b), making intervention via the gut an especially felicitous means of treatment for depressed mood. While conventional neuroscientific and psychiatric texts often posit a direct link from drug to brain, close attention to the details of drug absorption, distribution, metabolism, and excretion (what is called the drug's pharmacokinetics) shows that the viscera are also essential to how disorders of mood become instantiated and how they can be treated. Rather than validating a single central site of determination for mood (the brain), the pharmacokinetics of antidepressant drugs shed light on how depression is distributed, in both organic and psychic registers, all through the body. Too narrow a focus on the brain occludes other important events in antidepressant metabolism, making it difficult to think anew about the nature of body-mind relations.

For any orally administered drug, the gastrointestinal (GI) tract is the site at which the drug is absorbed into the body, and GI distress (nausea, delayed gastric emptying, and constipation) is a commonly experienced adverse effect. Because oral administration of drugs is so widespread, management of the gut's response to drugs has become a crucial part of pharmaceutical treatments. For example, there are numerous technologies available for controlling where in the GI tract drugs are released. Tablets can be specially coated so that they don't dissolve in the stomach (a low pH environment) but will dissolve in the intestine (which has elevated pH); or pills can be manufactured to float on the gastric juices, thus extending their time in the stomach (Jantzen and Robinson 2002). In most cases, the gut itself is not the target of therapeutic action; the drug is being released into the body some distance from its intended site of action (Katzung 2001). The pathways from the gut to that target site are often circuitous, and it is these pathways that have attracted my critical interest.

A drug like an antidepressant that is intended for the central nervous system (CNS) must first pass from the gut lumen into the bloodstream. Once it has passed though the gut mucosa, the drug is transported via the portal vein to the liver, where enzymes remove a certain amount of the drug (this is called first-pass clearance). From the liver, the remaining percentage of the drug moves into general (systemic) circulation in the body, where it is distributed into the fluid inside and between cells of the body's tissues and organs. The brain is targeted rapidly, as are the liver, kidneys, and other organs that are well supplied with blood. Eventually (this can take anywhere from several minutes to several hours), muscle tissue, the remaining viscera, the skin, and the body's fat will also be infused with the drug (Wilkinson 2001).[7] The physiological itinerary of an antidepressant takes in every organ of the body; so might we not wonder about antidepressant effects at these other sites?

The passage of a drug from systemic circulation into the brain is also quite an elaborate process. The brain is protected by a barrier (the blood-brain barrier) that prevents the transit of large molecules and potentially toxic solutes from the blood into the brain (Begley 2003). Serotonin, for example, cannot pass the blood-brain barrier (it is too large). Even though there are significant reservoirs of serotonin in the rest of the body,[8] the brain must synthesize its own serotonin from other molecules that are able to cross the blood-brain barrier. To put this in quotidian form: it isn't possible to increase serotonin levels in the brain simply by ingesting more serotonin. One of the ways in which the blood-brain barrier functions is simply obstructive—the cells that make up the walls of the brain's capillaries are so tightly packed together that drugs are not able to pass between these cells into brain tissue (as they would in other parts of the body): "The blood-brain barrier is the single most significant factor limiting drug delivery to the CNS" (Begley 2003, 85). Prevented from passing *between* cells, drugs must pass *through* the cells, and to do this they require some assistance from a chemical transport system. One of the most widely used methods for getting drugs to cross the blood-brain barrier is to make them lipid-soluble (Wilkinson 2001).[9] SSRIs are small molecules that are lipophilic, and they readily pass across the blood-brain barrier (Brøsen and Rasmussen 1996).

Once inside the brain, SSRIs are thought to increase the amount of serotonin that is available for neurotransmission (by inhibiting its reuptake in the synapse); and in turn, this increase in serotonin is thought to elevate mood. It has been conventional (in both biopsychiatric texts and the critical literatures that agitate against them) to focus on this particular destination of an antidepressant—as though the cerebral synapse were an antidepressant's natural or most important coalface. My interest has been diverted elsewhere—to the many biological sites and processes implicated in the ingestion of an antidepressant pill.[10]

BODY AND BRAIN

There are two issues that I would like to draw out of these data that may help inform feminist theories of body and mind.

First, drugs work with the whole body. While antidepressants may be intended for the brain, their therapeutic effects are gleaned from a wide variety of responses in other organs. Given that SSRIs and SNRIs are widely distributed in the body by systemic circulation and that they work effectively on synapses in the CNS, it would seem likely that they are also reaching the synapses of the nerves in the peripheral nervous system, especially the gut. Any pharmaceutical alleviation of dysthymic symptomology, then, cannot be attributed solely to effects in cortical and subcortical structures in the brain; it must also include the soothing and animating effects on the viscera (Wilson

2004a, 2004b). Pharmacokinetic data support models of the body in which simple lines of cause and effect (drug to brain to mood) are refracted, and these data are immensely valuable for feminism as it argues for more dynamic and expansive accounts of embodied psychic states.

Even though the gut is not mentioned as a target site for SSRI action in psychiatric or pharmacological texts, the effective pharmaceutical treatment of depression requires engagement with the organic periphery (especially the gut) as well as the brain. Perhaps because the gut is the delivery system for these drugs, it is thought of as simply a conduit for drug action and not as a participant in their therapeutic effects. Conceptual schemata that privilege the center over the periphery, or that draw radical distinctions between (active) agents and (passive) vessels have been the target of ongoing feminist intervention.[11] If the neurological and pharmacological sciences have been particularly potent sites for reinforcing these problematic conceptual structures, it seems to be despite the data they are generating, not because of them. Indeed, the neurological and pharmacokinetic data on antidepressants strongly indicate that the body as a whole is implicated in depressive states. The viscera aren't mere transfer stations for agents that will have their effects elsewhere. Rather, the liver and the gut provide the bioaffective tone of depressions: if your depressions are agitated, or soporific, or angry, or anorectic, that is due in no small part to the attitude of the visceral organs.

In fact, the formal psychiatric diagnosis of dysthymic depression is heavily reliant on somatic symptomology (see note 5). Dysthymia can be diagnosed when two or more of the following are present: poor appetite or overeating; insomnia or hypersomnia; fatigue; low self-esteem; poor concentration or difficulty in making decisions; feelings of hopelessness. There is some debate about whether the symptoms of dysthymic disorder in the DSM-IV are too strongly oriented toward somatic disturbance:

> A number of studies (including the DSM-IV field trial) suggest that Dysthymic Disorder may be better characterized by a wider array of cognitive and interpersonal symptoms, especially the following: generalized loss of interest or pleasure; social withdrawal; feelings of guilt; brooding

> about the past; subjective feelings of irritability or excessive anger; and decreased activity, effectiveness, or productivity. The DSM-IV Mood Disorders Work Group was especially conservative and decided that there was insufficient evidence to justify a change in the symptoms of Dysthymic Disorder. (First, Frances, and Pincus 2004, 203)

While it is commendable that the DSM describe the symptoms of depression in as exhaustive a manner as possible, the current (conservative) emphasis on somatic disruption does have the advantage of maintaining the visibility of the organic periphery, and it retains the memory of neurotic and hysterical conditions that have been gradually removed from the DSM. The addition of more cognitive symptoms need not broaden or refashion the conceptual apparatus of the DSM—it may have the effect of further entrenching the cerebrally centered and conscious-centered trends of biological psychiatry. It would also shift the practice of psychiatry even further away from psychodynamically oriented treatments toward short-term cognitive-behavioral treatments. The importance of retaining some interest in psychoanalytic knowledge when engaging with antidepressants is something I will turn to in the final section of this essay.

The second issue I would like to consider in the pharmacokinetic data concerns the brain and its interface with extra-cerebral systems. Just how isolated and autocratic is the brain? Are the biological bases of dysthymic states exclusively cerebral? Neurological and pharmacological descriptions of the blood-brain barrier (BBB) seem to stress the sequestration of the brain:

> The purpose of the BBB is twofold. Firstly, the internal environment of the brain, the brain interstitial fluid (ISF) and the cerebrospinal fluid (CSF) composition have to be controlled within extremely fine limits, far more so than the somatic extracellular fluid, so that neurons can perform their complex integrative functions. . . . Some amino acids in the blood, that are present in high concentrations, such as glycine, glutamine acid and aspartic acid, are potent excitatory neurotransmitters in the CNS and their levels in brain extracellular fluid must be very precisely controlled. Central neuronal synapses require this very stable background against which to function. Secondly, a major function of the BBB is that of neuroprotection. Over a lifetime the CNS will be exposed to a wide range of neurotoxic metabolites and acquired xenobiotics, which may cause cell damage and death. (Begley 2003, 84)

Such notions of the brain as an autonomous, self-contained organ are common enough in both the scientific and popular imaginary. However, the pharmacological data on the blood-brain barrier elucidate not simply the defensive nature of the barrier, but also its function as a system of communication with the outside. As we follow these data, we find that the brain is always necessarily implicated in relations with other organs and other extra-bodily systems. The blood-brain barrier is one particularly intensive site for those xenobiotic transmissions. For example, the brain doesn't manufacture serotonin internally and independently of the body. Rather, the synthesis of serotonin requires ongoing commerce between the brain and the gut and the cultural milieu. The basic building block of serotonin is tryptophan, an amino acid that is small enough to cross the blood-brain barrier. Tryptophan is an essential amino acid, which means it cannot be manufactured by the body—it must be supplied to the body as part of the diet. Chocolate, bananas, milk, meat, and fish are all high in tryptophan. Once tryptophan has been absorbed by the gut, passed by the liver, and released into systemic circulation, it crosses the blood-brain barrier into the CNS, where serotonin is synthesized in a two-step process: tryptophan is turned into 5-hydroxytryptophan (5-HTP), and this is turned into 5-hydoxytryptamine (5-HT or serotonin). Serotonin is then transported to the terminal endings of nerve cells, where it is used as a means of transmission across the synaptic cleft (Marsden 1996; Yuwiler, Brammer, and Yuwiler 1994).

The production of CNS serotonin is further complicated by the amount of carbohydrate that is ingested in the diet. Tryptophan is in competition with other amino acids as they cross the blood-brain barrier. The carrier that transports amino acids across the blood-brain barrier is limited in capacity, and tryptophan uptake can only be a percentage of overall amino acid transit. However, if the diet is heavy in carbohydrates (bread, cake, ice cream), the body will produce insulin in order to control high blood sugar. The insulin will remove most of the other amino acids from the blood, reducing competition at the blood-brain barrier, and allowing a disproportionate amount of tryptophan to pass from the blood to the brain (Wurtman et al. 2003).[12] This means that the level of serotonin in the brain is dependent on a number of extra-cerebral systems, for example, enzymes in the liver, conditions in the gut lumen, and the cultural and behavioral circumstances governing diet. No one of these systems entirely governs serotonin traffic. Rather, serotonergic activity is a network of relations amongst organs and between biological and cultural systems.

It is my argument that any regulation of the serotonergic system—including the ingestion of SSRIs to regulate mood—must grasp this network logic in order to be successful. Too narrow a focus on the brain as the sole biological source of psychological malady will obstruct the lines of connection that tie organ to organ and that underpin the biological possibility of recovery. To borrow from Winnicott—there is no such thing as a brain; there is always a brain and another system.[13] The biological disintegration of mood is a breakdown, not of the brain per se, or of the liver or gut, but of the relations amongst organs. The pharmaceutical treatment of depression has to be the management—not of a place or a center or even a neurological pathway—but of an organic capacity to connect. When they work, SSRIs reiterate the serotonergic networks that traverse the body, and they reanimate affinities between organs. Effectively administered, SSRIs can promote a profound, long-lasting, organic empathy.

BIOLOGY AND TRANSFERENCE

We may treat a neurotic any way we like, he always treats himself psychotherapeutically, that is to say with transferences.

—Sándor Ferenczi, 1909

In one of his key case histories, Peter Kramer (1993) discusses a patient (Lucy) who was helped enormously by both psychotherapy and SSRI antidepressants. Through psychotherapy, Lucy gained a certain amount of insight into the emotional principles that organized her experience of the world—she was very sensitive to rejection, and she could sometimes behave self-destructively. Despite the successes of the therapeutic alliance with Kramer, there were despondent parts of her emotional makeup that the psychotherapy couldn't budge. During one particularly distressing period, Kramer prescribed Prozac, and initially Lucy responded well. The drug seemed to stabilize her relations to study and to her boyfriend, rendering her more connected to the world and more psychically robust as a consequence. Then, like some other patients, she began to feel agitated, and eventually it was decided that she should discontinue with Prozac. Kramer reports that he might have started Lucy on another drug, except that she continued to improve without further medication. That brief period on Prozac seemed to have provided Lucy with insight: "We might say that the medication acted like an interpretation in psychotherapy" (Kramer 1993, 103). That is, Lucy was contained and reoriented by the medication in a fashion not unlike that provided by empathically based psychotherapeutic interpretation. Indeed, for Kramer, the action of medicating and interpreting are broadly homologous:

> It is now sometimes possible to use medication to do what once only psychotherapy did—to reach into a person and alter a particular element of personality. In deciding whether to do so, the psychopharmacologist must rely on skills we ordinarily associate with psychotherapy. (Kramer 1993, 97)

It has been usual to see medication and psychotherapy as agonistically related. The political battles over the treatment of depression often come down to a dispute about which of these methods is the more effective (psychologically and/or economically). I am using Kramer to move in a different direction: to highlight the affinity between biological and psychological registers. If the successful pharmacologist needs to act like the attuned psychotherapist, and if emotional insight can be gained somatically, this implies not simply a structural similarity between these processes but an intimate cohabitation of the biochemical and the psychological. Intervention in one register will reorganize patterns of organization in the other register, not because one determines the other, but because the two registers are ontologically connate. As I have begun to suggest above, there is a relation of sympathy between words and pills: the empathic and the organic are organized according to fellow feeling.[14] To put this slightly differently: interpretations are not events confined to a psychological (or cognitive) encounter. Nor are they simply actions that a cognitive system might visit upon a somatic system (a simplistic kind of psychosomatic suggestion). Biology too can decipher, parse, and appraise. The ruminations of the gut wall, the actions of the liver as is extracts a certain percentage of an antidepressant from the blood, the accounting of amino acids at the blood-brain barrier—these are moments of the body assaying its needs and limitations. If Lucy can be contained and rendered more emotionally robust by a short-term course of Prozac, this is because the interpretive capacities of her biology and her psyche are akin.

These notions are supported by the mainstream empirical research into the treatment of depression. There are two very robust findings in this literature. First, the combination of pharmaceutical and psychotherapeutic intervention seems to work better (on average) than treatment with either pharmaceuticals or psychotherapy on their own (de Jonghe et al. 2001; Keller et al. 2000; Pampallona et al. 2004; Thase et al. 1997). The effects of one seem to amplify or strengthen the effects of the other. The choice between Freud and Prozac, between talking and ingesting, is turning out to be less ideologically and medically definitive than we have been led to believe in the postwar, post-Freudian, pro-pharmaceutical years of the twentieth century. Psychoanalysis and psychopharmacology are not competing ideologies of depressive malady—they are different lines of attack into the same bioaffective system. Which line of attack, for how long, and at what level of intensity is an issue for each individual in consultation with their mental health practitioner and in accordance with the patient's circumstances, anxieties, and emotional preferences and the practitioner's frame of treatment. It is not an issue of principle or politics that can be adjudicated in advance (and for this reason it is exceedingly difficult for those not working at the psychological frontline to know whether or not antidepressants are being overused). The pro-Freud/anti-Freud, pro-drug/anti-drug debates that have occupied the political field since the anti-psychiatry movement of the 1960s are becoming less potent as we see growing sophistication (and increasing collaboration) in psychodynamic and psychopharmaceutical research. In the years to come, the difference between treating a depression biochemically and treating it psychologically may be less fraught than we currently suppose. With this future in mind, a desire for a greater variety of resources for treating mild to moderate depression need not also be a cry against psychopharmaceuticals.[15]

The second major finding in the research literature is that perhaps the most important variable in predicting a successful psychotherapeutic outcome for depression is not the mode of psychological treatment (e.g., cognitive therapy vs. psychodynamic therapy) but the quality of the relationship that the therapy provides (Hovarth and Symonds 1991; Klein et al. 2003; Krupnick et al. 1996; Martin, Garske, and Davis 2000). Irrespective of whether the clinician is cognitively or psychodynamically oriented, if a strong working alliance is formed between clinician and patient, we can expect a better-than-average outcome. To put this psychoanalytically: it is the transference that cures.

Definitions of transference have changed considerably since their early classical formulation. For Freud, the transference was a one-sided affair—the patient transfers old memories onto the analyst: "[Transferences] are new editions or facsimiles of the impulses and phantasies which are aroused and made conscious during the progress of the analysis. . . . [T]hey replace some earlier person by the person of the physician" (Freud 1905, 116). He initially thought that transference was an obstacle to treatment; it was a distortion of reality that the patient deployed unconsciously in the service of resistance. But later he came to see it also as "the most powerful therapeutic instrument" (Freud 1923, 247). This latter change (along with more sophisticated formulations of counter-transference) opened the way for many of the post-Freudians (e.g., Heinz Kohut, Michael Balint) to reconfigure transference as a relationship. This has broadened the base of psychoanalytic treatment from the classical transference neuroses (i.e., phobias, hysterias, and obsessional neuroses), and has facilitated treatment of what Freud had called the narcissistic neurosis (i.e., melancholia, manic-depression) as well as the psychotic fragmentation of personality disorders. In these contemporary formulations, transference is not simply the revivification of a past relationship; it is a rapport specific to the analytic dyad that requires attention in its own right:

> The relational approach that I am advocating views the patient-analyst relationship as continually established and reestablished through ongoing mutual influence in which both patient and analyst systematically affect, and are affected by, each other. A communication process is established between patient and analyst in which influence flows in both directions. (Aron 1991, 248)

What cures the depressive, in both classical and contemporary psychoanalytic modes of treatment, is an intervention into the patient's patterns of relationality. In depression, these patterns of relationality are usually dominated by loss: by the shock of actual losses through death or estrangement, by the incessant expectation of loss due to suboptimal care, or by an anxiety that one's own aggressive demands will instigate loss. The goal of working in a well-established transference is to re-establish the psychic capacity for connection that has been broken by a sudden loss, or perhaps never properly established due to early, chronic losses. The clinical transference is a provisional fabrication of a robust relation in the hope that it will eventually become self-sustaining and self-propagating.

This second research finding (the curative effects of transference) helps explain the first research finding (the successful co-assembly of pharmacological and talk therapies). That is, the successful imbrication of biological and psychological treatments of depression is due to the consanguinity of their methods; both are able to enliven through empathy and thus foster robust organic and emotional connection. The amplifying effect that pharmaceutical medication can have on the clinical relation ("we might say that the medication acted like an interpretation") suggests that transferences operate in biological as well as psychological registers. The organic relationality fostered by antidepressant medication (the quality of the relation between, say, brain and gut) resonates with the emotional connection that a strong clinical relationship can provide. Talk can strengthen organic connection, and drugs can facilitate inter-subjective affinity because the organic and psychic realms share a relational (transferential) logic. The breakdowns in dysthymia such as fatigue, poor appetite, guilt, and hopelessness are the result of losses—not of objects or organs themselves—but of relations to objects and organs. It follows, then, that dysthymic states can be most successfully ameliorated by restoring relationality in both emotional and organic registers.

This essay is an attempt to foster feeling for the organic in feminist academic writing. Without question, the early detachment of feminism from biological data and theories was a brilliant, indispensable political gesture. In recent years, however, the constitution of feminism's political foundations as axiomatically anti-biological has become too restrictive. By engaging so little with the vicissitudes of biological systems, feminism is closing itself off from a vibrant source of political agency and energy. Feminist projects that interrogate the heterodox character of the body's organs—projects that lean on and amplify biological data—can break new, vital ground for feminism. It has been my argument here that empathy for biology can generate fresh ways of thinking about the nature of depression and the politics of its treatment. The psychopharmaceutical data about the action of antidepressants, about the metabolism of serotonin, and about the traffic between the body's organs demonstrate sophisticated systems of somatic organization.

Interest in the vicissitudes of serotonergic systems doesn't mean compliance with the rhetoric and politics of Big Pharma, however. In fact, rather than giving the domains of biochemistry and neurophysiology to these corporate interests as their rightful property, curiosity about the pharmacology of mood can recapture biology for feminism. A feminism so informed about the character of biological substance will be better equipped to engage with the contemporary psychopharmaceutical scene.

NOTES

1. The new generation of antidepressants includes the selective serotonin reuptake inhibitors (SSRI) Prozac/fluoxetine, Zoloft/sertraline, Paxil/paroxetine, Celexa/citalopram, and Luvox/fluvoxamine. As well as the SSRIs, there are new "atypical" antidepressants that came onto the U.S. market around the same time: Serzone/nefazodone, Effexor/venlafaxine, and Wellbutrin/bupropion. These drugs are more heterogeneous in their pharmacological action—they are less specific to the serotonin system and act on other neurotransmitter systems, specifically norepinephrine (Potter and Hollister 2001). They are sometimes called third generation, heterocyclic, or serotonin-norepinephrine reuptake inhibitor (SNRI)

antidepressants. Nikolas Rose (2003) estimates that prescriptions in the United States for SSRI and related pharmaceuticals increased by 1300 percent from 1990 to 2000.

2. For similarly oriented feminist analyses of Prozac and biopsychiatry, see Blum and Stracuzzi (2004), Nicki (2001), and Zita (1998). As Metzl notes, the critical commentary on Prozac is now extensive ("a form so widespread it threatens to go generic along with the medication" (2003, 166). Amongst the most influential of these commentaries are: Breggin and Breggin (1994), Elliot and Chambers (2004), Fee (2000), Gardiner (1995), Kramer (1993, 2005), Healy (1997, 2004), *Hastings Center Report* (vol. 30, no. 2, 2000), *Journal of Medical Humanities* special issue on the cultural studies of psychiatry (vol. 24, issue 1–2, 2003), Masters and McGuire (1994), Rose (2003), and Solomon (2001). The astute feminist work of Mariam Fraser (2001) and Jonathan Metzl (2003) on Prozac, and Jennifer Radden (2003) and Juliana Schiesari (1992) on depression, has been particularly helpful for the arguments I make in this essay.

3. The most widely read of these are Elizabeth Wurztel's *Prozac Nation* (1995), Persimmon Blackbridge's *Prozac Highway* (1997), and Lauren Slater's *Prozac Diary* (1998).

4. I am using *deconstruction* here in two quite different senses. By "the deconstruction of biology" I refer to the now prevalent sense of deconstruction as a method for finding fault: the *Oxford English Dictionary* characterizes deconstruction as a means of "exposing unquestioned metaphysical assumptions and internal contradictions." In this sense, the deconstruction of biology would be an exposé of the ways in which biological knowledges are built with conventional binarized structures; I am less interested in that route. My second sense of deconstruction ("biology deconstructs") focuses on the dynamic nature of biological processes. How does biology fold, disseminate, fabricate, and breed? This latter use of deconstruction, which is laid out in detail in Wilson (1998), underwrites the analysis undertaken in this essay.

5. I limit my analysis here to the treatment of *dysthymia*—persistent, low-level depression:

> The essential feature of Dysthymic Disorder is a chronically depressed mood that occurs for most of the day more days than not for at least 2 years (Criterion A). Individuals with Dysthymic Disorder describe their mood as sad or "down in the dumps." In children, mood may be irritable rather than depressed, and the required minimum duration is only 1 year. During periods of depressed mood, at least two of the following additional symptoms are present: poor appetite or overeating, insomnia or hypersomnia, low energy or fatigue, low self-esteem, poor concentration or difficulty making decisions, and feelings of hopelessness (Criterion B). Individuals may note the prominent presence of low interest and self-criticism, often seeing themselves as uninteresting or incapable. Because these symptoms have become so much a part of the individual's day-to-day experience (e.g., "I've always been this way," "that's just how I am"), they are often not reported unless directly asked by the interviewer. (American Psychiatric Association, 376–77)

The Diagnostic and Statistical Manual of Mental Disorders (DSM) IV-TR distinguishes between Dysthymic Disorder and Major Depressive Disorder in terms of "severity, chronicity, and persistence" (374). Dysthymia is less severe but more chronic and persistent than a Major Depressive Disorder. It was first introduced as a mood disorder in the DSM-III in 1980, and up until the DSM-IV in 1994, it was also known as depressive neurosis. It is a rise in dysthymic diagnoses that has accompanied the phenomenal growth in antidepressant use since 1989.

6. Prozac/fluoxetine is also manufactured in liquid form. The other SSRIs and the atypical antidepressants are only manufactured in oral form (Potter and Hollister 2001). Some of the well-established tricyclic antidepressants (e.g., Elavil/amitriptyline and Tofranil/imipramine) can be administered by injection: "Intramuscular administration of some tricyclic antidepressants (notably amitriptyline and clomipramine [Anafranil]) can be performed under special circumstances, particularly with severely depressed, anorexic patients who may refuse oral medication or ECT" (Baldessarini 2001, 463).

7. This circuit is not the same for every antidepressant, making the differences amongst drugs a significant issue biochemically and psychologically. Each of the SSRIs varies in terms of how much of the drug reaches systemic circulation after having passed through the gut lumen and through the liver—this is called a drug's bioavailability. Bioavailability of an orally administered drug is measured as a percentage of the bioavailability of the same drug if it had been administered intravenously. By definition, an IV-administered drug has a bioavailability of 100 percent, since it has avoided both the gut and the liver and is fully available in the blood. Usually a group of subjects are given intravenous and oral doses of the drug on separate occasions: the bioavailability of the oral formulation is simply calculated as a proportion of the amount available when administered intravenously. The bioavailability of Paxil/paroxetine is around 50 percent, whereas Prozac/fluoxetine has a reasonably high bioavailability (70 percent). Luvox/fluvoxamine is even higher (greater than 90 percent) (Potter and Hollister 2001, 502). The differences in bioavailability are further amplified by the fact that the metabolites of the SSRIs (i.e., the substances produced by metabolism of the drug in the liver and elsewhere) can also have antidepressant effects: "Paroxetine [Paxil] and fluvoxamine [Luvox] do not produce any metabolites that, at least in therapeutic doses, are likely to make a significant contribution to their pharmacological effects. By contrast, fluoxetine [Prozac] and citalopram [Celexa] both produce pharmacologically active metabolites whose actions probably contribute to the antidepressant effects of their parent compound" (Leonard 1996, 42). Indeed, the metabolite of fluoxetine (norfluoxetine) is four times more potent as a serotonin reuptake inhibitor than is fluoxetine itself.

8. Ninety-five percent of the body's serotonin is stored outside the CNS—in the blood and in the extensive network of nerves that encase the gut (Wilson 2004b). In fact, serotonin was first discovered in the blood, where it was understood to be a vasoconstrictor (thus the name sero-tonin: a serum agent affecting vascular tone). It was some years before it was located in the brain and accepted as a neurotransmitting substance in both the central and peripheral systems (Gershon 1998).

9. Take, for example, the related compounds morphine, codeine, and her-

oin. Morphine has relatively low uptake across the blood-brain barrier. Codeine can be created by slightly altering the chemical structure of morphine (replacement of a hydroxyl group with a methyl group). This increases lipid solubility, and brain uptake is increased tenfold. A further lipidization of codeine (addition of two acetyl groups) creates heroin, which has a 30-fold increase in uptake into the brain (Begley 2003). While drugs can be injected directly into the brain, this method has a number of technical drawbacks, and it is not often used clinically. The nose can be an effective way of delivering drugs directly to the CNS: drugs can pass from the nasal mucosa to cerebrospinal fluid with relative ease. Antibiotics, insulin, AZT, and progesterone "have all been delivered to the CNS successfully via the nasal route" (2003, 87).

10. For critics like Peter Breggin (1994) this distribution of antidepressant effect beyond narrowly defined serotonergic pathways in the brain is one of the signs that drugs like Prozac are toxic substances. In the first instance, he disputes the selectivity of the SSRI antidepressants:

> The SSRIs, in fact, end up heavily impacting other neurotransmitter systems. Prozac, for example, has been shown to stimulate indirectly the adrenergic neurotransmitter system, resulting in significant, widespread compensatory changes within the receptors of that system. One of Prozac's most menacing side effects . . . is probably due at least in part to its effect on yet another neurotransmitter, dopamine. (Breggin and Breggin, 1994, 24)

And he sees this dissemination of drug effects as a kind of tyranny:

> Prozac has been shown to interfere with the functions of serotonin throughout the body, including the platelets in the blood, accounting in part for its wide variety of side effects.
>
> Overall, Eli Lilly's promotional line about Prozac's selective effects on the nervous system should be viewed with caution and skepticism. No one prescribing or receiving the drug can fully grasp Prozac's overall impact on the brain and whole body, because it's beyond our current scientific understanding. (1994, 26)

Like any drug, antidepressants can generate adverse biological and psychological effects. Patients taking tricyclic and MAOI antidepressants can report symptoms like dry mouth, gastrointestinal distress, constipation, weight gain, dizziness, tachycardia, and urinary retention. The MAOIs also force patients into fairly restrictive dietary habits: common foods like cheese can generate dangerously high blood pressure, which in some instances has been fatal (Potter and Hollister 2001). The SSRI and SNRI antidepressants have fewer side effects; and it is this, rather than any demonstrable increase in antidepressant efficacy, that underpins their therapeutic success (Baldessarini 2001). Some gastrointestinal effects are still evident with the newer antidepressants, and sexual dysfunction has emerged as a common problem with certain of the SSRIs. Most notoriously, there are reports of increased agitation and suicidal ideation with the new antidepressants, although the data pertaining to these events are still unclear and the political and legal situation remains heated (Healy 2004).

Breggin's work is politically ineffectual, in my view, because it doesn't use this dissemination of drug effect to rethink conventional models of the relationship between biological substrate and psychological malady. After all, the allegedly toxic effects of antidepressants are no less illuminating than their supposedly therapeutic effects. Does this data not provoke conjecture about the nature of sexual function or sleeping patterns or suicidal intent such that they may be rerouted by a molecule? If it is simply facile to say that psychology is fabricated beyond the reaches of biochemistry, or that psychology is entirely prescribed by biochemistry, then what models of biopsychic imbrication might we start to imagine? To the extent that Breggin accepts a very conventional model of direct and unwavering lines of influence from drug to behavior (Prozac made me kill my wife), he is more faithful to mainstream biopsychiatry than he suspects.

11. The work of Gayatri Chakravorty Spivak, for example, has been very influential in the feminist deconstruction of center and periphery (first world/third world), beginning most ferociously with Spivak (1988). She has argued that it is "this longing for a center, an authorizing pressure, that spawns hierarchized oppositions. The superior term belongs to presence and the logos; the inferior serves to define its status and mark a fall" (Spivak 1976, lxix). The importance of Spivak's work lies in her insistence (following Derrida) that it is never enough to simply reverse these conceptual structures (to privilege the periphery over the center, and so put the matter to rest). Rather, we are caught in an incessant inquiry into how each term in a hierarchy informs, destroys, and amplifies the other.

Evelyn Fox Keller (1995) spells out a similar analytic approach in her reading of twentieth-century embryology. She notes that "many debates about the relative importance of the nucleus [center] and cytoplasm [periphery] in inheritance inevitably reflect older debates about the relative importance (or activity) of maternal and paternal contributions to reproduction, where the overwhelming historical tendency has been to attribute activity and motive force to the male contribution while relegating the female contribution to the role of passive, facilitating environment" (1995, 39–40). Keller notes how contemporary developments in molecular biology complicate these conventional presumptions; not simply reversing an age-old dichotomy (activity/passivity), recent data reveal a dynamic system of biological influence: "The findings . . . point neither to cytoplasmic nor to nuclear determination but rather to a complex but highly coordinated system of regulatory dynamics that operate simultaneously at all levels: at the level of transcription activation, of translation, of protein activation, and of intercellular communication—in the nucleus, in the cytoplasm, indeed in the organism as a whole" (1995, 29–30). The analysis of brain (center) and gut (periphery) that I am building here and elsewhere (Wilson 2004a) follows this same general approach.

12. There seem to be links between carbohydrate craving and atypical depressions (e.g., seasonal affective disorder, premenstrual disorder). Moller (1992) suggests that "excessive carbohydrate intake by patients with PMS or SAD reflects a self-medication that temporarily relieves the vegetative symptoms [of depression] via an increased central serotonergic activity" (1992, 61; see also Fernstrom and Wurtman 1971).

13. "I once risked the remark, 'There is no such thing as a baby'—meaning

that if you set out to describe a baby, you will find you are describing a *baby and someone.* A baby cannot exist alone, but is essentially part of a relationship" (Winnicott 1964, 88).

14. The *Oxford English Dictionary* records the etymology of *sympathy* as from the Greek "to have fellow feeling" and gives as its first definitions of sympathy: "A (real or supposed) affinity between certain things, by virtue of which they are similarly or correspondingly affected by the same influence, affect or influence one another (esp. in some occult way), or attract or tend towards each other"; and, in relation to pathology, a "relation between two bodily organs or parts (or between two persons) such that disorder, or any condition, of the one induces a corresponding condition in the other."

15. This point is argued further in Wilson (2005).

REFERENCES

American Psychiatric Association. 2000. *Diagnostic and Statistical Manual of Mental Disorders IV-TR.* Washington, D.C.: American Psychiatric Association.

Aron, Lewis. 1991. "The Patient's Experience of the Analyst's Subjectivity." In *Relational Perspectives: The Emergence of a Tradition,* ed. Stephen Mitchell and Lewis Aron, 243–68. Hillsdale, N.J.: Analytic Press, 1999.

Baldessarini, Ross. 2001. "Drugs and the Treatment of Psychiatric Disorders: Depression and Anxiety Disorders." In *Goodman and Gilman's The Pharmacological Basis of Therapeutics,* ed. Joel Hardman and Lee Limbird, 10th ed., 447–83. New York: McGraw-Hill.

Barad, Karen. 2003. "Posthumanist Performativity: Toward an Understanding of How Matter Comes to Matter." *Signs: Journal of Women in Culture and Society* 28.3: 801–31.

Begley David. 2003. "Understanding and Circumventing the Blood-Brain Barrier." *Acta Paediatrica Supplement* 443: 83–91.

Blackridge, Persimmon. 1997. *Prozac Highway.* Vancouver, B.C.: Press Gang.

Blum, Linda, and Nena Stracuzzi. 2004. "Gender in the Prozac Nation: Popular Discourse and Productive Femininity." *Gender and Society* 18.3: 269–86.

Breggin, Peter, and Ginger Ross Breggin. 1994. *Talking Back to Prozac: What Doctors Aren't Telling You about Today's Most Controversial Drug.* New York: St. Martin's.

Brøsen, Kim, and Birgitte Buur Rasmussen. 1996. "Selective Serotonin Reuptake Inhibitors: Pharmacokinetics and Drug Interactions." In *Selective Serotonin Re-uptake Inhibitors: Advances in Basic and Clinical Practice,* ed. J. P. Feigher and W. F. Boyer, 2nd ed., 87–108. Chichester: John Wiley and Sons.

Cooper, David. 1967. *Psychiatry and Anti-psychiatry.* London: Tavistock.

Elliott, Carl, and Tod Chambers, eds. 2004. *Prozac as a Way of Life.* Chapel Hill: University of North Carolina Press.

Fee, Dwight, ed. 2000. *Pathology and the Postmodern: Mental Illness as Discourse and Experience.* London: Sage.

Ferenczi, Sándor. 1909. "Introjection and Transference." In *First Contributions to Psycho-analysis,* 35–93. New York: Brunner/Mazel.
Fernstrom, John, and Richard Wurtman. 1971. "Brain Serotonin Content: Increase Following Ingestion of Carbohydrate Diet." *Science* 174: 1023–25.
First, Michael, Allen Frances, and Harold Pincus. 2004. *DSM-IV-TR Guidebook.* Washington, D.C.: American Psychiatric Association.
Fraser, Mariam. 2001. "The Nature of Prozac." *History of the Human Sciences* 14.3: 56–84.
Freud, Sigmund. 1905. "Fragment of an Analysis of a Case of Hysteria." In *Standard Edition of the Complete Psychological Works of Sigmund Freud,* 7:3–122. London: Hogarth.
———. 1923. Two encyclopaedia articles. In *Standard Edition of the Complete Psychological Works of Sigmund Freud,* 18:234–59. London: Hogarth.
Gardiner, Judith Kegan. 1995. "Can Ms. Prozac Talk Back? Feminism, Drugs and Social Constructionism." *Feminist Studies* 21.3: 501–17.
Gershon, Michael. 1998. *The Second Brain.* New York: Harper-Perennial.
Griggers, Camilla. 1997. *Becoming Woman.* Minneapolis: University of Minnesota Press.
———. 1998. "The Micropolitics of Biopsychiatry." In *Vital Signs: Feminist Reconfigurations of the Bio/Logical Body,* ed. Margaret Shildrik and Janet Price, 132–44. Edinburgh: Edinburgh University Press.
Healy, David. 1997. *The Antidepressant Era.* Cambridge, Mass.: Harvard University Press.
———. 2004. *Let Them Eat Prozac: The Unhealthy Relationship between the Pharmaceutical Industry and Depression.* New York: New York University Press.
Hovarth, Adam, and Dianne Symonds. 1991. "Relation between Working Alliance and Outcome in Psychotherapy: A Meta-analysis." *Journal of Counseling Psychology* 38.2: 139–49.
Jantzen, Gwen, and Joseph Robinson. 2002. "Sustained- and Controlled-Release Drug-Delivery Systems." In *Modern Pharmaceuticals,* ed. Gilbert Banker and Christopher Rhodes, 4th ed., 501–28. New York: Marcel Dekker.
de Jonghe, F., S. Kool, G. van Aalst, J. Dekker, and J. Peen. 2001. "Combining Psychotherapy and Antidepressants in the Treatment of Depression." *Journal of Affective Disorders* 64: 217–29.
Katzung, Bertram. 2001. *Basic and Clinical Pharmacology,* 8th ed. New York: McGraw-Hill.
Keller, Evelyn Fox. 1995. *Refiguring Life: Metaphors of Twentieth-Century Biology.* New York: Columbia University Press.
Keller, Martin, James McCullough, Daniel Klein, Bruce Arnow, Janice Blalock, Frances Borian, Darlene Jody, Charles DeBattista, Lorrin Koran, Alan Schatzberg, Jan Fawcett, Robert Hirschfeld, Gabor Keitner, Ivan Miller, James Kocsis, Susan Kornstein, Rachel Manber, Philip Ninan, Barbara Rothbaum, John Rush, and Dina Vivian. 2000. "A Comparison of Nefazodone, the Cognitive Behavioral-Analysis System of Psychotherapy, and Their Combination for the Treatment of Chronic Depression." *New England Journal of Medicine* 342.20: 1462–71.
Kirby, Vicki. 2003. "Enumerating Language: 'The Unreasonable Effectiveness of

Mathematics.'" *Configurations: A Journal of Literature, Science, and Technology* 11.3: 417–39.

Kitzinger, Celia. 2000. "Social Constructionism." In *Encyclopedia of Feminist Theories,* ed. Lorraine Code, 451–52. London: Routledge.

Klein, Daniel, Joseph Schwartz, Neil Santiago, Dina Vivian, Carina Vocisano, Louis Castanguay, Brain Arnow, Janice Blalock, Rachel Manber, John Markowitz, Lawrence Riso, Barbara Rothbaum, James McCullough, Michael Thase, Franses Borian, Ivan Miller, and Martin Keller. (2003). "Therapeutic Alliance in Depression Treatment: Controlling for Prior Change and Patient Characteristics." *Journal of Consulting and Clinical Psychology* 71.6: 997–1006.

Kottke, Mary, and Edward Rudnic. 2001. "Tablet Dosage Forms." In *Modern Pharmaceuticals,* ed. Gilbert Banker and Christopher Rhodes, 4th ed., 287–333. New York: Marcel Dekke.

Kramer, Peter. 1993. *Listening to Prozac.* New York: Penguin.

———. 2005. *Against Depression.* New York: Viking.

Krupnick, Janice, Stuart Sotsky, Sam Simmens, Janet Moyer, Irene Elkin, John Watkins, and Paul Pilkonis. 1996. "The Role of the Therapeutic Alliance in Psychotherapy and Pharmacotherapy Outcome: Findings in the National Institute of Mental Health Treatment of Depression Collaborative Research Program." *Journal of Consulting and Clinical Psychology* 64.3: 532–39.

Laing, Ronald David, and Aaron Esterson. 1964. *Sanity, Madness and the Family.* London: Tavistock.

Leonard, Brian. 1996. "The Comparative Pharmacological Properties of Selective Serotonin Re-Uptake Inhibitors in Animals." In *Selective Serotonin Re-uptake Inhibitors: Advances in Basic and Clinical Practice,* ed. J. P. Feigher and W. F. Boyer, 2nd ed., 35–62. Chichester: John Wiley and Sons.

Marsden, Charles. 1996. "The Neuropharmacology of Serotonin in the Central Nervous System." In *Selective Serotonin Re-uptake Inhibitors: Advances in Basic and Clinical Practice,* ed. J. P. Feigher and W. F. Boyer, 2nd ed., 1–33. Chichester: John Wiley and Sons.

Martin, Daniel, John Garske, and Katherine Davis. 2000. "Relation of the Therapeutic Alliance with Outcome and Other Variables: A Meta-analytic Review." *Journal of Consulting and Clinical Psychology* 68.3: 438–50.

Masters, Roger, and Michael McGuire, eds. 1994. *The Neurotransmitter Revolution: Serotonin, Social Behavior, and the Law.* Carbondale: Southern Illinois University Press.

Metzl, Jonathan. 2003. *Prozac on the Couch: Prescribing Gender in the Era of Wonder Drugs.* Durham, N.C.: Duke University Press.

Millett, Kate. 1990. *The Loony-Bin Trip.* New York: Simon and Schuster.

Moller, S. 1992. "Serotonin, Carbohydrates, and Atypical Depression." *Pharmacology and Toxicology* 71 (Suppl. 1): 61–71.

Nicki, Andrea. 2001. "The Abused Mind: Feminist Theory, Psychiatric Disability, and Trauma." *Hypatia* 16.4: 80–104.

Pampallona, Sandro, Paolo Bollini, Giuseppe Tibaldi, Bruce Kupelnick, and Carmine Munizza. 2004. "Combined Pharmacotherapy and Psychological Treatment for Depression: A Systematic Review." *Archives of General Psychiatry* 61.7: 714–19.

Potter, William, and Leo Hollister. 2001. "Antidepressant Agents." In *Basic and Clinical Pharmacology,* ed. Bertram Katzung, 8th ed., 498–511. New York: McGraw-Hill.

Radden, Jennifer. 2003. "Is This Dame Melancholy? Depression and Past Melancholia." *Philosophy, Psychiatry, and Psychology* 10.1: 37–52.

Rose, Nikolas. 1998. *Inventing Our Selves: Psychology, Power, and Personhood.* Cambridge: Cambridge University Press.

———. 2003. "Neurochemical Selves." *Society* 41.1: 46–59.

Schiesari, Juliana. 1992. *The Gendering of Melancholia: Feminism, Psychoanalysis, and the Symbolics of Loss in Renaissance Literature.* Ithaca: Cornell University Press.

Slater, Lauren. 1998. *Prozac Diary.* New York: Random House.

Solomon, Andrew. 2001. *The Noonday Demon: An Atlas of Depression.* New York: Touchstone.

Spivak, Gayatri Chakravorty. 1976. Translator's preface. In Jacques Derrida, *Of Grammatology,* ix–lxxxvii. Baltimore: Johns Hopkins University Press.

———. 1988. "Can the Subaltern Speak?" In *Marxism and the Interpretation of Culture,* ed. Cary Nelson and Lawrence Grossberg, 271–313. London: Macmillan.

Szasz, Thomas. 1961. *The Myth of Mental Illness: Foundations of a Theory of Personal Conduct.* New York: Hoeber-Harper.

Thase, Michael, Joel Greenhouse, Ellen Frank, Charles Reynolds, Paul Pilkonis, Katharine Hurley, Victoria Grochocinski, and David Kupfer. 1997. "Treatment of Major Depression with Psychotherapy or Psychotherapy-Pharmacotherapy Combinations." *Archives of General Psychiatry* 54.11: 1009–15.

Wallace, Jo-Ann. 2001. "Where the Body Is a Battleground: Materializing Gender in the Humanities." *Resources for Feminist Research* 29.½: 21–42.

Wilkinson, Grant. 2001. "Pharmacokinetics: The Dynamics of Drug Absorption, Distribution, and Elimination." In *Goodman and Gilman's The Pharmacological Basis of Therapeutics,* ed. Joel Hardman and Lee Limbird, 10th ed., 3–29. New York: McGraw-Hill.

Wilson, Elizabeth. 1998. *Neural Geographies: Feminism and the Microstructure of Cognition.* New York: Routledge.

———. 2004a. "Gut Feminism." *differences: A Journal of Feminist Cultural Studies* 15.3: 66–94.

———. 2004b. *Psychosomatic: Feminism and the Neurological Body.* Durham, N.C.: Duke University Press.

———. 2005. "Correspondence [Response to Gail Bell's "The Worried Well"]." *Quarterly Essay* 19: 96–99.

Winnicott, D. W. 1964. *The Child, the Family and the Outside World.* Harmondsworth: Penguin.

Wurtman, Richard, Judith Wurtman, Meredith Regan, Janine McDermott, Rita Tsay, and Jeff Breu. 2003. "Effects of Normal Meals Rich in Carbohydrates or Proteins on Plasma Tryptophan and Tyrosine Ratios." *American Journal of Clinical Nutrition* 77: 128–32.

Wurtzel, Elizabeth. 1995. *Prozac Nation: Young and Depressed in America.* New York: Riverhead.

Yuwiler, Arthur, Gary Brammer, and K. C. Yuwiler. 1994. "The Basics of Serotonin Neurochemistry." In *The Neurotransmitter Revolution: Serotonin, Social Behavior, and the Law,* ed. Roger Masters and Michael McGuire, 37–46. Carbondale: Southern Illinois University Press.

Zita, Jacquelyn. 1998. *Body Talk: Philosophical Reflections on Sex and Gender.* New York: Columbia University Press.

14

CASSIE'S HAIR

Susan Bordo

LEARNING TO DO CASSIE'S HAIR

In the first year and a half of Cassie's life, her hair was basically not an issue because she didn't have much. Then one day she came home from day care with a dozen tiny braids marking a complex and delicate pattern on her tiny head. I was, first of all, mystified. I had no idea she had enough hair to do anything like this. Where had all that hair come from? How had her teacher gathered it up like that? And how had she gotten her to sit still long enough to do it?

When my friend Annice found out what had happened, she was indignant—for *me.* "What right did that teacher have to mess with your daughter's hair?"

I understood why she, as a black woman whose own hair had been braided by her grandmother and aunts, might have had that reaction. Why she, as a person whose ancestors had *their* parental rights ignored, would be horrified at the idea of another woman appropriating, without permission, such an intimate ritual of mother-child bonding.

But for me, with my very different personal history of mother-daughter hair care—basically, none—it didn't feel like an overstepping of parental rights, it felt like my daughter had been welcomed into a community. When I picked her up that day, all the black teachers were gathered around her, oohing and aahing, cupping her face in their hands. "Would you look at this gorgeous baby doll?"

She was, indeed, gorgeous. She also seemed, for the first time, undeniably black. Since infancy, Cassie, whose birth mother is white and birth father black, had been taken for many different ethnicities.

We'd eat in Indian restaurants, and the owners would ask if she was Indian. Asians thought she was Asian. And so on. "Where does she come from?" I'd get asked. People were often surprised when I replied, "Texas." But now, her head crisscrossed with cornrows, it was absolutely clear that Cassie was a black child. And I had been given a message, with or without intention on the part of her teacher, that as a mother I had two choices: get inside this world, *truly* inside, or remain a clueless white mom.

That was the last thing I wanted to be. Later, when Cassie was in preschool, I was privy to the black moms' bemused disdain for the white moms of black and biracial children who didn't know how to take care of their children's hair. One white mom, for example, was so intimidated by the very prospect of combing her daughter's hair that she had to cut it all off when, untended, it clumped into a mass of locked tangles. That woman was the subject of a lot of laughter, her daughter the object of pity. "That poor child." I never wanted my daughter to be the object of that kind of pity. Or me the object of that kind of scorn.

So I undertook the project of educating myself. I read, I asked, I looked, and I tried. Products that I'd never heard of before—pink lotion, braid spray, do-rags—became staples of my life. New terms: *tender-headed*—which Cassie definitely seemed to be; *kitchen*—that bit of hair at the back of the neck most prone to kinks and tangles, most resistant to combing through. "If there ever was one part of our African past that resisted assimilation," writes Henry Louis Gates, "it was the kitchen. No matter how hot the iron, no matter how powerful the chemical . . . neither God nor woman nor Sammy Davis Jr. could straighten the kitchen" (1994, 42). I first read these words from *Colored People* several years before we adopted Cassie. But now, with Cassie on my lap, the kitchen was no longer a fascinating piece of insider knowledge, but a precious marker of Cassie's ancestry—and a practical challenge to me, as the mom who had to deal with hers.

For practical instruction, I looked less to books than to Annice. I watched intently as she did Cassie's hair, marveling at her ability and her patience. Annice, the mother of a boy, claimed to be a terrible hairstylist; yet still she managed to get those parts straighter and cleaner than I ever could. Over and over she'd do them, until she considered my child fit to go out in public. I found it difficult to be as exacting. My fingers seemed less agile, and it felt, at times, as though I was lacking an inherited aptitude. I was amazed at the abundance of lotion that Annice (correctly) deemed necessary for Cassie's hair and—as someone who had grown up being told that greasy was something you *didn't* want your hair to be—had almost a bodily aversion to slathering it on in such quantity. My patience and endurance ran out sooner—these sessions can take hours, depending on one's dexterity and the complexity of the style—and I often sent Cassie off with braids that were only passable. It didn't bother me the way it bothered Annice, from whom I learned that my lack of anxiety over my child's being seen as less than perfectly coiffed (read: not respectable, not cared for, liable to being seen as a wild "animal") was a privilege of my race.

But there were also privileges conferred on the black mom, as I discovered when they became my privileges too. As I became used to setting aside at least two hours for doing my daughter's hair, I became addicted to the pleasure of unbroken physical closeness the ritual afforded. As she grew into a more and more independent and active child, I knew that I could count on at least two hours every week when I'd have her on my lap, her little body leaning against mine, sometimes (as I got better at combing) even falling asleep as she had when she was a baby. At first I was intimidated by every ouch, at the same time as it seemed like such a lot of work to take the time to do it carefully and gently, working from the ends on up. But I discovered that there is a kind of Zen to it. Once you give yourself over to it, everything else recedes to background as the closeness of one's child, the taking care, the permission to touch and smell and attend to her, becomes an absolute center, a place of peace and safety.

And then, too, there was the pleasure of community with other black moms, as we'd discuss the varying textures of our daughter's hair, their relative degrees of tender-headedness, and at what age, if ever, we'd let them straighten their hair. I never approached their level of expertise about any of it. But I knew, too, that they didn't regard me as clueless either. On one occasion, I even got a compliment on Cassie's twists and was asked how I did them. I proudly showed the mom, neglecting to mention that Annice had taught me how. But then, they had all learned from someone too.

THEORIZING ABOUT AND LIVING INSIDE

I learned something more than just how to do my daughter's hair. I had always imagined myself pretty savvy about "the intersections of race, power, beauty, and the body." I'd written articles critiquing the normalizing tyranny of Anglo-Saxon beauty norms; I had an enormous collection of slides, historical and contemporary, of hair-straightening products and skin lighteners. I knew all about historical practices like the brown bag test and the comb test, which were used to exclude darker-skinned and nappier-haired blacks from clubs and churches, and which are still employed, although rarely, in some black sororities today to limit membership to lighter-skinned women. I talked, in my classes, about contemporary court cases involving women who had been fired for wearing cornrows to work, and I showed slides of Sara Baartman—way before mention of her became politically obligatory in any discussion of race and the body. And so on.

It's one thing, however, to know about racist aesthetics and its history. It's another to have a black hairdresser recommend, in full earshot of your five-year-old daughter, that she should have her hair straightened. An issue that I had talked and written about was now something that I was living inside of. And living inside of it, it became far more complicated.

When it happened, Annice and I cast quick angry glances at each other. We were both aware of the fact that Cassie was already getting the same message from movies and television, where straight hair, straighter than I ever thought possible for *any*one to attain, now reigns absolutely. Every "transformation" on *The Swan* and *Extreme Makeover* includes a mandatory straightening for the black contestants. Late-night and early-morning infomercials for ceramic wands and miracle straightening lotions feature emotional before-and-afters of both black and white women with tousled and "natural" hairstyles miraculously transformed into sheets of sleek and shine. What's most incredible

The "miracle" of straight hair.

about these commercials is the women's reactions. They weep and speak of miserable lives redeemed, of dreams of beauty realized, of nothing short of deformity corrected, salvation achieved. Having straight hair has achieved a trans-racial beauty status almost as important as not being fat.

It pains me when Cassie tells me she hates her curls (as she calls them). But how could she not, when even Latifah—one of her idols—has hair like satin? In the doll world, there's been an explosion of "ethnic" and "urban" production and marketing, as dolls like the saucy and style-conscious Bratz have started to give Barbie a real run for her money (or rather, ours). But although some of these dolls have hair done in cornrows and braids, undo those dos and it's still the same old white-girl hair. Two exceptions are the high-fashion "urban hipster" Barbie (who has two enormous afro-puffs) and the "Treasures of Africa" Barbie—described in the FAO Schwartz catalogue as "richly drawn from an African model but completely defined by high couture," and sporting a dramatic Afro. These dolls are clearly an illustration of the principle that this culture mostly lets "difference" in by exoticizing it. These Barbies, not at all your everyday "American" girls, are the doll equivalent of the fashion world's inclusion of very dark-skinned models only when they are going for the drama, the "otherness" of their difference. (The black "American Girl" doll is a runaway slave girl).

At the same time as this has been going on, however, barely anyone—outside academia, that is—considers hair straightening to be a practice with troubling implications for racial identity and the preservation of historical memory. I look back on "Material Girl," an essay I wrote more than fifteen years ago that took issue with the diminishing of public consciousness of the politics of body practices such as surgical alteration of ethnic features, blue contact lenses, hair straightening, and so on (Bordo 1991), and realize that in the years that have passed since I wrote that essay, such consciousness has almost entirely disappeared. A current advertisement for African Pride hair products summarizes the prevailing attitude: "Some wear it straight. Some wear it natural. It all says pride to you." In other words, *what*ever.

In "Material Girl" I worried that obliterating such distinctions was also obliterating the memory of racist history and any awareness of continuing racial normalization. Today, however, I begin to wonder whether I am a relic of the sixties or an ivory tower academic who's grown out of touch with the culture. I am constantly aware, nowadays, not just of historical meaning and practices, but also of the contemporary reality of my daughter's life, within which some of her most powerful role models—Latifah, the Williams sisters, Lisa Leslie, Marion Jones—all have straight hair. Think of any highly public black female who doesn't—Whoopi or Toni Morrison, for example—and she's probably too old for my extremely athletic, aspiring-to-be-cool, six-year-old daughter to identify with. What are the implications of this for the future? I wonder. What extraordinary ethnic traditions may become lost? On the other hand, what would be the consequences of my challenging my daughter's identification with black women who are wonderful models of strength and creativity for her?

I also have become aware of the fact that my own former critique of hair straightening, being entirely "political" in nature, was in fact quite arrogantly oblivious to all the *practical* reasons why black people

straighten their hair. In my pre-Cassie days, like most clueless white people, I'd ooh and aah over the tousled hair of the children in Baby Gap ads. "How adorable!" I'd think—and I still do. I love Cassie with her hair loose and free—"flower petal billowy soft, full of frizz and fuzz," as bell hooks puts it in *Happy to Be Nappy* (1999, 3–4). But I also know that within a matter of days that delicious tousle will begin to lock and will become hell to comb through. Locks, once formed, can't be combed out; they have to be cut off (as that mom I talked about before discovered). So unless your child is old enough to choose locks, or you have enough time to devote an hour or so every morning to combing out her hair, or you have a personal hairdresser—that's how the adorable models manage it, of course—"natural" (unless very short) is not a very practical everyday style. You've got to "do it" in some way—even if it's just a pulled-back ponytail—or you can straighten it. When that hairdresser advised straightening Cassie's hair, it was, from her point of view, "to make things easier"—not to make Cassie look "more white."

The idea that straightening hair is about looking "more white" is an issue about which there is a great range of opinion among black Americans. Ayana Byrd and Lori Thorps, authors of *Hair Story,* emphasize that the quest for straight hair has never just been about "conforming to the prevailing fashions," but has been a recognition that "straight hair translated to economic opportunity and social advantage," both within slavery and after (2001, 17). Maxine Leeds Craig, in *Ain't I a Beauty Queen?* views the "social meaning" of hair straightening as about winning respect and respectability in a hostile environment by divesting the body of all signifiers of looseness, laziness, and hypersexuality (2002, 30–37). Poet Linda Hardnett, in a poem called "If Hair Makes Me Black, I Must Be Purple" (Ebong, ed., 2001, 80), protests the notion that straightening her hair is selling out her blackness:

> Yes, my hair is
> Straight
> But that don't mean that I ain't
> Black
> Nor proud
> All it means is that my hair is
> Straight.

On the other hand, numerous memoirs and poems recall, bitterly, the painful process of having "bad hair" normalized to white standards of beauty, as in Debraha Watson's "Good Hair" (Ebong, ed., 2001, 81):

> Early Sunday mornin' ritual
> I can hear Moma's voice saying
> Sit still girl
> Bend your head

> Unhunch them shoulders,
> So I can get to this kitchen
> Tight balled up hair
> Don'tcha want it to flow like dem white
> Girls
> My hair was stubborn
> It fought a hard battle against
> The straightening comb
> Defeated it uncoiled
> Fried into submission
> Burnt ears, sore scalp
> My cost for beauty . . .

Today, of course, methods of straightening are far gentler, and it's hardly only black women and girls that are making use of them. Just about every actress or model has straight hair—from Beyonce to the dramatically white (and formerly curly-headed) Nicole Kidman. "It's a girl's thing," as a commercial for hair conditioner makes explicit: "*My hair can shake. That's the number one girl thing.*" In line with this prescription, which doesn't displace racial meanings but powers up the gender differences that inflect those meanings, far fewer black men are straightening their hair nowadays than they did in the days when Malcolm X got his famous conk. The gender disparity is very clear in the world of black music video, a world populated by men with creatively individualized cornrows and braids, and virtually indistinguishable female sexpots with sinuous bodies and silken hair, both of which can do the "number one girl thing": shake. And it's also reproduced in the world of dolls: the only black doll in the Barbie line that has hair that truly looks and feels "natural" is a male—one of Malibu Ken's friends.

I often straighten my own hair nowadays—not chemically, but with a ceramic wand. When I was a young girl, Mary Travers and Judy Collins set the white-girl gold standard for the boys in my left-leaning crowd, and I was well aware that I was far from it: I had "big hair" (and even worse, red hair) at a time when it was aesthetically and politically incorrect for anyone except Angela Davis. I desperately envied my friends who, despite their Jewish genes, had long straight hair; and when I got to college, outside the purview of my mother (who probably wouldn't have cared anyway), I ironed my own hair in my dorm room. When Farrah Fawcett helped make a more layered, just-out-of-bed look fashionable, I finally had hair that did "naturally" what the culture wanted of it.

But the straight look, apparently, refuses to yield its cool hegemony over modernity. And nowadays it's even more difficult for most of us to achieve because it's both straight *and* layered, a bow to "the number one girl thing" (hair that swings from side to side) but "queered" by asymmetrical chunks (à la *The L-word*) or framing the face in descending lengths of absolutely wave-free, curl-free tiers. It's a style I can only achieve—just marginally, and only temporarily, until muggy weather makes it "go back"—with a lot of product and my *Chi* flat iron.

I feel younger and prettier when my hair is straightened—and troubled by the message I'm sending my daughter. It's not just the commercials and media images, of course, but also our own bodies, our own choices that are living, breathing advertisements to our children. I'm also aware of both how different and how alike the "hair piece" is for Cassie and me. Even with my thick hair, it's so much easier for me to switch back and forth between wild and straight, to treat these options as mere "fashion" choices. I get out of the shower. If I decide I want to go "natural" that day, I just spray a little foam, towel and don't comb my hair, and *voila,* it's fashionably messy (or at least relatively fashionably messy); it's nonetheless easy to brush out the next day. If I decide to go straight, it's at worst a half-hour with the ceramic wand. It will never be that way for Cassie; the choice to straighten or lock, go natural or braid, will always involve time, effort, and consequences that can't be turned around in one shower.

What Cassie and I share, however, although in the context of different racial histories, is the feeling of being "outside," peering at an ideal that seems to come effortlessly to those born with the genetic inheritance favored by "fashion." But no cultural ideal is ever "mere" fashion, as I've argued over and over in my work; all styles are laden with historical, cultural, political, and gendered meanings. When I was younger, I saw my hard-to-tame hair as "Jewish," and straight, swinging hair as among the many privileges of being Gentile. I may have been wrong about the actual genetics of hair (many Jews come by their straight hair naturally), but I wasn't wrong about the cultural associations and valuations. Cassie, too, *knows*—without historical knowledge, and perhaps in confused and fragmentary form—that straight hair is not "*just* fashion." I know she knows this because, despite her occasional wistful expressions of envy of straight hair, she insists on cornrows for herself. Living in a white family, with a WASP dad whose hair is naturally straight and a Jewish mom who uses a *Chi,* she nonetheless wants to look like L'il Romeo, not Hillary Duff—or Raven Simone. In this, I am convinced that in her inchoate, six-year-old way, Cassie is both resisting gender normalization and insisting on her racial identity.

THE LIMITS OF THEORY

When my white students read, in Maxine Leeds Craig's *Ain't I a Beauty Queen?* about the black woman student in the '60s—the first black woman to be accepted at her college—who was unable to fulfill the swimming requirement because to be in the swim class would mean to have to restraighten her hair several times a week, they are dumbstruck. The idea that concern about their hair would keep them out of the swimming pool is utterly foreign to them.

White people, even those who theorize with sophistication about "cultural difference" and the perils of ethnocentrism, are often clueless when it comes to the concrete, practical ways in which "race matters." We know little, for example, about the history of black aesthetics and its meaning within black communities. Poet Nikky Finney, in "To Be Beheld," her introduction to Bill Gaskins's book of photographs, *Good and Bad Hair* (1997), describes some of those meanings:

> We have adorned out heads from the beginning of time. It is ancient and black to crimp, coif, and curl in supreme celebration that part of ourselves that lives closest to the sun and other celestial bodies. That most high, most regal part of us has often been what we reach to elaborate on first when we have so much to say about who we are. We adorn

> this part of ourselves for ourselves mainly, but also for anybody else in the hemisphere needing the visual permission to create some audacious authenticity of style in their own life.
>
> We have tended to this particular body landscape that, consciously or not, holds the cultural jewels of an African sensibility that many have tried to tear from us. We have held on by way of different lengths of cultural memory we see as duty, as responsibility, as the children of genius and many a royal lot, to remember our contemporary lives back through our grandmother and great grandfather's bones. Yes, indeed, we remember ourselves through the ritual of doing and getting our hair done.
>
> Through the sweeping, stacking, locking, and soft methodical construction of our hair, we insist on being seen and we insist on proclaiming more of the knowledge of who we are that we never learned about in any school. This is but one way we catch history that boomerangs back to us and keeps our spirits free. Some of us adorn ourselves about the head more elaborately than others. Many of us have always been keen to differentiate our work-a-day hairdos from our festive world hairdos. Some of us in the tradition of ceremonial embellishing have needed to wait for specific occasions in order to attend to our hair, be it wedding, funeral, or Easter Sunday morning. But the more the world has tried (and succeeded on some levels) to alter the social and physical structure of our neighborhoods where we have not sat in the power seats, the more we bring our free, fancy, elaborate hairstyles to the primary shore of our everyday lives and the widest mosaic of American life, to say without question I will own the way I look. . . .
>
> I believe we have focused on and been obsessed with hair in order to keep our hands and sights on each other. I believe we stay in a groomed state with each other in order to remind ourselves of the language of touch as often as possible, in order to love on each other out loud, as the institutionalized racist world screams for us to turn on each other and keep spewing the hatred that way. At the very same time this world of barber and beauty shops—with names like *Amazon Hair Braiding, Africuts, Khimit Kinks, Brenda's Braids, The African Hair Gallery, Maxamillion* and *Ultimate U*—gives us physical place and spiritual permission to touch, to care, and to tend to each other, if only for a few pampering hours before we have to steel up our hearts again and head back out into that other world.

Today, editing this article after five days of watching footage of the ghastly aftermath of hurricane Katrina, I am reminded of the children who, amidst all the horror, had perfect cornrows. It is, as Nikky Finney says, an unbreakable practice of touching, caring, and tending—even in, *especially* in, a world that seems to be doing all it can to break you.

"The whole experience—the ritual of dealing with hair grooming—that's pleasurable. The sitting in, everyone remembers sitting in between some other woman's legs, having your hair brushed and braided. The feeling of knees on your cheek" (bell hooks). "Woman Combing Hair, Abidjan, Ivory Coast, 1980," Kent Reno.

African American hairstyling—the elegant and elaborate patterns of hip-hop, the ingenious twists, artfully interwoven extensions, sculpted and dramatically assembled locks, the myriad and infinitely individualizable combinations of rows and braids—is also about making high art with the body, in defiance of a culture for whom that body has been associated with everything untamed and primitive. "African American barbershops and hair salons," an article in the *New Yorker* says, "are hotbeds of anarchic and confident self-expression" (Thurman 2004, 144). So why, I wonder, do we never see this body-work discussed when white academics write about creative "body modification"—as for example, in Victoria Pitts's otherwise excellent *In the Flesh,* or Ted Polhemus and Randall Housk's book of text and photos, *The Customized Body* (1996)? Both these books deal extensively with the many ways—tattoos, piercings, scarification, head-shaving, and hair-sculpting—in which individuals and groups make use, as Pitts puts it, of "the body as a space needing to be reclaimed from culture" (2003, 7). Neither makes any mention of African American hairstyling.

Perhaps Pitts and Polhemus and Housk view contemporary black hairstyling as belonging to the realm of "fashion" rather than the "body as a space needing to be reclaimed from culture." If so, they have a lot to learn about the tangled roots, as Ayana Byrd and Lori Thorps call them, of black hair in America. The years of slavery, deprived of indigenous African implements and products for self care. The creative styles that evolved despite those harsh limitations. The racist politics of "good" and "bad" hair. The ongoing contest between "white" norms and reclamation of African styles. If this is all "just fashion," it is fashion that has developed in the context of ongoing struggle with a dominant culture, as it tries to carve out its own space within that culture.

Whatever the explanation, the fact is that despite their sophistication about cultural dynamics of "othering" and marginalization, both Pitts and Polhemus and Housk are in fact guilty of unconsciously reproducing those dynamics. Pitts is quite theoretically penetrating when she criticizes appropriations by "modern primitives" of tattoos, flesh hangings, and other tribal markings in order to "queer, blur, and unfix" Western identities. She reminds us that this subculture is composed almost entirely of white Westerners looking to "re-write" our bodies with culturally different, and—as we imagine them—freer identities. As Pitts points out, the "primitive others" whom we copy have no role other than for our white projections and consumption: "It is the white Westerner whose body appears as a blank canvas ready for self-inventive writing through various forms of consumerism. The bodies of non-Westerners, however, are not blank. Instead, they are already marked as 'exotic,' sensual, 'primitive' or traditional, and . . . read under a privileged Western gaze" (2003, 149).

"It is ancient and black to crimp, coif, and curl in supreme celebration that part of ourselves that lives closest to the sun and other celestial bodies" (Nikky Finney). Nineteenth-century drawing of Ethiopian women's hairstyle by Guglielmo Massaia; "Talk Shop," John Peden.

But Pitts herself—and Polhemus and Housk, too—seem to me to be guilty of precisely what she accuses the "modern primitives" of. The only difference is that in the landscape of contemporary body modification that they describe, it is American blacks rather than the "non-Western world" whose status as cultural, self-inventive, capable of appropriating their own histories, inventing dramatic and challenging new styles and statements out of them, is given no place.[1]

Would better theory have helped Polhemus and Housk and Pitts to see all that Nikky Finney sees in the hairstylings of African Americans? I don't think so. I don't think they needed better theory; I think they needed to be taken to a black hair salon. The equivalent of that, with respect to the cultural meaning of body shape, happened to me a couple of years ago. One of my public lectures that year was on the globalization of eating disorders, a phenomenon I had been charting for a decade. Among other examples in this talk, I brought up the case of Nigeria, which has recently seen a dramatic change in the incidence of eating problems, attributed by much of the U.S. media to a shift in beauty ideals. The story, as presented in the *New York Times* and paraphrased in my talk, was this:

> In Central Africa, traditional cultures have celebrated voluptuous women. "An African girl must have hips," says dress designer Frank Osodi. "We have hips. We have bums. We like flesh in Africa." For years, Nigeria had sent its local version of beautiful to the Miss World Competition, where the contestants did very poorly. Then a savvy entrepreneur went against local ideals and entered Agbani Darego, a light-skinned, hyper-skinny beauty. (He got his inspiration from M-Net, the South African network seen across Africa on satellite television, which broadcasts mostly American movies and television shows.) Agbani Darego won the Miss World Pageant, the first Black African to do so. And now Nigerian teenagers have begun to fast and exercise, trying to become "lepa"—a popular slang phrase for the thin "it" girls that are all the rage.

I gave this example at several campuses, where it was received without (verbalized) criticism. Western academics found it unobjectionable, I believe, because it acknowledged cultural "difference" in body ideals. I always got flack, during the 1980s and 90s, when I suggested that body image problems were not the exclusive province of white, overprivileged girls. Paranoia over "essentialism" and "universalizing," at the time, was a constant obstacle to people's seeing how culturally tenuous different aesthetic traditions are in a world of globally deployed images and an expanding technology of body alteration. People see the erosion of local aesthetics now—it's become just too obvious for them not to—although the acknowledgment of "difference" is still more warmly greeted than critiques of normalizing imagery. My point about Nigeria, acknowledging both the different traditions of black Africa and their erosion by Western aesthetics, didn't get anyone's dander up.

Then I gave the talk at a college whose audience included a Nigerian woman. She pointed out that Nigerian girls were dieting well before Agbani Darego won her crown, and that in her opinion, the trend was less about the allure of Western beauty ideals than about the rejection of traditional identities and the system of male dominance that they were anchored in. It was for men, she explained, that Nigerian women were encouraged to be full-bottomed, for men that they were often sent to fattening farms to be plumped into shape for the wedding night. Now modern young women were insisting on the right of their bodies to be less voluptuous, less domestically "engineered" for the sexual pleasure and comfort of men.

Hearing this was fascinating, illuminating, and a reminder that seeing something from the outside is bound to be partial vision at best. Paradoxically, though, what I hadn't seen was the *similarity* (rather than the "difference") between the young Nigerian dieters and the first generation of (twentieth-century) anorexics in this country. Many of them, like the young Nigerian women, were also in rebellion against a voluptuous, male-oriented, sexualized ideal—that of the post–World War II generation. Significant numbers of them had been sexually abused or had witnessed their mothers being treated badly. To be a soft sexual plaything, a Marilyn Monroe, was their horror; Kate Moss and others (like Agbani Darego for the young Nigerians) provided an alternative cultural paradigm to aspire to.

In "Feminism, Postmodernism, and Gender-Skepticism" (1990, 133–56) and other pieces, I've argued that instead of harassing and shaming each other for "essentialism" and the like, we ought to be putting our energies into practical transformations in our institutional and personal lives—transformations that would concretely (and not merely theoretically) enlarge the sphere of our knowledge of human culture and experience. Put simply, we need to spend less time "theorizing difference" and more time learning from and about the differences *and* similarities of each other's lives. That, however, is not so easy, perhaps especially not in academic communities. I was lucky to have a Nigerian scholar respond to my talk.[2] Unfortunately, academic communities are rarely diverse enough to allow for such interactions. And when they are, we're often too afraid of being seen as stupid, theoretically unsophisticated, or—worst of all—racist, to ask the questions we need to ask, or show the curiosity we naturally have about the worlds with which we're unfamiliar.

It's not surprising that people would hesitate to expose what they don't know, given the dogmatic, negative, and sometimes hostile position many theorists of "difference" have taken on the possibilities of the "dominant group's" understanding the "others." Ien Ang, for example, argues that "the subjective knowledge of what it means to be at the receiving end of racialized othering—whatever it means to individual people of color—is simply not accessible to white people" (1997, 60). She goes on to say that what this incommensurability of experience leaves us with, for the purposes of political affiliation, is what Jodi Dean has called "a solidarity of strangers," a solidarity that is "based on the statement 'I cannot know what it feels like to be racially abused, but I know that it hurts you.'" She proposes this "solidarity of strangers" as an alternative to the "solid, unified 'we'" that conventional politics, including feminist politics, used to imagine was possible.

Some of this seems right to me, and some of it doesn't. I want Ang's categories to be historicized and contextualized, for one thing, and for the concept of "white people" to be less homogenizing. I want to tell her that as a Jew, I certainly know what it's like to be on the receiving end of cultural othering, especially in the South, where I've lived for the last eleven years in an abiding, if not always acute, awareness that Christianity is the only real game in town. My daughter is already learning from the kids in the neighborhood that everyone who counts goes to church and that she's weird for not doing so. But it's also true that today, in this country, "othering" doesn't happen to me in the racialized way that it still does, routinely, for black people. The same, however, could not be said for my ancestors, including my mother, whose family escaped from a virulently anti-Semitic Poland before the death camps were instituted.

I'm not black and never will be. But what I *am* is not so easily "theorized"—and not only because of the hybridity of identity, which for me includes my Jewishness, a working-class background, and numerous other specifics that make my "whiteness" particular rather than generic (something that is true for all "white" people)—but also because I am now a member of a multiracial family, which, although nonbiological, has altered every molecule of my being. In connection with this experience, Ang's seeming denial that there can be inter-racial affiliations and from there, understandings, that go deeper than respectful acknowledgment of each other's differences both infuriates and saddens me. Surely, there are other possibilities beyond a "solid, unified 'we'" at one extreme and a "solidarity of strangers" at the other. The former—the "unified we"—is, of course, a myth—and, I would think, by now a dead horse among academics. But the latter strikes me as no less abstract, almost willfully obtuse, and utterly oblivious to the concrete realities of mixed race intimacy in this culture.

The epistemological power of loving, so far, hasn't been dealt with very well by academic theories of "difference." I do not know how it feels to be black, no, in the sense that I cannot step inside the subjectivity of a black person in this culture. But I could not step inside the subjectivity of my mother either. I heard stories, of course. I know that when she was a very little girl, she was dragged through the dirt by a pig that clamped on to her hand, smelling the porridge that had been cooling on the windowsill of their cottage and into which my mother had dipped her eager fingers. I could almost picture that scene; my mother's hand still had the scar. But other, more profound experiences were not even described to me. My knowledge of history tells me that her family had to have been affected by the pogroms that massacred thousands of Jews in Russia and Eastern Europe, but she never said a word. Nor did she tell me anything about her ocean-crossing and arrival in America. I can only imagine what it must have been like to be eight years old, headed for Ellis Island, bewildered and afraid in the hot, crowded, vermin-ridden quarters of steerage. But as incomplete and inadequate as my knowledge of my mother's life was, it cannot be compared to that of a stranger's life. We were intimates. I knew her everyday habits, the phobias and physical symptoms that visited her throughout her life, her cooking—an odd mixture of Eastern-European expertise and American convenience—the way she put on her makeup, the way she smoked her cigarettes, the way she told a joke. I knew the things that pleased her. I knew what her body felt like, as I leaned against her as we watched soap operas together.

To the degree that we have or develop or strive for this kind of intimacy with others, whether or not they are biologically related to us, the phrase "solidarity of strangers" rings cold and utterly inadequate. Cassie is black and I am white, but she is far from a stranger to me—indeed, she is the most beloved person in my life—and my relationship with her has created contexts that I didn't have before for relations of beloved intimacy with other black people, and indeed, with "blackness" itself in this culture. There is a line in Nikky Finney's piece: "The heart of loving myself always had to do with loving my Blackness." It's impossible for me to know exactly how I would have responded to this line before Cassie. I suspect, however, that it might have seemed dull and perhaps clichéd when compared to the arresting and poetic imagery of the rest of her piece. I do know that now, as a mother who wants more than anything for her daughter to grow up loving herself, I cannot read it without a wild surge of joy and hope.

COOL

The first time Cassie had her hair put in cornrows—something she had been requesting for quite a while—I took her to the local beauty school. It hurt terribly, and she could only bear it by pressing my head tightly against her the whole time. I'm sure we were a sight—my middle-aged butt sticking up in the air, interfering with beauty-school traffic, as Cassie pulled my head down to her chest. But the pain was worth it to her because she could emerge looking the way she wanted to: in a word, cool. After it was done, she swaggered down the street, so proud of herself that sunbeams seemed to be bouncing off her smile. Every day, as I watch her put together her own version of hip-hop styling, her own blend of tough and tender, I am reminded of Nikky Finney's words, "that no matter what, the circle will never be broken, that every generation will twist and turn the old ways into their own ways, and the next ones of us will step closer to the edge and nudge their locks higher toward the sun, but together we will never fall off or away from each other" (Gaskins 1997).

Cassie's cornrows, it is true, have interfered with the intimacy of our weekly routine, since I haven't learned to do them yet, but she has become miraculously less "tender-headed" now that I take her to Shamara's home rather than to the beauty school. The arrangement is better for all of us. The beauty school, at which Shamara was a student, didn't pay her one cent for her beautiful work. Yet she often stayed overtime to finish Cassie's hair. She rarely got the chance to do braids, she said,

Entire book cover from *It's All Good Hair: The Guide to Styling and Grooming Black Children's Hair* by Michele N-K Collison. Reprinted by permission of HarperCollins Publishers.

with so many black clients straightening their hair, and she loved doing them. As for Cassie, at the beauty school there was nothing to distract her. Now, as she sits on the floor, playing the Spiderman play station game with Shamara's son Antonio, she doesn't complain at all. I'm happy, too. Tajdzha, Shamara's daughter, has taken a liking to me and sits on my lap, bringing back Cassie's delicious baby days to me. Cassie isn't a baby anymore; now I'm going to have to develop much more elaborate skills to satisfy her tastes in hair.

So far, I haven't even tried. I'm afraid to—afraid of frustration, of failing. Watching Shamara, I can see how much dexterity it takes. Feeling inadequate and very white, I comfort myself with an article that we're reading in a class of mine. Called "The Art of the Ponytail," it's written by a young "third-wave" feminist who's given up both straightening and styling in favor of simply pulling her hair back in a ponytail. While conceding that "the time and attention some [African Americans] devote to their hair is a form of pride, a product of their creativity," Akkida McDowell nonetheless insists on the right of her ponytail to signify her own "casual nature." "Given the wide range of black people throughout the world," she writes, "we need to expand the boundaries of acceptance. Blackness is not (and should not be) defined totally by a hairstyle. I believe there is room for all our expressions," including the rejection of "the black beauty pageant" (1998, 130, 132). McDowell's piece, along with contemporary singer/songwriter India Aries's insistence, in her popular song, that "I Am Not My Hair," reminds me, not just that you don't have to be white to find black hairstyling challenging, but also that there are generational as well as racial and class meanings in our aesthetic styles, in what we choose and refuse to do with our bodies. Cassie, an extraordinarily active and sports-minded child, who prefers the ease of boy clothes to girlie fashions, may ultimately reject both cornrows and straight hair in favor of a very short style that requires little tending at all. The "differences" that emerge between Cassie and me—as well as the shared meanings and experiences—are unpredictable and will only be discovered through our life together.

The other night, Annice offered to help me take Cassie's cornrows out. I usually do this a week or so before she has them restyled and do her hair myself—or Annice will do it—in the interim. It's a long process. I was grateful for the help, and we've always had fun sharing my daughter's care together. Now, as many times before, we sit on the couch on either side of her, Sponge Bob on the television, and begin unbraiding. Halfway through I realize that I'm feeling oddly competitive. When Cassie yelps, I want it to be Annice's touch she's flinching at. I want to get more of Cassie's head done faster and with fewer tangles left than Annice. I reject a suggestion of Annice's to put Cassie's hair temporarily in a single braid, asserting my superior knowledge of what it will be like to deal with in the morning. I want to "win" in what has suddenly become a contest in my mind. I'm feeling a bit embarrassed by my proprietary feelings and actions, but Annice takes it all good-humoredly. Perhaps—or so I fancy—she's even pleased. At the beginning I had been so tentative, so respectful of my daughter as a separate individual who, by the most extraordinary grace of the universe, had been placed in my arms that I barely felt I had any "rights" at all. I know Annice has taken pleasure in watching me, since then, truly become Cassie's mom.

The next evening I finish braiding Cassie's hair myself. She and I have just taken a shower, and had each other in stitches trading songs as we soaped up our hair. "Stop singing that sixties stuff!" she screams when I offer, in my turn, Crosby, Stills, Nash, and Young's "Teach Your Children Well." When it's her turn, she tries to gross me out with made-up songs featuring extremities being cut off, butts, and farts. After we've slathered tons of lotion on our bodies (something we both need, dry skin being a tendency blacks and fair-skinned redheads share) and she's put on her Sponge-Bob bathrobe, we sit down to do the hair.

"Ow! You're hurting me!"

"Come on, it's not that bad. It hurts you much more when Shamara puts the cornrows in, and you never complain to her."

"No! It doesn't hurt when she does it! It only hurts when you do it!"

Now her lower lip is out, far out, and she's glowering at me. No one glowers like Cassie. But I'm not perturbed. It's my job and joy to keep my "hands and sights" on her, and I've been doing this for a long time by now. I know when I've hit a snag, and I know when she's just tired of sitting there. I know that I actually rarely hurt her and that she's just had a very long day and her body is longing to be set free to jump on the couch, play with the dog. I know that even if it hurts a little, it's got to get done. And I know, too, that whoever does her hair, I am the one whose touch she knows best, whose body she can fall asleep against.

NOTES

A version of this paper, entitled "The Trouble With 'Difference,'" was originally presented as a slide-illustrated talk in April 2005 at Grinnell College; I thank the students and faculty who responded so warmly to it at that time. "Cassie's Hair" was then the title of a short version that I was developing. When, without knowing about the short piece, Sandra Bartky said to me, "I wish you'd just call this piece 'Cassie's Hair,'" I realized that's what it was destined to be. My special gratitude to Janet Eldred, Kathi Kern, Binnie Klein, Ellen Rosenman, Paul Taylor, and Althea Webb for extremely helpful comments on earlier drafts of the written version; to Nell Painter for our e-mail conversations about race and beauty and for suggesting the (perfect) title for the last section of the paper; and to "Annice"—for everything.

1. In this context, it's striking that in the chapter on hair in Polhemus and Housk, the only photos of blacks are of cute twins with short "locks" and an older man with dyed blond hair. It's as though for Polhemus and Housk, as well as for Pitts, white people *own* postmodern practices of bodily self-definition. Black bodily styles can only be imagined either as the stuff out of which white people do that fashioning—as when *we* copy ancient African practices—or as what we think of as contemporary "primitive" forms—like locks—or as revealing aspirations to be like us (e.g., the old man who goes blond).

2. I have tried without success to find out the name of the person whose comments on Nigeria were so illuminating. I hope that the publication of this essay will allow her to identify herself so that I can adequately acknowledge my gratitude to her in future publications and talks.

REFERENCES

Ang, Ien. 1997. "Comment on Felski's 'The Doxa of Difference': The Uses of Incommensurability." *Signs* (Autumn): 57–64.

Bordo, Susan. 1990. "Feminism, Postmodernism, and Gender-Skepticism." In *Feminism/Postmodernism*, ed. Linda Nicholson, 133–56. New York: Routledge.

———. 1991. "Material Girl: The Effacements of Postmodern Culture." In *The Female Body: Figures, Styles, Speculations*, ed. Laurence Goldstein, 106–30. Ann Arbor: University of Michigan Press.

Byrd, Ayana, and Lori Thorps. 2001. *Hair Story: Untangling the Roots of Black Hair in America*. New York: St. Martin's.

Craig, Maxine Leeds. 2002. *Ain't I a Beauty Queen? Black Women, Beauty, and the Politics of Race*. Oxford: Oxford University Press.

Ebong, Ima, ed. 2001. *Black Hair*. New York: Universe.

Finney, Nicky. 1997. "To Be Beheld." Introduction to Bill Gaskins, *Good and Bad Hair: Photographs*. Newark, N.J.: Rutgers University Press.

Gates, Henry Louis. 1994. *Colored People*. New York: Vintage.

hooks, bell. 1999. *Happy to Be Nappy*. New York: Hyperion.

McDowell, Akkida. 1998. "The Art of the Ponytail." In *Body Outlaws,* ed. Ophelia Edut, 124–32. Berkeley: Seal.

Pitts, Victoria. 2003. *In the Flesh: The Cultural Politics of Body Modification.* New York: Palgrave Macmillan.

Polhemus, Ted, and Randall Housk. 1996. *The Customized Body.* London: Serpent's Tale.

Thurman, Judith. 2004. "Roots." *New Yorker,* 15 March, 143–46.

CONTRIBUTORS

Stacy Alaimo is Associate Professor of English at the University of Texas at Arlington, where she teaches courses in feminist theory, multicultural American literatures, environmental humanities, and cultural studies. She is author of *Undomesticated Ground: Recasting Nature as Feminist Space*. She has published articles in *Feminist Studies, camera obscura, Studies in American Fiction, ISLE, MELUS,* and other journals. She is currently completing a book entitled *Bodily Natures: Environmental Health, Environmental Justice, and Material Ethics.*

Karen Barad is Professor of Feminist Studies, Philosophy, and History of Consciousness at the University of California at Santa Cruz. She has a doctorate in theoretical particle physics. Her research in physics and philosophy has been supported by the National Science Foundation, the Ford Foundation, the Hughes Foundation, the Irvine Foundation, the Mellon Foundation, and the National Endowment for the Humanities. She is the author of *Meeting the Universe Halfway: Quantum Physics and the Entanglement of Matter and Meaning* and numerous articles on physics, philosophy of science, cultural studies of science, and feminist theory.

Susan Bordo holds the Otis A. Singletary Endowed Chair in the Humanities and is Professor of English and Gender Studies at the University of Kentucky. She is author of *Unbearable Weight: Feminism, Western Culture and the Body; The Male Body: A New Look at Men in Public and in Private;* and other influential books and articles. She is currently writing a novel. She apologizes to Cassie, who is now eight years old, for the references to lap-sitting and other "baby" behavior. Cassie was five when this essay was written.

Suzanne Bost is Associate Professor of English at Southern Methodist University, specializing in Chicana/o Literature and Feminist Theory. She is the author of *Mulattas and Mestizas: Representing Mixed Identities in the Americas, 1850–2000.* She has also published articles in *Aztlán, Mississippi Quarterly, Nepantla, Postmodern Culture, MELUS,* and *African American Review.* Her new book project, "*Encarnación:* Illness and Body Politics in Chicana Feminist Literature," analyzes the function of pain, illness, and disability in the works of Gloria Anzaldúa, Cherríe Moraga, and Ana Castillo.

Claire Colebrook is Professor of English Literature at the University of Edinburgh. She is author of *New Literary Histories; Ethics and Representation; Gilles Deleuze; Understanding Deleuze; Irony in the Work of Philosophy; Irony; Gender;* and *Deleuze: A Guide for the Perplexed.*

Elizabeth Grosz teaches in the Women's and Gender Studies Department at Rutgers University. She is author, most recently, of *The Nick of Time: Politics, Evolution and the Untimely* and *Time Travels: Feminism, Nature, Power.*

Michael Hames-García is Director of the Ethnic Studies Program and of the Center for Race, Ethnicity, and Sexuality Studies (CRESS) at the University of Oregon. He is author of *Fugitive Thought: Prison Movements, Race, and the Meaning of Justice* and co-editor of two books, *Reclaiming Identity: Realist Theory and the Predicament of Postmodernism* and *Identity Politics Reconsidered.* His current research focuses on the multiplicity of race, sexuality, and gender in cultural politics.

Donna J. Haraway is the author of numerous books and articles on science, technology, gender, and race, including *Modest_Witness@Second_Millennium.FemaleMan©_Meets_OncoMouse™: Feminism and Technoscience,* which received the 1999 Ludwig Fleck prize of the Society for Social Studies of Science. Her other books include *The Companion*

Species Manifesto: Dogs, People, and Significant Otherness; Simians, Cyborgs, and Women: The Re-Invention of Nature; Primate Visions: Gender, Race, and Nature in the World of Modern Science; and *Crystals, Fabrics, and Fields: Metaphors that Shape Embryos.* In 2000, Haraway received the J. D. Bernal Prize for outstanding contributions to the field of science and technology studies. She is currently working on a book called *When Species Meet.* She teaches in the Department of History of Consciousness at the University of California, Santa Cruz.

Susan Hekman is Professor of Political Science and Director of Graduate Humanities at the University of Texas at Arlington. She has published books on the methodology of the social sciences and feminist theory, including most recently *The Future of Differences* and *Private Selves, Public Identities.* She is currently working on a book called *The Material of Knowledge.*

Vicki Kirby is Senior Lecturer in the School of Social Sciences and International Studies at the University of New South Wales. She is author of *Telling Flesh: The Substance of the Corporeal* and *Judith Butler: Live Theory.* Her current book project, *Quantum Anthropologies,* considers the relevance of Derrida's work for posthumanism and system theories. She has recently been awarded an Australian Research Council Discovery Grant to investigate the linguistic turn in the life sciences.

Catriona (Cate) Mortimer-Sandilands is Canada Research Chair in Sustainability and Culture in the Faculty of Environmental Studies at York University. She is author of *The Good-Natured Feminist: Ecofeminism and the Quest for Democracy,* co-editor (with Melody Hessing and Rebecca Raglon) of *This Elusive Land: Women and the Canadian Environment,* and is currently completing a manuscript on sexual and environmental politics entitled *Pastoral Traditions, Sexual Subversions: A Lesbian History of Nature Writing.*

Tobin Siebers is V. L. Parrington Collegiate Professor and director of Comparative Literature at the University of Michigan. Among his major publications are *The Ethics of Criticism; The Subject and Other*

Subjects: On Ethical, Aesthetic, and Political Identity; and *Among Men.* He is also editor of *The Body Aesthetic: From Fine Art to Body Modification.* He has published essays on disability in *American Literary History, Cultural Critique, Literature and Medicine, Michigan Quarterly Review, PMLA,* and the MLA volume on disability studies. He is currently completing two books, *Disability Theory* and *Disability Aesthetics.*

Nancy Tuana is the DuPont/Class of 1949 Professor of Philosophy, Science, Technology, and Society, and Women's Studies and director of the Rock Ethics Institute at the Pennsylvania State University. Her books include *Engendering Rationalities: Feminism and Science; The Less Noble Sex: Scientific, Religious, and Philosophical Conceptions of Woman's Nature; Revealing Male Bodies; Race and the Epistemologies of Ignorance;* and *Women and the History of Philosophy.* She is editor of the Penn State Press series ReReading the Canon, and co-editor of Stanford Encyclopedia's entries on feminist philosophy.

Elizabeth A. Wilson is an Australian Research Council fellow in the Women's and Gender Studies Program at the University of New South Wales. She is author of *Psychosomatic: Feminism and the Neurological Body.* The essay in this collection is part of a project on depression.

Index

Page numbers in italics refer to illustrations.

Abram, David, 267–270, 273, 274, 283, 286n3
African-American hairstyling, 412–413, *414*
agency, 135, 148n7, 152n34, 325; distributed, 226, 230, 231, 233; human, 196, 197, 222–223; material, 5, 93–94, 142–144, 191, 194, 196, 197, 244–250, 253; of the natural, 188, 210
agential realism, 103–104, 105–106, 130, 133–134, 138–142, 144, 145–146, 151n26, 210n6, 248, 324–325, 327
AIDS, 342–347, 354, 358–359; quilt, 365, 367
Alaimo, Stacy, 4, 14
Alarcón, Norma, 349–350
Alcoff, Linda, 90, 96–98, 296
Allen, Barbara, 199
alphabetic technologies, 268–269, 273, 283
Althusser, Louis, 82n1, 181
Alzheimer's Disease, 271–272, 273–275, 276, 282–283
American Disabilities Act (ADA), 291, 292, 293, 304n1
Ang, Ien, 417
animal, animals, 160, 162, 165, 175–180
animal-industrial complex, 177, 178
animism, 269
antidepressants, 16, 373–374, 375, 377, 379–380, 382, 385, 387, 389, 390n1, 393n10; bioavailability of, 392n7
Antony, Louise, 90
Anzaldúa, Gloria, 340, 341–342, 345, 346, 347, 348, 349–353, 361, 368n5, 369n6, 370n13; online memorial for, 362–366, *367*
apparatus, 134, 137, 138, 140, 141
Aries, India, 421
Aronson, Joshua, and Claude Steel, 322
Aronson, Joshua, Steven J. Spencer, and Claude Steele, 326
assemblage, 79, 100
Austin, Mary, 240

Baldus, David, Charles Pulaski, and George Woodworth, 321
Barad, Karen, 6, 8, 11–12, 88, 102–106, 109, 210n6, 234n7, 248–249, 250, 324–325
Beltrán, Gonzalo Aguirre, 346
Bergson, Henri, 53, 54–55, 58–59, 79–80
Bernstein, Richard, 90
Bérubé, Michael, 208
Bigwood, Carol, 285n1
biochemistry, 258, 373, 390
biological determinism, 12, 241
biology, 23–24, 162–163, 179, 182, 219; deconstruction of, 378, 391n4; and feminism, 374, 390; and gender, 65, 69, 107; and politics, 377–379; queer, 241; and psychology, 386–387; and race, 313, 324, 333n6
Birke, Lynda, 241, 245
Blackwell, Antoinette Brown, 240
blood-brain barrier, 380–381, 383–385, 387
body, 54–55, 58, 59; and aesthetics, 405, 407, 409, 412–413; in Cartesianism, 216–217, 220–221; as conflated with woman, 215; disabled, 249–250, 296, 301; discourse of, 101, 106–107, 237–238; feminist considerations of, 90; and illness, 342–347, 356, 360–361; and

body (*continued*)
intra-activity, 141, 142; in landscapes, 283, 285n1; materiality of 1, 3–4, 15, 67–68, 127–128, 324; openness of, 255; pharmacokinetic models of, 382; in relation to memory, 281–282; relations among, 79; and sexual differences, 71; as site of perception, 267, 268, 270; toxic, 14, 260–262; viscous porosity of, 201–202
Bohr, Niels, 131–133, 137–138, 146, 150nn18,21, 325
Bordo, Susan, 16, 90, 243
Bost, Suzanne, 15–16
Braidotti, Rosi, 369n7
Breggin, Peter, 393n10
Brown, Wendy, 310–312, 315–316, 317, 329, 332n3, 333n4, 341, 360
Butler, Judith, 3, 65, 67–73, 80, 90, 104–105, 106, 115, 123–124, 126–127, 151nn26,31, 218–220, 221, 228, 229, 233, 246–247, 344, 359, 366
Byrd, Ayana, and Lori Thorps, 407, 413

Cantor, Charles, 171–172
Castells, Manuel, 316–318, 320, 321, 330, 334n15
Castillo, Ana, 369n9
Cartesianism, 125, 126, 131, 215, 216–217, 220–221, 230
Chicano nationalism, 340, 351; Aztec medicine as part of, 346–347
class, classism, 309–310, 313
Clough, Sharyn, 108
Coatlicue, *348*, 349, 350, 355
Code, Lorraine, 89, 192, 210
Colebrooke, Claire, 10–11, 107
Collison, Michele N-K, *420*
companion species, 167
compulsory heterosexuality, 161, 162
Conley, Verena Andermatt, 17n2
Connolly, Ward, 308
constructivism, 142–143, 151n26, 171, 172, 191. *See also* social construction, social constructionism
corporeal, corporeality, 238, 240, 244, 255–256, 259, 261, 342–343, 346, 349. *See also* trans-corporeality
Coyolxauhqui, 355
Craig, Maxine Leeds, 407, 410
cultural constructionism, 218, 224, 227. *See also* constructivism; social construction, social constructionism
cultural studies, 168, 237, 242; feminist, 243–244
cyborg, 85–86, 243–244, 257, 262n3

Davidson, Donald, 97, 108
Darwin, Charles, 10, 24, 169. *See also* Darwinism
Darwinism, 25–50, 74; and feminism, 39–46; natural selection in, 32–34, 36–38, 44, 47nn3,7, 48nn10,12, 73; and racial difference, 34–36, 44–45, 47n9; and sexual difference, 44–45, 49n16, 71, 73; and sexual selection, 33–38, 44–45, 47n7, 73; social, 47n7. *See also* Darwin, Charles
Davis, Lennard, 343
Dawkins, Richard, 49n13
Deen, Jodi, 417
Delaney, Samuel, 298, 299, 305n10
Deleuze, Gilles, 3, 52, 55–56, 100; on art, 77–78; on monism, 64, 75, 80
Deleuze, Gilles, and Felix Guattari, 76; on art, 81; on Becoming-Woman, 78, 81
Dennett, Daniel, 36, 39, 48n11, 49n13, 54, 74–75
Derrida, Jacques, 55, 219, 256; and *différance,* 224
deterritorialization, 78–79, 81
Dewey, John, 210n5
diabetes, 349–350, 352, 353, 365–366. *See also* illness
diffraction, 122, 147n3, 150n21
disability, 250, 329–330, 359–361; discrimination, 292–295, 298–299, 304; experience, 293, 297, 299; law, 298, 367; people with, 291–304, 305n10, 343; and reproductive health, 300; and sexual practice, 298–303, 305n11
disability studies, 10, 15, 249–250, 330, 343, 359, 360
disclosure, 110–112
discourse, discursive, 1–2, 3–4, 86–87, 100–102, 103, 136–140, 151nn25,26; as interacting with the material, 7, 104–105; as model of subjectivity, 246
Duncan, Goswell, 302
Dworkin, A., and R. Dworkin, 296
dysthymia, 381, 382–383, 389–390, 391n5

ecofeminism, 4, 46n1
ecology, 17n2, 246
ecopoetics, 270

embodiment, 53, 163, 190, 286n4, 349–350, 353
emergence, 52–53
emergent interplay, 189, 196
Eng, David L., and David Kazanjian, 370n12
entanglement, 223, 253
environment, environmentalism, 9, 14, 17, 173, 191, 238, 255, 258, 261, 262; politics of, 8–9; science and, 8
environmental health, 239, 255
environmental justice, 9, 10, 239
environmental philosophy, 14–15, 237, 244, 245, 251, 267, 268, 283
epistemic responsibility, 192, 196, 204, 210
epistemological sadomasochism, 163
epistemology, 2, 5, 89–90, 96, 97–98, 108, 122, 222, 238, 251, 252, 261; feminist, 90, 251; of ignorance, 204; of love, 418
essentialism, 4, 12, 28, 237, 239, 240, 241, 243, 416; anti-, 14, 17n1; biological, 179, 209, 373
ethics, 7–8; environmental, 245–246, 249, 256, 268, 269; of care, 360, 369n8
Eurocentrism, 318, 319, 322, 331
evolution, 25, 28–34, 38–41, 42–43, 45, 46n3, 53, 54, 55

feminism: Chicana, 15–16, 341, 342, 343, 347, 361–362, 364, 368, 369n6; corporeal, 18n3, 242; environmental, 4, 18n3, 237, 242, 251; Marxist, 18n3; material, 7–10, 12, 15, 17, 190, 243–244; multicultural, 173; postmodern, 18n3, 237
feminist social studies of science, 95
Finney, Nikky, 410–411, 414, 419
Fitz Simmons, Margaret, and David Goodman, 254–255
Foucault, Michel, 41, 60, 65–66, 104, 111, 113–114, 123; on bio-power, 66, 101; considerations of the body in, 127–128, on discursive practice, 100–101, 137, 151n25; heterotopia in, 303–304, on power, 231
Freud, Sigmund, 27–28; and *nachträglichkeit* (deferred action), 224; and transference, 388–389

Gardiner, Judith Keagan, 373, 374
Gatens, Moira, 106–107, 114, 253, 255, 256
Gates, Henry Louis, 401
genetic engineering, 170, 178, 239
globalization, 316, 318
Gomez, Gary, 205
González, Deena, 341
Gould, Stephen Jay, 47n5, 322–323
Gowaty, Patricia Adair, 25–26
Graves, Joseph L., Jr., 323
Griggers, Camilla, 374–376
Grosz, Elizabeth, 10, 71, 73–75, 80, 106

Hacking, Ian, 90, 124, 125
Hall, Lynda, 349
Hames-García, Michael, 15
Haraway, Donna, 4, 5, 12–13, 85–87, 102, 126, 147nn1,3, 251
Harding, Sandra, 5, 89, 179
Hardnett, Linda, 407
Hearne, Vicki, 165
Hegel, Georg Wilhelm Friedrich, 61–62, 69–70
Heidegger, Martin, 111
Hekman, Susan, 11, 368n4
Hennessey, Rosemary, 128
Herring, Cedric, and Verna Keith, 325–326
Hird, Myra J., 241
Hogan, Linda, 252
Holmes, Oliver Wendell, 298–299
hooks, bell, 406, 412
Housk, Randall, and Ted Polhemus, 413–414, 423n1
Human Genome Project, 158, 171–172
Hume, David, 69
Husserl, Edmund, 53–54, 55

identity, 216–217, 220–221, 230, 233–234, 296, 332n3, 344, 347; Chicana/o, 350–352, 361–362; *mestiza,* 349, 370n13; minority, 296–297, 298, 305n6, 330; politics of, 309–312, 314, 340–341, 342, 360; Project, 15, 317–318, 320, 328–332; racial, 15, 308–310, 313, 318, 327, 330–332
illness, 342–343, 345–346, 348, 350, 353, 359, 360; chronic, 250; mental, 377
incorporation, 254–255
interactionism, 191–192, 209–210, 210n5
intra-action, intra-activity, 104, 105–106, 109, 111, 133, 134–135, 138–141, 143–144, 146, 224, 248, 250, 261, 324–327, 331
Irigaray, Luce, 44, 49n16, 285n2

Katrina, Hurricane, 13, 188, 189, 190, 192–193, 194–195, 196–198, 203–209; and poverty, 205, 207–208; and disability, 207–208
Kaysen, Susanna, 374, 375
Keller, Evelyn Fox, 47n6, 394n11
Kirby, Vicki, 13, 68, 146, 255–256
Kitzinger, Celia, 377
Kramer, Peter, 385–386
Kuhn, Thomas, 91

Laing, R. D., 374
landscape, 14, 270, 277, 280–282, 283, 285n1
language, 1, 2, 52, 56, 59, 60, 64, 66, 68, 70, 72, 73, 76–77, 92, 98–99, 114–115, 120–121, 123, 131, 152n31, 216, 218–220, 224, 228–229; literary, 75–76
Laqueur, Thomas, 59–60
Latour, Bruno, 6, 87–88, 91, 92–93, 225–228, 229–234; on actor-network theory (ANT), 225–226, 235n9; on hybrid, 231–232; on quasi-objects, 225–226
Lauretis, Teresa de, 17, 242
LeGuin, Ursula, 160
linquistic turn, 1–2, 6, 87, 88, 92, 97, 98, 99, 109, 110, 214, 218, 242, 243, 244
Longino, Helen, 89
Lyotard, Jean-François, 294

Mairs, Nancy, 299–301, 360
Mann, Coramae Richey, 321
Manning, Lynn, 328–330
Margulis, Lynn, and Dorion Sagan, 182–184
Markowitz, Gerald, and David Rosner, 199, 211n13
Marxism, 60–64, 173, 175
Massaia, Guglielmo, *414*
materiality, 1–9, 244; and discourse, 52, 86–87, 88, 103, 104–105, 120, 138–140, 143, 151n26; of the human body, 127–128, 217, 220–221, 261, 324; and illness, 342–343, 348; and race, 321, 325, 331
material-discursive, 4, 106, 128, 134, 135, 140–141, 143–144, 248
materialism, 63, 65, 72; Cartesian, 57; dialectical, 11, 61–62; feminist, 56, 64; Marxist, 62–63; new, 17n3; nondialectical, 69, 70
material-semiotic interaction, 190, 191, 195–196, 199, 202–203, 249
material turn, 6–7, 243, 244
matter: Aristotelian conceptions of, 56–57; Cartesian conceptions of, 56–57; Marxist conceptions of, 61, 62, 63–64; performativity of, 70–71, 72, 378
McDowell, Akkida, 421
McKay, Don, 286n3
McWhorter, Ladelle, 247–248, 254–255, 256
mediation, 173–174
memory, 271–275, 279, 280–282, 283, 284, 286n6
Merchant, Carolyn, 245–246, 257
Merleau-Ponty, Maurice, 267, 285n2, 286n3
metaphysics, 55, 149n14; ancient, 59; Aristotelian, 58; atomistic, 130–131, 149n16; Platonic, 57–58
Metzl, Jonathan, 376–377
Michaels, Walter Benn, 312–314, 315–316, 317, 333n9
Millet, Kate, 376
Mills, Charles, 204
Mitchison, Naomi, 180–182, 184
modernism, 6, 91
Mohanty, Satya, 330
Moraga, Cherrie, 15–16, 340, 341–342, 345, 346, 347, 348, 353–359, 361, 362, 367–368, 368n4
Morris, David, 368n2
Morrison, Toni, 315
Mortimer-Sandilands, Catriona, 14–15. *See also* Sandilands, Catriona

nature, 12–13, 43–44, 73–74, 80, 142–143, 162, 173–174, 227–229, 230, 232–234, 238; as agentic, 4–5, 7, 145, 244–246, 254; Cartesian conceptions of, 217; as cultural construction, 218; in feminism, 23–24, 46n1, 237, 240–241; as other, 157–159; as performative, 146; politics of, 9; in science and technology, 110, 167–168, 171, 178, 196; and woman, 13, 215, 234, 239–240
Nelson, Lynne Hankinson, 89, 102
network society, 316, 317
Nietzsche, Friedrich, 121
Nigeria, 415–416
Noske, Barbara, 174–180, 186n7

OncoMouse™, 202
Onto-epistem-ology, 103, 111, 147, 249
ontology, 5, 86, 93, 95, 97–98, 103, 109–110, 111, 121, 122, 123, 151n26, 248–249, 267, 268, 378; interactionist, 188, 189–190, 209; social, 112–114
Orr, Deborah, 115

Peden, John, *414*
Peirce, Charles Sanders, 219
performativity, 68–71, 72–73, 94, 104, 121–122, 126, 147n2, 148nn7,8, 248, 378; posthumanist, 11, 104, 129, 132, 145–146, 148n6
pharmacokinetics, 379–381, 382
phenomenon, phenomena, 132, 133, 135, 137, 138, 141, 143, 191, 193, 222, 324–325, 326, 327
phenomenology, 268, 271, 275; eco-phenomenology, environmental phenomenology, 14, 268, 269–270, 271, 285n1
philosophy of science, 92–95; feminist, 89
Pickering, Andrew, 93–95, 148n7, 149n9, 209, 253; "dance of agency," 190, 198, 206, 211n12; and mangle, 94–95, 259
Pitts, Victoria, 413–414, 423n1
Plumwood, Val, 9, 257, 258, 262n1
polyvinyl chloride (PVC), 199–202
postmodern, postmodernism, 2–3, 99–100, 101, 242, 342
poststructuralism, 242, 243, 256, 293, 297
Price, Janet, and Margrit Shildrick, 359
productionism, 171, 172
Prozac, 258, 373, 376–377, 385–386, 387, 391n2, 392n6, 393n10
psychoanalysis, 27–28, 387–389
psychopharmaceuticals, 16, 257–258, 374–375, 376, 377, 379, 381, 382, 387–388, 389, 390
psychotherapy, 385–388
Putnam, Hilary, 97

queer theory, 2
Quijano, Anibal, 318–321, 331, 333nn11,12

race, racism, 15, 188, 205–206, 308–310, 312–316, 318–328, 330–331; aesthetics of, 403; and division of labor, 319, 326, 333n12; environmental racism, 203, 206; and poverty, 321; racial profiling, 308; scientific racism, 315–316, 318, 320, 322–323, 325, 328
Racial Privacy Initiative, 308–309
relata, 130, 133, 149n15, 150n20; within-phenomena, 248
Reno, Kent, *412*
representationalism, 108, 111, 121–122, 123–126, 130, 148nn6,7, 248
Robinson, Eugene, 206
Rorty, Richard, 109
Rosser, Sue V., 26–27
Rouse, Joseph, 95, 110, 124, 125–126, 148n5, 151n29

Sandahl, Carrie, 328–330
Sandilands, Catriona, 9, 251. *See also* Mortimer-Sandilands, Catriona
Sandoval, Chela, 361–362
Saussure, Ferdinand de, 2, 218, 223
Sayers, Janet, 25
Scheman, Naomi, 110
science studies, 5, 18n3, 91, 121–122, 124, 225, 234n8, 245; feminist, 5, 17, 102–103, 145, 242
Scott, Joan, 292–293, 294, 298, 304n2
Searle, John, 98, 190
Sedgwick, Eve, 342–343, 345–346, 365, 367
serotonin, 380–381, 384–385, 392n8
Shenk, David, 272–274, 284, 287n8
Siebers, Tobin, 15
Silverberg, Cory, 301–302
Singer, Linda, 342, 343–344, 345, 346, 347, 358–359
social construction, social constructionism, 1, 3, 5, 88–90, 91–92, 102, 104, 107, 112, 124–125, 237, 239, 242, 244, 286n4, 293, 294, 296–297, 298, 299, 312–313, 373, 377. See also constructivism; cultural constructionism
sociology of scientific knowledge (SSK), 88–89
SNRI drugs. *See* antidepressants
Spivak, Gayatri Chakravorty, 394n11
SSRI drugs. *See* antidepressants
Steingraber, Sandra, 201, 261

techno-science, 163, 167–168, 171
"thingification," 130, 249
Thomson, Rosemarie Garland, 369n8
Toadvine, Ted, 267, 268–271, 274, 285n2

trans-corporeality, 238, 252–253, 257, 258, 259–260, 262. *See also* corporeal, corporeality
trickster coyote, 247–248
Tuana, Nancy, 13, 241

Urquhart, Jane, 277–283, 286n6

Van der Tuin, Iris, 18n3
viscous porosity, 188, 189, 193–194, 196, 198, 199–202, 209
vitalism, 10, 52, 53, 56–57, 64, 81–82; anti-, 80

Wallace, Alfred Russel, 49n13
Wallace, Jo-Ann, 378
Watson, Debraha, 407–408
Weatherston, Rosemary, 355
Wendell, Susan, 249–250, 360–361
West, Cornel, 320
"white capitalist heterosexist patriarchy" (WCHP), 171
whiteness, 326–327
wildness, wilderness, 249, 252, 258
Wilson, Elizabeth A., 5–6, 69, 107, 237–238
Wilson, E. O., 233
Wittgenstein, Ludwig, 98–99, 115
world-systems theory, 318
Wurztel, Elizabeth, 391n3
Wylie, Alison, 102

Yarbro-Bejarano, Yvonne, 356
Young, Robert, 168–171, 173–174, 185n4